Hierarchy and Its Discontents

Hierarchy and Its Discontents

Culture and the Politics of
Consciousness in Caste Society

Steven M. Parish

PENN

University of Pennsylvania Press

Philadelphia

Library of Congress Cataloging-in-Publication Data

Parish, Steven M
  Hierarchy and its discontents : culture and the politics of consciousness in caste
society / Steven M. Parish.
      p.   cm.
  Includes bibliographical references and index.
  ISBN 0-8122-3313-1 (alk. paper). — ISBN 0-8122-1551-6 (pbk. : alk. paper)
  1. Newar (Nepalese people) — Social life and customs.   2. Caste — Nepal — Bhaktapur.
3. Hinduism — Nepal — Bhaktapur.   4. Bhaktapur (Nepal) — Social conditions.   I. Title.
DS493.9.N4P36   1996
306'.089'95 — dc20   96-3608
                                                                           CIP

To Rita

Contents

Preface and Acknowledgments

This book is a study of problems of meaning associated with life in a caste system. It explores the critiques of caste life that develop as members of caste society reflect on these problems. It is based on fieldwork with people of different castes in the Hindu city of Bhaktapur in Nepal, a town inhabited mostly by ethnic Newars; on fieldwork with untouchables in Kathmandu, Nepal; and on a reading of the literature of low caste life in India. I suppose it also reflects my own working class origins, and the problems of meaning and identity that the inequalities of American social life have posed for me. I think this sensitized me to certain issues pursued in this work, such as the ways people positioned in society in different ways may have different views of the society and culture they "share." In any event, I chose to include people of different castes in my fieldwork, from the highest to the lowest. Brahmans, untouchables, and others voice visions of caste life in this work.

Of course, we all bring lives and backgrounds to our studies of culture. I do not think my class origins bias or privilege me any more or less than a middle or upper class background would. They are simply different starting points. None of us can escape being positioned in relation to the human phenomena we seek to understand. This fact can lead to insight—or to the neglect of what we are not prepared to find meaningful.

Who we are makes a difference, whether we live at the bottom of a caste system or merely write books about those who do. In a lucid and penetrating study of violence and celebration in Brazilian cultural life, Daniel Linger acknowledges—as I would—that "my own biography and my own concerns helped shape both my fieldwork and this book; moreover, the shaping has been, I believe, in important respects unconscious, unknowable to me even in my most relentlessly reflexive moments." That there is inevitably a good part of ourselves in our work, however, does not mean there is nothing of others in it. As Linger goes on to say, "if anthropological knowledge is undeniably the contingent product of an encounter, as postmodern anthropological critics (Clifford and Marcus 1986, Marcus and Fischer 1986) have so forcefully demonstrated, I have not the slightest doubt that I encountered something with a life and dynamic of its own" (Linger 1992:255). I would echo this conviction.

Certainly the men and women I encountered in Nepal had an undeniable reality of their own—a gravity, a life—that justifies the effort to say something about them. Moreover, they were willing to explore a range of their experience with me, and worked at impressing their views on me. They shaped our encounter, just as I did.

Introspection regarding the practice of ethnography has, as Ann Gold (1988) writes, "swollen into a kind of torrent" in anthropology. It was intended, no doubt, to make ethnography more flexible, more nuanced, more able to do justice to other lives, other cultures. Some now fear, however, with some justification, that the torrents threaten to sweep away the other in the conversation that is ethnography, replacing the ethnographic exploration of other lives and cultures with a literary examination of the text and the author's self. We need to be more introspective about this trend and the interpretive turn inward that seems so often to come with it: the object of inquiry stops being people in the world, and becomes the experiences, craft, practices of the academic worker, as author, theorist, self.

I prefer a more extroverted ethnography, which has passed through self-analysis to a renewed engagement with people who live cultural lives, where the constructions of the ethnographic art point beyond themselves, seek to hear and understand the whispers of other lives, the voices of other cultures, the sounds of life beyond the insular world created by a reflexivity that has not achieved reengagement. If introspection means we get better at listening, good; if it becomes so self-absorbed that nothing is heard, if it consigns to silence the people who are in my view the only reason for ethnography, if it silences them *and* privileges the Western voice that was supposed to be critiqued in this reflexive movement, then I think great damage is being done. Has reflexivity, finally, been anything more than a reprivileging of Western voices? Leaving less room for others?

We should be able to avoid the worst excesses of constructing an essentialized "other" from our own standpoint without denying actual others—human beings whose lived worlds are different than our own—the agency, the dignity, of being our conversational partners. Moreover, finding an identity in the interpretive turn of the moment cannot be the sole raison d'être of ethnography. Where we pursued symbols yesterday, today we reduce all to what Foucault termed "the monotony of power," and detach "culture" from lived worlds, reifying self, life, and action into the arid and seamless one-dimensionality of "discourse"—while waiting for tomorrow's concept to slouch onto the scene.

I am not saying that we can ignore power, discourse, symbolic forms. Far from it; the analysis of power and symbolic forms, of moral and political discourse, remains essential. However, I do not think we can reduce human life to power, to discourse, even to culture. Life is bigger, more tangled, more nuanced and multi-dimensional than even the best of our theories allows for.

We overvalue theory, I think. I am not claiming we can do without it. At best, a well-tempered theory, grounded in the ethnographic study of cultural life, can clarify and illuminate, prompt us to strive, move us to wonder about the world, to ask questions, to look again. Yet today interpretive theory carries the risk of self-absorption, of radical closure around ethical and political terms. Insofar as social and cultural theory becomes a mode of ethical interpretation, it involves the risk that we might value it over and against actual human beings.

Theory may celebrate itself, but neglect to touch base with human worlds; it may display an ethical earnestness, and validate a moral stand, yet obscure the actualities and ambivalences, the urgencies and possibilities, of human life. At worst, the narcissism of theory erases "others," the concrete women and men who live cultural lives.

In the face of this danger, whether we wish to engage in ethical interpretation and document what we see as social evils, or wish simply and neutrally to understand the basic processes of social and cultural life (D'Andrade 1995:251), I believe we are best served by a commitment to grounded analysis. Whatever our vision or goals, the extroverted craft of ethnography remains indispensable. We need to do ethnography because it orients us towards actors, not away from them.

If ethnography is the total process of describing and interpreting cultural life, then cross-cultural ethnographic research is shaped by the way ethnographers—as human beings with lives, who themselves embody a culture—come to encounter forms of cultural life that embody premises alien to the ethnographer. We do need to be aware of what we bring to the ethnographic encounter.

Yet I believe we learn from others, and that most anthropologists are open to myriad influences. Often the most crucial of these influences flow not from our own lives, but from those we seek to understand. While sometimes scholars shrink into their scholarly languages, spinning esoteric, self-protective theories, I think they often reach beyond these, as in a dialogue that achieves new understanding.

Certainly, I have values that are not consistent with those of a caste hierarchy. The unavoidable fact is that I am a Western person, born and raised in an American milieu. When I lived in the Hindu city of Bhaktapur in the shadow of the Himalayas, I was an outsider, with alien values, with a moral sense attuned to the values and world view of my own culture. How did my moral sense, my values, my moral intuitions, affect this project? How did these shape the encounter with Newars?

Like any anthropologist, like any human being, I have been shaped by culture. My sense of justice, my concepts of equality, liberty, and my methodological cultural relativism are in part the products of a tradition. No doubt my moral sense bears the marks of what Mill thought about liberty and of Kant's universalizing moral philosophy. It has been shaped in ways I may not fully grasp by Plato, Darwin, Ibsen, Freud, and others. No doubt the values I have as a scholar have been shaped by the work of Franz Boas, Ruth Benedict, Edward Sapir and others in the anthropological lineage, by their critics, and by debates about relativism in the social sciences.

Quite honestly, I am not sure I can easily reconcile the values I have as a person with the values I have as an anthropologist, or indeed any of my core values with each other. Is my sense of justice commensurate with studying the values, and the human reality, of life in a hierarchical society? Should people have equality of opportunity only in my own culture? Not in caste society? Must I repudiate my concepts of justice to maintain a stance of cultural relativism? Conversely, must I repudiate relativism to maintain my own sense of justice?

Poor choices, perhaps. In practice, I am neither quite willing to give up my own sense of justice, forged in my own contingent culture though it is, nor quite prepared to take my own culture's moral tradition as providing absolutely privileged grounds for making moral judgments. In this hesitation, I am, I know, not alone.

In fact, I suspect I am caught up in one of the central quandaries of the ethnographic enterprise. As a person, I am concerned about justice: inequality and oppression anger me. At the same time, how can I know that my own culture's concepts of justice provide the best measure of the way the world ought to be? I can hardly assume that my own culture embodies universal moral truth in some absolute way, and so simply sweep aside the moral traditions of other cultures, denying out of hand that they offer any basis for moral intuitions different from my own.

Are there moral universals found in every culture that would provide the basis, a meta-language, for evaluating empirical moral traditions? Perhaps such universals exist. We cannot, however, base a universalistic perspective solely on the study of our own culture. Ethnocentrism offers no true escape from ethical relativism.

We need more comparative research on the lived moral worlds of human cultures. If we take up this challenge, perhaps the encounter with other cultures will push us to understand more fully and consciously our own values and lives. It could provoke us to reflect on them and to achieve insights within horizons larger than our own culture, perhaps move us to find a space of understanding that is not part of one cultural tradition or another, but emerges from the encounter, from the process of dialogue, from our principled reflections on lived cultural worlds, and on the implications of their co-existence. While it might not offer the comforting certainties of an absolute universalism or the simplicity of absolute relativism (Johnson 1993), this process might help provoke a process of rational reflection in which the ideas and values of distinct moral traditions are engaged, thought about, critiqued, incorporated in a "meta-culture" of judgment and insight that we may bring to bear on our own cultural lives.

In cross-cultural ethnography, we must wonder about the ability of the ethnographer to break out of his own culture, at least in a relative way, so that while the research will inescapably reflect the ethnographer's be-ing-in-culture, it is not totally predetermined by it. Here, the question becomes: did I let Newars be Newars? Another question involves the way the ethnographer is perceived by the people he or she seeks to under-stand. After all, the people the ethnographer seeks to understand are actively involved in the production of the ethnography. Their definition of the ethnographer and the research makes a difference. How did Ne-wars perceive me and how did this affect the way they presented them-selves to me?

I did not plan research into caste systems; my primary research focus was the cultural psychology of moral life, about which I have written else-where (1994). While I had read Dumont's seminal book *Homo Hierarchi-cus* (1980) and was aware of the efforts of his critics to refute him, I was drawn to the issue of cognitive responses to caste hierarchy in the course of fieldwork because of my encounters with Newars. I did not set out to find what I found, and did not find quite what I expected. Although I find it hard to admit now, I suppose I was prepared to meet *homo hierar-chicus*. What I found were men and women asserting and resisting hier-archy, as this formed a central social and personal reality for them. I did not find *Homo hierarchicus*.

What and who was I to Bhaktapur Newars? By virtue of being from the United States, I was a somewhat anomalous figure. I was both high status (the associations were with Western wealth, with the prestige of moder-nity) and low status (non-Hindu, impure); in some ways I was outside the system altogether. I existed as if I were three highly incongruent persons in one: one of the persons inhabiting me had an unearned aura of pres-tige; another was excluded and kept at a distance; the third was a streak of randomness wandering about the city, a culturally meaningless talking inkblot.

How strange was I? A complete stranger once pulled a hair off my arm to inspect, holding it up to the sunlight the better to see it. In some

neighborhoods, rarely visited by foreigners, curious crowds would sometimes gather around me to examine me as an unusual phenomenon, the
people on the outside pushing those nearest me into what I felt was my
personal space, up against my skin. I remember vividly a boy who seemed
absolutely stunned when I uttered a simple question in Newari, how he
stared at me as if a stone had spoken and then rushed away, shouting,
"He spoke, he spoke our Newari language!" Often I was strange enough,
enough of an outsider, that I could be disregarded, ignored as irrelevant
to the immediate business of life.

Like a low status person, there were places I could not go. Not everyone would eat with me, or speak with me. Like a high status person, I got
a certain amount of deference, more than I deserved. As an outsider, I
suppose I was an enigma. I did not have an absolutely fixed social meaning, a stable social identity, an "objecthood" in which I was contained
and conventionalized.

Under the circumstances, I have no doubt that Newars attempted
to make sense of me by mobilizing whatever concepts of the Western
person they had. (I know some of them played with the idea that I was
a German development worker, and some thought I might be an art
smuggler). Did they stress those values they thought might be acceptable
to me, and mute those they thought would be unacceptable? Perhaps.
However, I feel certain many of them did not have enough of a concept of Western attitudes, much less mine, to dissemble with total effec-
tiveness over the many hours I spent with them, as if they were perfect
chameleons, instantly understanding my values and displaying them in a
pitch-perfect performance. In these days before television descended on
Nepal (1982–85), not all of them were well versed in Western culture. I
do not deny that their sensitivity to me must have made a difference, that
my presence stirred things up, provoked thought. I do not think people
recreated themselves for me.

Once we have abandoned the notion that ethnographers have some
special power of empathy, and have recognized that we understand the
people of other cultures only by virtue of great, painstaking effort, if at
all, it does not then make sense to attribute special powers of empathy to
natives, so that they can read me easily, and effortlessly shift into a more
Western mode, even while I struggle painfully to understand them. Neither Newars nor I are chameleons.

In reality, of course, they could only respond to me in large part on
the basis of what they brought to our encounter, as Newars, as Brahmans,
or as untouchables. If they appropriated me to work on particular concerns, this still says something about how they see themselves in their
world. But of course they do invoke these concepts with each other, do
confront these issues in encounters with each other.

I was, I think, well enough trained in interviewing and in the presentation of self in ethnographic situations that I did not intrude my attitudes too sharply into my work, although I have little doubt they infused the encounter in subtle ways. I tended to be vague about what I thought and felt (one reason, perhaps, that people thought I lacked a certain cleverness, a certain sharpness, of the kind they associate with people who are good at articulating their views and desires). If anything, I now think, I may have erred by being so circumspect; possibly I would have learned more by occasionally being more challenging. In any event, I feel relatively confident people told me much of what they actually thought and felt at particular moments, not what they believed I wanted to hear.

While we need always to strive to understand the ways the ethnographer shapes the ethnography, I do not think we should exaggerate the role of the ethnographer or minimize the contribution of natives to the process of doing ethnography. Rather than having no option other than recreating themselves from scratch to fit the preconceptions of their Western interlocutor, people can, and do, respond in a wide variety of ways to the ethnographic encounter. It may cut at Western narcissism, but my impression is that the majority of Newars I knew were not impressed enough with either me or "the West" to want to reconstruct themselves. When they dissembled, and when they made themselves known, I think it had to do with their own concerns.

An ethnographer invites an exploration of various areas of cultural life and offers possible topics, but, if following the canons of qualitative, discovery-oriented, person-centered research as I was, he or she does not rigidly prescribe the direction a discussion will take (Levy and Wellenkamp 1989). In fact, the ethnographer may not be able to prescribe the direction of an interview or conversation no matter how hard he or she tries. Often enough, people will take the encounter as an opportunity to say things and affirm values they cannot express elsewhere and may have little chance to put into action.

These conversations with people provide a way of probing for values and thought that exists behind and beneath people's knowledge of the governing values of social practices. In the kind of interviews I conducted, one gets a sense not only of how dominant values are known, enacted, and experienced, but also a sense of how they are resisted, evaluated, seen from an ironic or dissenting point of view. You begin, in this way, to see people as more than reflections of the public order, as more than the products of discourse, to know them as agents of cultural lives.

Perhaps Newars expressed themselves in the ethnographic encounter in ways they might not have been able to with members of other castes, but I do not think they invented philosophies just for me. Newars asserted views and used concepts that are important to them, that have moral force in their own visions of self and society, even if they cannot always act on these because they are not tolerated in practice. If this is correct, then many Newars live in a kind of psychological tension with social reality.

I believe Newars mostly wanted me to understand, and worked to see I did. When I did not seem to grasp their ideas, Newars would often take a didactic turn, explaining at length about the kind of society they lived in, and their personal experiences and evaluations of this society. They would challenge me, take me to task, engage in further dialogue.

The fact is that their concepts and values differed from mine, and they had to work to make sure I grasped them. Even in those instances where their ideas resonated with my values, their concepts were often phrased in cultural terms that were surprising to me.

At times, too, they expressed ideas that I found disagreeable. For example, there were moments when they stigmatized human beings for what they were, not for what they did, in ways that violated my own ethic of striving to universalize respect. (In particular, I found some of the teasing of mentally retarded or mentally ill persons almost unbearable to watch—much harder to deal with than attitudes about caste.)

Moreover, Newar testimony was quite often contradictory. So where was I leading them, if I was? Where were they leading me, if they were? The blind were leading the blind, I suppose—groping to find the other, touching a face in the dark, finding unexpected features. What happened in the encounter, I believe, was more than an exchange of prejudgments. In fact, my experience was of having preconceptions upset.

Were the divergent attitudes, the apparent ambivalence, the inconsistencies, of the people who conversed with me the product of our encounter? An effect of their interaction with me? Perhaps. But if so, it seems to me that the consistency, the near-total consensus, reported by some other anthropologists are just as likely the product of an encounter. If so, which encounter should we privilege? Which best represents cultural life? Perhaps we need to take account of both.

I am keenly aware that the material of this book supports contradictory readings. In fact, I insist on it. I encountered a polyvocal discourse, in which the same person may both accept and reject hierarchy, may acquiesce to the social order and seek to disrupt it. It is this complexity I try to get across. I do not doubt that Newars were saying something significant about their experience and lives, however contradictory their testimony is.

If I stress the muted critique of hierarchy I encountered, it is because the literature of caste as a whole has hurried past indigenous critiques of caste life, not because I fail to recognize the dominance of hierarchical values. My job here is not just to be balanced in presenting constructions and counter-constructions, although I try; it is also to restore some balance to a literature that has for decades played down the critiques people make of their own culture and its dominant values.

In spite of my special concern with critique, I attest to the dominance of hierarchy, not only in the social arena, but even in the minds of many of the persons who critique it. What I try to do is candidly recognize the contradictions in my material as well as the contradictory arguments that can be made about it.

My argument, then, is not that critiques of social life are always effective, but that they are perennial and felt, and they animate consciousness in important ways. The fact that critiques of cultural life often, perhaps typically, lead to disappointment—yield failure, even tragedy—does not diminish their sociological significance. After all, they may call forth responses from the dominant order. Nor does a critique's impotence diminish its felt significance for self-identity. Identity may be forged in failure and irony.

Incidentally—or perhaps this is crucial—I liked all the high and low caste Newars I came to know. Perhaps this colors my feeling that we get nowhere by finding someone to demonize, to blame for the inequities of caste life. While caste domination has an undeniable reality, crushing hopes and lives, it may be the tragic consequence of the pursuit of other cultural goals and motives. Thus I believe that some of the structures of thought, feeling, and action I will discuss in this work have a double place in cultural life. They exist not only as systems of power and domination, but also as systems of meaning and practice that nurture and guide actors, that give meaning and significance to their actions and existence. The world-images and self-images that shape social action take on a form, and acquire a felt significance, that reflects the nature of the vision of a good life. Aspirations and power are deployed in light of all this. Reaching for the American dream, or seeking to live as moral Hindu householders, people can sometimes participate meaningfully in social practices that oppress others, perhaps even themselves.

I think the problem of caste is ultimately a problem of objective social structures of thought and feeling, of action and social relations. I do not think we can base our inquiry into social life on the premise that the "natural" condition of human cultural political life is a will-to-power with malice towards all, with generosity for none who is in any way "other." Hierarchy would then reflect a human nature capable *only* of oppression and other mischief, and there would be nothing to explain in terms of cultural life. I reject this convenient oversimplification.

Of course, mutual fear and loathing may indeed come to characterize human relations. This always has a cultural history. Fear and loathing, the whole dynamic of exclusion and dominance, are as culturally mediated as kinship or ritual. What matters most, I think, is the politics that grows out of cultural life, not as an expression of a primal impulse to dominate others, reflecting some transcultural will-to-power, but as a constructed sense of reality that endows social relations with a particular felt significance.

A caste system is a historical form of life, and while human actors make it and enact it, they may in fact do so without guilty minds. In part, they may not know what they do, and in part they may think they are only doing what they must do, and ought to do (Bourdieu 1977). Should they feel qualms or doubt or guilt, they can seek to resolve these within culture, finding cultural answers that absolve them of responsibility. Evaluating themselves by cultural standards, they may find it possible to "know" that they have done what life and society and morality require. But doubt is never banished, I think, at least not totally. One senses this, I believe, in the elaboration and insistence of the rhetoric that upholds caste hierarchy, implicitly sustaining a moral sense of self.

It is relatively easy for me to be objective about caste. I could leave Bhaktapur. I could go home, exit the world of caste. Those who live there cannot. This makes a difference. I can afford to see different points of view, can afford to speak neutrally of the political scene, of the social and cultural context, in ways that the actors involved do not. They have to be agents, not merely analysts. Embedded in caste society, it may be hard to be generous about motives, to be objective about what is, after all, your life. One may feel threatened in the most intimate ways.

An unforgiving hierarchy of power and privilege, of stigma and value, forms the social backbone of many societies, including the United States, with its racial, gender, and class hierarchies. I feel the psycho-existential quandaries posed by any system of hierarchy, although always culturally constituted, also have a certain universality. Certainly it is not possible for me to portray the problems of meaning and identity that caste hierarchy pose for men and women in India and Nepal as merely the problems of a faraway society, as if hierarchy and inequality had no sting in the United States. They do. My goal is not to distance us, but to unite the shock of recognition—for we face similar dilemmas—with a recognition of the role of culture, not only in constituting hierarchy, but in mediating felt responses to inequality. Thus this volume examines the psychocultural life of human predicaments that haunt every complex society, and can dangerously complicate the life of self in every such society.

A word on omissions. This book does not tackle the question of how life and thought is being reshaped in an encounter with the wider world. This will have to wait for later work. I should at least note, however, that many in Nepal and India see certain "Western" values—liberal, or marxist, political or technocratic—as potentially liberating concepts, worth discussing and perhaps experimenting with. They wish to test the powers and limits of these for themselves. Some might dismiss this as a case of "Western hegemony," arguing that non-western people adopt western values because of the projection of western power into their lives. In part, this states the obvious: undeniably, Nepal's encounters with the wider world have provoked thought and change. Contacts with Europe, the United States, Japan, China, Russia, India, with empires present and past, have had an impact on Nepal and its cultures.

Still, I do not think explaining everything in terms of "Western" influences quite captures the nuances of the situation. Moreover, such assertions sweep away the agency of non-western peoples. Ideas incorporated into a life, into practice, reflected on by the agents of a life, can be liberating even when those very same concepts help sustain colonial and postcolonial discourses that devalue "third world" actors. Such ideas—of justice, freedom, rights, equality—may help some actors emancipate themselves and transform their lives, even though, as history and the comparative study of social systems reveal, these ideas fall short of guaranteeing utopia, and are often absorbed into existing systems of inequality or used to justify new relations of dominance and exclusion. And yet, the concepts of democracy and feminism that some Nepalese have seized on and made their own may be liberating for them in the context of their experience of the class, caste, and gender hierarchies that exist in their lived worlds. But as I will show they have long resisted the caste hierarchy with their own indigenous concepts, and continue to do so.

I have also not addressed the problems of meaning that caste and gender hierarchies pose for women. As a male researcher, I was incorporated into the male world by Newars, and spent much less time with women than men. I may have been too diffident, but I worried that contacts with a male researcher would stigmatize female informants. At the time, moreover, I felt conducting ethnography with members of multiple castes without gravely alienating any of them seemed a delicate enough task, without also negotiating and possibly transgressing local norms regarding gender. I did, of course, attempt interviews with women, but these were constrained in a variety of ways. Using my usual interview approach, which involved intensive private meetings, might have led to stigmatizing gossip. In one case, chaperoned by an older Kathmandu Brahman, I did interview an untouchable woman, but we were only allowed to meet in the ground floor of his house. Obviously, this situation can hardly be considered conducive to a free and frank discussion of caste life. I could hardly expect her to speak frankly about her caste attitudes in the presence of a high caste individual, and the talk indeed veered into a discussion of the way men (in general but her husband in particular) neglect their duties, are lazy, drink, gamble, and leave women to work and earn a living. Skinner and Holland (in press) report that among Nepalese students, girls were more concerned with gender hierarchy, boys with caste; possibly this holds for the interviews I had with this Sweeper woman. But perhaps her diffidence about caste and outspokenness about male inadequacies was simply an artifact of the interview situation. However, in a life-history project that I have begun to work on with Rita Shakya, the gender hierarchy does seem more salient than the caste hierarchy, so perhaps women do tend to forge their critical consciousness first and foremost in terms of gender experience. Certainly the kinds of constraints, humiliations, and violence that men experience primarily in the context of caste, women experience in the context of gender and caste. Perhaps this means some women may maintain an even more complex critical consciousness that men. I do think women may share the ambivalence, the discontents, concerning caste that I document for men, but they are also often ambivalent and discontented with gender roles.

In some cases women surely maintain a multiple consciousness regarding both gender and caste, rejecting and accepting elements of it in ways that reflect the development of their self-concepts, their aspirations in a changing society, their life-histories and their reflections on their experience, as well as their position in society. One elderly untouchable woman I encountered was quite frank about what other members of her group sought to disguise (they were veiling their historic status, attempting to blend in with a higher status untouchable group). She spoke as if their status and their stratagems hardly mattered at all, and yet exuded a sense of futility, as if they did matter more than anything, reiterating that there was no good in talking of such things. She impressed me as fatalistic almost to the point of despair, unwilling to care any more, and yet angry, her fatalism perhaps masking rage.

Inter-caste marriages bring the issues of caste and gender together in revealing ways: as old restrictions fade, and old sanctions lose their power, what often remains are rifts in families and contested identities. One younger high caste woman I know rejected caste, as many of her generation did, forming bonds with members of multiple castes in school; but her mother, siblings, and sisters-in-law affirmed caste boundaries, maintaining that it took generations to be born into their caste, and worried about what neighbors and other members of their caste would think about the kinds of inter-caste ties this younger, more "modern," member of their household forged. For this woman, a desire to be "a good daughter" (dutiful and loving and loved) conflicted both with a desire for greater personal autonomy and with a belief that caste did not matter. Her parents wanted to arrange a marriage for her with a man of their caste; she wanted to choose her own husband, if she married at all. She acted on her desire to make her own choices, but the price was a lingering sense of guilt and a break with her parents, brothers, and sisters-in-law that only slowly healed.

On women's critical agency in South Asia, I refer the reader to Raheja's and Gold's work with Indian women (1994) and to Holland's and Skinner's account of political songs associated with the Nepalese women's festival of Tij (1995). These ethnographic studies are important contributions to our general understanding of culture and agency, as are some of the theoretical concepts they deploy. In particular, Holland and Skinner's article "The Co-Development of Identity, Agency, and Lived Worlds" (in press) has inspired my use of the phrase "lived world." More graceful and more accurate than the expression "life-world" that I have used in previous work, lived worlds are the products of the dialectical engagment of human agency with culture and society. The concept embraces diversity, since multiple lived worlds can inhabit society, continually emerging, developing, and dissolving, and I believe also gives due weight to the play of agency in cultural life. These worlds are actively fashioned and lived, not passively enacted. They develop in history, and reflect actors' struggles to make lives for themselves.

In my readings of the Hindu epic the Bhagavad Gita, I find many of the themes I attempt to pursue in this work. It uses the evocative and persuasive powers of language in a magnificent attempt to restore commitment to an envisioned social order. But its narrative structure pivots on questions that pose real life dilemmas for many of those interviewed for this ethnography: How do you respond to the conflicting imperatives of cultural life? How do you deal with the dilemmas that a moral order generates? Here is life: what should you do? Who are you?

Arjuna, the human interlocutor of God in the Gita, despairs because his moral order poses excruciating dilemmas for him. Faced with the choice of doing his duty and killing men he feels kinship with, or not doing his duty, he confesses that "My nature has been infected by the fault of pity / My mind is confused about duty (dharma)." He does not want to fight.

Arjuna has the opportunity to question god about his dilemma, since Krishna reveals himself in a theophany. Krishna offers a religious justification for acting in conformity to the imperatives of the social order. After receiving Krishna's counsel, Arjuna's inner conflict is resolved, and he enters the battle. Perhaps we are supposed to feel that Arjuna must do his duty, that there is nothing else to do, that the world is the way it must be, could scarcely be any other way (Bourdieu 1977). A vision of ultimate sacred reality resolves very human ambivalences.

Actual human beings do not always achieve the closure on problems of meaning that Arjuna does. Very often, I think, we do not resolve moral quandaries posed by cultural life but are forced to live with them. Often, like poor Humpty-Dumpty in the nursery rhyme, neither all the king's men nor all the king's horses, and not even Krishna manifest in his cosmic form, can put a human self together again, make it undivided, produce a single unambivalent consciousness of self and society, once the moral self has splintered into fragments in its encounter with a "moral order."

Efforts to justify self and society, to make them seem unified, coherent, necessary, natural, and absolute, can of course, develop into politically significant exercises in cultural hegemony. Seeking to resolve their doubts, to achieve coherence for themselves, to overcome their ambivalences, people may be willing to impose much on others—an attitude of "my way or no way" may develop. Differing moral positions can threaten the self-images, the world-images, and the illusion of closure with which those who hope to inhabit these images seek to grace both. Since persons and groups may nurture these images and illusions as the expression of an intimate desire for moral vindication and social legitimation, this can lead to a politics of culture and values.

The kind of rhetoric found in the Bhagavad Gita helps legitimize the moral order of caste society. As an ordered and ordering narrative of ultimate reality that affirms hierarchy as necessary and natural, defining it as an expression of God's sacred being, the epic asserts that people must conform, must do their own duty. It imagines a foundation in ultimate reality for the social order, making it truly a moral and sacred order. It advises you that it is better that you do your own duty poorly, rather than do another's duty well, for if you do what arises from your own inherent nature, you will avoid guilt. But do people so easily avoid guilt and ambivalence? I believe they do not, as hard as they may try. I believe the moral order continues to pose problems for actors, placing them in quandaries that they struggle to work out for themselves, sometimes by taking a leap of faith into the ideology of hierarchy, sometimes by attempting to challenge dominant premises, and sometimes in other ways. In this work, we will see actors attempting various resolutions, as they struggle with the problems of meaning and practice that caste life poses for them.

Acknowledgments

I am grateful to my Newar friends for their guidance and forbearance. Robert Levy inspired me to work with Newars, and I owe him much, as a mentor and a friend. For conversations and kindnesses I wish to thank

Roy D'Andrade, Melford Spiro, Aaron Cicourel, Allan Hoben, Tom Barfield, Charles Lindholm, Dan Linger, Eugene Kumekawa, Ernestine McHugh, and Rebecca Joseph. I have benefited immensely from their provocations, readings, help, guidance, and criticism.

The discussion of narratives in Chapter 5 was first presented as a paper at the 1988 American Anthropology Association meetings in Phoenix, Arizona, and received useful critiques by Nicholas Dirks and Vincent Crapanzo. I wish to thank Al Pach and Debra Skinner for keen comments on a later version of the same paper. Several anonymous reviewers offered readings and critiques that I found invaluable. Naturally, I have not always listened to suggestions and criticism, and the interpretations I make here are my own.

Rita Shakya helped with translations from Newari, and Joy Chen Lewis produced the maps. The epigraphs and quotes from the Bhagavad Gita have been translated for this volume by David Eckel.

Portions of Chapter 1 first appeared in Parish, *Moral Knowing in a Hindu Sacred City: An Explanation of Mind, Emotion, and Self* (New York: Columbia University Press, 1994). Copyright © Columbia University Press; reprinted by permission of the publisher. The poem "Devara Dasimayya" is reprinted from A. K. Ramanujan, *Speaking of Shiva* (New York: Penguin, 1973); reprinted by permission of the publisher.

Note on Transcriptions

I have disguised identities by changing names and by omitting or blurring certain details. The testimony presented in the interviews in the text is taken from my tape-recorded interviews. I have edited these materials for ease of reading. Diacritical marks have been omitted.

Having first shown that everyone is a philosopher, though in his own way and unconsciously, since even in the slightest manifestation of any intellectual activity, in "language," there is contained a specific conception of the world, one then moves to the second level, which is that of awareness and criticism. That is to say, one proceeds to the question—is it better to "think," without having a critical awareness, in a disjointed and episodic way? In other words, is it better to take part in a conception of the world mechanically imposed by the external environment, i.e., by one of the many social groups in which everyone is automatically involved from the moment of his entry into the conscious world. . . . Or, on the other hand, is it better to work out consciously and critically one's own conception of the world . . . choose one's sphere of activity, take an active part in the creation of the history of the world, be one's own guide, refusing to accept passively and supinely from outside the moulding of one's personality?

—Antonio Gramsci

Here is the purest rhetorical pattern: speaker and hearer as partners in partisan jokes made at the expense of another. If you "internalize" such a variety of motives, so that the same person can participate somewhat in all three positions, you get a complex individual of many voices. And although these may be treated, under the heading of Symbolic, as a concerto of principles mutually modifying one another, they may likewise be seen, from the standpoint of Rhetoric, as a parliamentary wrangle which the individual has put together somewhat as he puts together his fears and hopes, friendships and enmities, health and disease, or those tiny rebirths whereby, in being born to some new condition, he may be dying to a past condition, his development being dialectical, a series of terms in perpetual transformation.

—Kenneth Burke

I see you touching the clouds, sparking with many colors.
Your mouth is agape, and your wide eyes are on fire.
My inmost self is shaken,
O Vishnu, I find no solidity or calm.

—Bhagavad Gita

Introduction: Culture and Its Critique

History shuffles the deck for all of us, but it stacks the deck against some. Often, we are not even aware of the invisible hands dealing our cards.

Many fear the idea of social fate. Who wants to be prodded by invisible hands? Who would wish to be picked up and crushed as if they barely existed? Even the thought of it diminishes us in our own eyes. A vision of such a reality might shatter us. If history appeared before us, in the form of a terrible god, swallowing up humanity in holocausts, grinding people to dust at the bottom of society, we might lose our moral bearings, find no refuge to shelter our most fundamental illusions about ourselves and the world.[1]

While some of us may at the odd moment experience oceanic feelings of unity with the universe, I suspect few people want to vanish forever into some gigantic quaking landscape of capricious social forces that act in ways we cannot grasp, or even perceive, that offers nothing but an uncertain existence, or the threatening certainty of suffering. Yet who can really doubt that history embraces more than what I know, whoever I am? It embraces much more than I can control.

History and society do determine the basic terms of my existence. Perhaps my struggles can make a difference, perhaps not, but the struggles do begin with a historical reality, with a world I did not make. No wonder some think that human agency means nothing, that all that matters can be explained in terms of mechanical social "forces" that mock our intentions, sweeping our aspirations away with a careless hand.

Yet history and social life also show how reluctant people often are to accept their determination. This perennial, stubborn unhappiness with social facts makes a difference—it stands as a social and historical force itself.

Human unhappiness with history, with social reality, is dealt with in various ways by the human mind. In the moral imagination, I would argue, our sense of reality becomes entangled with a sense of what might be, and what should be. Discontents inspire moral fantasy, a reimagining of the world. This reimagining can take many forms which yet have a kind of underlying unity: there are dreams of justice, reveries of revenge and reversal, the musings that define aspirations, the poetics of utopia, the value-statements of social critique. In all these ways and many more, people imagine themselves whole, or contemplate a world where they could be whole, where they might not suffer, might have justice. They dream of possible worlds. The fantasy stands in counterpoint to an actual world, where some might fear even to whisper their discontents.

We must not romanticize the discourse that develops among those who experience firsthand the terror of history and the injustices of human societies. Surely, suffering drives people to despair and madness more often than it lifts them up and ennobles them. Those oppressed by society typically cannot afford to be moral paradigms—not for us, not for themselves.

Moreover, discontent and its cultures may evolve in destructive and self-destructive ways. Wounded in the imagination and robbed of a future, brutalized by society, by violence, by ethnic cleansing, by the depredations of those more powerful, people may step from history as nightmare into cultural hallucination in their desperation to get the world to turn out right.

Facing the destruction of their worlds, the loss of their homes, facing real oppression and injustice, world history's victims may become possessed by the incantatory and hallucinatory language of prophecy, act out the rhetoric of millenarian or irredentist movements, stalk the promise that a lost world will be restored to them, a better world created, their homes and lives restored. They may bring history violently home to others in the process. As fantastic as such cultures of justice may seem, they are not to be mocked or dismissed lightly. Nor are the psychocultural responses of those with more power to withstand the events we call history or even make such events happen. Isolating themselves in a separate but parallel reality, the more powerful may live in a state of denial and develop a culture of denial. The historical sociology and psychology of the moral imagination must pay attention to these "cultures" within culture.

Of course, the discourse provoked by discontents may sometimes take a more constructive turn. Moral fantasy may help fuel the work of critique, of thought and practice that has the aim of reinventing the existing social world. People struggle to interpret history and society in the light of a sense of moral possibility and necessity, framed in terms of their cultural ethos and experience. Such discourse rejects what is, the way society is; it aspires to define what might be and what should be, putting culturally imagined possibilities into conceptual play, pitting actuality against ideals, defining aspirations and hopes that may be felt with a certain intensity, however unreal they are in practical terms. What people imagine might be and should be are key aspects of human consciousness.[2]

Inevitably, the world often disappoints human desires. The gap between what people want, and what they get, can be immense. The reality may be that the ideals people cling to are rarely embodied in practice; the actuality may be that their political or religious values fail to alter the course of history or transform society. Nonetheless, the desire to remake the world—to make the pain go away, to realize dreams of justice, equality, liberty—is perennial. That such desires are disappointed almost as often as they arise does not diminish their significance; the moral discourse they propel may have other effects, may reveal much about the structures of feeling and power that animate cultural life. Whatever else it does, exploring such moral discourse discloses the subterranean desires that must be understood in any powerful sociology and psychology of human culture.

In fact, I suspect we all experience this gap between desire and reality where discontent brews in a cauldron of fantasy, hope, and despair. It seems to me integral to human life. We embody it: it is the self-contradiction that signals our humanity. We confront our own multiple consciousness with varying degrees of awareness, irony, pain, or wistfulness, and we attempt to cope in terms of our own values and experience. For example, we may be keenly aware that life is not fair, but still possess a kind of will to believe that it should be. In Western cultures (or perhaps only in some of the more comfortable suburbs of Western society), we may believe in freedom and justice—that is, we think these ought to constitute the basic terms by which we judge society and our own fate—yet fully appreciate that freedom does not exist for many, and that not everyone receives justice. We may see social injustices, but believe that we should aspire to justice, that it should determine the structure of society and our relation with others. Thus, while we know with felt certainty that justice often does not characterize the human condition, or our personal situations, we may be unwilling to say, "This is the way it should be, and this is the best of all possible worlds, the utopia at the end of history."

Tacitly at least, we imagine a world that might better embody our hopes and values, and believe that the human world has some meaningful order, that our actions mean something, even when our sense of reality does not provide evidence for these hopes and wishes. We feel the world should be a certain way, should conform to our values (which we may not recognize as cultural values), even if it does not. Justice should exist, freedom should. We are not easily reconciled to the reality that human history is the story of millions of lives crushed at the bottom of human societies, that thousands march to meaningless deaths even now, and that those who have claimed to solve the problems of history and inequality have probably condemned more to death and suffering than they have saved.

The problem is not just wish-fulfillment in the face of the nightmares of history; if we are to give a fair account of the human condition, we cannot only look at the way our history and societies transcend our humanity, our consciousness. We must deal with the fact that we do suffer as individual agents, that we do feel, do hope, do strive. Women and men in many societies do grope for emancipation—not from history as such, perhaps, conceived as a vast social process that involves variables neither they nor social scientists fully comprehend, but rather from the limits of their life situations. They may suffer much in the process. I do not doubt that history and society constitute, like the universe as a whole, a story queerer than we can imagine, either in our wildest dreams or in our most robust and expansive theories. But we can imagine and live our suffering, our pain, our frustrations, our struggles to survive and lead lives that mean something. This is surely one thread in history: a story woven in life and thought, by men and women capable of responding to what they experience, who, if unable to grasp fully all of the circumstances that create their life-situations, are nonetheless both agents and subjects of cultural lives. They have no choice. They have to live. This means they must grapple with the cultural world in which they live.

Bhaktapur and the Newars of the Kathmandu Valley of Nepal

While this study draws on important studies by others who have worked in India and Nepal, my first hand experience has been with a people called the Newars. Most of the Newars quoted in this work live in the largely Hindu city of Bhaktapur in the Kathmandu Valley of Nepal. I also interviewed people in Kathmandu itself, in the city of Patan, and in the town of Panauti on the edge of the Valley.

The Newars are caught up in not one but two caste systems: they have their own caste system, which separates and unites them internally, and they are part of the caste system codified and long sanctioned by the state of Nepal (Hofer 1979). The state system reflects Hindu theory, politics, and the administrative needs of a state that during a expansionary phase had conquered quite diverse groups; the state's caste system throws together tribes, castes and ex-nations, groups of different religions and with fundamentally different social organizations, in a kind of Alice-in-Wonderland way for political and administrative convenience. The result is an odd juxtaposing of different kinds of societies. Buddhist and Hindu groups are brought together and have their identities reconstituted; groups aligned culturally with Tibet are thrown together with those oriented toward India; and communities with no internal history or experience of centralized power find themselves placed in the national "caste" hierarchy along with Newar civilization, with its long historical experience of castes and kings (Hofer 1979; P. R. Sharma 1977). In contrast to the state system, the Newar's own caste system appears more organic, a system where the parts have been honed to fit together in a general symbolic unity, at least for some strata, despite eruptions of dissent.

The Newars' own caste system, which is the one which will primarily concern us here, is a kind of home-grown product, in the sense that it was made (Bhaktapur Newars today maintain) by their own kings when there still were Newar kings, in consultation with Brahman advisors, although of course it reflects general South Asian conceptions. The other system was imposed by the group that conquered the Kathmandu Valley city-states in 1768 and 1769 (Stiller 1973). In the state system, Newars are generally ranked in the middle of the system. In their own system, Bhaktapur Newars divide themselves into more than twenty status levels ranging from Brahman to untouchable (Levy 1990).

This massive yet intimate social construction shapes the macro-structure of society and the micro-reality of everyday life. Newar Bhaktapur, even today, is a city of castes, of culturally valued inequalities; the social and symbolic life of the city is organized in terms of these inequalities. They form a moral order, making possible a dynamic system of hierarchical interdependence. Many Newar Hindus who inhabit this city believe that without hierarchy there would be violence and disorder; without interdependence there would be no society—no one would know what to do, how to live with others. For them, hierarchical interdependence makes social life possible; it is the moral basis, the essential principle, of traditional Hindu civilization, and of their lives. And yet this poses problems for the moral imagination, because people know more than, and other than, what a particular ideology establishes as "reality." Along the margins of the dominant order, there is ambivalence and dissent. Bhaktapur is thus also a city of moral fantasies, of equalizing rhetoric.

Cultural perspectives on caste life are multiple: as one changes point of view, aspects of caste life are differently perceived, in ways that transfigure the way caste is known. Caste life complicates moral knowing, because caste is a fundamental value, and yet it disturbs the moral imagination. I explore this by examining what some actors—Brahmans, untouchables, and others—say about caste life, incorporating their testimony in the form of extensive quotes.

My aim is to enlarge and enhance our understanding of the place of moral discourse in the legitimation and delegitimation of a social order. I have attempted to unite features of psychoethnography and critical ethnography as a means of exploring psychocultural responses to political culture (Strauss 1990). My work here is only a tentative beginning, but I hope it will participate in the evolving rapprochement between critical theory and cognitive theory, showing that the study of cultural psychology and of cultural politics cannot be neatly compartmentalized. Psychological anthropology cannot ignore the politics of culture.

Moral Knowing and *Homo Hierarchicus*

Caste systems have long been a central preoccupation—some would say obsession—of anthropological studies of South Asian life. There are reasons for this. Caste is a social fact of the greatest significance for millions of people. It has shaped their lives and their fates. In South Asia, save for the family, no other social institution has had so deep and all-encompassing an influence on so many over so many centuries.[3]

Numerous anthropological accounts have focused on the ideology of caste, and especially on its apparent contrast with the official moral ideologies of the Western world. Louis Dumont (1980), in particular, has conjured up an image of the Hindu as *Homo hierarchicus*: absorbed in hierarchical interdependence, individuals have no "being" or "value." This account offers an important insight; it captures a central ideological note. Yet it yields a profoundly incomplete image of cultural life. If taken as a comprehensive image of the Hindu person, as a "totalizing" interpretation that accounts for everything, this view dangerously obscures the actual diversity of human experience in Hindu cultures. It precludes a discussion of a culture's discontents, of agency and resistance within culture, of the tensions and quandaries of cultural life.

I believe that, too often in the literature on caste, the ideology of caste hierarchy has become a black hole in to which all of personal and cultural life has been collapsed. No information can escape from a black hole, because the grip of gravity is so intense that nothing, not even light, can escape: very little information on lives and selves escapes the grip of ideology.

This is, sadly, also true of many scholarly studies that have examined the ideology of caste life. If ideology transforms human beings, making them one-dimensional, mere reference points for cultural practices or polemics, rendering them stick-figures suitable for rhetorical purposes, for justifying some vision of society, then too often this process of over-simplification has been echoed in and implicitly ratified by academic studies. In small measure, I intend this study to struggle against this current.

Ideological glosses on humanity, and academic glosses on ideology, leave out too much of what men and women themselves find most meaningful: their aspirations and discontents, much of their suffering, the texture of their lives and the flow of their experience. We need to explore such experience, and not just the ideology of caste.

Actors may challenge the premises and practices of their culture, and in doing so, they may also confront the premises of self, of their own lives and feelings. When they reject a cultural practice, they may have to struggle with the way they have been involved in that practice, with the way it has shaped who and what they are. When culture, at whatever level, is contested, it is often not just a struggle with others, who pursue different commitments and interests, but also an inner conflict—a struggle of self against self. In this work, I argue that the symbolic forms and values of caste hierarchy are created, recreated, and contested, in minds and lives. I term this the "politics of consciousness."

The politics of culture is not just a matter of maneuvers in social arenas, of one group disseminating ideas and values that another group rejects. Group politics may be the crucial context for re-examining cultural premises and practices, but the most painful and difficult part of questioning and reinterpreting culture may be the process of self-examination, of scrutinizing the way self is involved in the dynamics of the social world.

In my view, then, the politics of culture is more than the cultural production of critique and ideology by contending groups, whether dominant cultural elite against critical minority, those with great power against those with little, or Brahman ideologues versus low caste critics of Brahmanical ideology. As crucial as the cultural productions of such groups are, the politics of culture has a more intimate side. It is a politics of self. Identity and consciousness, mind and experience, reflect conflicting visions of reality, self, life. Who I am, what I am, is grounded in culture: the process of contesting culture encompasses an inner politics of consciousness.

Cultural constructions of personhood often constitute an objecthood: they define some people from the outside in, painting them as inferior or superior, assigning them a social value that stigmatizes. Yet, as powerful as they may be, these social constructions do not necessarily determine what people think of themselves. Even as they are "sealed in that crushing objecthood" created by the images others have of them (Fanon

1967), individuals struggle to define themselves and their place in society, from the inside out, contesting the way they are socially constructed, trying to recreate culture to make meaning for themselves.

This book offers ideas about their work of culture, about problems of meaning that motivates this work. Caste life poses psychocultural quandaries, dilemmas of existence that are virtually inescapable. If we want fully to understand people attempting to make lives for themselves in caste systems, human consciousness, identity, and the work of culture must be seen in light of these quandaries of social existence. I will suggest the way some actors seem to develop an ambivalent multiple consciousness of self and society: their consciousness is a composite, a compromise formation, at once hierarchical and critical.

This situation arises, I argue, because consciousness of self and society develops within and for hierarchy, and so reflects hierarchical values and premises; yet moral consciousness also develops *against* hierarchy, in resistance to it. An ambivalent humanity lives in caste society. Their cultural consciousness reflects the way they internalize the premises of hierarchy, engage in the practices of caste hierarchy, are influenced by the ideology of hierarchy; it also reflects the way they reject these premises and practices. The men and women I knew are not the *Homo hierarchicus* proposed by Louis Dumont, hierarchical in essence, constituted solely by hierarchical premises—but neither do they somehow, magically, escape being influenced by the values of hierarchy.

Cultural consciousness is much more than a political construction, but mind and experience do reflect political ideas. People bear the marks of struggles to shape what they know—and do not know—about themselves and the world. Every social order produces a politics of consciousness, a politics of culture, that advances politically significant concepts of life, society, and self, instilling them with a powerful sense of reality— while much else is kept out of sight, out of mind.

Caught up in political tensions, caught between opposing definitions of reality, tangled up in conflicting moral visions, people may evaluate and experience themselves and their worlds in shifting, often contradictory, ways, developing a multiple consciousness of self and society. Weaving a world-creating web of rhetoric, defenders of a dominant order attempt to make that order seem natural, necessary, even sacred—and surely they often persuade themselves. Dominant groups produce legitimating concepts of reality that obscure the capricious foundations of social life, making it possible for social actors to believe, at least some of the time, that they live in a just and moral world.

Even those oppressed by the dominant order may at times experience the order that oppresses them as fair, as embodying justice, since they, too, wish to believe they live in a moral world. They may find it difficult, as well, to dispute the hegemony of other groups or challenge the cultural concepts that stigmatize them. Politically weak, they may not be in a position to dispute the constructions of reality that more dominant groups produce and disseminate, at least not openly. Moreover, since in some sense they share culture with the politically dominant elite, they may actually collude in the production of the sense of reality that stigmatizes them. They may conspire with the dominant culture to make the social order that oppresses them appear objective and unalterable, natural and moral—even just. They may join in the process of making their social fate appear deserved.

This cultural labor of mystification often succeeds in obscuring the political and economic realities of the social order, even though it may require a significant degree of deep self-deception. The effort may also succeed because it is done massively and redundantly; much social energy may be expended, great political skill used.

And yet, it often fails. The power of culture to blind people to political reality is limited, not absolute. People have moments of insight into the social order, moments in which they see through the cultural presentation of a "moral" order to the arbitrary foundations of social practices. In these moments of insight, they may see that the established order of their lives is a human construction, and may even catch themselves in the act of "naturalizing" the arbitrary.

When they do so, they face a choice. They can either explore the insight, or make themselves forget what they know. Often enough, actors work to make the dominant order's often capricious foundations seem moral and necessary, and natural (Bourdieu 1977:164). Frequently, this requires that people produce in themselves a degree of cultural amnesia or blindness. For to see clearly how a social order—and one's own fate and identity in society—has arbitrary foundations may undermine commitment to society and one's sense of the unity of self and life. It might even threaten the social order with dissolution. Hovering on the edge of such insights, people must often find ways of not knowing what they know. They may seek to force themselves and others not to build on de-mystifying insights. This cultural dialectic of insight and blindness—a politics embodied by the cultural self—is the most general subject of this volume.

The blindness and the insights run deep. People shift between different visions and rhetorics of self and society for many different purposes. Race, caste, class, and gender are only the most obvious and powerful vectors of multiple consciousness of self and society. In the context of any of these, not only do people sometimes have the political equivalent of religious conversion experiences, they shift and adjust perspectives as they confront the realities of their everyday lives, and attempt to fine-tune their social existence. While our concern here is with Hindu Newars as Brahmans and as untouchables and as human beings seeking mutual recognition, I believe multiple (un)consciousness characterizes cultural life in any complex society.

We need theory and ethnography that looks at, looks through, and looks beyond, the ideology that constructs and justifies a social order. To be sure, such critical ethnography must present much material on the construction of the social order; the construction of hierarchy in pageants and rituals, in moral and political discourse, in the practices of everyday life, and in the context of the sacred, must be explored in any study of caste society. Yet the psychoethnography of critical consciousness we need would also probe insights into the arbitrary foundations of the social order. It would examine imagined worlds, envisioned as better than the "real world," showing how these imagined worlds help constitute a "critical self" in relationship to the actually existing social order. Such a critical psychoethnography could explore the ways a plethora of mental spaces and conflicting models exist within a culture—including spaces where people rethink the social order, even rethink themselves, challenging dominant concepts of reality.

I attempt tentatively here to explore a few such mental spaces, such critical moments, documenting ways in which some of the human subjects of caste society both participate in and demystify the social order, both justify society and propose alternative grounds for it. Using ethnography, we can trace some of these movements, shifting focus from constructions of order to personal, narrative, and ritual subversions of caste hierarchy, and back again. Description and interpretation "tack" between conflicting perspectives, moving from legitimation practices to subversive thought, from disruptive acts to the re-closure of the ideology of hierarchy over the wound of insight, seeking in this way to arrive at a fuller understanding of the cultural life of inequality, in one culture.

Critique co-evolves with ideology, so that you cannot fully understand one unless you understand the other. Spun out of the moral imagination, critiques and the aspirations they represent are an integral part of culture: currents of counter-ideology (Lynch 1969) and anti-hegemonic thought (Williams 1977) affect the historical development of culture and society, shape the development of ideology, influencing even the cultural development of the self. Thus, they warrant close examination. Over the long run, they orient social actors to change, prepare them for social transformation, and provide the grounds for resistance and protest. Dominant groups attempt to counteract these potential catalysts for change, seeking to weed them out before they can develop, to make them costly in a social and psychological sense, to co-opt and redirect them. This conflict is played out in the interactions of groups and in transactions among individual actors, but also in the psychological worlds of actors. In every complex society, there exists an unending struggle at the core of consciousness, at the heart of self-experience.

People limit and neutralize their own insights into the social order, as they attempt to survive in a hierarchical society and find meaning in their own experience. Insight melts away, only to be recaptured at another time.

Every political consciousness creates a corresponding "political unconscious." Every time social actors "know" themselves and their society in terms of particular models of self and society; they must "not know" themselves and their world in terms of other models (of and for reality) available to them. In these states of dynamic, dialectical amnesia, people can no longer recall much of what they know; they may not be able to recognize the nature of the social processes that determine their experience and life-chances, may not be able to challenge, question or repudiate the legitimacy of institutions; they may defeat their own efforts to transform themselves and society, collude with their own oppression. Nevertheless, what is suppressed often remains a potential way of knowing self and society; this body of suppressed insights and values may regain consciousness, forming the basis for discourse and action that resists the grip on mind, self and emotion of dominant concepts of reality.

Indigenous Critical Theory, Its Cultural Traditions and Cultural Psychology

As vital as the analysis of ideology and hegemony is, more is required if we seek a full understanding of the experience and dynamics of caste life. Thus, while one locus of this work is the debate between Dumont and his critics on the nature and place of hierarchy in South Asian life, a larger issue emerges: the relationship of cultural tradition and critical discourse. This volume, then, is an ethnographic essay that explores an area of inquiry defined by the dialogue and principled disagreement of Hans Georg Gadamer and Jürgen Habermas.[4] I attempt to show how critical consciousness emerges when the thought of a dominant group has achieved near-total hegemony, shaping common sense, moral tradition, and the practices of everyday life. An inquiry into the critical perspectives of actors gives a wider sense of cultural life. Critique, irony, and utopian reimaginings are modes of subjective self-constitution that may prepare actors for cultural resistance, perhaps at some moments in history forming the cultural basis of political resistance. More often, perhaps, they make life more bearable, provide a way of dealing with painful dissonances, with the "crushing objecthood" that threatens self (Fanon 1967).

Indisputably, Newars "have" a culture that values caste hierarchy on many fronts, generating understanding of caste inequality as natural, necessary, moral. The values of hierarchy are integral to an interlocking system of social structure, thought and practice that constitutes an inescapable lived reality. For Newars, the generative schemes of caste hierarchy—of habitus and consciousness alike—are constituted both within the taken-for-granted world of common sense knowing and practice, and within the numinous, not-taken-for-granted world of "marked" sacred symbols (Levy 1990). Hierarchy is thus an obvious fact of life, of nature, of reality. Hierarchy is at once prosaic "common sense" and a divinely sanctioned ultimate fact, grounded in a cosmos-constituting mythos. Granted the power of this—how do Newars ever not succumb? More precisely—how do they both participate and resist?

Dumont's project was to isolate an ideology and show how it constituted the structure for social life. My goal is to isolate the critique of ideology in everyday consciousness. How does a critique of ideology grow out of ideology itself? How do minds in the grip of culture ever break free of it? How does moral discourse begin to cut against the grain of a dominant ideology, against the values and practices that have cultural hegemony? These are difficult questions, and I do not claim to offer final answers, but rather only provocations and speculations that help illuminate these perplexities. My data are not texts but the testimony of persons positioned in an actual caste system, who voice both ideology and critique. I think the relatively "experience-near" material I present reveals that ordinary people engage in critiques of the ideology of caste, however powerless they may be to change social practice.

Since culture encompasses ideology and critique, it is not enough to isolate an ideology and declare we understand a way of life because we have grasped its central ideological principle(s). It is also necessary to explore a people's critique of themselves and their world. Dumont's project, while if great value, is radically incomplete.

Of course, the notion that culture embraces a critique of itself poses some basic questions. How do people as cultural subjects go beyond what culture (as ideology, hegemony, tradition, subject-position) constitutes as knowledge and reality, as value and self, for them? How does critical consciousness, critical reflection on culture, society, and self, develop in the course of cultural life? What is the nature of the critical consciousness of cultural subjects, themselves culturally constituted? How do they think critically and culturally about the culture they are, since it takes form as, and gives form to, their own minds and selves, lives and realities?

As my phrasing suggests, I see the human subject as—in part—culturally constituted. If so—if in fact we are all the products of powerful processes of enculturation and cultural experience—we cannot take the easy way out, and simply assume actors stand outside of culture with minds innately prepared to interpret and critique it. We cannot pit natural reason against cultural tradition, if reason reflects culture, if it is in part cultural cognition. While all thought must be embodied in neural and cognitive processes, we do not find the ideology or the critique of caste hierarchy "wired into" our brains. If we have to strip away all the rich cultural premises, models, and experiences people think with and about, in order to arrive at a pristine, culture-free mind—one magically developing and working in splendid isolation from the lives people live—I fear we will only find mental processes so abstract they will shed little light on what Brahmans and untouchables think about caste.

When exploring critical discourse that defines itself in its opposition to cultural tradition, we must not assume that this critical discourse is culturally unconstituted. Where else could it be constituted except in culture? The skepticism that has developed in anthropology, psychology and other fields about the assumption of culture-free minds seems more than warranted. Persons are always persons in social and cultural contexts, and embody culture in their experience, thoughts, and actions.

In making room for accounts of critical discourse, and of the critical subjectivity constituted in such discourse, we should not falsely portray men and women as having a simple power and freedom to reject culture and to emancipate themselves from it that they do not actually possess. If it is false—or at least dangerously one-sided—to portray social actors as simply the more-or-less passive products of culture, it is equally so to depict them as having acquired an immunity to culture, as having the power to isolate their minds, bound their experience, quarantine their selves, in such a way that they remain apart from culture, untouched by it (Ortner 1989; Parish 1994). I do not believe such isolation is possible. People cannot excommunicate themselves from culture and become critics "from the outside"—they can only become critics "from the inside."[5]

What we need to explore is precisely the way men and women may develop critical stands "from the inside," as cultural beings, in dialogue with culture. We should see how we can locate their mental agency in culture, not apart from it. While people are in part the products of culture, they may also know and experience themselves and their world in terms of their critique of culture, a critique which they actively develop—and themselves with it—because it expresses their interest in emancipation from cultural practices, their desire to transform the conditions of their existence.

Rather than imputing a false freedom and distance from culture, I believe what we need to do is to place this crucial aspect of subjectivity in relation to the total interpretive work of men and women. If we use the metaphor of a dialogue with culture to forge our conceptual terms, we might say cultural tradition "speaks to" people, who find themselves and their sense of reality in it. However, in this "dialogue" people may also feel compelled to "speak against" culture—as against a misrepresentation or threat. In "dialogue," then, people weave themselves into and out of cultural tradition, relating and re-relating themselves to it in different ways, both internalizing it in the form of generative schemas for self and social practice, and distancing it as not self, as distortion, as not the way things "ought to be."

The view I propose we take of actors draws on the insights of both Gadamer and Habermas: actors generate themselves out of their cultural tradition through their interpretive work, but also generate critical discourse that "reflects" on culture and goes beyond received tradition. Consequently, our goal as analysts should be not only to see how actors merge with cultural tradition, constituting themselves within culture, deriving their power to interpret themselves and their worlds from it, but also to look at the ways they seek and achieve critical distance, shifting cultural perspectives and activating contradictory cultural schema to generate distance and dissonance, re-relating themselves to culture, formulating hew ideas, often rejecting the status quo in the process.

I am not sure we should rush to "reconcile" these apparently conflicting perspectives; we might achieve a premature crystallization, when it would be more fruitful to explore the tension. In any event, whatever theoretical resolution we propose, the interplay in cultural life of tradition, ideology, hegemony, and critique deserves attention—and we should keep in mind that their relationship in a given culture may develop in ways unanticipated in our philosophical speculations.

"Critique is also a tradition," Paul Ricoeur (1990:306) observes, in one possibly-too-easy resolution, echoing Gadamer's insistence that tradition and reflection cannot be sharply opposed. This seems correct, at least up to a point, for even as critique breaks with tradition—it remains a cultural perspective. Drawing on Habermas, the view I take is that critical thought is not independent of culture, but rather one expression of a thread of interest in emancipation and transformation woven integrally into cultural thought and practice. It does not stand alone—sovereign—the product of culture-free minds. However, if we must be careful not to minimize the cultural embeddedness of critique, we must be as careful not to reabsorb critique in culture in such a way that we misrepresent its distinctive character and place in cultural life. Thus, while I understand many of the points Gadamer urges against Habermas's criticism of hermeneutics, I believe there is a measure of truth to what Habermas (1977:

357) says when he acknowledges that understanding is always grounded in tradition. Understanding, he declares, "cannot simply leap over the interpreter's relationship to tradition"; but he insists nonetheless that we can distinguish between critical and non-critical thought. Critical reflection is grounded in cultural tradition but, "in grasping the genesis of the tradition from which it proceeds and on which it turns back reflection shakes the dogmatism of life-practices." I agree.

Ethnographically, the situation is more complicated than Habermas's comment suggests, since people may have to neutralize their own critical insights: such insights pose dangers, may get in the way of living a life. The person who shakes the dogmatism of life-practice—or who even thinks skeptically about it—may also have to participate in those practices. Obviously, it is not an exaggeration, in many social systems, to say that people may need to do so in order to survive. As a result, people may suppress what they know—put it out of mind so they can act without needing to cope with the immediate burden of cognitive dissonance and self-reproach, and without exposing themselves to the risk of being condemned for their insights. Critical traditions may have to go underground.

Given that people have learned that dissent may expose them to danger, may stigmatize or isolate them, we can understand how they may wish to keep their critical thoughts to themselves. Often, they may hide their less-than-orthodox attitudes and practices even from the relatively gentle scrutiny and incomprehension of the anthropologist.

Of course, this poses a problem of method for the anthropologist (Berreman 1972). As one untouchable told R. S. Khare (1984:12): "I may talk with you but not inform, and may inform but not really share my mind. I may inform as well as misinform you until I am sure you are honest in your intentions." If critique is kept "out of sight, out of mind" when the anthropologist visits, a vital part of culture is rendered invisible, while socially acceptable ideology stands out. What it is safe to say, what it may be unsafe to say: this divides a culture into regions. We need to explore both, if possible. The danger exists, in the most unfortunate case, that anthropologists may be tempted to identify culture too closely with a dominant ideology.[6]

Plan of the Book

Let me state what this book is not intended to be. It is not primarily a contribution to Newar or Kathmandu Valley studies, even though some chapters plunge the reader into this cultural world, and incorporate testimony by Hindu Newars of various castes, from Brahman to untouchable, in the form of extensive quotations from interviews. It is not a study of traditional social organization; it does not dissect Newar social structure in its totality, nor does it attempt to present an exhaustive account of caste structure or practice.[7] The book is an interpretive ethnographic essay, rather than a descriptive ethnographic monograph. It explores some aspects of everyday moral discourse, of social criticism directed at caste, and I hope it also conveys a sense of the "ambient" discontents of caste life these express. At the same time, it asks why so much culture theory leaves so little room for actors and their discontents.

By tacking between the testimony of actors and the critique of theory, I aim mostly to enlarge and sharpen our sense of what actors are up to, and what they confront, as they struggle with cultural life. But of course I also hope to define the *kind* of theory that would do justice to actors' discontents, to their efforts to reimagine themselves and their worlds, as these are revealed in words and deeds.

Since the work takes this interpretive turn, I do not hesitate to speculate when I think it will provoke thought or point out areas of puzzlement. Throughout the work I contemplate—with both a measure of enthusiasm and a critical eye—theoretical perspectives that promise insight into caste experience. True, we do not yet have theory that permits us to deal easily with both society and mind, with the phenomenology of the moral and the politics of consciousness, with self poised in culture. Yet ideas and speculations abound that can help us rethink caste hierarchy as flowing from a politics of consciousness that grips minds as it shapes practice. Because of my focus on actors' felt quandaries and their cognitive responses, however, I discuss certain points only in endnotes, and have omitted much else entirely.

Chapter 1 follows a festival through the city of Bhaktapur, using this as a way to introduce the ethnographic setting and to evoke the texture of cultural life in a caste-bound community. The chapter begins the process of revealing how massive and yet intimate a construction caste hierarchy is, how much cultural work goes into making it seem natural and necessary, sacred and moral. Chapter 2 introduces the interplay of concepts of hierarchy and equality in the thought of some Newars, suggesting that not all of them coalesce into the figure of *Homo hierarchicus*. Some of them recognize equality as an ethical principle, making use of it in ironic and utopian counterpoint to the practice and legitimation of hierarchy.

Chapter 3 offers a critique of Louis Dumont's theory of caste hierarchy. It examines the impulses and limits of anthropological constructions of "India" as hierarchy. Returning to the experience-near testimony and life-circumstances of actors in Chapter 4, I discuss the ambivalences that I see as central to caste life. I sketch in what I am tempted, following Fanon (1967), to term the psycho-existential structure of the caste system, speculating on how this might generate felt quandaries and multiply moral perspectives. I believe the contradictions and tensions of caste life are such that "self" and "world view" can never coalesce into a single, coherent vision. Instead, in narratives and action, actors seek ways to confront the social and moral contradictions that produce quandaries for them: conflicts in self-identity, dilemmas for the moral imagination. To do so, they make use of conflicting models of self and society, continually reformulating what they "know" of themselves and their social world. Chapter 5 builds on this. It begins as an exploration of multiple justifications for the caste system. I argue that Newars make sense of caste in terms of certain incommensurate constructions: they possess not one, but several layered and interwoven world views, a multiple ethos. In this chapter, I also suggest how disorder creeps up on the "moral order" I examine the eruption of resistance/disorder associated with city-wide rituals of order.

Chapter 6 reaches out to India again—but where Chapter 3 looks at Western academic visions of "India," this chapter focuses on untouchable accounts of what seems like a very different country. Untouchable responses to the ideology and practices of caste in India parallel the responses of Newar actors in some respects: significant regional continuities exist both in its ambivalences people experience and in the critique they make. Some Indian untouchables' readings of "India" and "Hinduism" tease out contradictions in and unravel the text of Indian and Hindu culture (Khare 1984), exposing it as what we would call cultural hegemony, formulating a critique of the dominant culture without ever escaping it.

A concluding chapter evaluates some of the issues raised in the book, reflecting on the politics of consciousness. It argues that hierarchy and equality co-exist in an uneasy, mutually subversive, but nonetheless vital, complementarity. Each offers a vision of justice that can be challenged and destabilized from the perspective of the other.

In a postscript, I reflect briefly on the significance, limits, and discontents of key concepts—culture, self, power, hegemony—found in contemporary theory. Speaking of justice, I believe all books necessarily do an injustice to their subjects. An ethnography can never fully describe cultural life; an essay such as this does not even begin to flesh in the contours of life, even as it brings one facet of it into sharper focus. To more fully understand Newars, I urge a reading of Robert Levy's masterful study of Bhaktapur's urban Hinduism (1990). Levy's study makes it possible for me to focus on a *special range* of Newar culture and experience. Without it, I would not have been able to write this exploration of hierarchy, its hegemony, its discontents, and its critique.

Even though one of my primary goals is to show that hierarchy does not have an absolute grip on the Newar moral consciousness, I have some qualms about writing a book that focuses on caste and hierarchy, precisely because of the way these have been a central preoccupation of Western thought about South Asia. I would not want to inadvertently reinforce the construction of "India" as static hierarchy, of South Asians as *Homo hierarchicus.* My intent is the opposite: I wish to contribute to an emerging orientation in South Asian studies, where there is a developing body of work that, as Arjun Appadurai puts it, attempts to explore "self-making and culture-making . . . without capitulating to the hegemony of hierarchy as a dominant image" (1986:475). I will show that Newars do not necessarily capitulate to the hierarchical ideology and practices of their own society.

Even so, I am concerned about the relatively narrow focus of this book, the way it zooms in on hierarchy and its effects, neglecting other aspects of cultural life. I would not want anyone to think that South Asians as a whole or Newars in particular are "defined" in some total way either by the caste hierarchy, or by their resistance to it, as if this was all they were. They are more than this.

In other work (Parish 1994), I have explored other aspects of Newar life: rituals as vehicles of consciousness and socialization, emotions as part of the cultural and moral order, the way lives and symbols are joined together in family life. While I found tensions in all of these areas of life, they are in many ways less bitterly contested than caste life. This is a judgment relative to the caste system, not an absolute judgment. Certainly, the members of a Newar family are not always at peace, even though their culture provides rich resources for understanding and identifying with each other—harmony does not reign supreme as an extended family breaks up. Nonetheless I believe there is some relative truth to this relative judgment. My other work better captures a sense of the way Newars are "at home" in their culture.

This book, as a study of the caste hierarchy and its discontents, explores values and practices that Newars are much less at peace with. Caste life arouses disquiet, and passion, and fear; it involves suffering, and power, and domination. Thus, where my other studies are, in essence, explorations of the "dialogue that Newars are," this volume explores as well "dialogues of what might be, and ought to be" as imagined by some Newars and by Indian untouchables.[8] For many, the caste system is not just an objective social fact, but a disturbing social fate, a problem of meaning. They critique the stubborn, often brutal actuality of caste, and speak of possible moral worlds.

Chapter 1
God-Chariots in a Garden of Castes

My Kingdom is the Garden of the Four Varna
and Thirty-Six Castes
—King Prithivi Narayan Shaha of Nepal

The Journey of the Chariot I

In Bhaktapur, myth comes to life with the music of drums and the clash of cymbals. A festival marks the turning of the year. To celebrate it, the gods and goddesses of the city leave their temples to journey through its streets, to rest beneath the eaves of their god-houses, to receive offerings from their worshippers.

Each spring, in rites that mark the passing of the year, the people of Bhaktapur pull two Tantric divinities, Lord Bhairav and the goddess Bhadrakali, in chariots through the streets of the city, and then out to the edge of the city. Before they set out, expectant crowds begin to gather in the square of the five-storied temple where the journey begins, several days before the new year. The celebration fills the town with joyful crowds, with a sacred tumult, as other divinities are also taken in procession.

During these festivals, I have seen the deities associated with various quarters carried in torchlit processions on the shoulders of ecstatic, intoxicated men. Carried away, they sometimes surge through the crowds that have gathered in the narrow streets; the rush of the men carrying the litter holding the divinity adds to the general commotion and excitement. Those who live along the procession's path crowd into their doorways and lean out the windows of their multi-storied houses to watch the gods go by.

The festival's main event, however, is the journey of Bhairav. At rest, waiting for its ceremonial progression to begin, his chariot is an echo on wheels of the two monumental pagoda temples that flank the city square where it sits. Standing motionless, the chariot rises into the air above the heads of the crowd. It is a mobile temple, a god-house on wheels, several times the height of the people who gather around it to watch and worship. Lord Bhairav is a powerful Tantric divinity, and one of the central divinities of the city.

Moving, the chariot of the god surges through the crowd like a ship on the ocean, parting swirling masses of people, who stream away from it on nimble feet to avoid being crushed beneath its great wooden wheels, each taller than a man. The wheels have painted eyes. The chariot has a kind of prow that stretches forward and up, where an image of another god is attached, a mask that stares outward with blind eyes.[1]

The men of the city pull the chariot by ropes attached front and back. In one of the central acts of the festival, they pull it first forward, then back, chanting the rhythm of their efforts, in a sacred tug of war. The men of one half of the city vie with those from the other half, each group attempting to pull the chariot and the god it houses into their section of the city. Each side wants the blessings of the god, and the honor of being the first to take the god through the streets of their part of Bhaktapur.

Having the chariot pass through the city is considered a form of *darsana*, an opportunity to view the god. The journey of the divinity is a kind of ritual epiphany, offering Bhaktapur's people a way of coming into the presence of the deity. The ride of the god on his chariot over the brick streets of the city is one of many ways that the inhabitants of Bhaktapur have of approaching divinity, of making the sacred palpable. They live in a sacred city. Bhaktapur embodies a religious conception of reality: permeated with sacred images, saturated with religious meaning, the city itself exists as a sign of sacred realities, calling them to mind.

We will return to the procession of the god-chariot, for it takes us through the city, not only as a physical place, but as an "imagined community" of a special kind (Anderson 1983; Levy 1990; Parish 1994). But before we rejoin the chariot on its journey, I want to sketch in and begin to define the kind of place Bhaktapur is, as a Hindu city, a city of castes and divinities, where Hindu Newars "inhabit the world they imagine" (Geertz 1983:155).

The City

Bhaktapur sits on a rise above a river, a bit south of the center of the Kathmandu Valley. Viewed from the south, from the fields where Bhaktapur's farmers grow rice and wheat, the city presents a face composed of red-brick houses thrust up like a kind of urban cliff, breached by narrow streets that climb up and into the interior. Above the rooftops of houses rises the tiled pagoda roofs of the five story temple that towers above each year's ritual tug of war in the center of the city; above that, beyond the city on the other side, rise the snow peaks of the Himalayas.

Measured by the grandeur of the Himalayas or the vastness of the contemporary world, Bhaktapur is a small place, a diminutive sacred city, a grain of sand. Physically, its maze of streets and houses rest on a tiny, insignificant fraction of the globe, packed into an area not much more than half a square mile. Yet in terms of meaningful human existence, Bhaktapur constitutes a world in itself.

It is a world built up in the human imagination and social life out of layers of religious and cultural meaning, constituted as an intricate, and compelling, lived world. Considered in this way, Bhaktapur stands on its hilltop as a kind of never-ending story, revealing more and more meaning, as layers of culture and history unfold, exposing more levels of dynamic organization. Indeed, Bhaktapur can seem virtually infinite, at least to the finite minds of those who try to understand its history and culture. Bhaktapur is a universe-in-a-city, a cultural universe as intimate as the scenes of a miniature Rajput painting, but unbound, moving, living, changing. It is barely a whisper in the tumult of the post-modern world. It would be lost in a corner of modern Cairo, or New York, or London, despite the some 40,000 people packed into its half square mile, giving it a population density that rivals many of the densest cities of the world.

Indeed, this population density makes Los Angeles look like a vacuum, like a city that is not quite there, a mirage lining the freeways of Southern California. Although a small place, Bhaktapur has a density of meaning, too, that makes it a palpable presence in life, not just a place where life is lived. Urban form and the use of space, the city's art and architecture, and its city-wide rituals, all help shape a sense of identity, embody a world view, and propose ways of defining self and society. Life in Bhaktapur has qualities that make existence seems coherent and compelling to many of its inhabitants. It is a place that has harvested much of the meaning, much of the sense of reality, generated in South Asia over the centuries. It embodies the Hindu cultural tradition in its space and form, makes them part of life in myriad ways (Levy 1990, Parish 1994).

Considered in terms of the meanings, traditions, and practices that make its cultural life possible, Bhaktapur stands as a work of art, a work of culture. It is as much a city imagined, dreamed up, and conjured into existence by people working with the symbols and meanings that constitute their sense of reality and purpose, as it is a place built of timbers and bricks by its carpenters and masons. For along with the physical density of its population, generated by extended families packed into rooms in three and four story houses, Bhaktapur has a density of felt meaning and living tradition that rivals any city, a thickness of meaning layered on meaning that also seems to make Western cities like Los Angeles appear tenuous, not-quite-there, unsure of their own identity or significance.

Before it was incorporated into the larger kingdom of Nepal more than two centuries ago, Bhaktapur was once home to kings who ruled a minute city-state, the kind of place you could walk across in a day or two. In a way, however, Bhaktapur was, and remains, vaster than empires, if looked at in terms of its human meaning. Built out of orange-red bricks made from the rich soil of the Kathmandu Valley, Bhaktapur as a work of culture draws on a rich mother lode of meaning. Ancient and still unfinished conversations of the human imagination in South Asia supplied images and meanings for the symbolic construction of Bhaktapur, shaped and sustained its cultural development.

You can see signs of this harvest everywhere in the city. It is made palpable in art and architecture, in celebrations that fill the streets, in the routines of everyday life.

For me, walking through the maze of streets of Bhaktapur is much like walking through a maze of narrow desert canyons in Arizona or Utah, with light slanting down making one wall of the canyon bright, the other shaded. In the morning or late afternoon, the sunlight does not reach the flagstones or bricks of Bhaktapur's narrow-streets. It only touches the upper stories and eaves of the houses high above the heads of passers by. If you look up, there is a thin river of blue sky running between the overhanging eaves of the house.

The difference, of course, is that these urban canyons are inhabited; people lean out windows to watch, indolently stroll or purposefully stride by, busy with their lives. You do not see chariots of Hindu gods moving on ritual journeys in the canyons of Arizona. Bhaktapur's streets and squares, plazas and courtyards pulse with human life, with activity. Early in the morning, farmers march out of the city to till their fields. Untouchable Sweepers enter the city, to clean. Men stroll to the main market, or visit the tea-shops. Women carry water-pots or babies balanced on their hips. Entering a courtyard, you might see a woman sitting at a spinning wheel, with a baby sleeping on her lap. At places along the streets there are arcades (*phalca*) where old people and children lounge in the afternoon. In the morning, you might come across one occupied by a devotional group playing religious music, hymns to the gods.

Shops line the streets with enough regular foot traffic to justify opening a business; other lanes seem deserted, giving no clue to the domestic activity that goes on in the three and four story houses that line them. These houses, inhabited by extended families, typically encircle courtyards where other households of the same patrilineage or sub-caste group may dwell.

These streets and squares can come to life. On one day, a lane may be jammed by a wedding procession with a band playing proudly, bringing a bride to her husband's house. On some other day, a funeral procession might travel down this street, on its way out of the city to the burning grounds along the river. A religious procession might wind down a street, stop at some shrine, move on, with drums and flutes. In some streets or squares, at certain times of year, a troupe of god-possessed masked dancers might pass by in the night, pausing to perform some rite. In the moonlight, before the troupe disappears around a corner, you might witness a sacred dancer spinning with a sword.

In the morning, a solitary small girl might appear, walking to a nearby temple with a plate of offerings. Every neighborhood has at least a shrine of the god Ganesh. Walking these streets, you might find your way to the potter's quarter, where you might see pottery set out in the square to dry, and pause to watch young boys making pots on a whirling potter's wheel. In another neighborhood, brightly dyed cloth hangs on bamboo poles set up along the edges of a wide artificial pond. In certain seasons, people rake out grain or set our bright red hot peppers on straw mats to dry on sunny days, in public squares and courtyards, on streets and roof-tops. Sacred cows roam the streets, but not so sacred that they won't be chased away from the drying grain. Along some streets, you will hear barely a whisper, but if you go on a ways, turn a corner, you'll walk into a wall of sound, as hammers beat cacaphonously, bang-clang-clash, the din and clamour echoing in the narrow space of the street as men in ground-floor shops pound metal to make copper and brass pots.

If you walk through the city with high-caste persons, you may detect a flicker of disgust crossing their faces when you enter certain neighbor-hoods. Glancing around, they will say, "Butchers live here," or "This is where untouchable live." I have had this experience on several occa-sions.[2] What Raymond Williams (1977) called "structures of feeling" go along with structures of exclusions: here urban space and social emo-tions reinforce each other.

Urban space is filled with images that invite and provoke religious feel-ings: with sculptures, myth-in-stone. It fills with festivals—the chariot fes-tival is only one of many, although one of the most important. A troupe of ritual dancers dance myths in the streets of the city (Levy 1990). The felt presence of divinities permeates Bhaktapur; the city deserves its epi-thet—the city of devotees. From its own religious perspective, Bhaktapur embodies Tantric Hinduism, as its inhabitants engage symbols and par-ticipate in rites that make religious conceptions of life, self, and world palpably present and powerful.

Bhaktapur is a backwater, or the center of the universe, depending on who you talk to among its inhabitants and what mood they are in. Both perspectives apply. Bhaktapur has not been part of the main current of world history (if there is such a thing) that has swept great masses of humanity into the vast cities of the urban-industrial world-system. It has little in common with Calcutta, Cairo, Chicago, Shanghai, and similar urban conglomerations. Rather, Bhaktapur was, and is, imagined in religious terms, built up in the minds of its inhabitants in terms of a Hindu vision of the cosmos and society. Bhaktapur as a city embodies much of this vision, becomes a kind of symbol itself, in the minds of some of its inhabitants, standing for and making palpable the religious vision that pervades life lived there. Bhaktapur's religious ethos is expressed in its temples, festivals, rites, in its sacred geography, its art and architecture, in the consciousness, experience, and everyday practices of its citizens, assembled into a vision that is more real than history to some who live there.

The Journey of the Chariot II

The priests do not always have an easy ride during the journey of the god through the streets, either during the tug of war or afterwards. I have seen the chariot pulled with such energy that it collides with houses along the street as it does not quite make a corner, gouging holes in brick walls, damaging the chariot itself. The priests complain that the chariot is not pulled with the decorum or discipline that should be applied to the task, as it once was; but Bhairav is a dangerous god of force and motion, and the force with which his chariot is drawn through the city seems somehow appropriate, as a kind of metaphor for social and psychological forces that pulse just beneath the surface of Bhaktapur. Composed of human emotions and dissatisfactions, these forces sometimes break through the redundant constructions of reality and common sense that help establish a cultural and political order for Bhaktapur.

The chief Brahman priest of the Taleju temple rides the chariot, carrying a sword that represents the royal power. According to Levy (1990: 469), this Brahman priest becomes a surrogate for the Newar's Malla kings; Brahman becomes King, for the purpose of the festival. Another Brahman rides with the king, representing the king's own Brahman priest and royal advisor, his guru-purohit. Thus, the apex of the caste hierarchy is represented in the (symbolic) persons of king and Brahman. They ride with divinity: their proximity to the god declares their status, and lends it an aura of legitimacy.

Their importance is dramatized in the way they make an entrance onto the scene, with pomp and ceremony, before the ritual tug of war and hauling of the chariot through the streets begins. Shaded by a ceremonial umbrella carried by an attendant, accompanied by music, they march with dignity from the Taleju temple in the old palace complex to the temple square where the chariot waits. Arriving in the square, the priest-king commands that Bhairav's image be brought.[3] The image of the god is placed in the chariot and the "king" worships it. The Brahman representing the king takes a seat on the god's right. The Brahman representing the royal priest takes a seat on the left. Members of other castes take positions in the chariot that reflect their positions in society. Four carpenters stand at the four corners. An Astrologer and a non-Brahman priest seat themselves behind the priests representing the king and his royal advisor. A *jyapu*, a member of the farming castes who make up a majority of Bhaktapur's inhabitants, also takes a seat behind the king, the royal Brahman priest, and the god. In this way, a kind of self-image of Newar caste society is composed, and then pulled through the streets of the city.

The Caste Hierarchy in Newar Life

Nurtured by Hindu kings over the centuries, caste civilization flourished in the Kathmandu Valley. In many ways, traditional Newar society came to embody the *ideal* that men are unequal. The Newar cities grew to become extravagant flowers in royal gardens of caste, representing a cultural efflorescence of the idea of hierarchy, as caste practices were propagated and cultivated as the essence of the body politic. Taken up as part of the larger harvest of South Asian culture, the propagation of ideas and images of inequality as legitimate and sacred values not only shaped the structure of society, of social relations, but also the intimate consciousness of men and women.

After the defeat of the Newar Malla kings and Bhaktapur's incorporation into the larger kingdom of Nepal, the early Shaha dynasty and the succeeding Rana regime continued to give legal support to caste hierarchy. By the middle of the twentieth century, the larger social and political context was quaking with radical structural change, but change tended to come later to Bhaktapur than to other cities, and caste continued to be one of the key cultural axioms of local social existence even as the legal and political foundations for caste were swept away. By the time I arrived in the early 1980s, some castes had vanished or abandoned their symbolic roles,[4] but the caste *system* as a symbolic and moral system survived in Bhaktapur, and continued to grip people's minds, to define their social identity.

What we term caste, Newars call *jat*. However, although the word jat denotes those hierarchically organized divisions of society designated by the word "caste" in English, it refers also to occupational and ethnic groups and to gender—or to any other distinct category. It is used broadly to mean "kind." When used in the sense of "caste," Newars say there are as many as thirty castes in Bhaktapur. Some of these may recently have disappeared as families left Bhaktapur, and a few may be present only cognitively and symbolically—they are there in thought, not as actual groups. In terms of ethnic identity, most of these castes are considered Newar, but some belong to other ethnic groups.

No one, not I, and not any of the Newars I know, would deny that the opposition of pure and impure is one basis for the caste hierarchy (Dumont 1980), one of the key models for social relations, although it is only one among several. States of purity and impurity separate Newar castes, and purity is one key idiom of rank: higher castes are relatively more "pure" than lower castes. Among Newars, this situation is expressed concretely in a number of ways. As in much of South Asia, food is one medium; patterns of sharing and not sharing food and other items have hierarchical implications. High caste Newars will not accept boiled rice or certain other foods from individuals of any caste lower than their own; they will accept nothing, not even water, from members of some still lower castes.

Some castes are dangerously impure (*asudha*) or untouchable (*tiya ma tya phu(n)*, those who must not be touched). Members of these castes cannot enter the upper stories of houses of high caste Newars (the bottom story being conceived either as outside the house or impure in its own right). They are barred from entering certain temples, though some untouchables have the right to act as attendants at certain other shrines.[5] They perform stigmatizing roles: accepting polluting offerings in death rites, handle excrement, kill animals for a living.

In the past, exclusion was practiced in a variety of the ways. For the most part, the higher castes lived in the center of the city, while lower castes lived on the peripheries. Some of the more stigmatized castes lived in separate neighborhoods; the untouchable Sweepers, the Pore, lived outside the traditional boundaries of the city, in an area near the river, across from one of the city's cremation grounds. This location resonated with their symbolic association with filth, decay, and death. Certain occupations were reserved for certain castes; occupational mobility was limited. Education was limited to members of high castes. Members of the lower castes were required to wear distinctive dress. The untouchable Sweepers could construct only one-story houses with thatch roofs, among other legal disabilities. Untouchables could not use the same water taps as pure castes. Untouchables could not enter the city after sundown. These rules were enforced by royal will, by state power. In the past, many Newars recalled, any wealth untouchables might accumulate would be seized by the old kings. Power and force kept untouchables in their places in the caste hierarchy.

The state no longer enforces this system of exclusions, which so powerfully symbolize hierarchy, but the basic pattern persists, suggesting that it is not only the actions of the state that sustain caste. Given the social, economic, and political changes in Nepal, the persistence of the caste system is remarkable. It is eroding, however. In Bhaktapur, untouchable sweepers still live outside the city. Untouchables now use water taps once reserved exclusively for use by the traditional "high" and "pure" castes, but may still be met with verbal abuse, made to feel unwelcome and inferior. Members of the traditional "pure" castes of Bhaktapur object to untouchables entering tea shops in their neighborhood. Traditionally they could be served outside, and would wash their own utensils. They would risk being beaten if they did not accept these exclusions, if they did not conform to expectations held by members of other castes. Many high and low caste Newars recalled such incidents of violence for me.

Practices that exclude or stigmatize people, that put or keep them in their place in the caste hierarchy, may no longer receive the active support of the state, but groups, households, and individuals remain under pressure to conform to such practices or else leave Bhaktapur altogether. Although legal and political constraints have eroded, the social and cultural constraints of caste life continue to have power, to be central to people's lives.

Many traditional low caste people still perform their traditional stigmatizing occupations. They may be refused employment outside of such occupations if they are recognized as belonging to a stigmatized jat, as they would be in Bhaktapur. They may be barred even from such lowly work as office "peon," a position in which a person performs miscellaneous chores and menial tasks, because, informants report, untouchables filling this post would have to serve tea to high caste office workers.

But change is reflected in educational aspirations for children, in the improved economic circumstances of a few groups, in increased tolerance by some members of other castes, and in the absence of explicit legal sanctions supporting the traditional caste order. Stories are told about individuals who have been successful in the modern sector, and of rare cases of low caste solidarity that have produced concrete gains.

Even with such changes, much of the life of the city still rests on its complex caste system; the caste system constitutes a division of labor, not only for economic activity, but for city-wide ritual activities (Levy 1990). Brahmans and other religious specialists have essential roles in the temples of the cities, and officiate at some of the domestic rites of families. Several castes have symbolic roles that are stigmatizing, but essential to the traditional social and symbolic life of the city. The impurity and inauspiciousness of untouchable Sweepers, for example, is necessary to the purity and fate of the city; the impurities, misfortunes and suffering of the city are conceived to flow into the untouchables, who live in a separate area outside the old boundaries of the city. Their impurity thus defines the purity of the city.

In a sense, they suffer for the city: they absorb in a symbolic way the suffering of the city. Their symbolic presence helps relieve the existential anxieties of higher caste actors; through some process of symbolic displacement they become living symbols that condense meanings and possibilities that high-caste actors want to cast away, reject, throw off, keep away from self. In the words of one high-caste Newar, untouchables "soak up" impurities and inauspiciousness, "like a sponge."[6] They are seen as having a "nature" that fits them for their work of collecting dirt, feces, and garbage.

In a set of conventional stigmatizing stereotypes, the people of low and untouchable castes are seen as dirty, disgusting, impure; as highly sexual and promiscuous; as ignorant and lacking the discipline and mastery of language that would make them truly human. In total, they embody an "otherness," for high caste actors, that is disturbing and yet reflects a moral order that is necessary, ordained by the very structure of the universe. High caste actors view low caste actors, individually and collectively, as deserving their fate. The low castes are polluted, that is, naturally defiled, a notion based on a complex physical theory of the flow of person-defining substances; they are also viewed as realizing the fruits of the sins of previous lifetimes—their fate is justified by karma and ordained by dharma, the moral order of the universe, which caste society embodies.

In sum, a hierarchy constituted by power (the king and state) fuses in experience and in practice with a ritualized hierarchy constituted in terms of purity and impurity with a moral hierarchy of action and knowledge, of sin, virtue, and fate, and with a religious hierarchy of proximity to sacred values and access to spiritual power. In my view, caste hierarchy is all these, locked together in a dynamic propelled by struggles for domination and emancipation.

Lower caste actors (farmers and below) often resent the way they are stigmatized and excluded in the caste system. For them, the garden of castes yields a harvest of discontents. In the past, however, there was often not much they could do about their discontents, since the state weighed in on the side of keeping them in their place. Despite the formal removal of legal sanctions, there is still not much they can do to escape being stigmatized, to escape the caste system. Overcoming the initial set of life-chances determined by their caste standing remains exceedingly difficult, and for most perhaps virtually impossible. Since the invidious distinctions of caste are linked to subsistence and survival, the historical reality is they could not readily act on whatever analysis or critique of caste society some of them may have developed. Furthermore, since caste life generates a sense of moral community, shapes personal identity, and offers a number of meanings and satisfactions, it is not surprising that Newars are ambivalent about caste society, Moral discourse in caste society does not reflect ideology alone; it expresses profound, often self-shattering, ambivalence.

Bhaktapur is much more than caste. We should not identity Bhaktapur, or Newars, with caste hierarchy, as if this is all they were—and not living human beings and a complex culture that is, and can become, more than any one anthropological study can describe. If we keep this firmly in mind, I believe we can explore caste life as central to the lives of people living in Bhaktapur, and examine Bhaktapur as a place where caste has a central role in organizing life. But we must keep this tentative, not claim it is the whole story, or the last word, on a community that has many aspects, and continues to form and transform itself.

In this chapter, I describe Bhaktapur's caste hierarchy as a living, and lived, social reality, but this does not mean it as an absolute of Bhaktapurian identity, the be-all and end-all of their social existence. Such a characterization would be wrong, as powerful as caste is as a social practice. Caste practices are potent forms of life and thought: they help constitute psychocultural realities, lived worlds, for actors. As such, they pose quandaries for the moral imagination. Some actors find their social fate disturbing, find their powers or powerlessness disturbing. They are disquieted by cultural life, even as they live it. Such perplexities and quandaries haunt the imagination of any complex society, including my own racially polarized and class-divided society. Exploring them in the context of a radically different kind of society—as different as Newar Bhaktapur is from the United States—invites us to reflect once more on how the rifts of a society complicate the ways actors imagine themselves, how the cultural evaluation of actors enhance or wound their identifications with society, ultimately disturbing their sense of self, making cultural life not a self-affirming shared project but a self-dividing quandary they must live, whatever they feel and think (Fanon 1967).

Perhaps the symbolic action of Bhaktapur's chariot festival helps quiet the disquieted imagination. Perhaps it helps reassure some social actors that the way things are represents the way they ought to be, affirming their identities and practices, guaranteeing privileges and compensating for subordination—perhaps. In any event, the festival does display, for social actors to see, images of a sacred and moral order. These images affirm hierarchical interdependence as the basis of social reality.

The Journey of the Chariot III

At one point, the ritual progression of Bhairav and Bhadrakali takes them out of the city; at least, they leave the city's symbolic core as high caste actors define it. After their progression through the two halves of the city and certain other events, the chariots descend the hill on which the greater part of the city is built, down a steep, crooked street, down to a wide field on the edge of Bhaktapur, near the river that passes by the city.

This passage to the edge of the city is not difficult for the smaller vehicle of the goddess, but can be a dangerous process with the larger chariot of Bhairav. Two special ruts have been built of stones in the surface of the street to guide the wheels of the chariot and keep it on track. Even with this, the chariot sometimes rushes out of control, endangering bystanders.

I used to watch from the window of one of the houses that line this street. I once observed the chariot break away and rush with great speed and force down a stretch of the road. A man ran alongside the chariot as it crashed down the street. He sped downhill in the narrow space between the chariot and the houses lining the road. Running all out, he virtually bounced off the walls of the houses, and careened back into the chariot, pumping his legs fiercely all the time to keep up with the chariot. I had no doubt that he was at risk, that he could fall and be killed.

I am not sure what he thought he was doing, although he may have been one of those responsible for seeing the wheels did not get stuck in the ruts built into the road for them. (They were in no danger of doing so in the moment I saw him). I am even less sure how he managed to survive. He looked out of control, pacing the chariot as it accelerated out of control. Running along with the chariot seemed to have taken possession of him. Caught up in the moment, he appeared in the grip of an adrenaline rush if not in the grip of some spiritual fervor. Others are swept up in the excitement of the festival as well, are pulled out of their everyday lives and mundane selves, if not as intensely and dangerously. In a variety of ways, festivals offer excitement, danger, and stimulation, generate palpable sacred thrills. Experienced actively or vicariously, these are encompassed in a religious context, making the body's arousal a sensual chord in the mytho-sacred performance, a felt sign of the presence of the sacred.[7]

At the bottom of the hill, where the street issues into the open area on the edge of the city, a crowd will have gathered to watch the chariot arrive. It emerges suddenly, burst out of the city, plunging down the hill, rolling with great force and speed. The crowd nearest it scatters to avoid being run over.

The chariot rolls to a halt in the broad field at the foot of the hill that spreads out towards the river. One corner of the field adjoins the segregated ward of the untouchable Sweepers, the Pore. When the chariot rolls to a stop, men again pick up the ropes to pull it into position for the next stage of the festival. Bystanders toss coins at it as it passes, offerings for blessings.

A few days earlier, in the forests east of the city, a goat had been turned loose, to wander until it rubs its head against a tree. "The goat is then sacrificed to the tree" Levy writes, "and the tree is cut down" (1990: 467). After removing most of its limbs, men of a particular caste drag the tree trunk back to the city. Newars call this trunk *yasi(n)*. They see it as a deity. Envisioning the tree-pole as a kind of body, Newars ritually install or awaken divinity in it. The branches of the tree are removed when it is cut down, except at the very top, where some are left to represent the god's hair. A cross-bar made of part of another tree is attached near the top of the pole, representing the arms of the god. Branches and leaves are tied to the arms to represent the god's hands and fingers. Two banners (*pata*) are tied onto the god-pole. According to a Newar quoted by Levy, the chariots of the god and goddess are pulled near the site where the god-pole will be raised "so that the two deities can watch" (Levy 1990:476).

Each year a crowd gathers to help raise the god-pole, which may be as tall as seventy feet (Levy 1990:476). The base of the pole rests in a hole that has a wall built around it, with a slot open on the west side. The people helping raise it push up on the trunk with poles, and from the other side pull on long ropes attached to the yasi(n) tree, bracing the tree as they go, until it swings upright, the top of the tree swinging in the sky above. The raising of the pole represents the old year; lowering it the next day, the new year.

The ropes attached to the pole represent the protective goddesses of Bhaktapur, the Astamatrka, whose shrines encircle the city. After the pole has been raised, young men climb these ropes, and make an offering of coins to the knots at the top. I was told they did this to get a blessing, and no doubt also they did it for the thrill of the climb.

The chariots are pulled close to the god-pole. The surrogate king and his royal Brahman, and some of the others who ride in the chariot on its ritual journey, have watched the pole raised while still seated in the chariot. They now get off, circumambulate the Bhairav chariot, circle the

Bhadrakali chariot, and finally the Yasi(n) pole, taking prasad at each. The king surrogate and his Brahman advisor then depart for the Taleju temple in the old royal palace (Levy 1990:482).

As part of the festival, people make offerings and sacrifices to the divinities. Throughout the city, gods and goddesses are taken from their temples and god-houses and put on public display. These include the city's protective goddesses. Blood sacrifices are made to these goddesses, and several of them have processions and festivals of their own at this time (Levy 1990).

Thousands of people gather for the taking down of the yasi(n) god, going first to take a ritual bath in the river. After esoteric and secret rituals are performed in the Taleju temple, the king surrogate and his Brahman advisor, carrying the royal sword, leave the temple and go out through the golden gate into the royal square. Joined by their charioteers and musicians, accompanied by an attendant carrying the royal umbrella, they return to the field where the chariots have been left and the god-pole stands. After some preliminary rites, they take their seats in the chariot. From there, they watch the yasi(n) pole lowered.

Levy's account describes the process this way: "First the Yasi(n) is rocked back and forth in an east-west direction, in motion called "rocking to sleep." The god is said to be tired, . . . for "he has been standing all year." (1990:485) The ropes represent the city's protective goddesses. Seeing the god-pole now as Bhairav himself, and these goddesses as his consorts, Bhaktapurians interpret the rocking of the pole and motion of the ropes as sexual intercourse between the god and the goddesses. Levy goes on: "The pole is slowly rocked back and forth, and finally, after perhaps ten minutes to half an hour of swaying, eased down to the west. . . . People who wish a son try to pull one of the leaves from the yasi(n) or its crossbar, and if they get one they will not only have a son, but he will be an important man. When the pole falls, the new year begins."

This is a high-point of the festival, one of its key moments as a signifying practice. While the festival has complex meanings, as Levy's more detailed account makes clear, one aspect is crucial for our purposes in this volume, as it is crucial to the thousands who witness and participate in this city-wide event: the festival is a ritual construction of order. The order it constructs has universal dimensions: it is social and moral, cosmic and sacred. These aspects of order are linked; the ritually declared connection to the cosmos and divinities helps give legitimacy to the royal and caste order. Human and divine actors witness the beginning of the new year, participate in it. In later chapters, I will describe a year in which this construction of order was disrupted and disturbed by what might be called rituals of disorder; but for now we should appreciate that this festival is, among other things, a pageant of hierarchy and a spectacle of order, in which, as Levy says, "the king and his entourage and the god Bhairava are moved by immemorial ritual order, as the sun moves through the year" (1990:493).

Much of the ritual activity of the festival takes place not far from where Bhaktapur's untouchable Sweepers, the Pore or Po(n), live. What part do they play in the festival? Levy (1990) describes an event that seems to signify much about dominance and subordination, inclusion and exclusion:

Now some of the [untouchables] take hold of the ropes at the back of the chariot, and other men, mostly Jyapus [farmers], take hold of the ropes at the front. Again a tug of war begins to determine the direction in which the chariot will move. The Jyapus are trying to pull the chariot back toward the city, while the Po(n) are trying to keep the deity in yasi(n) field, which adjoins the "Po(n)twa": [Sweeper word]. the area where they live, just outside the symbolic boundaries of the city. This struggle does not (at least in the memory and expectation of present informants) lead to fights, and gradually the more numerous Jyapus with the advantage of the two extra ropes at the front of the chariot prevail (Levy 1990:486).

In contrast to the tug of war between the city halves, where one side or the other might prevail, it seems unlikely that the untouchables could ever "win" this tug of war. They are less numerous and they have fewer ropes to pull: the deck is stacked against them. We should perhaps see this as a ritual of social positioning that acknowledges their existence but asserts their subordination and marginality. They were not allowed to participate in the other tug of war, in which only men from higher castes pulled on the ropes. Unlike the two halves of the city, they do not get to draw the chariot through their quarter, which Levy notes is symbolically "outside" the city. The unequal contest asserts the power of the castes of the city over those outside the city, the untouchables. The god and goddess are pulled away from the untouchables, back into the city.

Some Actors

Let me offer several brief sketches of individual actors. I wish not only to convey a sense of the way they are positioned in caste society, but also to acknowledge their individuality. Such an acknowledgment reminds us to be wary of reducing them to abstractions in the rest of the work. Since the sketches present individuals from the "top" and "bottom" of the caste system, they also begin to give a sense of the range of experience of actors in the caste system. For three of the sketches, I draw on material that appeared in my book *Moral Knowing in a Hindu Sacred City* (1994), where I explored the moral psychology of Newars. Here I will begin to reflect on the ways caste hierarchy shapes their lives. Let me stress that I do *not* think persons are in any simple sense totally determined by their place in society, although the way they are positioned surely constitutes a powerful and inescapable influence on them. We cannot, however, simply substitute knowing a person's position in society for knowing the person. To do so risks doing some injustice to actors, reducing them to social constructions when they are more than this.

In Bhaktapur, I lived in the upper floors of a house owned by a Brahman. The entrance was on the second floor; to get to the door you had to walk up a flight of stairs. In Newar culture, this is a walk up to a state of purity; the upper stories of a house are considered purer than the ground floor. Low caste people are barred from entering the upper floors of a high caste house. I had two friends who would sometimes come to see me, to help me by talking about their thoughts and experiences, by discussing a variety of cultural topics. They had very different ways of making their presence known when they arrived at my house, and I believe this fact expresses, in a small way, the reality of caste differences. Shiva Bhakta, a high caste man, would run confidently up the steps, pound vigorously on the door, call out my name in a loud voice. Kancha, an untouchable, would come into the tiny courtyard of the house and sit down on a stack of lumber. He would quietly smoke a cigarette, waiting until I came down or poked my head out the window to see if he was there. I asked him to come to the door and knock, so that I would know that he was there, but he refused. He did not refuse directly—he always bobbed his head affirmatively when I explained to him that he should do this—but he would not make the journey to the top of the stairs. I would poke my head out the window the next time we had arranged to meet, and would find him sitting at the bottom of the stairs, smoking.

The contrast was striking. Some of Kancha's behavior was a public presentation, intended for a possible high caste audience; when he got to know me, he would in private let much of the diffidence drop. In our interview sessions and conversations, he usually voiced his opinions in a direct and self-confident manner. He did not possess the self-assurance and authority that characterized Shiva Bhakta, but he was not at all passive. He felt it necessary to present himself as yielding—as unchallenging—in public. What we see in his behavior is the culture of dissimulation that develops in caste society and perhaps in any stratified society where power may be used in arbitrary ways.

Kancha did not, dared not, assert himself in public; he embedded himself in socially and historically determined patterns of behavior in which he found safety. I did not observe such a radical split in high caste friends and acquaintances, although they too had public faces and private selves (both cultural). Shiva Bhakta, far more than Kancha, could both assert himself and embed himself in historically determined patterns of group behavior without radical self-contradiction.[8]

Kancha—an untouchable

Kancha is a middle aged man, usually dressed in dirty, ragged clothes and carrying the tools of his trade as he goes about his business. He is an untouchable, a Sweeper, a member of one of the very lowest castes, the Pore. Sweepers like Kancha are employed by the Bhaktapur Town Committee (Nagar Panchayat) to clean the streets, and by private householders to clean their courtyards or latrines.

As an untouchable, Kancha exists on the margins of society, lives on the underside of hierarchy, in its stigmatizing depths.

One way this is expressed is by where he lives, and the meaning given to the area where he lives. The Sweepers live in a separate quarter, which is considered to lie outside the city. There is a place you can go and look out over the houses of the Sweepers' quarter. Unlike the houses of others, many of these houses have thatch roofs. In the old days, these untouchables were not permitted to have tile roofs, or to live in houses as tall as those of other castes. Kancha knows he is marginal. He knows that his work stigmatizes him, that for others, his work is what he is. To survive, he feels he must live his life on the terms given in the caste system, and this shapes his view of his world. He struggles to reconcile a sense of self with the burden of his social identity. He expresses some ambivalence, and resentment—he recognizes that he is stigmatized, rejects some of the implications of hierarchy for himself, but knows, too, that his survival and that of his family depends on his relations with high caste people.

Kancha undergoes a social metamorphosis as he leaves his home and goes up "into" the city to work, walking up the same street the god-chariot came rolling down and "out" of the city during the festival. In the social gaze of high caste actors, who bring a hierarchical sensibility to what they see, he undergoes a transformation. They see an untouchable.

At home, he finds meaning in domestic life, finds a measure of psychological security—"my caste is good for me," he will tell you. There, he sees himself (and wants to be known) as a good father, a husband, a head of household, and a person with aspirations for himself and his children, but he must leave this psychological cocoon to make a living. As he leaves the untouchable quarter and enters the city, he enters a world where his presence and being have other meanings. He walks the streets not as himself but as a symbol. Here, in contrast to the domestic scene, he has no active role in constructing his own meaning: he simply exists for others as a living symbol of hierarchy. High caste people "know" and experience him as a member of a functional category that performs needed, but degrading, work. They see that his hands and clothes are dirty from contact with feces and filth. I have seen people shrink away, assume disgust faces in the presence of untouchables. Being harangued, ordered around, by words hurled across the social distance that separates them, may be his dominant experience of interacting with high caste people.

Arguably, for the high caste community, the Sweepers have a special, psycho-symbolic value—the untouchable is one of many "others" who define "self" through contrast and complementation (Sartre 1963). In caste culture, Kancha is a source of impurity, a polluting presence, but perhaps even more critically, he absorbs, soaks up, the most disgusting, dangerous, contaminating residues and effluents of higher caste bodies and selves. He is a receiver of impurity, of inauspiciousness, of what others reject and seek to keep away from themselves. Kancha's caste is associated with an inauspicious planet, Rahu, responsible for eclipses and human misfortunes, and I was told by an older high caste informant that the goddess of cholera used to dwell in their quarter, near one of the cremation grounds.

As we will see, Kancha does not seem bitter about his status. At times, he defends the caste system; indeed, at times, he defends it more vigorously than some high caste Newars. How, he wants to know, would he survive without it? But he wants something else for his children, and there are moments when he denies that the caste hierarchy has any moral reality, any ultimate justification.

Shiva Bhakta—a high caste Chathariya

If Kancha is a marginal man living on the margins of the city, Shiva Bhakta inhabits the center, in a physical and social sense. Indeed, Shiva is a man of many centers, within a lived world that contrasts sharply within Kancha's world. Some of Shiva's many centers, his personhood and status, his prospects and possibilities, his class and caste position, are defined in part by where and how Kancha lives, by what Kancha is. Shiva is not Kancha—this is an existential and social fact of no little significance.

Shiva is a dweller in the city, the head of household of one of the large houses in one of the central neighborhoods of the city. In the local status system, only the Brahmans are higher in status, and even they may not be more central to the social and economic life of the city, although they are to the religious and ritual life of the city.

Befitting his status and prosperity, Shiva dresses neatly, with a kind of precision, in traditional fashions. With a formal black hat settled on his graying hair, there is nothing of diffidence about Shiva. He is a merchant, and relatively prosperous, with a social network radiating out through and beyond the community. He lives in a larger social world than Kancha, who has few contacts outside of the city.

One center of life for Shiva is the modern economy, and the opportunity it represents; he tells me life is getting better, that you have to seize the day. He applies this philosophy to business and pleasure. He has a certain zest for life.

If one center of Shiva's life is commerce, the effort to generate wealth and through it prestige, he is also centered in a moral world, in the traditions of family, religion, and city; he identifies with the dharma, the moral order and rightness, integral to each of these. I believe this gives him what Erik Erikson calls an "ordering core"; for Shiva this ordering core is socially and psychologically attuned to the moral order of his city, his family line, integrating past and present, himself and significant others through whom he integrates self and culture. As the key concept of the Hindu moral order that Shiva identifies with, dharma offers Shiva a firm basis for his sense of self, and yields him moral insights for living his life, yet also helps constitute a society that oppresses others, such as Kancha.

Shiva's confidence, his ordered and ordering core sense of self, also, I think, reflect what Robert Coles, writing of the American elite, termed a sense of "entitlement"—an "emotional expression," not just of money and power, but also of caste status and family history, combined with the sense of purpose and fulfillment that doing dharma gives. Shiva characterizes himself as *calak*—vocal, articulate, clever—and I think he is right. Language, the power to use it to express social values and achieve goals, is another one of his centers; he is a man of words and means, grounded in dharma and family, who speaks and acts from the center of a community and tradition.

Kesar—a Jugi

A member of the Jugi caste, Kesar is an angry man, unafraid to voice his fear and loathing for the caste system, his contempt for what he sees as the bad faith and illusions involved in it. He voiced rage and a sense of powerlessness, too, in a less veiled fashion than some others. Unlike many other low caste informants, he consistently rejected caste, stressing its oppressiveness and his impotence to change it. He often spoke with irony and sarcasm, pointing out what he felt was bad faith and hypocrisy, insisting on a kind of dual perspective: that he felt the caste order had no moral reality for him, but that it nonetheless formed a social reality that he could neither ignore, nor deny, nor totally break free from. His goal was clearly freedom: he wanted to break from caste interdependency, to become a man of independent means. He expressed great pride in a small entrepreneurial business selling chickens and goats, which he felt made him relatively free of his group's former dependency on caste roles. It may be this relative capacity to support himself that made him feel free to scorn the caste system, in ways that others somewhat shared, but would temper and hedge, worried about what others might think and about their own need to perform caste roles in order to survive. Perhaps it is because he had come to think of himself as a man of independent means that he also insists on defining himself through his own independence of thought. He was willing to concede, even underscore, his powerlessness in the face of the realities of caste. Why would he stress this, if he has achieved more independence than many? Perhaps because in his "inner" world he imagines and strives to create himself over and against the caste system. By claiming that he did not make the world of caste, he emphasizes that he did make himself, in defiance of the caste system and the place it allotted him. He values his hard-won, relative independence, the freedom of choices he has earned. These contrast with his sense he lives in a world that he did not make, and would never have chosen.

Krishna Bahadur—a Gatha

This jat is on the borderline between pure and impure. Krishna Bahadur dances myth in the city, as a member of a ritual troupe that visits each neighborhood to perform rites that protect the city and its inhabitants. He has danced in the streets of Bhaktapur as a divinity. This role is his center, offering him an ordered and ordering core, a sense of identity. He wishes for his son to follow him, to share this identity, to dance for the city, to have a sacred role. Yet this identity is not without its cost, for it cannot be separated from his low caste status. He is highly critical of the "closed" hierarchy of caste, and proposes an "open" hierarchy based on knowledge—such as he himself possesses of sacred dances and Tantric divinities, knowledge of the kind he knows he has the capacity to master. A thin and intelligent man, brooding and yet gentle, he has given some thought to these matters, and speaks with some rhetorical force. Yet I do not think he can be said to have resolved anything; perhaps this is why he broods.

Dharma Raj—a Brahman

A priest and a reflective man, Dharma Raj sees the city in terms of the religious meanings that compose and integrate it. He supplies others with interpretations of cultural tradition, of religious reality. He performs domestic rites for people, using Sanskrit texts, as he was taught by his father. Like Shiva Bhakta, he sees the city as his; his caste provides the chief priest of Bhaktapur's main temple, in the old royal palace complex. In the days when Bhaktapur was the capital of an independent kingdom, members of his priestly caste served as advisers to the kings. In that role they shaped the ritual cycle and religious landscape of the city. Indeed, as we've seen, Brahman priests have in some ways been amalgamated to the old Malla kings, blending the symbolism of king and priest together in ways that help sustain the Hindu core of Bhaktapur (Levy 1990).

Dharma places himself in a line of teachers and students, predecessors and successors, from whom he received the knowledge of tradition (including secret religious knowledge), and those who will receive that knowledge from him. His most important teacher was his father, but other Brahmans also shared their knowledge and helped shape his view of the world.

His concern about the changes affecting Bhaktapur runs deep. He foresees that Hinduism will become more and more a private matter—religion will be confined to the household, and no longer centrally involved in the life of the city, as it is today, as it was in his father's time. Caste is the focus of some of his concerns; he needs other castes to be what and who he is. People will still need Brahmans for domestic rites but they will not care about the web of rites that link divinity to the life of the city, with many castes working together to please the gods and goddesses and perform the obligatory rites. Caste is still a powerful social reality, but a breakdown of caste relations seems inevitable as more and more people break away.

With this withdrawal of commitment, the means of maintaining the public ritual system of the city will vanish. He does not expect the caste system to vanish, only to change; it is the city-wide ritual system based on caste specialization that he sees as threatened. Rather, he expects, with some reason, that the caste system will survive as the basis for identity and exclusion, competition and politics, but will no longer unite the city into a religious community. Already, gaps have grown where once special castes performed symbolic roles; so far, the system has enough resilience to absorb these losses. Dharma Raj lives in a state of quiet, anticipatory mourning, grieving for what is passing, and for what is still to pass.

After the Festival

The god and the goddesses return to their temples, the people return to their homes, the chariot is dismantled and stored by the side of the Bhairav temple. The passing of the old year and the coming of the new year have been celebrated. The order of life has been displayed. People have had their chance to come into the presence of divinity, and to view a kind of tableau vivant of the caste order, a living symbolic display of hierarchy in which members of certain castes get to pose as themselves. The tableau presents an eternal, unchanging image of the way things are—hierarchical, fixed, sacred. It proposes that actual life is no different, that each actor is also symbol in everyday life, an element in the cultural order. If this display cannot actually contain reality, if disturbing elements and ambivalences enter stage left, nonetheless life must go on. Having seen world-images and visions of themselves, people return to their routines, settle back into the habits of everyday life. Krishna broods, Dharma reflects, Mahila goes up into the city to sweep in the morning. The farmers work in their fields, and the Brahmans perform their rites.

Chapter 2
Equality and Hierarchy

When I spoke with Newars, they would sometimes turn to me and pro-claim, "I am a person, you are a person." Taken out of context, the phrase seems simply to announce the self-evident; but I didn't think these intelligent people needed to reassure themselves, or me, about the obvious. I was strange, out of place, anomalous, and they recognized this, but I am sure no one doubted I was a person of some sort, except myself on days when I could not seem to understand anything. Why, then, did so many Newars confront me with the fact that they were persons, and I too was a person?

I came to understand that the phrase signified and constituted a whole mode of moral discourse for Newars. It was a declaration of equality, an invocation of mutual recognition, voiced by high and low caste Newars alike. They often said it with great emphasis. One man, a Brahman, used to bounce up and down in his seat, pointing to himself and then to me as he recited the phrase, leaning into his words, getting his body behind them, embodying his engagement. Another high caste man used to make crisp gestures with his cigarette, leaving a trail of smoke to mark his words. Indeed, many of these high and low caste Newars were chain-smokers, filling the room where I interviewed them with clouds of smoke; but they used this declaration of what they took as an ultimate fact to clear the air of clouds of mystification—the reality, they'd insist, was that they were just as good as anyone, and that everyone was enough like everyone else, a person, to deserve equal and fair treatment. Floating in my own cloud of culture shock, I would look at them through their clouds of cigarette smoke, and think to myself "This is not *Homo hierar-chicus*, not right at this moment, anyway." Indeed, all in all, it was not quite what I expected, not after reading the works of Louis Dumont.

For the Newars I conversed with, invoking this principle of equality was usually a prelude to speaking of treatment experienced as unfair—of being coerced or ordered about in a peremptory way, of being insulted,

cheated, or exploited. By declaring the moral equivalence of human beings, my Newar acquaintances asserted their conviction about the ultimate basis of justice; if persons are alike, if they are the same in morally
relevant ways, then they deserve to be treated the same. If I am a person,
and you are a person, if we are interchangeable, then if you should actually be transposed with me, placed in my life and circumstances, you
will feel what I feel, know what I know, and suffer what I suffer. What
harms me would harm you, and you would reject treatment that I reject, for we are persons. Since we are alike, you would want to be treated
in the same way I want to be treated. Thus, for Newars, invoking the
moral equivalence of human beings constitutes and deploys a sense of
justice. Moral discourse, Newars were telling me, begins with mutual
recognition.

How are we to reconcile this affirmation of equality with the image of
Homo hierarchicus? I feel that the preoccupation with ideological constructions of hierarchy fails to do justice to the range of ways that men
and women in South Asian cultures know themselves and evaluate their
society. In this chapter, I will join in the efforts of a number of scholars
to restore some balance to the way South Asians are represented, by describing the interplay of concepts of equality and hierarchy in Newar
moral discourse. Newars make use of both perspectives.

Many Newars have doubts about the ideology of caste hierarchy, about
what it means for themselves and others. Some of them find meaning in
concepts of equality and solidarity, asserting that these, not hierarchy,
are the ultimate moral grounds of social life. They use concepts of human equality and solidarity to resist some of the implications of hierarchy. They identify themselves with society, and commit themselves to
social practices, on the basis of these ideas, not exclusively on the basis
of concepts of hierarchy. Sometimes they justify hierarchy as a functional
expedient, or reject it as an imposed order, ultimately encompassed in
higher order solidarities.

For many Newars, the hierarchy of purity and impurity is merely one
way of viewing self and society. They play with the idea of alternative hierarchies, based on other principles, which, if enacted, would give them
a different place in society. The relationship of Newars to the dominant
caste hierarchy—and to equality as well—is perhaps best described as
one of ambivalence. In action, in terms of actual social practice, hierarchy is dominant. This dominance, I think, can only be fully understood
when we see it as the outcome of a long-term struggle to overcome the
sense of justice and equality evoked by mutual recognition. The ideology
of hierarchy itself bears the marks of this struggle.

If so, the ideas that the ideology of hierarchy opposes must be present;
they must have a source in culture, and some kind of place in culture,

even if only in some kind of cultural underground. In this chapter, I will attempt to locate and explore ideas that have a certain subversive potential in Newar thought.

To do so, I will quote a number of Newars. These informants belong to the more traditional part of Newar society, but the ideas they express may be modern, in the sense that opposition to hierarchy may have been voiced in different ways in the past. Though modern, I do not think their ideas are in any simple sense derivatives of Western thought, though clearly contact with other societies (China and India as well as Europe and America) provide some of the impetus for contemporary developments within the Newar tradition. Their contacts with South Asia have presumably always challenged Newar society to assimilate new ideas and practices.

My Newar acquaintances were not all chain-smokers, but they were all heads of household. They were all older than forty. None of them could be described as marginal figures; on the contrary, most of them could more aptly be characterized as "pillars of society," at least in their own status and reference groups. All conformed to caste practices, at least in public, whatever they said about it in private. Their personal views are interesting precisely because they are those of ordinary householders of different castes—not those of spiritual renouncers or political activists.

A word on the nature of the testimony is in order. Equalizing rhetoric is public, and accessible to study, in a way that obscurely experienced, culturally disowned, emotions are not. One can rather easily recover the words in which low caste people reject hierarchy, because they voice something of their protests, doubts and reactions. Here and elsewhere I examine both high and low caste testimony, but I stress low caste accounts, because they were more often volunteered, and because they seem more open to interpretation as responses to the problems of meaning, identity, and practice that caste status poses. Then, too, some of the most influential anthropological accounts of the caste system have not given these voiced sentiments the weight they deserve (Dumont 1980).

I am using the term "equality" advisedly to refer to constructs used to critique aspects of caste practice, or to dispute dominant ideas of hierarchy. Some Newars—and possibly most of them, at least at some moments—reject the organization of social life, and express a variety of discontents. Some, not all, of them attempt to neutralize concepts of hierarchy—not very often directly, in confrontations, for there would be a high price to pay for such gestures, but in their imagination, in moral rhetoric. While they may not invoke concepts of equality in the course of everyday life, out of fear of the practical consequences of confrontations, they rehearse them in critical discourse that actively imagines ways to abolish differences and to dissolve hierarchies. Their concepts of equality, in other words, are often expressed as critical and negative concepts, although, on the constructive side, they assert or invoke a common "being," not an equality of opportunity or condition, but of mutual recognition. In their rhetoric, if not always their practice, Newars declare and affirm the nature of a higher ethical reality. Such assertions of a common "being" are, of course, also incorporated in hierarchical discourse, but in the framework of exclusion and difference.

Let me re-emphasize that the values of hierarchy, not equality, shape Newar inter-caste social relations. Hierarchy is the dominant value because it is enacted with respect to other castes, and because it frames and gives meaning to equality within caste and kin groups. Yet equality is present, felt, and significant in a number of ways. My argument is not that equality has an equal place with hierarchy in Newar culture—that would be a false symmetry—but that the values of equality and hierarchy exist in dynamic, uneasy complementarity.

Newars do not possess an ideology of "equality" analogous to those found in the modern Western world. In fact, I believe their concepts bear only a remote family resemblance to secular Western concepts of equality. Although perhaps some form of the equality of mutual recognition may be found in many different cultures I do not argue that universal and invariant, much less Western, concepts of equality are present in South Asia. My point is that cultural concepts of equality are found in Newar Hindu culture; equality is present, but transmuted into distinctive cultural forms, embedded in indigenous meaning systems.

The task before us, then, is not to discover moral universals by some process of abstraction, but to explore cultural differences in the way that "equality" is constructed, and to examine the place of equality and hierarchy within the moral discourse of Newars of different castes. Newar notions of equality—often fragmentary and personal, as one might expect of a discourse driven underground by fears of violence and ostracism—cannot be understood in terms of the interpretive approaches applicable to the secular democratic ideologies of Western industrial polities.

The way that ideas of "equality" can be expressed in terms of importantly different belief systems is a familiar phenomenon within the Western tradition. The statements "All men have equal political rights" and "All men are equal in the eyes of God" both assert equality, but the equality asserted means different things. The statements derive from different, although Western, belief systems: the first from secular democratic ideology, the second from Christian thought (Williams 1969:158). Newar concepts of equality cannot be simply reduced to some universal idea of equality; their concepts of equality are *culturally* different. Such cultural differences shape the way the underlying idea of equality is used and experienced.

The range of different concepts of equality (and hierarchy) seem to me to be cultural response to concerns that must, I think, be experienced by human beings in any stratified society—if we are to credit human beings with any sense of self or capacity for agency at all. These varied concepts respond to the fundamental threat to human identity posed by inequality. Newars voice these basic concerns in words like these: "How am I less than another?" and "Am I not the same as others?"—questions often answered with the declaration, "I am a person." These questions are meant as rhetorical challenges; but they also express the irreducible, existential threat to self posed by the inequality and unfairness of life.

Equality in Newar Moral Discourse

The vocabulary of equality in Newar discourse includes abstract terms for equality such as *samanta* (n., equality, likeness, sameness 'Skt&). Such terms were used only rarely in interviews, and only by the most educated of the traditional Brahman intellectuals. Khare (1984) reports that untouchable intellectuals in Lucknow, India, do use such abstract terms.

More common among Newars were adjectives such as *barabar*, or *saman* both with the sense of "equals, alike." The word *uthae(n)* "same, equal" was also used to assert that people are the same or equal. There were a number of common propositions about mutual recognition used to undermine hierarchical constructions of difference. As I noted above, Newars would frequently make statements of the form "I too am a person, you too are a person" to establish that the distinctions of caste or wealth were not the only relevant factors in relationships. This declaration distinguishes the category of "person" or "people" from caste role, economic status and so on, substituting undifferentiated humanity for hierarchical differences. Some Newars evoked equality through the imagery of "blood" and "flesh"; the blood and flesh of people is the same, not different. Other Newars advanced the idea of a kind of transcendent, spiritual equality.

For example, an untouchable, asked why his *jat* now performed life cycle rituals (*samskara*) previously done only by the upper castes, defended his right to do so by saying that all have "the same blood, the same flesh" (*wa-he-hi, wa-he la*). He also insisted there were other groups still lower than his. Such an equivocal stance is common. Assertions that all people are the same, alike or equal, in morally relevant ways, are often made by low caste Newars who will, in the next breath, assert their superiority to other low caste groups, who are just as stigmatized, and suffer the same disabilities. But it would be wrong, I believe, to interpret this as a commitment to a shared ideology of caste hierarchy. The vacillation and equivocal values of low caste men and women reflect the ambivalence of cultural experience, not the structuring of mind by ideology.

Ways of deflecting the personal implications of caste status are more of a concern for low caste informants, but most of them defend some aspects of caste, and all of those interviewed conformed to various hierarchical practices directed at persons held to be still lower (even when, as we have seen, the lower category is transparently constructed). Assertions that all are equal, or "the same," are equivocal in this regard. Hierarchy is likely to be canceled in an upward direction, and maintained in a downward one.

High caste individuals may defend hierarchy, or take inequality for granted—several informants reported they had never considered the point of view of low caste individuals—but some express sympathy with ideas of social equality. Informants are aware that the law has established equality. Some modernized Newars did make statements judging the caste system based on such contemporary innovations. For example, one young educated Newar called the abolition of the legal supports for caste the most important development in recent Nepali history. I am here concerned with relatively traditional individuals. The legal status of equality does not typically, however, serve as a unifying conception in their discourse on matters of equality and hierarchy. My informants did not speak of equality in terms of legal or human rights.[1]

Equality of Moral Worth and the God Within

In the following interview transcript, I have asked a Brahman, Dharma Raj, to explain the difference between the worship of the god Shiva and the worship of the god Vishnu. Dharma Raj chooses to make some points about hierarchy and equality, stating that the *dharma* (moral law, religious ethic) of the god Vishnu-Narayana does not make hierarchical distinctions; he maintains the "way" of Vishnu-Narayana does not divide people into "high" and "low," but rather makes it possible for people to transcend hierarchical social distinctions by acquiring the "inner knowledge" of Narayana through devotion. I was not probing for such commentary; I had expected him to focus on differences in rituals or myth, not speak of an ethic of spiritual equality.

"In the dharma of the god Narayana [Vishnu], it is enough to do *bhakti* [devotion]. In that dharma, caste is not necessary. In Narayana's dharma, there is no caste. There are no high castes, no low castes—

they are equal. Narayana says they are equal. This is Narayana's word. What Narayana proclaims is this—although a person is a Brahman, if he does not trust in this [inner] knowledge, he is low. Although a person is low caste, if he possesses knowledge inside, then he is high. There is [spiritual] knowledge inside. If that knowledge is sufficient, a person is high. In his way, Narayana has lifted up many who were low. Narayana has said, there is no caste. The main thing is knowledge." (a Brahman)

This argument represents a kind of dissenting, minority view in Newar culture, which in practice is organized in terms of hierarchical values. The view that maintains that caste is unreal, unimportant, or wrong, is, however, an articulate alternative. High and low caste informants are familiar with such views. These views may be "modern," but they are not Western. A concept of equality is often expressed by asserting that the god Vishnu (Narayana) dwells inside each person.

"Vishnu is in my heart. He is in your heart also. He is in the heart of others. He is everywhere. Since he is everywhere, we are with everyone. We are all equal. One man is a pundit, another is an idiot, but this is the outward thing. For inside the pundit has Narayana, and the fool, he too has Narayana inside him. In this way there is equality. There are two sides to this. In terms of knowledge, this person has knowledge, while another does not. In terms of wealth, he has wealth, but he does not. Or take the example of strength—he is strong, but he is weak. They are different. Weak or strong, having knowledge or not, having money or not, within the person dwells the same Narayana." (a Brahman)[2]

The implication is, I think, that every person has moral worth (for this deity has worth, as a defender of the moral order) regardless of empirical individual differences. Empirical differences co-exist with an image of the way people are alike: an invisible spiritual identity that unites them despite obvious surface differences. This kind of notion of a spiritually grounded equality of moral worth has the potential of being used to attack class and caste differences; it could be used as a 'leveling' ideology. Several informants made a point of sharply contrasting the state of "equality" that having a god dwelling within confers—envisioned as an "ultimate" reality—with the injustices and inequalities of real life, as they experience it. Kesar Lal, of the "impure" Jugi caste, is one who does.

("You [Newars] speak of a 'heart god' don't you?") "Narayana. Narayana is with you too, is the same. He is with me too, the very same."

("The same for all?") "The very same. [He pauses.] "If he is the same, then the Narayana that dwells within wants to be rich too. The God that dwells within you is the same God that dwells within me, but you have wealth, and if you must say or do something, you can quickly do it—you are ready and able. I do not have wealth. Because I am not rich, even though the Narayana that dwells within me is of one mind, even if I want to do something, I cannot." (a Jugi)

It is easy to tape record and transcribe people's words, but it can be difficult to judge their mood, to characterize their voice, or to define their attitude towards their own words. If I am any judge of linguistic cues and meta-communications across cultural boundaries, I would say Kesar Lal was being ironic. The irony is simple, even heavy-handed, playing the idea of the way things should be against the way they are: people are the same because God dwells in each of them, but their life-situations are different. The idea of a spiritual equality is other-worldly, concerned with ultimate reality; Kesar Lal wants to reverse this, and make the God within the source of desires and needs in this world, where inequalities rule. This highlights injustices. Kesar Lal's words are energized by anger and bitterness. He contrasts the immanence of Narayana in each person with the social reality of unequal access to the resources needed to act. People are equal (by virtue of having Narayana dwelling within) but their freedom of action is limited by poverty in the social world. People share the same needs or disposition to act, but only some can act. Kesar Lal resents this; he feels he is denied the world of action.

I think Kesar's words here should be seen as actions. He is not just explaining a cultural concept: he is bringing it home to me, challenging me, a person he associates with the high castes, to see reality. The question creates an opportunity for him; he takes advantage of it to confront me and to create irony, taking us outside of everyday reality to a spiritual perspective, revealing the injustice of daily life, asserting a sense of ulti-mate reality and of social futility in the same breathe. He points out that while equality exists absolutely, as a religious fact, it is not realized in the material world of riches and poverty.

Kesar Lal's words play on deep frustrations, and give form to an essen-tial moral tension: the idea of ultimate moral equality cannot easily be reconciled with hierarchical social reality. This "equality" is both real and unreal. While low caste informants such as Kesar Lal may use the idea of a God within to pose their critique of society, they also expose the unreality of the idea of equality. To invoke the concept is to show that it is not achieved in practice.

A Brahman, Govinda Raj, shifts equality into the transcendent real, thus keeping it out of social life. He acknowledges the concept of an ideal spiritual equality, but sees it as separate from ordinary, everyday life—that is, life within social structure.

("Then why isn't wealth divided equally?") "That is social behavior. You can't do that—dharma and behavior are different. There are those who say that—but the reaction to that will be, if you think that, I will take the money from your pocket. Don't get angry. Narayana is with me, with you, we are equal. And he puts your money away. This is disturbing. So although the proposition is true [in dharma], you are unable to put it into practice in worldly affairs. Only those who have renounced the world (*sannyasi*), only they can practice it." (a Brahman)

This shifts "equality" into an "otherworldly" mode. Hindu Newars generally do not, today, view renunciation as a possible moral career, as a valued path in life, whatever Newar involvement with it may have been in the past, and contemporary Bhaktapur Newars rarely become ascetics.

Asked to list their "most important" duties and wants, the Newars I interviewed typically answered in terms reflecting the value of the life of the householder (*grihasthi*). They never mentioned renunciation. Ascetics are, if anything, a negative reference group. As a householder, a Newar is expected to maintain caste rules regarding marriage and food. While the theoretical "ultimate value" of the spiritual life of world-renouncers may be acknowledged, Newars often express doubts about how authentic particular mendicants are, and seldom speak of it as a way of life that they admire or might wish to follow.

The contrast of householder and ascetic is sometimes used as a moral control. A Brahman told me that Newars should not become world-renouncers; rather, a Newar must bear the burdens of the life of the householder, which he said were very hard, and involve many religious and social duties. A Brahman, he added, who complained excessively about the hardship of the life of a householder (*kuldharma*) might be told: "If you feel the life of a householder is too difficult you can become a renouncer. Who is stopping you from being an ascetic? But if you don't want to be a renouncer, then you have to do these things." This rhetoric attempts to suppress criticism of, and to head off commitment to values that threaten, the hierarchical way of life of the householder.

This statement plays on the contrast of ascetic and householder, splitting them into separate and opposed realities. More research is needed on the relationship of Newars to renunciation, now and in the past. However, when informants set the life of the ascetic and of the householder in opposition, it is possible to speculate that the rejection of renunciation is tantamount to a rejection of equality and anti-structural

dissent. This follows from the identification of self and hierarchy: to reject hierarchy is to reject "self." We might interpret the steps as follows:
"equality," as an idea that potentially has radical consequences for the
distribution of wealth, prestige, and freedom of action, is first defined
as something that cannot occur in the world of the householder. Rather, equality is an ethical mode of behavior that can only be realized in
the world of the renouncer; equality is an "otherworldly" mode of being. This shifts anti-hierarchical possibilities outside the ordinary social
world. This makes "equality"—the collapse of hierarchy, the abolition
of differences—a theoretical spiritual possibility, but exiles it from the
world of practice. This religious idea of a non-hierarchical way of life is
something Newars know about, but not something that has personal
meaning for most of them. The world of the renouncer exists on the
other side of a chasm from ordinary values. The freedom that the renouncer has from the restrictions of hierarchy presupposes withdrawal
from society, from family and kinship, from the domain of political action, of social esteem, of prosperity and pleasure. The life of the renouncer is a cultural possibility for Hindu Newars, but they can find
meaning in it only by estranging themselves from what they have known
and lived. For them, the world-renouncer is the "other" who defines the
"self" of the householder; Newar householders can affirm the value of
their way of life by rejecting the values that the ascetic represents, and
find their own identities in this rejection. Furthermore, certain of the
general values of transcendence (although not of equality) associated
with asceticism (especially religio-magical power) are duplicated within
the social system and monopolized by priestly Hindu Brahmans who
have a vested interest in sustaining hierarchy.

World-renouncers are not precisely what Newars imagine them to be.
If the general theoretical position I have outlined is correct, then one
would predict that actual world-renouncers will, as often as not, seek to
neutralize equality and assert some significant degree of hierarchy
among themselves. I am not here concerned with the actual life of any
group of renouncers—in which I would expect to find an interplay of
hierarchy and equality—but with Newar representations of the world-
renouncer, and with the role of these representations in their moral discourse and rhetoric. Recent research points out that social divisions and
hierarchy are indeed found among some groups of renouncers and de-
votionalists (Burghart 1983; Van der Veer 1987). Whatever the world of
renouncers is actually like, Newars use their image of world-renouncers
to structure and emphasize their own commitments as householders.

To summarize, the contrast of renouncer and householder poses a psychological dilemma for high caste persons who are ambivalent about the
hierarchical life of the householder. They can be invited to become as-

cetics, where (they assume) anti-hierarchical values can be realized. But this involves self-abnegation, a surrender of much of what is cherished in life, a breaking out of the web of relatedness into existential aloneness. To reject hierarchy in this way is to lose the "self." But efforts to rebel against hierarchy in other ways, while attempting to remain part of the ordinary social world, invite social and economic sanctions, even the use of force or violence. These are hard choices. To frame a choice in this way arguably has a precise ideological value. Once a person becomes a world-renouncer, he becomes materially dependent on society, but morally superior to it (Dumont 1980). The Western sense of "equality" is wholly obviated in the process.

From the point of view of the Newar householder, the moral system is structured so that a person may not coherently lead an ordinary social life and seek to avoid or level hierarchy: a person is either in "this world" completely or out of it altogether. The life of the householder (hierarchy) and the life of the renouncer (characterized by absence of hierarchy and withdrawal from family life) are hard to reconcile. Their disharmony may be useful, providing a conceptual structure for rhetoric and practices that allow defenders of the normative order to divert or undermine egalitarian challenges to an elite's place in the hierarchical social system.

The interesting thing is that, despite this powerful cultural destructuring, this exile of equality into the world of the renouncer, equality continues to reappear in Newar thought in various forms, voiced by householders, Brahmans and untouchables alike. Ideas of equality are evidently not easily displaced from moral discourse. Before we turn again to the ways Newars voice concepts of equality, we should look at another cultural system for neutralizing equality. The rhetoric of karma also displaces equality from (potentially politically charged) moral discourse.

Karma and Hierarchy

It is easy to see how the idea of the in-dwelling of God in the "heart" of each person could form the basis of a "leveling" ideology; one also easily imagine that any such radical ideology might be refuted in terms of the doctrine of karma. None of my informants directly attempted to reconcile the idea of spiritual equality with the concept of karma, although some of them attributed low caste status to the action of karma; but I do not think that it is a mere coincidence that these ideas, which seem so fundamentally opposed, coexist in Newar thought. Certainly, as has long been noted (Weber 1958:118–123), the doctrine of karma rationalizes inequalities. It provides a means by which a concept of justice that applies to individuals—the idea that people should get what they

deserve—can be invoked in a social context, where the issue is distributive justice, and used to justify the unequal distribution of misery and
opportunity, reward and hardship. This crossing of two kinds of justice,
so that the question of social, distributive justice is reframed in terms of
what individuals deserve, is crucial—it makes karma a powerful political
concept, and a fundamentally conservative one.

The coupling of these two types of justice is not, however, what makes
the concept culturally distinctive—and so psychologically powerful. It
is the idea of transmigration that fleshes out the concept, and acts
to establish, maintain and validate the link between these two justice
concepts. According to karma theory, the sins (*pap*) a person commits
are punished in this and subsequent lives, while acts of dharma are re-
warded. Persons who may, in previous lives, have been of equal status
or moral worth, and whose spiritual essence is of equal worth, are,
through actions for which they were responsible, reborn into different
life-situations. The conditions of life of high and low castes are thus the
just desserts for actions for which persons were morally responsible; they
get what they deserve, and the status quo is justified.

Karma links individual choice and the notion of moral desserts into a
causal law. Misery is not random, arbitrary, unfair; it reflects the inherent,
objective moral structure of the universe. Suffering is the inexorable, just
result of the persistence of moral responsibility beyond death and into
new lives. Some suffer without seeming to have done wrong in any tangible sense; others enjoy privileges despite the fact they did nothing evident to deserve them. What appears to be a gratuitous distribution of
good fortune and misery becomes intelligible, when seen in terms of the
ideas of transmigration and the karmic conservation of the moral consequences of individual actions. Newars retain the doctrine of karma as a
one of several explanations of why low castes have their present position
in society. The theory of karma seals status boundaries, just as the idea of
the presence of God in each person tends to make them permeable.

The concept of karma may have developed outside of political discourse, as a way to give meaning to suffering. It answers the question,
Why me? Why has this happened to me? Why has my wife or husband
died, why am I blind or sick? It seems likely that karma was brought into
political discourse, in efforts to establish the justice of inequality, as soon
as inequality became enough of a moral problem to require elaborate
justification. We are perhaps safe in presuming that social hierarchy or
inequality was either under attack or arousing resistance or ambivalence.
We can speculate that there must have been some need to mobilize support for hierarchy: a need to counter reformist pressures and to maintain
commitment to the system. There have been periods when challenges to
hierarchical systems were particularly intense—the emergence of

Buddhism is the obvious example—but it is reasonable to think inequalities were always challenged and dominant hierarchical systems under constant, if uneven and equivocal, pressure. The rhetoric and criticism of several informants reported here I offer as evidence of the way such tensions are inherent in a stratified society. The cultural history of hierarchy cannot—as some have assumed—be written without writing the history of resistance to hierarchy, which in turn requires an evaluation of indigenous concepts of equality.

The content of anti-hierarchical discourse may well have been different at different periods—in the discourse reported above, placing God in the "heart" of every person is a symbolic act, a way of looking beyond the "differences" that separate people. This vision of the presence of Narayana, a form of Vishnu, is used to speak of equality in the context of a community in which the dominant group of castes are Saivite. In other times and settings, Saivite forms may have lent themselves to opposition to hierarchy. The figure of Shiva has a number of traits hard to reconcile with hierarchy and the life of the orthodox householder (O'Flaherty 1973); he is an ascetic, and in Bhaktapur is often said to have affinities with the Pore untouchables. Vishnu, on the other hand, is often associated with hierarchy; Hindu kings are defenders of hierarchical society and forms of Vishnu. It would seem that the moral and polemical uses of members of the pantheon evolve, and that opposition to a dominant elite and its orthodoxy influences the way in which a deity is imagined and presented in discourse.

We can now turn again to the words of Newar informants; equality has not disappeared from their constructions of their world and experience. It has a key place in their critical thought, which often focuses on the tension between equality and hierarchy.

Equality

Hari of the Jugi (or Kapali) caste still performs his stigmatizing traditional work for high caste informants—"if they are polite." He defends this as a duty, telling me how he rebukes his adult son and daughter when they turn away high caste people seeking his services; he tells his children, "Our caste has done this from long ago." He has his own way of seeing people as both the same, and different. People are the same in essence; what makes them different is their role in society.

("How are Kapali and other castes different?") "But as people there is no difference. Our rites and our practices are different. Looked at in terms of what we do and the rites we observe,—this is a Barber, this is a Jugi, so it is said. We need the Barber caste to purify us by cutting

our hair and nails, and we need a Brahman to perform our death rites
[*sraddha*]. And so it came to be [that social life] was organized in this
way." ("Humans are not different, their work is different") "Their
work is different, but men are nowhere different. They have a nose,
they have legs, they have eyes. When any one is cut, when you are
cut—then you bleed blood, and I bleed blood too. You do not bleed
milk. If I say that you are a great man, you will still bleed blood. And
so will I. But here we have the order of high and low. People must
worship, and so they need the Tantric priests. The auspicious times
for worship and ritual must be found. Therefore, the caste of Astrologers is necessary. . . . To create order, the system of high and low
arose." (a Jugi)

For this informant, people are essentially or originally the same. He
does not accept the view that caste hierarchy expresses natural differences, differences in the nature, substance or moral "being" of people
of different castes. He corrects the implication in my question that his
caste and others are different: "But as men, there is no difference." He
views hierarchy instead as a construction that makes a certain way of life
possible. In part, it is an adaptation to sacred reality; a division of labor
is necessary for the performance of rituals. This is a matter of social practice, however, not of "nature" or "substance." Castes develop because of
pragmatic social need; people do what they do, not because that is "what
they are," but because someone has to do it. Since people are not naturally different, social differences are constructed for social ends, to create functional interdependence. Speaking in this way, he rhetorically
and psychologically clears the ground for rejecting the stigmatizing implications of his own position in the caste hierarchy. He "neutralizes"
hierarchy; he reassures himself that it does not reflect his nature or
being. There must be some psychological satisfaction in this for him,
even if others insist he is constituted by the hierarchy. He also gives
reasons for the existence of a caste hierarchy, reasons that give it some
legitimacy. It creates an order, and this order is pragmatically necessary.
Thus, he does not see his essence, his ultimate identity or being, as constituted by the caste hierarchy; he rejects the implication that it constitutes him (or anyone) as a "person." But he is prepared to accept
hierarchy on other terms; for him, the caste hierarchy is not an expression of human nature or natural law, but it may be necessary.

The necessity is moral as well as pragmatic and political. A Brahman is
necessary to perform one part of the death rites that are of deep cultural
and emotional significance in Newar culture; the informant's own traditional, highly stigmatizing role in the funeral rites is also necessary if the

deceased is to gain salvation. Members of his Jugi caste are called on to receive an offering to the dead on the fifth or seventh day. To accept this is highly polluting. The social pressures and economic incentives for continuing to perform this stigmatizing role have been greatly reduced in recent years; Hari must actually resist pressure from his own children to stop participating in high caste death rites. He does so in part because he sees the role as an ethical one. Although Hari expresses negative feelings about the high castes, he thinks that his caste's role in death rites is indeed necessary to ensure the salvation of the person who has died, and that there is nothing wrong, and much that is right, in helping "save" them. In addition, the informant identifies with his *own* caste, even though it is stigmatized. He finds value in its traditions. The necessary ritual roles of his caste give the Jugi a place in the system that may partly compensate for the experience of being stigmatized. For example, their caste is intimately connected with the deity Shiva. They embody certain aspects of Shiva and act as a kind of symbolic functional equivalent for asceticism. Hari is prepared to find meaning in much of this; indeed, he asserts it as a reason his caste is "high"—in an "alternative" hierarchy that he imagines.

The theme of differentiation through ritual, work, and social practices is important, and I will take it up again later. Social differences are culturally constructed; and Newars are aware, in their own ways, as "positioned subjects," of this process of construction.

Confrontations

In constructing themselves in opposition to the way dominant groups construct them, low caste actors create cultural forms for themselves that juxtapose their own central intuitions about themselves with concepts and constructs derived from high caste life. Low caste actors do not live in a self-contained "culture" of their own, entirely apart from high caste culture, nor do they seamlessly share a "culture" with high caste actors. Rather, they struggle to know themselves in terms of a double encounter: they encounter the difference between their constructions of self and the way high caste actors stigmatize them; they respond creatively to this by juxtaposing and orchestrating cultural perspectives and thus attempt to encounter high caste "culture" on their own terms. While this constitutes a significant response to the quandary posed by the way they are stigmatized, and asserts their own moral intuitions about self and society, reconstituting the encounter may only reconstitute the quandary, not resolve it. Low caste actors may continue to live in the gap between cultural perspectives. While they may resent the way they are stigmatized, it is hard to be "at home" in their own self-contained cultural perspective, because it is neither wholly self-contained nor unaffected by high caste values and judgments. They have to live defending and affirming themselves.

Doing so, untouchables often construct a highly equivocal world for themselves, at once opposing and embracing cultural practices that constitute hierarchy. Let me offer an example of this. Certain Newar castes have the right to claim the offerings left at certain shrines. At a goddess temple in Kathmandu, doing so is a prerogative reserved for the Pore or Po(n). Accompanied by a distinguished, gray-haired Brahman assistant, I used to visit this temple seeking untouchables to interview. One day, one of the untouchables we approached got angry at a question; evidently it struck a nerve. I'd wanted to know about certain rites of passage that are central to high caste life, and which had been adopted by untouchables; he responded with the vehemence of someone who felt I was challenging his right to perform them—not my intention at all. Squatting on his heels beside his sleeping baby—I remember clearly the flies crawling on the baby's face, and on the pile of food offerings he'd collected to take home to eat, images that perhaps reenforce stereotypes in high caste observers of such scenes—he spoke forcefully about the moral justification for his caste's emulation of high caste practices. He affirmed a moral identity in contradiction to his caste identity. Echoing other low caste actors, he spoke of being "the same blood, the same flesh" as others. By claiming a common humanity in this way, he asserted he had as much right to practice these rituals as anyone else.

Now, any untouchable who declares, "I am of the same blood, the same flesh, as high caste people, and so I perform the same rites as they do," arguably places him- or herself in radical self-contradiction. On the one hand, such untouchables are making a declaration of an equality of moral worth; they claim the right to appropriate high caste practices. On the other, the rites they adopt help constitute the caste hierarchy. Among other things, the rites celebrate the exclusion that low caste people so often seek to overcome. Hungering for recognition, untouchable actors may not appreciate the irony, the self-subversion, involved; what they assert is that they are the same as everyone in such a way that they are entitled to make their own the very rites that make everyone different: the rites they claim on the basis of equality endow differences with value and meaning, giving felt reality to the separation of castes—and so contribute crucially to the reproduction of hierarchy (Parish 1994).

Of course, the untouchable I encountered in Kathmandu acts out of self-affirmation. He has critical insights. What he does not possess, perhaps, is a fully developed, robust critique of the cultural matrix of caste.

Viewing himself as ultimately the same as everyone else, this actor may not see that these rites are affirmations of caste. He claims the rites as his, too—he is as good as anyone, constituted of the same stuff as they are, why shouldn't he practice these rituals?—but may not appreciate how powerfully these rites help crystallize and catalyze the idea of caste differences in cultural consciousness (Parish 1994, chap. 5).

I was impressed with his candor and forthrightness: it takes some courage to challenge a distinguished-looking Brahman and a foreigner, to seek to correct them, to enter into a cultural argument with them, not just as persons, but with all they might represent. If we came as interlocutors, we also came as symbols of the caste order. He contested what he believed we embodied. He was passionate as he spoke out against the felt weight of hierarchy, against the construction of his existence by high-caste actors. While he was clearly angry, I have come to think he not so much angry with us for asking ill-conceived questions, as he was outraged at the social order we represented in his mind. Moved by this moral anger at perceived injustices, I imagine he spoke not only to us, but through us to the social order itself, constructing a kind of ultimate audience: he spoke out against the ways the caste hierarchy constructed him, excluded him, and confined him to a stigmatized social identity.

In one case reported to me, an untouchable Sweeper was cleaning up a courtyard when a woman who lived in one of the surrounding houses returned. As she crossed the courtyard, a man shouted down from a window that she should be careful not to touch the Sweeper. The untouchable looked up at the man in the window and declared, "I am a person, you too are a person."

Untouchables who refused to wash their own dishes at tea-shops would say the same thing. Several Newar women reported that, at the public water taps where many people get the water they need for drinking, cooking, and bathing, high caste people would say to untouchables, "Go away, we need pure water. Don't touch us." Some untouchables do retreat, but others challenge: "I am a person, you too are a person. Why are you treating me like a dog? If you are afraid of touching me, why don't you go away?" Reporting such incidents, some high caste actors invoke the idea of an age where moral virtue has vanished: "It is the Kali Yuga that they say these things."

While everyday life is a crucial context for asserting and challenging identities, for constructing, experiencing, subverting and resisting hierarchy, it is important to remember that often real risks are involved in directly challenging high caste actors. Low caste actors have been beaten, but even more than this they may fear the loss of their livelihood. The fear of hunger may be a greater force than the fear of violence in keeping people silent.

Low caste statements that they are the same, that they are persons, the same blood and flesh, often lack the "thickness" that anthropologists so often feel they must find in culture (Rosaldo 1989). Nonetheless, I would suggest that such axioms of existence have moral force. It may be that actors who feel this way do not have a platform for elaboration, a forum in which they could "thicken up" this basic idea. Perhaps it simply seems self-evident, and they feel it needs little justification. They may feel they have made their point, have expressed it with such economy and force of expression that little or no elaboration is necessary. Refuting these points may be what requires elaboration.[3]

In terms of practical effect, confrontations such as these seem to have relatively little enduring impact on the caste system—and they don't change many minds. Perhaps more cathartic than socially effective, such encounters have obviously not led to a dissolution of the caste system, although perhaps they do set limits (drawing lines about how far higher castes can go in excluding and stigmatizing) and test limits (exploring what assertions of equality are safely made). Such encounters may thus reveal much about relative power to caste actors, high and low.

Efforts to change relative status may be more successful than sweeping egalitarian claims. Historically, some caste groups have endeavored, in legal cases and in public opinion, to change their relative status within the system, usually claiming their traditional low-status was a mistake that needs to be rectified. Pursued vigorously, such claims of higher status within the conventions of the caste system may have an impact, gaining ground for the group even if they do not win full social acceptance of their view of their own place. Of course, such efforts tend to affirm the idea of hierarchy; they challenge only relative rank, not the value of ranking groups in a caste hierarchy. While they may dispute the right of groups they have long deemed low to claim higher status, many members of the upper castes seem perfectly aware that such efforts to raise status tend to energize hierarchy as a value and a practice, reinforcing the system in which they stand unchallenged as the highest groups. The egalitarian claims of the lowest, impure and untouchable castes, are shrugged off, neutralized with counter-constructions.

Equality Unmade

If low caste Newars try to recover a sense of self by neutralizing the stigmatizing implications of hierarchy and asserting equality, high caste Newars seek to neutralize equality and to reconstitute hierarchy as the governing principle. Asked why castes are divided into "water acceptable" (pure) and "water unacceptable" (impure) groups, a high caste individual replied:

"They are at a lower level, they are low. Because they are lowest—the Shoemakers, the Jugi, the Sweepers. As a matter of fact, as far as it counts for me, you have blood, I too have blood, we are people, aren't we? I think this [the caste system] is nothing. But what to do? This tradition was established long ago, and people have feelings about it. They feel uneasy. Although on the outside we say this [that people are same], in our minds, we feel troubled. For example now, consider the untouchables, the Shoemakers, the Sweepers. They are dirty. There is the Jugi. Their work matches their kind." (A Pa(n)cthariya)

Notice how complex this is. In a brief passage, the informant asserts a social reality ("they are low"), recognizes and embraces equality ("you have blood, and I too have blood, we are people") and so cancels caste ("this [the caste system] is nothing"); he then reconstitutes caste by being fatalistic ("but what to do") and appealing to tradition ("this tradition was established long ago") and using that as grounds for emotion ("and people have feelings about it"). He goes on to establish inequality as an inner feeling, whatever the outward pretense. He then returns to the cultural codification of reality ("consider the untouchables") and points to a stigma ("they are dirty") and drives it home: "their work matches their kind." Equality is neutralized; hierarchy is re-established.[4]

In this passage, we are seeing hegemony from the inside out. Notice how hierarchy is not a given here, a taken-for-granted reality, but a value in relationship to other values. The informant actively constructs his commitment to hierarchy; he appeals to several different constructions of hierarchy, and defends inequality from several different lines of attack. Clearly his consciousness is not simply constituted in terms of hierarchy; he has access to other ideas, and engages in argument to invalidate or neutralize these ideas, which, he implicitly acknowledges, represent an alternative moral consciousness. He works to overcome these ideas, to master them, and to maintain his commitment to hierarchy. His psychological work is also cultural or ideological work, coming together in a rhetoric that reproduces the hegemony of hierarchy in his mind.

Coda

Not the cultural construction of hierarchy, but the inward cultural life of critique has been the main focus of this chapter. I do not see the egalitarian moods of Newars as mere vagaries of the moral imagination. They have an essential place. Nor do I see them as more or less modern introductions.[5] Rather, I see them as fragile expressions of human agency, as the responses of the moral imagination to the "violent strangeness" of a social reality where people are set apart and against each other, made into different kinds of humanity. Culture and self act and react on each other in a dynamic fashion: people have some capacity to re-interpret the meanings that shape the way they imagine the world, and they may be motivated to do so, because of naked self-interest, or be-cause they are engaged in an "endless struggle to think well of them-selves,"—in a phrase Unni Wikan (1980) takes from T. S. Eliot.

If people's relationship to tradition is in some basic sense hermeneu-tic, and existential, what choice do they have but to interpret? Women and men may be moved to interpret culture and self on the basis of per-sonal experience or personal reflections about the meaning of experi-ence. They may be moved by anxiety, or by doubt, which they feel because of the nature of their life-situations. Thus, even while society must "think itself" in the individual—as Dumont at the beginning of his *Homo Hierarchicus* (1980:5) puts it—at that very moment the ideology of caste, although objectively linked to social structure, risks having the in-dividual rethink society.

Against the metaphor of "society thinking itself," we can set the views of Gadamer and Habermas, who, however much they disagree, would agree, I think, that human subjects live a dialogue with culture. Persons capture culture not in an entirely unmediated way, as if self and culture always form an identity, but rather grasp particular meanings in terms of other meanings, relate experience to experience, all in ways that reflect the fashion an actor actively engages a life that is always so-cially situated. Models derived from cultural tradition grow in the mind, develop, enter into new models. The self exists within subjective hori-zons that are not identical with a given ideology. The actor—as interpre-tive agent—grasps ideology through other meanings and experience, through a translation "into" consciousness, and a translation "out of consciousness": an active interpretive process both ways.[6] This is espe-cially true in caste society, where life-situations vary radically.

Newars actively interpret their own culture and society, arraying one cultural perspective against another, positioning themselves within this shifting array of attitudes and interpretive vantagepoints. They may seek to neutralize hierarchy, to modify it in their own minds, even if they can-not or do not achieve this in practice. The brute reality of power and scarcity makes a difference: men and women can think against the grain of dominant thought and practice, but fail to change these, if others are prepared to use force, ostracism, and economic sanctions to preserve existing institutions. That protest and resistance are recurrent phe-nomena tells us that people's minds are not so absorbed in ideology that they cannot think critically. It tells us they are highly motivated to dis-sent.[7] Social movements not only have a dynamic of their own, based on a variety of factors—the psychological aspects of which can properly be studied in a cultural psychology of social movements—but also a kind of figure-ground relationship to the experience of everyday life, and its "ambient" discontents. We should not so privilege the drama of protest and rebellion that we fail to see the roots of dissent in the experience and thought of cultured actors involved in everyday life (O'Hanlon 1988).

What makes it possible to dissent from hierarchy? What basis is there for critiques of hierarchy? The task of rethinking society, of redefining the moral grounds of social life, is difficult for individuals, but the practice of thinking against dominant institutions, the act of resisting the subtle blandishments of hegemony and the seductive appeal of ideology, are just as much part of culture as conformity and belief. For example, Khare (1984), in his important work with Lucknow Chamars, has described the way the critical response to hierarchy forms a deliberate intellectual tradition. Here I have discussed the sort of everyday thinking that I think ultimately prepares people to find meaning in efforts to transform society, even if these are stillborn or doomed to failure: the intuitive, fragmented beginnings of a critical response to the dominant ideology of caste life. These beginnings are embedded partly in cultural tradition, but disclose something of the interpretive, the cognitive, work of individuals.

Both family and caste in Hindu Bhaktapur have ethics of hierarchical interdependence, with ranked solidarities that are encompassed in a higher order solidarity. Hierarchy is encompassed in "love" or in the "body" of the patriline in the kinship system, and it is encompassed in renunciation and transcendence in the caste system. The way people are "the same" and "different" is mediated in different ways in different contexts. People share substance in kinship contexts. In moral discourse that seeks to subvert, or to encompass, the hierarchical differences, exclusions and complementarities of the caste system, other devices are used to represent the way people are "the same." Although they are of different castes, they are as one in terms of the god within each of them. Differences are transcended in this vision. Other Newars argue that Brahmans as well as untouchables are constituted as bodies and of blood, making them the same.

In Newar families, the problem is to generate differences from a matrix of sameness—to create authority and structure within kin attachments and identifications. In the caste system, constructions of hierarchy and solidarity are, at once, less certain and more absolute. The problem is again to generate differences from sameness: to make people who are alike, as human beings, into different "natural" kinds. In the caste system, the special characteristics of the kinship domain no longer limit the making of differences. In the caste system, this can be done absolutely—

at least in theory. No principles of kinship stand in the way of reifying (constructed) differences into a vision of the stigmatized "other." Neither love nor the feeling of kin and family as constituted of the same essence as self apply. Invoking the dominant ideology of the caste system, actors can freely construct, essentialize and objectify differences, so that socially manufactured differences are seen as differences in nature, in substance, in moral being.

The importance of ideas of solidarity and equality in Hindu experience has been played down in much Western analysis. When recognized at all, solidarity and equality are interpreted as subordinate principles, domesticated and contained in the social units—families, castes—embedded within a hierarchically ordered whole. "The principle of hierarchy in Indian society explaining vertical relationships among units," Fruzzetti, Östör and Barnett (1982:29) say, "is complemented by equivalence within each unit." This is a valid statement. But we can restate it in ways that are also valid for traditional South Asia, or at least, for Newars. First, it should read "principles of hierarchy." Second, we have seen that some Newars "trump" hierarchy by appealing to concepts of equality and solidarity; they invert conceptually the relationship that has been most often assumed in Western studies. In this discourse, the appeals to solidarity encompass and limit hierarchy by defining people as "the same"—and so as fundamentally related, and equally deserving. I do not claim priority for solidarity and equality over difference and hierarchy.[8] What I want to emphasize is the dynamics of their relationship: Newars invoke both hierarchy and equality, in different contexts for different purposes. Diverse principles of hierarchy (Raheja 1988; Wadley 1975) are complemented—and at least rhetorically subverted—by diverse conceptions of solidarity, equality, and identity.

Since Newars at once affirm and critique hierarchy, we need not restrict our analysis to a unit of meaning (the opposition of the pure and impure) as registered in official, dominant ideology, but need also to explore processes of meaning-construction that challenge the dominant ideology (Khare 1983). Not surprisingly, such challenges in turn trigger counter-constructions. To adapt a distinction from Kenneth Burke (1962), not only the symbolism that sustains a sense or order and consensus, but the co-evolving rhetorics of assent and dissent require analysis: warring forces of meaning exist in cultured minds and cultural practices. Our unit of analysis need not be confined to ideology per se, to the opposition of pure and impure, but can embrace the wider field of cultural and psychological conflict, where even the most dominant ideology confronts muted yet audible critique and dissent.

To make the caste hierarchy work requires that someone be made to embody differences. As Dumont might insist, the prototype for relations of difference may be the relation of a Brahman and an untouchable. The code, however, must be made flesh; and the flesh, we know, may resist, may stray from the path set for it, may feel pain. This is what Dumont fails to recognize and Frantz Fanon (1967) recognized so well.

Yet the system of oppositions exists; the society exists: someone must be made to assume these contrasting identities, must live these differences in the flesh. A low caste or untouchable person exists not as a kind of semiotic ghost in culture but as a living, breathing, thinking person.

While caste actors are, in a sense, figments of culture—for without the specific cultural meanings that define them, they would not exist as they do or be perceived as they are, or face the problems they do—culture theory as much as the dominant ideology does them an injustice when it treats them as less than themselves, as just cultural constructions, mere "sites" for cultural discourse, figments of an ideology, symbols in a cultural system. Not just symbols, they are symbols made flesh, symbols who live.

Such symbols, as persons, may resist their semiotic fate. Yet whatever they think about it, they have symbolic values in the caste system, and they may not be able to escape the objecthood this confers. Whatever they do or feel, they signify, they possess meaning for others. The ideology that constructs them has social and psychological correlates: it may threaten the self. Nonetheless, we cannot assume they simply are what caste culture proposes, nor do we have the right to presuppose that they totally confuse their social meaning and their felt being.

Yet as symbols, they do embody meanings, at whatever cost to themselves. The person of Mahila in his ragged clothes carrying his tools as he walks the streets signifies the caste system, renders it palpable: he represents one pole of reality, one fate, what a Brahman called a hell-on-earth, an excremental existence. In such cases, while they cannot validly be viewed as simply the same, no doubt social meaning and felt being cannot be kept neatly apart, either. They may pull and tug on each other: perhaps this tug-of-war threatens to divide the self, even to shatter it into fragments of contradictory consciousness.

Yet so embodied in living symbols, the differences that link yet separate Brahman and untouchable, each caste from every other, do form a constructive code for caste society, constituting some of its practices and many of its moral and psychological dilemmas: pure, impure, high, low, valued, devalued. These oppositions do create a world, what Dumont calls a structural universe. Chains of difference, uniting and opposing the most diverse elements—knowledge, purity, sacredness, honor, diet, dirt, bodies, moral substances, sexuality, urban space, ritual time, and religious power—do underpin the attitudes of caste life. Yet, like any organizing principle embodied in practice, the chains of difference that separate, unite, and rank castes react with the existential, the political, the pragmatic conditions of practice, with human agency and psychology.

The values that, for Dumont, seamlessly constitute hierarchy erupt into the moral imagination as quandaries and rifts in the world that self experiences. These problems of meaning require some response, and each response fleshes in the dilemmas and possibilities that attend the values of hierarchy. Whatever their grounding in such oppositions as pure and impure, the experience of caste relations and of caste ideology shape world-images and self-images that are lived, used, felt in the most intimate way. Inevitably, the values of hierarchy intersect and draw meaning from other values and motives. For actors viewing the world from within the dominant ideology, hierarchy binds almost chemically with the will to believe in a just world (Lerner 1984). High caste, low caste, Butcher, Brahman, Sweeper: you deserve your fate; your caste identity determines and justifies it; for there must be a just order to the world, not an arbitrary one (or how could I justify my fortune or hope for a better fate?). This linking of status, fate, and justice becomes intelligible and appears real in terms of specific cultural concepts. Despite certain ambiguities in the concept, the idea of karma makes it possible to believe that low caste people are getting what they deserve. Concepts of purity and impurity enshrined in "common sense" make differences seem natural. The Hindu idea of dharma, of a sacred, natural, moral law, can be used to make hierarchy seem necessary, by postulating an objective ethical structure for the world that embraces the caste system.

As this chapter shows, some resist this process; they problematize the construction of hierarchy. Their dissident voices and subversive concepts may provoke reactions, be countered and overcome in further hierarchical discourse. This is a living moral debate, not a monologue, a discourse of disembodied ideas unfolding in monolithic ways, imposing a single construction on reality. Nor is it a cacophony of monologues, with each caste the "site" of different discourses—as if there was no one really there to speak for or against different definitions of self and world. In reality, people speak for and against hierarchy at every status level. The caste hierarchy does not spontaneously generate itself as much theory would seem to imply. Caste society is made and enacted by actors, who, in their concrete life-situations, experience it and relate themselves to it in a variety of ways. We have little basis for assuming that any ideology or discourse, dominant or subversive, entirely determines what social actors think and feel: as if actors did not have lives, minds, interpretive powers.

If the pageantry of hierarchy celebrates caste society as a natural and sacred order, spinning a legitimating semiotic web of and for consciousness, actors also may reject this as travesty, mere cobwebs, illusion. They speak of caste relations in ways variously critical, ironic, and utopian.

In conclusion, then, let me emphasize the inner ambivalence of cultural selves in a caste system—the theme to be explored along different tangents in subsequent chapters. People may exist in hierarchical society without being *Homo hierarchicus*. If the caste hierarchy is prismatic, so that the Newar mind-in-culture refracts people into different natural kinds, Newars are also able to reconstitute people as "the same," as like self—as equal persons who are potentially owed justice and care. Some Newars are merely acquainted with such ideas, and many reject them. Others affirm them as an ultimate moral reality, but say they must submit to social reality, constituted by what other people think and do. Even Newars who reject, on moral grounds, the basic tenets of caste hierarchy have to find ways to live within caste society. Moreover, even as they reject hierarchy, it has a grip on their emotions, and shapes the ways they know themselves.

Chapter 3
Constructing Hierarchy: India as "Other"

Who is *Homo hierarchicus?* If the men and women I spoke to, even the Brahmans and untouchables, are not, then who is? While the self-images of Newars have much to do with their cultural experience of hierarchy, and much of their testimony and behavior reveals the grip of the value of hierarchy on their consciousness, the image of *Homo hierarchicus* does not fit them. It is not a self-image, but an image fashioned by others. *Homo hierarchicus* is the product of Western minds, an apparition that mirrors the way the West has imagined India.

This image has a long history. Ronald Inden (1990) has traced some of it, showing how this Western discourse constructs images of India as "other," as what "the West" is not. These images of India draw much of their force from a peculiar Western assumption about the nature of reality. Deeply embedded in much Western thought is the idea that things possess an inherent basic nature, an essence of some kind, that constitutes what they are, constitutes their irreducible identity. This guiding idea shapes thought about other cultures, not just things and persons: each civilization must have a basic nature, a stable essence that defines it, as if cultures were natural kinds, like species—or as if they embodied a master principle, a principle that makes them what they are.

Cultural differences are not just recognized in such discourse—they are reified, distilled into essences. Human agency and history, the inner diversity of cultures and the process of making culture, are neglected. Instead, researchers working in this paradigm seek to discover distinctive cultural patterns, and interpret these as constituting the essence of a culture, that which gives it coherence and unity, an identity. This interpretive manoeuver in turn shapes a comparative project: since differences define essences, the nature and identity of a culture can be discovered by describing it in exotic contrast to other cultures. As a result, as Inden argues (1986:402), the conviction developed that "the essence of Indian civilization is just the opposite of the West's." In the Western imagination, India embodies what the West is not.

In such discourse India is constituted as "other," defining the identity, or "self," of the West by contrast. Inden (1990) makes a case for this thesis in his important book *Imagining India.* He argues that "India" and "the West" have "dialectically constituted one another" (1990:3) in much Western thought. "European discourses," he suggests, distinguished "self" from "other" by constructing a set of contrasts in which "the essence of Western thought is practical reason, that of India dreamy imagination, or the essence of Western society is the free (but selfish) individual, that of India an imprisoning (but all-providing) caste system." He then asks: "But is this really so?"

The question is crucial. Do we know India? Do we attempt to know ourselves through India, twisting India into shapes that speak to the ambivalence of our own self-images? Does India appear to be the opposite of the West because it is, or because our images of India reflect efforts to construct and validate self-images that are emotionally and politically charged in the most intimate ways?

Certainly, as a chorus of critics of Western thought have proclaimed, we need to explore the possibility that we reconstitute actual cultural differences to satisfy cultural needs to define or redefine ourselves. As Inden says, "[Western] discourses create a strange, lop-sided complementarity between the Western Self and the Indian Other. . . . We have externalized exaggerated parts of ourselves so that the equally exaggerated parts we retain can act out the triumph of the one over the other in the Indian sub-continent" (1990:3).[1]

While the terms of contrast that constitute this "strange complementarity" have varied over time, the quest for opposing essences continues. In the past few decades, this quest has often focused on hierarchy and equality, holism and individualism. In this imagining of India and the West, hierarchy fuses with holism, equality with individualism, to yield diametrically opposed values: the dominant principle of "India" is hierarchical interdependence, while the essence of "the West" is egalitarian individualism. Once again, India is "caste," the West is "the individual."

Louis Dumont (1980, 1985), of course, has been the leading contemporary figure in this project of distilling opposing values for India and the West, of defining them through contrast and oppositions. His work, a vigorous hybrid of elements of social anthropology, structuralism and Indology, in many ways represents the culmination of the "essentialist" tradition in Indian studies. As Arjun Appadurai (1986:745) writes, Dumont has "composed an elegy and a deeply Western trope for a whole way of thinking about India, in which it represents the extremes of the human capability to fetishize inequality."

Homo hierarchicus is Dumont's image; it conveys what he thinks of India, his view that South Asian men and women have no real identity, no being, apart from caste. Hierarchical interdependence absorbs them, leaving no basis in culture for actors who challenge caste hierarchy, or for values they might use to challenge it. The problem is that such actors exist, do critique culture.

Now, Dumont's ideas are original, subtle, and important; this is undeniable. I do not challenge all of them. Indeed, I think there is much that is valid in his characterizations of some bodies of South Asian ideology; he has identified and theorized about concepts and practices that help constitute structures of order and domination in "traditional" India. What I challenge is the hegemony of his concept of hierarchy and the distortion of complex histories, cultures, and selves that ensues from reifying hierarchy. This reification blocks recognition of the actual diversity of South Asian cultural experience and plays into the construction of India as "other."

Whether Dumont intended it or not, his effort to capture what he saw as distinctive about caste relations in India has conjured up a sort of specter, with his vision of *Homo hierarchicus*. From a certain point of view, and in a limited way, some of Dumont's characterizations of Indian life seem valid—they capture a central ideological note. Blown up and exaggerated, however, defined as the essential facts of South Asian life, taken as the master pattern of all South Asian reality, Dumont's views distort, and easily decay into stereotypes. Dumont, surely, would not want his ideas overextended or misapplied, but the image has acquired a life of its own, animated by the way India has long been defined as exotically alien, and identified with caste. We cannot easily exorcise the apparition of *Homo hierarchicus*, because it so powerfully symbolizes the central tendency of Western discourse about India—thus, although we know it is a phantasm, a metaphor, not to be taken too literally, a metonymn that substitutes part for whole, the image of India as caste haunts our imagination, becoming the metaphoric key through which we channel our efforts to understand a whole civilization, millions of people, centuries of diverse cultural experience. Even when repudiated, the imagery invades our discussions as a virtually inescapable subtext: India is caste, India is other, the opposite of the West.

Contrasts need to be drawn with great care, for they can conceal as much as they reveal. Dumont's work has given important insight into some of the ideological formations of traditional Indian society. But there is more to Indian history, culture, and experience than the caste system. Men and women can value hierarchy, and struggle to come to grips with the reality of living in a hierarchical world, without becoming *Homo hierarchicus.*

As important as concepts of hierarchy are, they co-exist with felt concepts of equality, solidarity, and injustice—as suggested by the testimony in the last chapter. Even equality exists in South Asia, as Parry (1979) puts it, "as a stressed principle in its own right rather than as a mere adjunct of hierarchy." Since India has been identified with hierarchy however, we know relatively little about the cultural construction of equality in India, about the role, however muted, or culturally different, that it might play.

We may even know less than we thought about hierarchy in India. More than one model exists for constructing and organizing inequality in South Asian cultures, as many studies have shown (Greenwold 1975; Dirks 1988; Raheja 1988; Wadley 1975). People invoke multiple models in cultural life and in moral discourse (Strauss 1992). What people know and feel does not reflect a cultural consensus based on a single model, as some of those following Dumont have argued, a consensus capable of exerting a near total grip on consciousness, which extends from the highest to the lowest castes (Moffatt 1979).

My main interest in this volume is with the mental foundations, the preconditions, of practice. How do people develop the ability to reflect critically on cultural formations that act on them, to reimagine the "forms of life" in which their lives are largely embedded? How does a critical tradition develop within a culture that enables people to evaluate and reimagine social and political life? I believe we can fully understand how people resist and seek to change social and political structures only by looking at the totality of what people know, by probing the ways their experience equivocally transcends the bounds of a political structure and its attendant ideology and world view.

Understanding the dynamics of the moral and political imagination— as it operates in culture—is a necessary theoretical and ethnographic prerequisite to understanding processes of social change and political transformation. We can understand these fully only by coming to grips with what people actually think and feel, as complex and multiply-constituted selves, not by assuming they are entirely constituted by the social and political structures or "discourses" in which they are "embedded," although these may indeed shape much of what they think and feel, know and do. To understand commitment and resistance to cultural practices, we need a cultural psychology of ideology and critique, a cultural anthropology of the "embodied knowledge" of social actors, that is sensitive to politics and economy (Linger 1992).

Thus I am concerned in this volume not with social action, protests and mass movements, as vital as these are, but with the ultimate roots of such phenomena in everyday life and thought. Resistance begins with mental acts that decenter self from the dominant world view, shifting consciousness away from the sense of reality that sustains the dominant order. This cognitive restructuring involves revising and redeploying cultural models that mediate the way actors identify with society, and find identity for themselves in culture. Ultimately, if often equivocally, commitment is withdrawn from the social order, from its ideology and its rhetorical forms, and from the common sense that makes the ideological constructions of reality, self, history, and society seem natural and necessary. Before people can ever act to change society, they must turn a critical eye on the practices in which they participate. They must re-feel and re-tell the world. If persons find coherence and meaning for themselves in hierarchy, they may nonetheless remain open to finding meaning in alternative visions of self and society. As we saw in Chapter 2, some Newars have ways of liberating themselves, at least temporarily, from hierarchical modes of thought and self-definition. But they rarely totally escape it.

I will use the term "hierarchy" to refer to any practice or meaning system through which inequality or dominance is culturally organized, conceptualized, and valued. Ranking groups or individuals requires a cultural code, some principle of inclusion and exclusion, superiority or inferiority—a hierarchy-making principle. Yet there is no single principle of hierarchy in Newar culture. Multiple, overlapping symbolic frameworks organize inequality. Thus, although Newars sometimes speak of the caste hierarchy as constituted in terms of relative purity and impurity, they also understand and experience inequality in terms of other cultural concepts. Identifying hierarchy exclusively with relative purity and impurity obscures the other ways that caste rank, dominance, and intercaste relations are organized and evaluated. Raheja (1988) has recently argued that dominance and inter-caste relations in a North Indian village are not structured solely in terms of a hierarchy constituted in terms of conceptions of purity and impurity. Dominance in this village is also organized in terms of conceptions of giving and receiving that constitute the ritual "centrality" of a dominant non-Brahman caste. She points out that her informants often do not view their central concerns in terms of purity and impurity. This is true of life in Bhaktapur as well. Hierarchy-constituting concepts of purity and impurity (as understood in Dumont's terms) are crucial, but so are transfers of inauspiciousness that stigmatize and degrade, and concepts of religious power and knowledge that elevate. In Bhaktapur, all of these concepts help organize and valorize inequality. They are also resented, resisted, and criticized.

Dumont Contemplated

However we read Dumont in the past, today we must read Dumont as not Gramsci, not Gadamer, not Habermas, not Bourdieu. In area studies, he must be read against Dirks, Inden, Raheja, Marriott, Levy, Khare—just as we may need to read ideology against critique, or Dalit (untouchable) perspectives against high caste Hindu ones. Perhaps Dumont would appreciate the irony: rather than consider his argument purely on its own terms—as an individual, as it were—we must treat him in relation to a whole, and place his work in relation to a universe of discourses that define themselves in part in opposition to his positions.

In 1908, C. Bouglé wrote that "the spirit of caste" involves the separation of groups, hereditary specialization, and hierarchy. Dumont (1980: 21) begins with this definition. He reduces these three "principles" to "a single true principle, namely the opposition of the pure and the impure" (p. 43), which forms the basis of hierarchy.

This opposition underlies hierarchy, which is the superiority of the pure to the impure, underlies separation because the pure and the impure must be kept separate, and underlies the division of labour because pure and impure occupations must likewise be kept separate. *The whole is founded on the necessary and hierarchical coexistence of the two opposites.* (Dumont 1980:43; italics in original)

He argues, tellingly, that the purity of the Brahman is inseparable from the impurity of the untouchable (p. 54). Surveying the empirical situation, he finds that "the multiplication of the criteria of status"—e.g., vegetarianism vs. non-vegetarianism, forbidding or allowing widow remarriage—is related to the "fundamental opposition" of the pure and impure (pp. 55–57), which he insists is "beyond question and universal in its operation." He goes on to define hierarchy in general as "the principle by which the elements of a whole are ranked in relation to the whole" (p. 66). In the case of South Asia, not power, he says, but religion "provides the view of the whole" (p. 66). In this connection, he reaffirms the link he has made between the principle of hierarchy and "the opposition between the pure and the impure," which he identifies as a "religious" concept (pp. 66), not as an aspect of the reality of the "natural" world as understood culturally (Levy 1990:376, 386). Thus, for Dumont, the caste system resolves itself into the hierarchy of the pure and the impure, and he admits no other basis for hierarchy—he rules out power and exchange as factors. Ideology here is the ordering principle of thought, and of social reality, not a distortion of that reality, not a false consciousness. Ideology is not the product of rhetoric, of efforts to advance a vision of the world, a means of defining and leveraging commitment, asserted against inertia and resistance, but a mental structure, constituting thought seamlessly. In his structuralism, Dumont cannot accept the multiplicity of culture, the inner diversity of culture—he insists on unity. Since *only* relations matter—not relations *and* agents, not wholes *and* parts, he cannot easily imagine actors engaged in dialogue with culture, or engaging in critique of culture.[2]

Dumont claims that it is "by implicit reference" to the opposition of the pure and impure that "the society of castes appears consistent and rational to those who live in it" (p. 44). But does it? Perhaps it appears incoherent to some; what of them?

People may exist in a state of violation; they can think and feel against the grain of the dominant concepts of reality. To do so, they may have to work around dominant concepts of reality; but since mental life and social existence are fluidly and multiply structured, not absolutely determined by a single ideology, or social structure, people find ways of doing so.

Objective Ideology, Objective Ambivalence

I think we must turn away from Dumont's formulation of "a single true principle," which is "beyond question and universal" and explore instead the multiple cultural models people bring to caste relations, and the relations between these models. To illustrate this point, I want to look at a "playful" cultural text in the eclectic light of ideas drawn from Bourdieu (1977) and Jameson (1981). My goal is not so much to analyze the text, but to model the process of analysis, so that we can reflect on the way analytic choices shape how and what we understand.

This child's rhyme captures a sense of the way the Newar world is hierarchical; the rhyme has faintly disturbing nuances, an undertone suggesting hidden ambivalences. My translation lacks the resonances of the original, the tone and associations it would have for Newars, but I think it conveys something of what you have to "know" in order to be a competent member of a traditional, complex, and hierarchical culture. The rhyme can be performed; two children, or two groups of children, sit facing each other, and take turns reciting the lines of the rhyme. One child hides his or her arm, and the other asks, "Where has your arm gone?" The reply is "A rat (or a bird) took it." The rhyme continues with queries and responses:

(How much blood came?)
   Eight parts came.

(Who'd you give the blood to?)
   I gave it to the little Butcher woman.

(What'd she give for it?)
  She gave milk.

(Who'd you give the milk to?)
  I gave it to the betel seller.

(What did the betel seller give for it?)
  He gave betel.

(Who'd you give the betel to?)
  I gave it to the king.

(What'd the king give for it?)
  He gave a horse and an elephant.

(Where'd you put the horse and the elephant?)
  I put them on the ground floor.

(They aren't on the ground floor.)
  I put them on the second floor.

(They aren't on the second floor either.)
  I put them on the third floor.

(They aren't on the third floor either.)
  I put them on the fourth floor.

(They aren't on the fourth floor either.)
  I put them on the roof.

(They aren't on the roof either.)
  They fell off the roof and died.

Notice the commercial nexus and the social hierarchy—the movement from butcher to king is a passage from near the bottom to near the top of the Newar caste and class hierarchy. The exchanges begin with blood and end with an elephant and a horse. These are incommensurate somehow, they are not there, in the story, on any of the floors of the house; they are not part of the life of ordinary people, in the real world. Is there a certain symmetry between caste hierarchy and the vertical dimension of the house? (The Newar house is a symbolic structure, where higher floors are more pure than lower floors.) The rhyme begins with a wounding—the loss of an arm. It is blood that begins the exchanges; blood whose loss would mean death becomes a commodity. This is used to acquire what ordinary people don't ordinarily have—horses and elephants. These are not anywhere; they are gone, negated. They fell down and died (the children collapse in a pile).

   This children's rhyme contains an implicit analysis of Newar society. In one sense, the rhyme is a representation of the organization and orchestration of the relations among objective social groups (butcher, king, merchant). The interactions of social agents form the narrative structure, but what is most clearly communicated is the way that their *interactions* are "defined by the objective structure of the relations between the groups they belong to" (Bourdieu 1977:81). The rhyme's actors are socially positioned in relationship to each other; they appear to be nothing more than figures standing for the hierarchically structured relations among groups. The story stimulates and represents the workings of society as a place where social persons encounter each other, engage in exchanges, and are ranked hierarchically. Its implicit analysis converges with some of Bourdieu's views; for example, when he says that biological individuals carry their "present and past positions in the social structure" with them "at all times and places, in the form of dispositions which are so many marks of *social position* and hence of the social distance between objective positions." The rhyme shows how social structure brings people together in the interactions that embody that social structure—where each person is present, not "in and of themselves," but "through and for" the objective structures of their society, which they reproduce in their structured interactions.
   The rhyme is therefore a narrative map of social structure, clearly marking the central significance of hierarchy and exchange. But the rhyme also contains tensions, elements somehow at odds with the representation of social structure. What of the loss of an arm? The exchange of blood? The inability of the house to contain the product of the exchanges? These are markedly ambiguous—they verge on being disturbing. What do they represent, what meaning do they have? Are they a kind of protest against, or subversion of, the social structure represented in the interactions of the narrative? Do they suggest that a kind of violence is inherent in social structure? They are too ambiguous to say for sure; but this ambiguity has an effect. It prevents the rhyme from achieving closure, a final "meaning."
   Perhaps the meaning is not totally contained in the text, but also relates to life. Of any cultural text or signifying practice, we can ask: what is here, but not here, that we can "read as what the text represses"? (Jameson 1981:49). This rhyme invites us to read into it what it does not declare overtly: an ambivalence attuned to structure. If we make the relatively modest assumption that a narrative may bear traces of the pain and quandaries of a social world, then perhaps we can reconstruct this rhyme not only as a rendition of structure, but as allusion to the reification and commodification of self.
   If so, the rhyme whose surface so elegantly maps social relations can

also be read as having latent, implied meanings, if we appreciate that its narrative structure, to borrow from Jameson again, "far from being completely realized on any one of its levels, tilts powerfully into the underside or *impense* . . . in short, into the very political unconscious, of the text." Texts relate to life, if they have any meaning for people, but may point away from pain and oppression. They can conceal as much as they reveal, may misrepresent, evade, falsify, presenting a selective image of self and world that omits much that is lived and practiced.

In a general sense, the political unconscious of a text may point us to the political unconscious of culture, that is, to an ethos and world view not fully disclosed in dominant ideology and practice. This fugitive ethos and world view, its models of self and society, its forms of thought and life, reflects the lived worlds and experience of some actors, even as these are kept out of the public eye, and often enough "out of mind." What gets suppressed may, of course, vary. But in general, narrative and symbolic practices require a kind of double reading, looking inward to the text and outward to culture life. For as narratives or practices, such as the chariot festival, declare their meaning overtly they also resonate with, and yet suppress, other meanings. They "contain" meaning in both senses of the word: they convey a message, transmit a body of knowledge and values, and also set limits on what can be known and valued. Even as they seek to set boundaries and define a world, filling it with meanings and motives, they suggest other possible worlds of experience, other aspects of life, often tacitly registering and insinuating what they implicitly deny. Approached in this way, cultural texts and practices—rituals, narratives, even children's rhymes—may "direct us to the informing power of forces or contradictions which the text [or practice] seeks in vain wholly to control or master" (Jameson 1981:49).

In this light, the collapse of the children at the end of their game can be seen as a "silent" but powerfully contextualizing and critical metastatement on the social structure so lucidly modeled in the rhyme. In any event, whether a joint child-adult construction, or a piece of children's culture, the rhyming game embodies society, "only to destroy it" (the house falls down, the children collapse into a heap)—opening up the possibility that there is more to life and reality than the socially-constituted normative order (Sutton-Smith, quoted in Schwartzmann 1978:124).

The festive collapse of kids into a pile seems more authentically childlike—a game—than the rhyme's rendition of social hierarchy. The modeling of a hierarchical ladder of exchanges seems more an adult paradigm, perhaps constructed by adults for children to participate in. For while reification may be experienced by a child, the specific form of self-commodification, giving an arm in exchange, seems to speak more of adult experience: I have little doubt that this rhyme resonates with adult concerns in a form that may strike a chord in children, who must of course surrender part of themselves to the dominant parental order.

As I worked with Newars of different castes, I was duly impressed by the significance of hierarchy in their lives. It would have been easy to see them only in these terms—and to selectively present them only in hierarchical terms, to be tempted into a too-easy totalizing approach (Bourdieu 1977:106–7; Trawick 1990:137). I began to see, however, that this would falsify aspects of Newar self-experience and meaning-construction that had felt significance for many Newars, but that contradict the ideology and mood of hierarchy. Newars would often invoke other values—even reject hierarchy altogether. It was rather like being in the rhyme: informants would build up a hierarchical structure in their discourse, floor by floor; and then they would collapse the hierarchical structure itself, leaving elephants and horses, anthropologist and *Homo hierarchicus* to fall ambiguously.

If the child's rhyme, or selected ideological texts, were our only data, it would be easy to portray the Newar moral world as totally hierarchical in character, and the Newar as Dumont's *Homo hierarchicus*. The nuances in the rhyme are only nuances, after all — although I think they should alert us to the possibility of ambivalence—and not the dominant image. But note too that the rhyme says nothing of purity and impurity: it speaks of blood going up a ladder of exchange, not of a hierarchy predicated on purity and impurity; moreover, there is a king but not a Brahman; taken as a whole, the rhyme seems to speak to the moral ambiguity of unequal exchange—life's blood for an elephant on the roof—in a hierarchical world, not to the ritual acts of the purity complex that separate and rank. No doubt Dumont could find a way to reveal the opposition of the pure and impure in it. No doubt I have overinterpreted the cultural text.

This is, of course, precisely the problem. It is easy to select and overinterpret a narrow range of texts and practices, which reveal some of the images people have of themselves and their society, and say, "This is what they are, and this is the single principle that gives form and coherence to their world." If I do this, however, I run the risk of ignoring or excluding other texts, commentary, and practices that make it possible for those same people to know themselves and their world in other ways. If like Dumont we insist on "a single true principle" as the basis of cultural life—or even merely of its "intellectual coherence"—we may miss much, if in fact social actors are prepared to find different things meaningful at different times, in different contexts, for different purposes.

If Brahmans and untouchables, kings and butchers necessarily live "through and for" the world of hierarchical practice, they also live "in and of" what the symbolism and ideology of such practices denies—their agency, their suffering and loss, their resentments, fears, and hopes, their discontents. Despite what so much classical culture theory has implied, social actors exist not only within and through dominant structures of mind and practice, but also in resistance and counter-point to these. If actors recognize the coercive structure of social life and its costs, if they internalize this as a generative schema for their own lives and practice, they also achieve enough distance to ironically comment on it, to critique it and resist it with some subtlety.

Hierarchy and *Homo Hierarchicus*

Little or no room is left for agency in Dumont's structural universe, yet he does not see it as an iron cage, as legitimating practice that develops to overcome cultural resistance to inequalities. His theory suppresses the critical consciousness, the "critical self," that I believe exists in every complex culture. In fact, despite evidence to the contrary, much culture theory assumes that people are so absorbed in "culture" that they cannot react to it, act on it, in ways we might call critical, ironic, utopian. That culture comments on culture, as people take different (cultural) perspectives on cultural practices, engage in cultural debates, giving culture a dynamic, critical side, gets lost in the assumption that culture globally constructs everything, does everything. When human agency is dismissed, only culture has agency.

For example, in their preamble to an illuminating discussion of concepts of the person, in which they quite appropriately invoke Dumont's ideas as inspiration and critical foil, Fruzzetti, Östör, and Barnett (1982) offer this succinct summary of Dumont's vision of India, which also, I think, concisely exposes its weaknesses and limits:

Dumont puts the problem thus: the ideology of caste encompasses and thereby situates all aspects of Indian culture. Caste ideology is holistic: the ultimate focus of value falls on the society, not on particular, abstract individuals as in Euro-American society. Castes are ranked not as autonomous units but as dependent parts of an independent whole (for Dumont the analogy is parts of the body, each necessary, none sufficient). The principle of ranking is ultimately the opposition of the pure and the impure, seen unambiguously in the opposition of Brahman and untouchable, so that castes are ordered along a scale of relative purity. . . . Oddly, the criticism that has gained the most currency seems the weakest: that Dumont's constructions represent Brahman (read oppressor) notions and so cannot be generalized as Indian culture. . . .

In this view lower castes see through the Brahman mystification and reject those views that make them inferior. However, those same lower castes replicate the caste system among themselves and participate in local life. As Lukács wrote [1971:257]: "The organs of authority harmonize to such an extent with the [economic] laws governing men's lives, or seem so overwhelmingly superior that men experience them as natural forces, as the necessary environment for their existence. As a result, they submit to them freely, which is not to say they approve of them." (Fruzetti, Östör, and Barnett 1982:9)

We need to challenge or severely qualify almost all these assertions. I do not think the ideology of caste hierarchy "encompasses and thereby situates all aspects" of South Asian culture, even where caste is a dominant social form. In making hierarchy the central principle of Indian life, the principle that gives an identity to India, I think Dumont's paradigm has substituted a part (the opposition of the pure and the impure) for the whole (South Asian life as a dynamic moral and political ecology), and this keying of whole to part produces serious distortions in the way we envision India—for despite critiques and challenges, Dumont's views achieved a kind of preeminence in South Asian studies and has reinforced one-sided popular conceptions of India as "caste."

Of course, this does not mean we should fail to recognize Dumont's real contributions. In fact, this volume attests to these contributions, even as it offers a critique. Dumont has gotten a grip on part of the reality, and part of the self-serving self-imagery, of caste life.

So, while caste hierarchy and its *multiple* ideologies are crucial for any full understanding of South Asian cultural life, I doubt that any culture anywhere can be encompassed and harmonized in its totality by a single value or a single ideology. Castes are ranked, and Newars sometimes involve the metaphor "*society is a body,*" but there are alternative views of society. Moreover, if the caste system is like a body, it is like a body whose parts think and resist. One Newar caste has attempted to relocate itself in the Bhaktapur caste system through various stratagems: if we extend the analogy to incorporate the behavior of this group, we have a leg that denies it is a leg and maintains it is really an arm or shoulder; it wants to assume (what it insists is) its rightful position, and seeks to be acknowledged as an arm; it voices the opinion that it got a rotten deal when it was made a leg, that it was tricked into being a leg; it petitions for redress and agitates for a rearrangement of parts into a differently configured whole. Moreover, people may not see rank solely in terms of the principle of the opposition of purity and impurity (Raheja 1988), although this conceptual opposition may be used to simulate an unambiguous and incontestable ranking, to give closure to the construction of hierarchy.

What I find odd is not the criticism that what Dumont presents as the singular key to a civilization is the ideology of a particular group (or a number of groups), but rather the notion that this criticism can be so easily disarmed. The criticism seems weak to Fruzzetti, Östör, and Barnett (1982:9); they note that lower castes "replicate the caste system among themselves and participate in local life" as if they always had someplace to go and wouldn't leave if they could, when in fact when they can exit the system, they often do (Mahar 1972; Khare 1984; Freeman 1979). What I think odd is not the criticism that Dumont has elevated to absolute preeminence a chunk of ideology that seems most favored by, and to serve best, those in a dominant position in society (however widely shared elements of this ideology are) but that this criticism was not pursued as far as it should have been—as far as we can today. It is a fact that some lower caste people may, at some moments, reject "those views that make them inferior." Like others, I document this. Newars have, as we've already seen, various kinds of critical, utopian, and ironic views on inequality. It is also true they participate in caste life. People can and do see through mystifications, but must also find ways to contain and neutralize these insights.

For indeed, low caste actors must participate in the caste system; what would it mean to *not* participate in local life? Low caste Newars are quite clear about what it would mean—hunger and suffering. Thus one must ask of the passage quoted from Lukács, what it means to submit freely. The phrase seems ironic on its face; coercion and agency takes many forms and have a dynamic dialectical relationship. Perhaps men and women submit unfreely—and approve. Perhaps they reject and accept, subvert and yet collude, resist and yet in their resistance reproduce what they resist (Willis 1981). The permutations are, if not endless, many, and productive of myriad cultural and subjective formations. Is freedom only the absence of naked force? Or is it present only when there are alternative structures, mental and social, that permit a degree of reflective choice? Perhaps we need deeper philosophical scrutiny of our terms.

Our terms are no clearer about what seem to be self-evident facts—that lower caste people enact caste relations. Doesn't this "fact" compel us to say they "share" an ideology with the higher castes? Perhaps. Clearly, what people say and what they do are not always the same; what they do, often, is participate in caste relations they verbally reject. Fruzzetti, Östör, and Barnett note as evidence that low castes do not see through and reject caste the fact that the lower castes *replicate* the caste system among themselves. Truly, if taken at face value (an odd maneuver for structural analysis) the replication of caste system by the lower castes would seem to certify the existence of a consensus about caste on the part of the highest and lowest castes (Moffatt 1979).

But what does it mean to *replicate* the caste system? Perhaps we risk assuming too much with this word. Do the lower castes copy someone else's system, absorbing the ideology that supposedly encompasses all, or do they produce their own caste system, which for them ultimately has its own meaning, and serves some of their own interests?

Is the caste system of the lower castes precisely the same as the caste system of the higher castes—or does it only seem so? Is it inwardly the same or only outwardly? Perhaps they enact caste relations in a different spirit, or for purposes of their own. Perhaps it constitutes a different intentional world, both like and unlike the world of caste of dominant castes. How would we know? A focus on abstract structural relationships (parts and wholes) that skips from surface to deep structure without pausing to contemplate other, more concrete aspects of meaning and experience can obscure much (what caste means to self, its political value, its quandaries and ambivalences). A philosophical analysis of our terms and a psychocultural analysis of the felt reality and meaning of social facts can be salutatory.

The replication of caste relations on the part of low-caste actors may further the interests of the higher castes; no doubt it does at times. At the very least, the extension of exploitative relations helps validates the entire system of oppressive relationships and helps ensure that the lower castes remain entrapped in the total system. They are complicit, know they are complicit, can be charged with complicity if they protest. This may blunt their critiques of the caste system.

Yet they do reject and critique caste life, even in the face of the authority and legitimacy and sense of reality it appears to have. I believe the organs of (cultural and moral) authority harmonize imperfectly, with each other and political economy, and always in the face of discord. Naturally, they can more or less harmonize, and there can be more or less discord—but some dissonance seems integral to social existence. Perhaps many individuals do experience the visions of reality of caste life as natural, necessary, and irresistible—even as fair. Still, empirically, dissent exists, at least if the Newars are any guide. As I will show in later chapters the harmonizing of the organs of authority in the chariot festival in fact works imperfectly, does not totally quiet the imagination of actors, quell their discontents, or bring them into harmony with their society. As their testimony in chapter 2 suggests, disquiet about caste life stirs the imagination of Newars (Brahman as well as untouchable). A process of reimagining occurs, often privately, occasionally in public— which stimulates reaction, and leads to efforts to defend and maintain the ideology that *is* in crucial ways constitutive of social reality, but does not so overwhelm minds that the terms on which it attempts to constitute society and self are never questioned.

This struggle goes on within the cultural order and within individual hearts and minds as part of the cultural order. In complex societies, at least, cultural subjectivities stand not fixed and encompassed in a single ideology but move fluidly in the mutually entangled webs of meaning that are ideology and critique. Each of these unravels the other, and each requires continual maintenance and reweaving. Thus what I would term "the critical self," itself diverse and positioned, is an integral part of cultural life, a mode of thought and action that men and women can animate. Interpreting and acting persons are not so absorbed in ideology that they vanish, disappear into the culture they internalize: nor do ideas and critiques or the process of thinking and reimagining exist apart from cultural meanings, experiences, and practices.

Thus, although Bhaktapur is a city where castes are integral features of civic life, it is not a city inhabited by men and women whose essences are somehow constituted by hierarchy. Bhaktapur is not home to *Homo hierarchicus*, but to men and women who try to live their lives in the context of the powerful hierarchical ideology and hegemonic cultural formations of a complex caste system.

While there are a few significant exceptions, the anthropological preoccupation with caste has not produced a comprehensive body of research into the problems of meaning and identity posed by caste life. We know much about the cultural ideology of caste, but less about how caste life is experienced and evaluated by social actors. This means that our understanding of caste society—as a moral system—is incomplete.

When Newars spoke of caste life, they evaluated it, defended it, and criticized it, speaking as Brahmans, high caste merchants, farmers, untouchables. Many of them spoke out against the implications of caste ideology—resisting psychologically, if not politically. They worked at reimagining the caste system, proposing alternative forms of hierarchy and equality. In a sense, they were making a critique of culture; they were developing, multiplying, and exploring cultural perspectives on the moral order that were critical and potentially transforming—even when they could not put any of this into action.

If they cannot act on them, why have them? I think these morally and politically charged ideas are put forward by people who want to justify resistance or wish to distance themselves from oppressive practices, who need to critique the social order so they can think better of themselves, who need to find hope, to find a way to go on enduring a life they find in many ways intolerable. Notions of equality exist in an uneasy relationship with the ideology and legitimating practices of caste hierarchy. While in the field, I could see, as Dumont said, that hierarchy implied equality, but what use did people make of that relationship? If they imply and support each other, what form does this take? I began to question whether it was enough to observe that hierarchy implies equality and then focus almost exclusively on hierarchy. This leaves equality unexamined, when it clearly exists, at least as a kind of fugitive body of culture that infiltrates thought and feeling, even if only to face immediate neutralization. What is the nature of the interplay?

In this volume, I explore some aspects of the interplay that have to do with persons, with the way they relate themselves to the social system. But we need to ask, what are the theoretical implications of this? To state it baldly: the relationship of hierarchy and equality is dynamic, not static and passive; if they imply each other, then both are available for use in moral rhetoric, and each can be used to resist and place limits on the other. The hierarchical concepts of Hindu cultures reflect this. If hierarchy implies equality, and equality can be used to subvert hierarchy, then the cultural construction of hierarchy will involve efforts to prevent this subversion, to counter egalitarian ideas. Therefore, the relationship of a dominant ideology of hierarchy with egalitarian concepts will never remain one of absolutely passive implication, but will always involve an active animosity. This antagonism inspires rhetorical actions, efforts to undermine the opposing value. This may develop into more sustained political polemic; this can lead to further elaboration of an ideology. The rhetoric and argumentation developed out of this ideological work constitute tools in struggles—however glacial they may be—to shape and control the social order; ideology, rhetoric, and polemic may be mobilized to help *overcome* egalitarian thinking. Since hierarchy always implies equality, this cannot be done with absolute finality. Thus equality blossomed in the poetry of *bhakti* devotionalism and is voiced passionately today in critiques that untouchables make of the caste system.

Gangadhar Pantawane (1986) writes of the development of Dalit—as many untouchables in India have chosen to call themselves in the self-consciousness their protest movements give them—identity and culture as arising out of a rejection of the institutionalized inequality and oppression, and as arising in confrontation with oppressive "Hindu culture." He quotes the Dalit poet Harish Bansode:

> We have begun a new life
> We have found our own temples
> Regained our lost faith
> All are equal here

In a Dalit movement song, equality is also invoked:

> Rise, people, rise up now, break the chains of caste
> Throw off the corpse of slavery, smash the obstacles,
>   Rise people—
> We may be Maratha, Mahar, Brahman, Hindu, Muslim, Christian,
> Humanity is all one, all are brothers.[3]

The song attacks the practices of discrimination, and also the cultural tradition of which those practices are part, identifying it as "the eternal culture that was offended even by the touch of our shadow." The lyrics speaks of "the deformity of purity which crushed humanness" and says "the volcano that was cast outside the village has erupted." The language is plain enough; these are not voices constituted in terms of the opposition of the pure and impure, but in opposition to it and all that it stands for in terms of social oppression and inequality. They do not find caste society somehow rational by reference to the ideology of the purity, but irrational and oppressive (Dumont 1980:44).

Of course, Dumont would perhaps say it was not his intention "to fail to recognize more or less modern movements" (1980:xxi). Against this, Dalit intellectuals might say their movement is not only modern but that their tradition, the past of their movement, has been erased (Khare 1984). Possibly they only invent a tradition for themselves in this way. However, there is evidence that the caste hierarchy was rejected in the past—if the whole history of Buddhism in India and Nepal is not enough evidence. (Of course, rejection was often restructured back into hierarchy, which, after all, represents the dominant order.) A. K. Ramanujan (1990:54) says of bhakti—not just a modern movement—that it "defies all contextual structures: every pigeonhole of caste, ritual, gender, appropriate clothing and custom, stage of life, the whole system of *Homo hierarchicus* ("everything in its place") is the target of its irony." In support of this, he quotes this poem from the tenth century:

Did the breath of the mistress
have breasts and long hair?

Or did the master's breath
wear sacred thread?

Did the outcaste, last in line,
hold with his outgoing breath
the stick of his tribe?

What do the fools of this world know
of the snares you set,
O Ramanatha?
      (Devara Dasimayya, tenth century)

Alternate cultural perspectives, if not alternative social actuality, have long been available within South Asian cultures. If, as Newars harvested the culture of South Asia to make their own culture, they adopted the ideology of caste hierarchy, they also adopted something of the critique of ideology that is also part of the South Asian tradition, so that today they may invoke the idea of a deity in every heart who transcends human distinctions, their image of an ineluctable unity that corresponds to the poem's "breath" that bears no marks—no stigma—of distinction and rank.

The epiphany of unity with divinity—and through this, unity with all humanity—does not necessarily last very long in the face of necessity before being "structured" back into rank and inequality, that is, into the hegemony of hierarchy. C. J. Fuller, in a book that gives a thorough account of the place of hierarchy in popular Hinduism,[4] offers an example of this, suggesting that the apparent commitment to equality in the Radha-Krishna *Bhajanas* of Madras studied by Milton Singer (1966) sustain relations of inequality while seeming to overcome them. However, Fuller's analysis here does not seem strong enough to sustain his important thesis. He claims that the associations of mostly middle class Brahmans such as these "help to define and maintain social boundaries, and hence promote an internal solidarity among people whose own identity is perceived to be at risk" in the face of the urban problem of maintaining social problems (1992:161).

This analysis does not, however, explain why these Brahmans need to profess any concept of equality at all, much less demonstrate a commitment to it in word and deed, as context-specific and limited as this demonstration is; they could affirm their identity, generate solidarity, and reassure themselves about their status without doing so. Others surely do so. Fuller seems more eager to get equality out of the picture than to account for its actual—but highly equivocal—place in the minds, experience, and lives of the members of this association. Why any concept of equality, and why any demonstration of commitment to it, however limited? We need to understand the value and sentiments express in relation to their limits, not dismiss them because they are limited and are reabsorbed in hierarchical systems. Is this concealed affirmation of their self-definition as Brahmans a chameleon-like reaction to anti-Brahman political currents? Although as Fuller points out, since very few non-Brahmans participate, it cannot be argued that caste divisions are actually overcome, professing equality might provide protective camouflage (one can say one believes in equality even as one does not practice it). Or does equality have a rational appeal or moral resonances that can be acknowledged in this way without requiring much effort or actual loss of hierarchical status? Do these Brahmans perhaps seek to immunize themselves against the rational or political appeal, the felt resonances, of equality through a kind of cultural vaccination—innoculating themselves with just enough equality to develop a resistance to it? Actors may need to play with homeopathic doses of what they ultimately want to reject, in order to have enough experience of it to speak against it, and to formulate a rhetoric that overcomes it.

One speculative interpretation is that egalitarian behavior here is a kind of ritualized "play of mastery." Equality is a disturbing concept in a socially disturbed urban world; through ritual play, perhaps they "encompass" it, making it part of their repertoire—they "master" it. They define it; it does not define them. By ritualizing it in the ways they do, they effectively neutralize and encapsulate it. This would not preclude the possibility that ritual professions of equality provide protective "cover" in an environment where equality is valued by some—these Brahmans can assert that they are egalitarian if situations arise where doing so might prove advantageous. They have provided the grounds for believing that they are, after all, even as they continue to assert their superiority to audiences receptive to that claim. They have a (ritual) egalitarian self encompassed in a hierarchical self.

Thus, Fuller's basic point is well-taken. Anti-hierarchical and egalitarian ideas, impulses, and sentiments tend to be sealed off or restructured back into hierarchy. The material here—and the phenomena—cries out for deeper analysis in terms of hegemony, power, self-representation, structures of ambivalence, rather than in terms of the functionalism of Fuller's discussion—perhaps along lines suggested in Linger's analysis (1993:3) of the way "embodied knowledge," as "an amalgam of thought and sentiment" can at once "fuel varieties of protest and rebellion" and "divert them into politically innocuous channels" within "an unyielding political structure."

Fuller (1992) seems to be in agreement with Dalits who see Hinduism as fundamentally conservative and supportive of inequality, "notwithstanding," as he says, "the contribution made by devotionalism to Indian egalitarianism." Despite the words of one of my high caste Hindu friends, who protested that Hinduism has nothing to do with caste, I think this link with religion—this mobilization of divinity and ritual—stands at the heart of the cultural hegemony of hierarchy in caste society.

However—as I think the Newar testimony in Chapter 1 suggests—no ideology can make equality or hierarchy unthinkable. The possibility of shifting between "hierarchy" and "equality" always exists—whatever the dominant ideology says, and whatever degree of cultural hegemony has been achieved for one or the other.[5] This is due in part to the fact that hierarchy and equality entail and presuppose each other. Locked into a mutual complementarity that is always potentially mutually subversive, equality and hierarchy appear to be transcultural categories that are culturally interpreted, given meaning in a concrete social scene, a lived world. In part, the way people shift between the perspectives of equality and hierarchy reflects the ambiguity and ambivalence of human beings in the face of moral and political rhetoric. Anyone can always claim that anyone else is are the same, or different, in morally relevant ways.

Values of hierarchy and equality confront each other, not only in moral and political rhetoric, but in the minds and experience of men and women. Low caste actors often resent caste practices, and experience emotional pain as a consequence of their stigmatized identities. This is not surprising—unless one has too deeply absorbed the assumptions of some schools of culture theory, which ignore the diffusely political nature of cultural life as well as the emotional pain and material deprivation that cultural life can produce. It does, however, pose an important question: what happens to the moral and political "energy" that this resentment represents? How is it expressed in culture and in self?

To an outsider whose outlook is shaped by the liberal tradition of the West it may seem obvious that low caste actors will reject the caste system and desire to abolish or transform it; but this is not entirely true. Low caste women and men may affirm hierarchy. Low caste actors often invoke both hierarchy and equality as they seek to formulate strategies and tactics, pragmatic and psychological, for making their way in life—and for making life more bearable, perhaps even redeemable. They search for meaning, and seek to survive, by shifting perspectives on self and society.

Dumont (1980:265) himself acknowledges the co-existence of hierarchy and equality in any society: "each," he says, "implies the other and is supported by it." Yet he fails to explore the nature of their relationship. As Parry (1979) observes, "aside from his observation that hierarchy inevitably implies equality within . . . hierarchically ranked units, Dumont finds no significant place for egalitarian values in his model of traditional Indian society."[6]

In a way, this is surprising: Dumont's own definitions would seem to allow one to find a significant place for equality in Indian culture and society. One abstract definition of hierarchy he gives is this:

What I call a hierarchical opposition is the opposition between a set (and more particularly a whole) and an element of this set (or of this whole. . . . This opposition is logically analyzable into two contradictory partial aspects; on the one hand, the element is identical to the set that it forms a part thereof (a vertebrate is an animal); on the other hand there is a difference or, more strictly, contrariety (a vertebrate is not *solely* an animal; an animal is not *necessarily* a vertebrate). (1986:227; emphasis in original)

He thus defines hierarchy in terms of the relations of identity and contrariety: as "involving a distinction within an identity, *an encompassing of the contrary*" (1986:279; emphasis in original). In my view, people make use of differences, oppositions and "contrariety"—but also construct moral arguments on the basis of relations of identity. They can turn Dumont's hierarchy inside out, making difference, or contrariety, into the subordinate principle. They can collapse differences into identity, and so recover equality as a basis of solidarity. They can (and do) recover equality (relations of identity) for critiques of social rank, asserting that human identity encompasses human differences. This is manifest in cultural thought. As Newars say: "I am a person, and you are a person."

Thus, it seems to me one can recover relations of identity, equality, solidarity from the relationship of part and whole. Ironic, critical, and utopian discourse may recover these and make use of them, constructing an "egalitarian" reading of the root themes of Indian culture that challenge socially and politically dominant "hierarchical" versions (Khare 1984). Attending to the way caste actors do this simply extends and completes Dumont's project. Doing so, we "decenter" the hierarchical reading of Indian society, tone down the exaggeration and caricature associated with *Homo hierarchicus*, and problematize the "strange, lopsided complementarity" of Western discourse that constitutes India as hierarchical "other."

We must, of course, continue to attempt to understand the place of hierarchy in South Asian cultural life—as defined in ideology and in critique—but I agree with those who feel we need to displace Dumont's vision, making room for more subtle theories. No one I imagine—not I, certainly not most untouchables—would deny the centrality of hierarchy in Indian society. I do think we understand hierarchy's place in society better if we see it in relation to its indigenous critique, if we explore the way it is multiply constituted, and if we explore it as a political and cultural production, not as a given of cultural tradition.

Since equality exists in traditional South Asia—at least as an implication of hierarchy—we can ask, what place does it have in South Asian cultures and lives? We should not aim to show *that* equality and hierarchy co-exist, but to say something about *how* they co-exist. In my view, their dynamic relationship develop under conditions of social and ideological struggle, where hierarchy reigns as the dominant principle of the dominant ideology as dominant groups seek hegemony for it, and equality is a concept used in critique and resistance.

It would be impossible in a brief volume to do justice to the critical work on Dumont, which by now amounts to a vast and varied body of writings.[7] I will concentrate instead on three contemporary critics of Dumont's vision of the nature of hierarchy and its place in South Asian life: Gloria Raheja, Nicholas Dirks, and Arjun Appadurai.

Raheja: Mutuality and Centrality

Raheja writes that "the deeply entrenched Western interpretation" that sees hierarchy as "the sole ideology defining relations among caste" was "set forth most starkly and most persuasively by Louis Dumont." The origins of this interpretation, however, were found in the European conceptions of the colonial era, when "Brahmanic textual formulations" were elevated to "unqualified hegemony over other traditions and other sets of values." (1990:79) Raheja's work helps restore some balance by exploring other indigenous constructions of caste identity and relations.

Dumont insisted that caste derives from a single ideology, whose governing principle was the hierarchical opposition of the pure and impure. For him, caste relations cannot have any other form or meaning; the relationships of caste cannot have any other value or meaning for people. Noting that Dumont criticized other accounts of caste—such as Hocart's effort to derive caste rank from kingship and associated ritual, and Wiser's account of the "reciprocity" of *jajamani* relations—Raheja argues he "dismisses these other aspects of inter-caste relationships precisely because he sees these alternate emphases and values as being incompatible with his postulation of a single encompassing ideology of hierarchy." (1990:81) I agree with this assessment. Singularity is the key themata of Dumont's work, the self-imposed transcendental condition of his mode of interpretation. We are not, however, compelled to accept this, or the totalization of the experience of a sub-continent based on it. Indeed, it is vital to see what the South Asian cultural world appears like under multiplicity rather than singularity (S. Daniel 1983).

Rejecting Dumont's position as being "incapable of comprehending the contextuality, circumstantiality and shifting emphases that characterize ongoing social life in India," Raheja argues forcefully that "there are several contextually shifting ideologies of inter-caste relationships apparent in everyday village social life. Meanings and values are foregrounded differently from context to context, and they implicate varying configurations of castes" (p. 81). I agree.

Raheja further conceptualizes caste relations in terms of "centrality" and "mutuality." The dominant Gujar caste in Pahanu, the village she studied, give gifts or make donations (prestations, in anthropological parlance) to other castes, including Brahmans and others who provide services. Such giving expresses ritual centrality. The locally dominant caste, the Gujars, are jajmans who have the right to give *dan*; the other castes involved in the prestations have an obligation to accept dan from them. Not just payments for services, dan "is always given in the context of ritual actions." Giving promotes well-being; it transfers the "evil" (*pap*), afflictions, faults of the giver to the recipient (p. 82). By giving, the donor transfers "inauspiciousness" to the recipient of the gift: "through the giving of dan in the proper ritual contexts, these negative substances 'come out' [*utarna*] of the donor and may then have their effect on the recipient in the form of 'disease' [*rog*], madness, a diminishing of his 'power' [*sakti*] or his 'fiery energy' [*tej*], or in the form of a general decline of his family and lineage" (1990:82).

Other prestation do not transfer evil and inauspiciousness. "Dan," writes Raheja (1990:88) "is always given to those who are seen as 'other' [*dusre*] precisely in order to 'move away' [*hatana*] the inauspiciousness afflicting the jajman." But those who are "other" in one context are termed "one's own people" in other contexts. As such, they "are given prestations that imply a mutuality of service rendered and payment received, or simply a 'sharing' that is deemed appropriate among 'one's own people.'" In this type of prestation, she notes, the recipient does not so much have an obligation to receive as a right to expect the gift (88–89).

Raheja argues that these prestations, and not hierarchy constituted in terms of purity and impurity, are key to caste relations in Pahansu. Prestations do not conform to the hierarchical rank conferred by the values of purity and impurity. As Raheja puts it, "there are no situations in which a prestation is made precisely because of a hierarchical relationship" (1990:92). Rather, prestations express or constitute inter-caste relationships independently of the values of purity, on their own terms. The hierarchy constituted in terms of the opposition of purity and impurity provides "only a limiting parameter or a presupposed set of assumptions concerning the media in which prestations are made." Prestations reflect other values and meanings, and define relationships in other terms. An exclusive focus on the hierarchy-constituting opposition of purity and impurity obscures the role of dan and other prestations in constituting relationships. Raheja makes a convincing case for ritual centrality and mutuality as key grounds for inter-caste relations.

Raheja argues that the transfer of inauspiciousness is not a matter of "hierarchy." This is true, if hierarchy is defined in Dumont's terms, as ordered by relative impurity and pollution. But in Bhaktapur, at least, the transfer of much inauspiciousness—sin, evil, astrologically induced misfortune—stigmatizes the recipient, and has hierarchical implications. What I see in Raheja's data are at least two interdigitating constructions of hierarchy. She notes that some of her informants resist receiving prestations that transfer inauspiciousness to them; this suggests ambivalence at least. They may not resist it because of any direct hierarchical implications. What is transferred is, after all, inauspiciousness—

and they may not want it. So why would they ever accept such transfers? Because the dominant caste is dominant? Because it holds the most land (as Raheja reports) and so holds the most power?

Another possibility is that giving and receiving is done in an ethical mode of mutuality; people receive inauspiciousness because it promotes the well-being of those they have important relationships with. Such motives indeed exist for high and low caste Newars, but may help construct dominance and subordination: transfers of inauspiciousness have stigmatizing hierarchical implications for Newars. These transfers, like the separation and ranking imposed by purity and impurity, can organize and valorize inequality. I would venture to guess that their relationship with human experience and agency is equally problematic. From an untouchable's point of view, a system construed in terms of centrality and of transfers of inauspiciousness is likely to end up being as stigmatizing and limiting as a system construed in terms of purity and impurity. However, the elaboration of concern with auspiciousness and inauspiciousness may be more unconsciously "hegemonic" and less consciously "ideological" than other hierarchical concepts. That is, people may make the connection between concepts of purity and caste status, but not be as articulate about, or aware of, the constitutive connection between inauspiciousness, well-being and caste differences and domination. Hegemonic formations are lived social processes; people are not necessarily aware of the implications of these processes. They may act much of the time in good faith, out of moral motives, and yet enact an oppressive hierarchical ordering of life chances.

Raheja (1988:46) notes that her informants explicitly separate concerns about inauspiciousness from discourse about purity and impurity, with only the latter having to do with caste ranking. In Bhaktapur, the stigmatizing, hierarchical implications seem to be more transparent than in the North Indian village she describes. Newar untouchables receive variously conceived sorts of inauspiciousness, negative qualities, and impure substances—and their stigmatizing occupation is seen as consistent with their degraded nature. They are seen by some as receptacles and receivers of filth, dirt, sin, impurities, *and* inauspiciousness. If you are the receptacle of all this, perhaps in some ways—as an existential situation—it will not matter much to you whether people "transfer" impurity or inauspiciousness. From an untouchable point of view—and especially from the point of view of some of the critiques they have formulated of the caste system (Khare 1984)—the distinction of impurity and inauspiciousness may be existentially and politically irrelevant, whatever cultural nuances it discloses or high caste psychocultural needs it expresses.

One of the primary values of Raheja's work is that it shows us that multiple ideologies may help constitute and organize caste relations and the way people cognize and experience these relationships. By neutralizing the single-mindedness of Dumont, with his vision of a singular all-encompassing ideology, Raheja provides a richer account of caste relations, one that accords better with my own sense of the multiple constructs Newars use to perceive and evaluate caste relations.

Raheja does not, however, fully take up questions of power and self. Like Dumont, her principal concern is with ideology and its practices, not with the critique of ideology. The meanings and values she speaks of sustain caste relations; they are implicated in the cultural production of dominance. We hear no dissenting voices, speaking out of a critical consciousness, which reject this dominance. Her analysis is situated within hegemony, not within critique. The ideologies she identifies and documents as central to caste relations are evidently naturalized in the minds of her informants. They come across as natural, necessary, moral, not as imposed, resisted, and morally problematic. Downplaying "hierarchy" in Dumont's sense, she also seems to downplay power. The role of power is not scrutinized; the way people may experience this as oppressive is not explored. Since her work is situated inside a quasi-hegemonic world, her analysis of ideology shares with the ideology she analyzes the quality of rendering almost invisible questions of power. We learn of the dominant caste, but not of domination.

This does not detract from the value of her work—the analysis of the multiple ideological constructions of cultural life is vital. Ultimately, however, a dual analysis, of ideology and of critique, seems necessary. I believe we need to see ideology and critique in relationship to each other if we want to understand how cultures change and how power infuses culture. This involves—and perhaps generates—the kind of shifting multiplicity Raheja speaks of; thus, we need to look at both ideologies, and the critiques of ideologies as mutually defining cultural modes, as elements of a process, a struggle to control culture and produce culture.

Perhaps we have multiple ideologies because they must confront critiques along moving fronts in struggles to achieve, or resist, hegemony and dominance. This occurs under particular economic and political conditions, and takes form in terms of particular social practices. Ideology and critique as cultural phenomena are not exempt from history, but are themselves historical phenomena, the results of constructive and destructive labor by cultural subjects.

If a multiplicity of ordering concepts defines relationships in different terms, but in ways that confirm the basic terms of relationship of two groups, then multiple ideologies provide redundancy for political structures and controls. If the legitimacy of one set of values and practices comes into question, caste identity and the terms of relationship are still given in other values and practices. It may be harder to break through into critical consciousness when multiple concepts, organized and fore-grounded in different contexts, animate practices and relationships and generate interlocking definitions of reality, each of which must independently be broken to achieve demystification; it may be harder to sustain a critique in the face of multiplicity.

A terminological note. I think Raheja has surrendered the word "hierarchy" to Dumont, rather than seeking to give it some other meaning—she reserves the word to mean by it what Dumont means by it. I do not want to quibble over definitions, but there are dangers in letting Dumont have the term. Her terms "mutuality" and "centrality" flatten out what is after all a set of unequal relations. Not terming these relations hierarchical makes the possibility of viewing them as in part non-hierarchical emerge, but this seems to mute what is also there, relations of rank and constructions of dominance and superiority. What Raheja terms mutuality and centrality seem to be a culturally constructed nexus that brings together relations of rank and preeminence with relations of reciprocity and interdependence. Actors are joined together by these relationships, not opposed as pure and impure—there is an element of reciprocity. Nonetheless, these constructs position castes in relationship to each other in ways that are unequal. That is why I would prefer to define them as alternate constructions of hierarchy. They are not necessarily gentler, kinder, versions of hierarchy, either—at least not for everyone.

Even more dangerously, Raheja's restriction of hierarchy to hierarchy in Dumont's sense of the term plays into the difficulty some people will have with her important thesis of multiplicity. C. J. Fuller, for example, quotes her as saying "hierarchy . . . is not the encompassing value of caste society," (Raheja 1988:519) only to dismiss her position as a "revisionist thesis lacking support from the mass of evidence" (1992:255). The reader is not told what Raheja means by hierarchy. Fuller's dismissal mischaracterizes by omission: Raheja's thesis is about hierarchy as constituted in Dumontian terms, as the opposition of the pure and the impure. For Newars, at least, I do not think that hierarchy constituted in terms of the opposition of the pure and impure is the single, all-encompassing value of Newar society.

I am not alone in this judgment. S. M. Greenwold first demonstrates that "the Newars in fact possess a caste structure that conforms most stringently to Dumont's definition" (1978), then shows they have at least two models of caste, one based on concepts of purity and the role of priests, the other relating to power and kings. He thinks both models are necessary and that neither one can stand alone, unsupported by the other; rather, each involves "internal contradictions which necessitate reference to the other" (1975:74).

Similarly, summarizing the material on purity and status for Hindu Newars, Levy argues that although the basic social units of Bhaktapur are "arranged in a hierarchy" with Brahman at the top and untouchable at the bottom, purity and impurity are constitutive only for some groups, like Brahman and untouchable, while others, like the king, farmers, craftsman "are fitted into the system by a kind of unstable tinkering. Their hierarchical position, rationalized into the purity system, is based in part on other often more obscure factors, deriving from history and power and class." Mutuality and centrality seem to play a part, too. As important as purity and impurity are for segmenting the social order into a hierarchy, whatever "intellectual coherence" they offer, they do not represent the only way Newars understand and build hierarchy (1990: 396–97).

Dirks: Power and History

"While Dumont is not wrong," Nicholas Dirks writes, "to insist on radical differences in the 'ideologies' of India and West, the irony is that the way in which he postulates the difference is based on a fundamentally Western ideology, in which religion and politics must be separated" (1990: 60). Dirks does not separate power and religion, but sees them as coming together within history as a cultural process to provide ways of constructing and ordering caste relations.

Dirks views the separation of politics and religion as pivotal to Dumont's interpretation of caste hierarchy. If caste is religious, and religion and politics are separate, then politics is not part of caste life—politics and power do not provide the grounds on which caste relations develop. In Dumont's view, the Brahman embodies the religious, since he possesses the greatest purity possible, and is superior to the king. The king embodies power, and is inferior—thus, the religious "encompasses" the political. For Dumont, caste is not a matter of power, but of the actualization of purity. Dirks acknowledges the evidence for Dumont's view, but points out that the texts that provide evidence for it are in fact equivocal. These texts portray the Brahman as superior to king, but the same texts also show the king as superior to the Brahman in some ritual contexts, as in the royal consecration ceremony.

Dirks sums up his position in these words: "the social relations that made up Indian society, far from being 'essentialist' structures predicated on the transcendence of a set of religious principles, were permeated by 'political' inflections, meanings and imperatives" (1990:74).

Moreover, the caste system that has been the object of so much anthropological study is in significant ways a "colonial construction, remi-
niscent only in some ways of the social forms that preceded colonial
intervention." I would add that even as social relations were determined
by the politically inflected meanings of a dominant ideology—so that
caste takes form in terms of the cultural construction of power—Indian
consciousness was not constituted solely in terms of the poetics of power,
whether played by Hindu kings or colonial Raj, anymore than it is exclusively dominated by the opposition of the impure and the impure. Critique co-evolved with ideology, resistance with efforts to achieve cultural
hegemony. These must have a place in ethnohistory as well.

If Dirks does not accept the way Dumont separates power and religion,
and then privileges religion as providing the key ordering principle of
the caste system, his skepticism extends to some of Dumont's critics, who
would also separate power and religion, but would privilege power—and
treat it as unmediated by culture, as not formulated, held and, exercised
in cultural ways, on cultural terms. Dumont and his materialist critics,
Dirks argues, view India in terms of Western dichotomies that are ill-
equipped to capture the cultural dynamics of power in Indian cultural
life (Dirks 1990:60; see also Dirks 1987, Appadurai 1981; McGilvray
1982). Dirks argues further that neither a cultural emics that denies
power nor a materialist etics that denies culture will serve: "The form
and relations of power in southern India efface social scientific distinctions of materialist etics from culturalist emics, for even an analysis of
ritual action and language suggests the complex and conjectural foundations of hierarchical relations" (1990:61). Here Dirks, in my view,
makes a major contribution, by insisting we see power and culture together, as a unified field, not as discrete analytic concerns or distinct
domains of culture.

Dirks sees power as central to caste, but not power in the abstract, as
some kind of extra-cultural phenomenon. Rather, for him power is constituted in cultural ways. For Dirks, power is not the same everywhere,
but requires explication in terms of culture. The perspective is synthetic:
power is not the product of material conditions that bear no trace of
culture, but the products of such forces mediated by culture, as they take
form in culture. Dirks offers a "cultural poetics of power" in which elements of discourses such as chronicles and ballads reveal "persistent mo-
tifs, events, narrative forms, tropes, and images" that express organizing
conceptions that are also "realized in historical processes." Dirks sets out
to reintroduce "power, hegemony, and history into studies of culturally
constructed structures of thought." He finds that the purity complex is
not the only configuration of meanings that endows hierarchy with form
and significance. Not only purity and pollution, but also "honor, order,

royalty, command" are involved in "practices that produce and reproduce hierarchy" (71).

Dirks' insights can be extended in a number of ways. Dirks speaks to history and power. We also need to speak to power and self. I think that it is vital that we examine power, culture, and self together. Without knowing something about how actual persons actually link cultural constructs together, deploy them in practice, and use them to interpret self, society, and world, you do not have the context needed for either ethnosociology or ethnohistory. Just as Dirks read texts to discover the cultural poetics of power, I found that personal testimony helps illuminate the way actors construct and experience caste hierarchy, and reveals their discontents as well. Freeman's (1979) telling life-history of an untouchable also shows that person-centered ethnography and life-history studies can illuminate much. Moreover, as Khare's (1984) work suggests, we also need to take account of critiques of the culture that constructs hierarchical relations. These critiques are themselves cultural, and part of cultural experience, not detached from cultural life, not free-floating in a disembodied pool of discontent that is somehow "outside" of cultural life. Critical discourse, too, requires cultural analysis, and cannot be artificially detached from power, religion, economy, or cultural psychology.

Dirks helps us realize that we must get beyond the expectation that different castes will have oppositional and entirely distinct cultures. This is naive and essentializing. There are, rather, patterns of similarities and differences. We can now easily avoid the naive logic that suggests if high caste and low caste share anything, they have the same culture, or if they differ on anything, they have different cultures. As Sapir long ago informed us (1934 [1985]), culture is not so cut-and-dried.

Appadurai: Displacing Hierarchy

Some of the most cogent criticism of Dumont's thesis of *Homo hierarchicus* has come from Arjun Appadurai (1986, 1992 [orig. 1988]) in two telling articles probing the substance and genealogy of the idea of hierarchy as the defining image of India.

Appadurai asks how certain images of places and cultures become dominant and defining—as he says, "hegemonic in, and confined to, certain places" (1992:43). By what process of conceptual synthesis and deployment did hierarchy become the key metonym for South Asian life, the part that we substitute for the whole?

While this production of dominant images of parts of the world presupposes the power to produce such images, it also reflects styles of thought that have a long and checkered history in various Western intellectual traditions. It reflects, he says, the needs of readers who form the audiences for anthropological works. In Dumont's vision of hierarchy as "the key to caste society," Appadurai argues,

> we see the convergence of three distinct trajectories in Western thought. . . . First there is the urge to *essentialize*. . . . This essentialism, which has a complicated genealogy going back to Plato, became for some Orientalists the preferred mode for characterizing the "other." . . . The second tendency involves *exoticizing*, by making *differences* between "self" and other the sole criteria for comparison. . . . The third trajectory involves *totalizing*, that is, making specific features of a society's thought and practice not only its essence but also its totality. Such totalizing probably has its roots in the German romanticism of the early 19th century and comes to us in all the variations of the idea of the *Geist* (spirit) of an age or a people. Canonized in Hegel's holism, its most important result was the subsequent Marxian commitment to the idea of totality, but it also underlies Dumont's conception of the "whole."
>
> Hierarchy, in Dumont's argument, becomes the essence of caste, the key to its exoticism, and the form of its totality. (1992:39; emphasis in original)

Appadurai's work is especially valuable in the way it traces links in the development of Dumont's thought and in the acceptance of his thought, showing how the concept of India as hierarchy builds on efforts to conceptualize other parts of the world—ancient Rome, Africa, Arabia, Ceylon, the South Pacific—by figures such as Hegel, Mauss, Bougle, Evans-Pritchard, and A. M. Hocart, each propounding theories and concepts "criss-crossed" by still other influences (1992:41–43). While Dumont confines hierarchy to a particular part of the world—arguing that it is the central, all-encompassing feature of South Asian life—his concept of hierarchy has cosmopolitan roots in concepts and theories deployed to understand other parts of the world. There may be nothing intrinsically wrong with this perhaps unavoidable process—until concepts are reified, and become the dominant image of a place that shapes what can be thought and said about it. Confining a culture to our congealed concept of it, a concept certified by our own essentializing and totalizing discourse, confines our ability to describe and understand that culture. I agree with Appadurai: knowing that concepts which pretend to characterize the essence and totality of places and cultures are in fact composed out of ideas from many places allows us to resist the dominance of these concepts when they threaten to obscure the richness and diversity of lived worlds (1992:44).

The acceptance of images for regions and cultures of the world—hierarchy for South Asia, honor for the Mediterranean world, individualism for Euroamericans—as *defining* images poses the problem of the process by which such images become dominant, becoming defining, become the organizing themes of scholarly work and popular perceptions. As they do, gripping the scholarly, the popular, and the political imagination alike, such images may obscure "the diversities . . . of local worlds" (1992:43). Many people rightly object to the media tendency to project images of African-Americans as inner-city criminals when in fact diversity characterizes African-Americans and inner-city life. Yet anthropology has long produced, accepted, even celebrated, images that take part for whole, that construct a single identity for places and cultures characterized by diversity.

Hierarchy is *part* of South Asian life. What Appadurai asks of us is that we should recognize parts as parts, and not take them as wholes. We need to be able to recognize hierarchy and inequality as part of South Asian life, without obscuring how much more there is to culture and self, power and experience, in South Asia.

If the colonial project produced certain defining—and politically convenient—images of India in terms of caste, as Dirks and others indicate, this process was no doubt, as Appadurai suggests, reinforced and influenced by the reception of the images and ideas in Western centers of thought, in terms of relationships or resonances with "discursive needs of general theory in the metropolis" (1992:44).

Hierarchy in many senses is central to cultural life in Western countries; holism too has a pervasive presence; these seem to me to be obvious facts about Western life, only thinly disguised by cultural rhetorics of equality and individualism. Since hierarchy and holism are also a striking and problematic feature of life in South Asia, "India"—not India as it was or is, in its actual diversity and complexity, but as imagined in singular, essentializing, exoticizing, totalizing and Orientalizing terms—became a place where a thoroughly Western preoccupation with these perhaps inescapable aspects of life in a complex society could be worked out in terms of another culture.

By displacing Dumont's unifying vision of hierarchy from its dominant position, Appadurai, like Dirks, Raheja, and Inden, invites an exploration of the diversity of South Asia. Appadurai, rightly I think, urges us to compare *polythetically*, exploring the many ways people, places and cultures are alike and different (1992:44).

The Hedgehog and the Fox

We face a choice that will determine how we go about attempting to represent the cultural life of India, of Nepal—indeed, of any culture anywhere. Let me pose the choice in terms of the concept of values, although the basic conundrum applies equally to other key terms, such as consciousness, mind, and experience. The problem is this: Should we affirm that there is an irreducible plurality in the domain of values, or should we seek some unifying premise? For my own values? For the values of others? Much hinges on the answer to these questions. Like Isaiah Berlin, and unlike Louis Dumont, I have decided in favor of plurality.

That is, Dumont and I possess—or perhaps we are possessed by—different thematic commitments, as the historian of science Gerald Holton (1973) termed them in his seminal study of the scientific imagination. Dumont believes in the unity of culture, while I believe there is an irreducible plurality to cultural life. Dumont looks for unity given by a dominant value or master principle, while I see a plurality of values as characterizing cultural life, a plurality that is the product of human agency engaged with culture.

In a small way, this echoes a persistent division in Western thought. Isaiah Berlin (1978) writes that a "great chasm" divides those thinkers who possess a "central vision" based on a "single, universal, organizing principle" that lends significance to "all that they say and are," and "those who pursue many ends, often unrelated and even contradictory, connected, if at all, only in some *de facto* way . . . related by no [single] moral or aesthetic principle." These pluralists, he notes,

lead lives, perform acts, and entertain ideas that are centrifugal rather than centripetal, their thought is scattered or diffused, moving on many levels, seizing upon . . . a vast variety of experiences and objects for what they are in themselves, without . . . seeking to fit them into, or exclude them from, any one changing, all-embracing, . . . unitary inner vision. (1978:22–23)

Berlin quotes a line from a Greek poet: "the fox knows many things, but the hedgehog knows one big thing." Conceived this way, Louis Dumont is a hedgehog, along with Plato and Hegel. Berlin goes on to acknowledge, as he must, that this classification is over-simple and if pressed too far become absurd. Nonetheless, there is something to be said for disclosure of such basic interpretive commitments, as these organize our explorations and narratives of cultural life.

In the interest of such full disclosure, let me say that my own intellectual background draws on strands of Western thought that imply a different perspective on cultural life. Certainly, Dumont's implicit Hegelianism and rationalism contrasts with my own interest in the thoughts of such thinkers as Kierkegaard, Freud, and Sapir about "actually existing individuals" who of course live cultural lives. I do not believe I can disembody people and ignore history to construct a culture for people.

Such disclosure as this reveals that a deeply Western epistemological controversy (perhaps it is universal, but I do not know that it is) swirls around the different ways that Dumont and I approach cultural life. The way Dumont and I encounter and interpret caste life reflects divergence of opinion about the nature of culture, mind, and person that perhaps reflects the habit of dualism found in much Western thought—Dumont sits on one side, I on the other, and never the twain shall meet in synthesis.

Naturally, since I am on the side of the foxes, I think our differences also reflect differences in Western thought, and so expresses the diversity of Western culture that parallels the diversity of South Asian culture. Although each of us is deeply embedded in the Western intellectual tradition, we draw on contrasting strands of that tradition—Kierkegaard vs. Hegel, Sapir vs. Mauss. Thus we encounter South Asia in radically different ways, each pursuing a Western vision, perhaps a Western illusion, but not the same one.

I think my vision involves less illusion, but I cannot demonstrate this in a fashion that would produce mass conversion to my views on the part of those who see the world in a different way. I cannot prove that my commitments are superior to Dumont's, that they do more justice to cultural life, even though I believe they are, and that they do—I am not sure what proof would work, given the way deeply held interpretive commitments shape perceptions.

No doubt it is fairly rare for foxes and hedgehogs to convert each other. While it would be imperious indeed—or perhaps more like a kind of academic fundamentalism—to proclaim that the perspective of the foxes is the only true way of apprehending cultural life, I do think I can fairly assert that fox-like thinking has as much claim to our rational attention as the unitary perspective of hedgehog-thought. While I recognize that foxes and hedgehogs alike are perhaps Western creatures, pursuing themes inherent in Western thought, I feel that taking the perspective of the foxes engages the diversity of South Asia and permits the kind of polythetic analysis that subverts oversimplifications.

Moreover, while Dumont and I make different choices, the question of which premise we should pursue—unity or plurality—confronts any Western observer. Should we make a virtue of the quandary and look simultaneously for the unity and the diversity of India? I might prefer this approach, if so much effort has not been expended on defining a unity for India, for Hinduism, and for caste systems. In the face of this massive construction of an identity for South Asia, which has shaped the way "India" is imagined in the West, I feel it is important that we explore more fully the diversity of cultural life in South Asia. Perhaps later we can overcome the dualism implicit in this shift from one Western perspective to another. At the present moment, however, I believe we need simply to restore some balance.

Dumont's concept of hierarchy still has stalwart defenders who rightly insist that it does shed light on some key facets of cultural life (D. Gellner 1992:344, Fuller 1992). His critics understandably may find his paradigm more tattered than others do (Raheja 1998b). But the overarching, single-minded vision cannot be sustained: *Homo hierarchicus* is dead. Hierarchy as imagined by Dumont does not define the essence or constitute the totality of Hindu cultural life, although it mediates much, shapes much, and poses problems of meaning. We must look elsewhere for theory that can illuminate the interplay of critique and ideology, that can do justice to the dynamic of hierarchy affirmed and hierarchy resisted. Dissolving the totalizing image, we see more of the diversity, and agency, of cultural life. *Homo dialecticus* lives on, incarnated in culture, encompassing both *Homo hierarchicus* and *Homo equalis.*

Chapter 4
Ambivalences

One of my low caste informants, an Untouchable, claimed on several occasions to be satisfied with his caste position. The refrain was, "Our caste is good for us, the Brahman's caste is good for the Brahman." At other times, he seemed uncertain. Asked whether, if he had a choice, he would want his son to be high caste or low, he replied that he would want his son to be high caste. Asked whether he would want to be reborn an untouchable or in a higher caste, he said he would want to be born high, not low. "Who," he asked, his face contorted in a grimace, "would want to be born low?"

A pointed question: who indeed? Certainly, high caste actors agreed with him. The fact that this untouchable found the questions absurd and distressing, the answers self-evident and better left unsaid, the fact that virtually everyone around him would find his replies self-evident, tells us something basic about his life and experience. By asking what he might want, the questions expose what he cannot have. The questions pained him, touched a raw nerve, bared his powerlessness. I think we can trace his answers and feelings back to the quandary caste life poses for him: he finds himself trapped in a world where he must live a life he rejects, where he must labor with an identity he would reject, if he could. It is not easy to escape, or he would have left long ago, made his rebirth in this life, found for himself what he wishes for his son—a better life.

The caste system condemns many people to lives they don't want to live. For them, hierarchy is not simply a value, an abstract principle of reality, but a threat to self, the fate that condemns them to suffer, forcing them to surrender hopes and desires. Threatened in this intimate way, they seek to reply to the threat. This influences their dialogue with culture—the dialogue they "are," that constitutes the core of their identity. They struggle to know themselves in other terms, by reimagining the moral grounds of social life. As we have seen, one way they may do so involves appealing to ideas of equality. But there is more to it than this.

Although some Newars reject hierarchy, and even speak of equality in counterpoint to hierarchy, they do so ambivalently. If, for some purposes, they shift from hierarchy to equality, affirming the ultimate reality of equality and denying hierarchical differences, for other purposes they shift back again, making hierarchy real and equality illusory. People seem intent on having it both ways. They want to be equal, to be acknowledged as the same as others, and not "lower"; and yet they desire to be "higher" than others. This contradictory set of desires reflects the essential ambivalence of caste life.

Newars tend to invoke more ideas of solidarity and equality when they are "looking up" at those who have more wealth, power and freedom of action than when "looking down" at others who define (and might challenge) their relative status. Looking up, they speak against the ways they are deprived and stigmatized. Caste life denies most people much of what they most want from life (to be as good as anyone, to be able to do what they want, to think well of themselves, to be thought of as good persons, to be remembered); it does, however, give people something to defend, a relative status (in which, at least, they are better than some). But they could lose even this. Newars typically define caste as necessary (to maintain order, to provide work for themselves, to constitute a division of labor), but wish to avoid the stigmatizing implications of being lower; at the same time they may want to assert and enjoy their relative preeminence over others. This ambivalent stance causes various complications in the way people view themselves and society.

Anxious Symmetries

High caste informants also felt that no one would want to be low. This is the one certainty of caste life, the center of the moral problems posed by caste life, around which assorted anxieties and quandaries revolve.

The quandary for low caste people is to respond to the place assigned them in society: to find value in their caste identity, and to find grounds for rejecting it (at least in fantasy), because it threatens their sense of their own worth. They need to recover a sense of their own value in the face of ideologies and practices that stigmatize them. They have to find ways of *knowing* themselves that neutralize the way they are defined as social persons in terms of their caste identities. High caste actors, in contrast, need to maintain their sense of the order and justice of the caste world, of the moral goodness and existential safety of self. This is achieved through the cultural construction of the "otherness" of the low castes. The low castes are viewed as different in ways that make a difference—so that they deserve their social fate. The high castes need to reassure themselves that they do not deserve the same fate; they must defend the differences that make them different. They find ways of *not knowing* that low caste people are like themselves.

In contrast, low caste people (and especially the very lowest groups) often seem engaged in a struggle to know themselves as men and women like others, as morally the same—they often seek to neutralize stigmatizing hierarchical "differences." They must also be pragmatic, and find ways to cope with the ways the caste system excludes them.

Inequality multiplies perspectives on self and society; it offers radically different points of view. Being part of *this* caste cuts one off from *that* caste—and, except at the very top or bottom, belonging to a particular *caste* makes some persons less than others; but it also makes them higher than some. Except at the top, and, much more ambiguously, at the bottom, of the caste hierarchy, shifts in point of view, from "high" to "low," and back again, can be found in a single person. Some middle or low caste Newars reject caste, or their place in the caste hierarchy, because they are deeply threatened by being made lower than others; and yet they value their relative position, and defend the integrity of their own caste against the threat of having their lives joined to others of lower caste status (through marriage or by sharing food). They do not want to be lower than anyone else, but they want to be higher than someone, anyone, even if, to achieve this, they have to make them up, constructing a fantasy "other" who is lower than self. Only at the very apex of the hierarchy, with Brahmans and the highest secular castes (who concede the Brahman's religious standing, but have reasons to see themselves, as the descendants of kings or royal functionaries and as the traditional employers of Brahman priests, as having the highest standing in their own sphere), does solidarity not coincide with inequality.

These highest castes too are opposed to solidarity with other castes, but they are not free of ambivalence. The play of emotions is different. For those highest in the caste hierarchy, emotional tensions are not provoked by the stigmatizing implications of caste standing, for they are not stigmatized. The identity that the caste system supplies for members of the highest castes is self-affirming. And yet this identity is also a possible source of anxiety, for a person might lose the prized place in society that constitutes that identity. One can "fall"—be excluded from caste, and be forced to assume a stigmatized identity. A person can be polluted. If low caste actors seek to recover a sense of self because they have been stigmatized, then higher caste actors seek to preempt the loss of self by sacrificing something of their existential freedom and possibility; they conform and accept constraints to ensure their place in the hierarchy and preserve their identities.[1] This presupposes the possibility of becoming like the other—of solidarity. Newars know that you can become like people of lower status: if you eat with a person of lower status, you become like them. Marriage with a person of lower caste standing can affect status and alter an identity. In such cases, some Newars argued, you can avoid (or at least deny) loss of status by claiming that you never eat the food the lower status spouse prepares; this works as long as the lower caste spouse is only marginally lower, and not a member of one of the highly "impure" or untouchable castes, such as Butchers or Sweepers. Prolonged proximity with those of much lower and highly stigmatized status can also transmute self into other; but eating food prepared or touched by lower caste people is the quickest way of becoming like them. High caste men and women fear such "solidarity." They must labor to maintain the vision of the lower castes as less than themselves in the face of the threatening knowledge that the boundaries between "self" and "other" are not absolute.

The struggle of high and low caste persons to know themselves reflects their relative social positions; the forms their quandaries take are symmetrically opposed, but equally irreducible and charged with anxiety. However people struggle with these quandaries, they probably have no final resolution within the structure of caste society.

For the patterns of ambivalence express existential concerns within the structure of caste society. These concerns are very basic. People need a place in society; they are dependent on others. They seek solidarity with others because they desire to survive, to find meaning for their existence, and to experience what their world offers as vital, good and necessary. Since society creates the human world, and defines the scope of human action within this world, people must come to terms with it. Social relationships are primary because they give people access to the resources and meanings of the socially generated world. The experience of solidarity is a powerful symbolic affirmation of the need and right to exist. It links personal existence and society. It affirms the possibility of meaning. In this way, people claim the power to act within the social world. They identify with society in order to empower themselves, to make it possible for them to live, to have full and meaningful lives. But in caste society, solidarities are ranked, and interdependence is hierarchically organized. Constituting hierarchy means manufacturing inequality, making "differences" matter. People seek solidarity to make themselves whole, to draw power to themselves, to make life in the fullest sense possible—yet hierarchy threatens each self with the incompleteness I have described.

The Ideological Form of Caste and Ambivalence

The ambivalence of caste life also has something to do with the ideological form of caste. "The spirit of caste," wrote Célestin Bouglé, "unites . . . three tendencies, repulsion, hierarchy and hereditary specialization, and all three must be borne in mind if one wishes to give a complete definition of the caste system." Formulating this diagnosis in 1908, he went on to say a society has a caste system "if it is divided into a large number of mutually opposed groups which are hereditary specialized and hierarchically arranged—if, on principle, it tolerates neither the parvenu, nor miscegenation, nor a change in profession" (1971[1908]:9).

This phrasing of the ideological form of the caste system is relevant to the Newar case. Newar jats are organized in a hierarchy, and informants agree on the general form of this hierarchy, if not on all of its details. Newar castes have traditional occupations that signify their status in the hierarchy. Newar jats are rigidly separate and endogamous if they are not components of the same status level. One should qualify the notion of "repulsion" to note that while upward mobility is in principle rejected (despite its covert, empirical presence), downward mobility to join lower groups is not only possible, but an important sanction. Transgressors of caste rules traditionally could "fall"; in the contemporary scene, violation of caste endogamy still triggers sanctions such as ostracism, although "outcasting" is no longer legal. The "repulsion" is not entirely mutual, but always more in the direction of preventing the upward mobility of lower groups. Lower groups and individuals do at times attain higher status despite the ideal norms and the sanctions of the dominant groups opposing such mobility, but only when they have shed the stigmatizing associations of their origins; this involves much social identity manipulation (see Rosser 1979; Bailey 1957).

Part of what motivates conformity by those of high caste status to a strict code of conduct is fear of becoming like those lower in the system; they want to avoid losing their place in the world. Some think that losing caste (*jat wannigu*) entails a deep alteration of self. The principle is simple. If you are connected to lower caste people through food, sex, love or simply by extended contact, you become like them. One account from my notes goes like this: A young high caste man loved and married an untouchable woman. He lived with her. After awhile, "he did that kind of work [sweeping]. Slowly, he became like them."

The low status person, in contrast, wants to become like the high caste person—not simply to be like them, but to gain what they have. The low castes *need* to possess the material, social, cultural *goods* the high castes control, even while resenting the gap between them.

Ambivalence and the Structure of the Newar Caste Hierarchy

The traditional place of individual Newar castes in the caste hierarchy is relatively clear—at least from the point of view of knowledgeable high caste Newars. The principles in terms of which rank can be evaluated and substantiated (should any question arise about relative status) are also clear. Things are muddled in practice, since some individuals and groups reject their "traditional" place in the hierarchy, and others attempt to raise their status by disguising their origins and adopting a high caste life style (Rosser 1978). To more fully understand the personal and ideological constructions of hierarchy in Newar life, including efforts to disguise or reconstruct identity that reveal much about the structure of ambivalences in caste life, we need a fuller sketch of the social and conceptual organization of the Newar hierarchy. My purpose here is not to provide an exhaustive description of the Newar caste system, but to show how central and massive a reality the caste system is, as a "structure" that poses problems of meaning and identity for the Newar "self."

The rule is that one should not accept boiled rice (and certain other foods) (*calae maju*, lit., "should not move") from all castes lower than one's own. This partitions society into those at one's own level and above, from whom boiled rice can be accepted, and all those lower, from whom it cannot. Other phrases that mark differences in status are

1. *napa (n) cwani nae maju.* This expresses the restriction on commensality, "cannot stay and eat with"; equivalent to no. 2.
2. *tiye nae maju*: lit., "touch and eat not-should" = should not be touched while eating. A bar on commensality, in practice, this is equivalent to 3.
3. *na calae maju*: lit., "water move not-should" = "water unacceptable" In practice 2 and 3 means no food can be accepted, "not even water." This "water line" (Rosser 1978) is perhaps the most important phrase indicating separation.
4. *thiye maju*: lit., "touch not-should" = "untouchable." This refers to Newar castes that are untouchable by Newar criteria.

The criteria of "untouchability" divides the group of "impure" castes into two divisions, those who are impure but touchable, and untouchables. The division into "water acceptable" and "water unacceptable" groups does not, however, rigidly divide society into pure and impure groups. The point in the hierarchy where the "water-line" is drawn is relative to an informant's position in society and degree of orthodoxy.[2] The "water line" is a key divide, but I think for many Newars it is occupational impurity that segments society more absolutely. These groups (especially, perhaps, the Butchers) mark the beginning of those groups whose impure status has a more fixed, innate quality, existing by "nature" and by virtue of their role in the caste structure. The impurity is not "relative" in the same way water-unacceptability is. Newars may also speak of "big, great" (*thadhangu*) or "small, little" (*cidhangu*) castes: "compared to us, they are great."

Caste Ranking: A Traditional "Ideal" Hierarchy of Newar Castes

If asked, informants are able to rank order the numerous named *jat* of their community. The list produced will not be absolutely agreed on by all, but will reflect the social position and degree of orthodoxy of informants.

What follows is an idealized rank ordering of Newar jat. The list notes the occupations traditionally reserved for each group. This list is most applicable for Hindu Bhaktapur. I have not included Buddhist "castes," the Bare, consisting of the Vajracarya and Shakya, and the Tuladhar, since it is not clear in what sense the Buddhist groups and Hindu castes constitute a single hierarchy. The list is based on the rank-ordering worked out with Newar Brahman informants by Robert Levy (1990); an earlier version was reported in Gutchow and Kolver (1975).

HINDU CASTES: TRADITIONAL OR RESERVED OCCUPATIONS: SYMBOLIC ROLES
1. Brahman (Rajopadhyaya) (priests)
2. Chathar or Seysya (merchants)
2a. Joshi (astrologers)
3. Pa(n)cthar (merchants, shopkeepers)

These levels include the traditional Newar elite. Historically, most would have been landowners with tenant farmers from lower groups. Many of the class of shopowners and businessmen would have been from levels 2 and 3.

4. Tini (purifying ritual roles)
5. Jyapu (farmers)
6. Tamrakar (metal workers in brass and bronze)
7. Prajapati (Kumha) (potters and awal bricklayers, masons)
8. Jyapus (farmers of lower status than #5)
9. Sika:mi (woodworkers); Baidya (healers); Loha(n)ka:mi (stoneworkers)

Craft groups may intermarry with farmers; most Prajapati work as farmers, as do many members of other craft groups. In all, those engaged in agriculture comprise approximately 65% of the population in Bhaktapur (Acharya and Ansari 1980: 109, Table 6). In Bhaktapur, only 3.2 percent of the Chathar and 10.9 percent of the Pa(n)cthar were reported to be farmers (Acharya and Ansari 1980:111, Table 7).

10. Chya (Cyo) (ritual role in funeral rites)
11. Chipi (merchants, government service); may have had stigmatizing ritual roles in past; claim higher status

Groups below this level are stigmatized in various ways. Level 11 is "water unacceptable" for some, as is level 12.

12. Dwi(n) (sweepers for Taleju temple courtyard, palanquin bearers)

Levels 13–22 are a "borderline pure" category of roughly equal status (from the point of view of the highest castes). The "water unacceptable" levels start at levels 11-13 for some orthodox high caste (that is, level 1 & 2) individuals. The separate groups 12–22 are endogamous. For less strict informants or for groups under level 3, the "water unacceptable" level begins with level 14. This level is heterogeneous. The ranking here is mine, based on conversations with selected low caste informants, not one agreed on by all members of these groups, who often dispute their relative status.

13. Gatha (Banmala) (ritual performers in a major ritual sequence, the Navadurga dances) (Levy 1990); the Gatha sell flowers to higher castes
14. Nau (barbers); needed for purification by upper caste individuals; they do not perform such services for any group in this level or lower
15. Bha (stigmatizing ritual role in funeral rites)
16. Kata (cut umbilical cords and dispose of afterbirth)
17. Cala(n) (role in funeral rites; bell ringers)
18. Kau (blacksmiths)
19. Chipa (dyers)
20. Citrikar (Pu(n)) (painters of religious images)
21. Kusa (litter bearers; act as priests for butchers (?)
22. Sa:mi (oil-pressers; previously lower in status)

"Impure" levels begin with 23, but 23 and 24, at least, are not "untouchable" in terms of strictly indigenous criteria. I am uncertain as to how to treat levels 25 and 26. All these are "water unacceptable" and highly stigmatized. There is a clear break with 23, the Butchers, but it does not have a label. The occupations themselves stigmatize the groups.

23. Nay (butchers; stigmatized for killing animals)
24. Jugi (ritual roles)

The Jugi are stigmatized for accepting polluted offerings during high caste death rites. This group probably originated in a renunciate sect; they traditionally buried their dead sitting upright and did not perform the *samskara.*

25. Do(n) (played a kind of horn)
26. Kulu (leatherworkers and drummakers)

The next two jat are "untouchables" by Newar criteria (*thiye maju-pu(n)*).

27. Pore (or Po(n)) (sweepers)
28. Cyamkhala (sweepers; no longer present in Bhaktapur)

More than 60 percent of "untouchables" were employed as sweepers in Bhaktapur in 1977 (Acharya and Ansari (1980:111, Table 7). Employment is possible with the municipal government (the Nagar Panchayat), the military, in offices of the national government, and for private individuals.

29. Halahulu

The bottom category of Halahulu seems to consist of the poor and landless of higher castes and their descendants who have "fallen out" of the system. Unlike the levels above them, they seem to have no solidary institutions, symbolic roles or indexical occupations of their own, but live by begging or by cleaning like members of levels 27 or 28. I was unable to locate any individual who would identify him- or herself as a Halahulu, though members of levels 27 and 28 attributed membership in this category to certain persons.[3]

It should be stressed that this "ideal" ranking falsifies reality by imposing an order that is not wholly accepted by all. Not everyone would agree with the ranking; in particular, many would reject the position of their own group. In addition, the caste system is not necessarily experienced as—or even always thought of—as a rank ordered whole. Informants more typically deal with the caste system either in terms of dyadic interactions (as when a high caste person hires a sweeper) or in terms of hierarchically organized ensembles of castes gathered for some ritual purpose (as in traditional high caste funeral rites or in religious festivals). The ability of informants to rank groups into a single system does, however, strongly suggest that the hierarchical system conceived as a whole has a place in informants' understanding.

Substantiation of the Newar Hierarchy

A Newar will not accept boiled rice from any jat lower than his or her own; Newars who take a spouse from a lower jat will be degraded if they accept cooked food from their lower caste spouses.[4] Food carries "impurity"; because it does, rank within the caste hierarchy can be shown by determining who takes, and who refuses, food from whom. If food carries impurity, the lowest jat are the most impure because they accept food, even polluted food, from all higher jat; they are the end point of a system of unilateral transfers of pollution. They can also be ranked with respect to each other. A passage in the Muluki Ain of 1955 (the legal code of the Hindu state of Nepal before legal and political reforms led to more egalitarian constitutions) uses the principle of food transactions to rank impure castes. McDonald translates an illustrative section:

1. In that they eat food left over (*jutho*) from the *jat* of the Upadhyaya to the *jat* of the Pore, the Cyamakhalak are the lowest *jat* (literally "the smallest," *sabai jat bhanda sano*).
2. In that they eat food left over by other *jat* with the exception of the Cyamakhalak, the Pore are higher than the Cyamakhalak. In that the Badi, who make a living by begging, singing and dancing even inside the homes of those with whom contact requires purification by sprinkling of water, do not eat food from the hands of the Cyamakhalak and the Pore, the Badi *jat* is higher than those two. (McDonald 1975:281–82)

This legal substantiation of a hierarchy reflects an actual cultural principle; it is one that I found untouchable Newars of the Pore and Cyamakhala jat used. However, they did not accept the ranking described here; instead they maintained their own group had a higher rank among impure groups. They claimed other groups accepted food from them, including a polluting death offering. The Cyamakhala I spoke to in Kathmandu denied accepting this from Pore, and stated they gave it to the Halahulu. One Pore went as far so to rank his jat higher than the Jugi, a bold claim given the ways Sweepers are stigmatized. (He may have assumed that I would not be familiar with the general high caste consensus about how to rank Newar jat.) The untouchables accept the principle that food transactions "prove" the relative positions of two groups, use it to claim a higher status than groups close to them in status, and reject the position in the hierarchy assigned to them by other jat using that principle.

Though the acceptance of boiled rice and other foods is important, there are other criteria for differentiating jat. For example, schematically the Jugi and the Pore may be compared and contrasted as follows:

JUGI	PORE
Water unacceptable	Water unacceptable
Touchable	Untouchable
Live inside city	Live outside city
Have mantras	No mantras
Take polluting offerings	Take polluting offerings
Accept boiled rice from higher jat	Accept boiled rice from higher jat including Jugi (some deny this)
May take dead person's clothes	May take dead person's clothes
Symbolically form of Shiva	Symbolically form of Shiva (for some)
Collect donations as form of Shiva	Collect donations during eclipses
Play music in temples, at funerals	Fishermen
	Clean feces and dirt

Both groups are impure, but they have different roles in the larger social and symbolic system. Both are removers of pollution, but the contrast between them has a number of elements, not just that of different degrees of purity or impurity.

In Bhaktapur (where the Cyamakhala are apparently no longer found), the Pore sweepers are the end point of the system of unilateral transactions. They accept boiled rice from everyone above them; accept polluting offerings during eclipses; take the clothes of the dead; and are defiled by their work as sweepers, which requires them to handle feces.

Much of this is consistent with McKim Marriott's theory that in Hindu culture people feel that food (and certain other media) absorb a person's "coded-substance," "essences, residues or other active influences" (1976:111), which can then be transmitted to others. Hindus act as if the "moral nature" of a person were contagious; one person can receive the morally coded substance of another, mingling the "essence" of the other with self, and so absorbing something of the qualities of the other, in a diluted, hybrid form. This (culturally constructed) fact in turn has implications for constructing hierarchy. To receive, or to refuse to receive the biomoral substance of another determines relative status. Marriott argues: "In the absence of reciprocation in the same or an inferior medium of substance-code, those who give are to be recognized as differing from and as standing in rank, power and quality of substance code above those who take: the takers are thereby recognized as inferior, but are also made partly like the givers" (1976:112).

We can compare this theoretical statement with the comments of a Brahman, Govinda, on the Pore. We have been discussing the Pore and their various roles. During eclipses, Govinda says, Hindus must do *dharma* (religious acts) to bring the cosmos back into equilibrium. When an eclipse occurs, Newars should purify themselves by bathing, and must give offerings or gifts (*dan*) to the Pore, who represent the dark planet Rahu responsible for eclipses. (Rahu is "stealing" or "eating" the sun or moon.) Govinda then comments: "The person who gives religious gifts (dan) goes to heaven, but the person who takes dan goes to hell. During Rahu, the one who receives dan goes to hell. But this rule does not apply to the low caste. They are poor, they are low. Going to hell is not so painful for them. For the low caste, this world is already hell."

Govinda explains that for the Pore, "there is no place to fall. They are already on the ground. The Pore have finished falling. Therefore they take dan." He says that those who give dan go to heaven, while those who receive it go to hell; this suggests a transfer of "sin" or "inauspiciousness." We could interpret the "gifts" given to the caste associated with Rahu as an attempt to placate this entity—and this impulse may indeed be present—but looking at a range of similar Newar practices suggests that the transfer of inauspiciousness, impurity and evil is a basic underlying concept. The ill fortune is diverted from the higher castes to a low caste, who suffer instead of the high castes.

Much of this seems broadly consistent with Marriott's theory. An unreciprocated act of giving distinguishes the parties involved; the giver is elevated (goes to heaven, does not suffer) while the taker is lowered (goes to hell, suffers). The form of the transactions described by this Brahman are consistent with Marriott's characterization of the form of "Hindu transactions," although these transactions concern inauspiciousness rather than impurity. Apparently inauspiciousness, like impurity, can be transferred from one party to another (cf. Raheja 1988). But we can see, in this account, that such transactions do more than define relative status. They divide the world into those who suffer and those who do not. The image of heaven and hell is used in the informant's testimony to contrast the concrete experience of the high and low castes; the informant sets up a construction of some of the low castes as absorbers of impurity. For the transactions are not neutral; they stigmatize. They help condemn some to a life of suffering, and make this seem necessary and natural. The context of these hierarchy-constituting transactions is a construction of the low castes as repositories of filth, impurity, and inauspiciousness. This construction is justified in various ways. This "liberal" Brahman only defines these untouchables as accustomed to suffering; they have hit bottom, and so are not made worse off when "misfortune" is transferred to them. Others feel the low castes deserve their fate.

Mobility and Social Identity

Newars are often keenly aware of having multiple social identities, of being many things to many people. In Newar culture, a person may be a Brahman, an eldest son, an elder brother, a husband, a father, a priest, a man of honor and good judgment, a Newar when dealing with other ethnic groups, and so on. In some groups on the margins of Newar society, multiple ethnic identities are possible (Leach 1954)—some individuals conceive of themselves as Newars, on some occasions and for some purposes, but deny being Newars at other times, for other purposes. High caste Newars do not typically have multiple ethnic identities. They do not attempt to construct multiple caste identities for themselves, either. A Brahman is always a Brahman; not sometimes a Brahman and sometimes a Shrestha. High caste Newars have little reason to disguise or change their caste identity. At work in some modern setting, such as a government agency or some nontraditional business enterprise, caste identity may be kept in the background. It may be stressed in other contexts. But it is implicitly a constant; it is not highly stigmatizing to be known as a Brahman. Hiding this caste identity offers no gain.

People of relatively low status may attempt to alter their identity. Newars known by their village neighbors as *jyapus*, members of the farming castes may assume high caste surnames when they go to work in a government office in Kathmandu. Generally this is a simple shift, as with the office worker who uses a high caste name at work, but reverts to his original identity in his home village (Rosser 1978:94).

These sojourners in another social identity may decide to become permanent residents of a higher status. I was told of one man who had been born to some very low caste—no one recalled exactly which one anymore—who had been successful at creating a higher status identity for himself. As a boy he became a conductor, collecting tickets on buses. Later he became a bus driver, a position that paid more and offered more prestige. Eventually he became a taxi driver. Still later he started a business with some others and became relatively wealthy. He adopted a high caste name. Of course, he had not completely obscured his origins, or I would never have heard of his case.[6]

At very the bottom of the caste hierarchy, multiple identities are common. A person is less "located" or fixed in social space at the bottom of the Newar caste system, at least in the Newar cities. Many high caste informants cannot or do not distinguish among the Sweeper sub-groups (although others can). Members of these groups may seek to avoid being attributed their conventional "lowest" status by attempting to "pass" as members of marginally higher groups. Thus I had some initial difficulty locating a Cyamakhala community in Kathmandu, because certain Cyamakhala chose to identify themselves as Pore. An elderly woman finally identified her locale as being a community of "Cyami" (Cyamakhala), to the evident embarrassment of a "Cyami" resident who has just identified it as a Pore settlement. These people admitted that "these days" some Cyamakhala trespass and poach on niches that were traditionally reserved for the Pore. While doing so, they become Pore for others. For high caste people, it does not make much difference if a Pore or a Cyamakhala cleans their latrines or the street, or which one shows up to receive traditional donations.

One man—a squatter at one of the system of shrines (*pitha*) that encircle Kathmandu—identified himself as a Sanyasi. He meant not that he was an ascetic, a renouncer, but that he belonged to the Indo-Nepalese caste called Sanyasi. (*Sannyasi* is the term for world-renouncers; the Sanyasi caste is said to arise from renunciates marrying and having children.) He said he was originally from an outlying district, and had migrated to Kathmandu at the age of nine when his parents died. He started begging in Kathmandu to support himself. He claimed to have spent some time in the army, and to have been in India for three years. Upon returning, he said he began working as a sweeper for the city.

Others identified him as belonging to other castes. Some termed him a Jugi. A Farmer woman said he was a Cyamakhala; she had hired him to clean her latrine. Others said he begged donations during eclipses. This is traditionally done by the Pore, and people who gave him rice or clothing at such times defined him as a Pore. Pore informants identified him as a Halahulu, and said they gave him polluted food. By this, they declared he was lower than they were.

In counterpoint to the multiple identities he has in the eyes of others, he also claims several identities for himself. The caste identity he asserts when speaking to me is the highest one he can get away. It is not a Newar caste, but simply an available identity. At this level in the social system, it is possible to have a Newar caste identity without being a Newar, or to be a Newar at some moments, but not at others, by using different criteria for self-identification. Members of impure and untouchable castes may deny being Newars, as a way of distancing themselves from the traditions of the dominant castes, even though they identify themselves as Newars in other contexts.

This man had adopted a different stance. Speaking fluent Newari, he presented himself as a "Newar," ignoring the fact that a Sanyasi is not a Newar caste. (He may have been playing on the ambiguity between Sanyasi(n) as ascetic, and Sanyasi as a caste.) This reflects a strategy of exploiting economic and cultural niches available at the "bottom" of the Newar caste system. He also filled a need in the Newar caste system. For the Pore, he was a Halahulu—a jat which accepts polluted food (including an offering during death rites) from them. By accepting food from the Pore, he made it possible for them to replicate the caste hierarchy, and be "higher" than someone else. For his part, he found it useful to accept the ways that others define him as a "Newar" untouchable—he is whatever it takes to live, situationally Jugi, Pore, and other. His interests do not coincide with having a single, fixed social identity.

People such as this man make possible what Michael Moffatt (1979) has termed the "replication" of hierarchy among the lowest Newar castes. Such people serve as the raw material out of which low caste people can construct a "caste" that is lower than their own. They seek to make this "lower" group perform stigmatizing services. In this case, this man does perform services for them that the Newar high castes have traditionally exacted from low castes—the relations are analogous. Moffatt sees this as supporting a consensus model of the relation of the lower castes to hierarchy: the lower castes replicate hierarchy because they share the values of hierarchy held by the higher castes. I will discuss this process of replications in Chapter 6. I do not see it as reflecting a consensus among high and low caste actors on the value of hierarchy, but as an expression of the structure of ambivalence of caste life. No one wants to be "on the bottom" of the caste system.

I was unable to find anyone who would identify him- or herself as a Halahulu. The Halahulu may still exist, since, as I noted for the Cyamakhala, members of the lowest castes may seek to pass themselves off as members of higher castes. However, I think that it is quite possible that the Halahulu do not exist (or no longer exist) as a group in the way other Newar jat do. All Newar jat down to the Pore have clear occupational, institutional, or symbolic roles in a larger system, although some of these are marginal to a changing society. Many groups have multiple links (such as the Jugi, who play musical instruments, are symbolically a form of Shiva, accept a polluting offering during high caste death rites, and are tailors). Informants can define the place of most of these castes in society. The Pore are not only sweepers, but attendants at the city-encircling Goddess shrines. They also have internal institutions; some of

these are of considerable scope. For example the Pore have an association (*guthi*) that regulates the turns of members as attendants at a single
shrine (*pitha*) in Kathmandu. Informants gave estimates of about 300 to
360 members in this guthi, drawn from three named funeral associations
(*si-guthi*, "death" guthi) from one area of Kathmandu.

The Halahulu do not have this kind of organization and integration
into society. They are listed as Sweepers in various lists of Newar castes,
but they do not seem to have other specific roles to play in Newar life.
The social identity attributed to them by Newars of other castes is vague.
Some say the Halahulu arose from the marriage of a Cyamakhala and a
non-Newar of low caste (a Sarki or Damain), or consist of people who
have fallen or been thrown out of their caste. Some said the Halahulu
consisted of poor and landless people forced to live by begging. A Pore,
asked about the Halahulu, gave this reply, pointing to people around the
area of the shrine.

The replication of hierarchy among the lowest caste groups seems to
require, not an actual group that is lower than the Pore or Cyamakhala
untouchables, but only the fantasy of such a group.

Narrative Subversions of Hierarchy

Newars express their anxieties and work through their ambivalences
about caste life in many ways. If seeking to disguise and alter their identity is one way, yet another strategy is to expose the arbitrary foundations
of the caste hierarchy.

One way they do this is by telling stories. Newars of all castes use stories
to construct moral arguments.[7] In general, narratives have special characteristics that lend themselves to making critical judgments. First of all,
narratives provide a way of overcoming the transparency of culture, the
way culture is "not there" to common sense, because it presents itself to
experience as natural, as reality, simply the way things are. Narratives
make culture "visible," an object that can be thought about and evaluated. Stories involve "detached" meanings, meanings that can be worked
on, can be manipulated as opposed to meaning so embedded in the
practices of everyday life that it easily eludes conscious reflection and
narrative formulation. Stories exist at a certain distance from cultural
life: a story represents a world imagined or considered, mediated by the
narrative process. It does not present a world apprehended directly, immediately, with the sense of reality that every culture instills in enculturated subjects. Marked, self-conscious narratives dis-embed or extract
meanings: they reapprehend the world. With narrative crystallization,
meanings become available for scrutiny, can be explored, manipulated,
and recomposed.

Moreover, a story is told by a person, who can manipulate the materials the narrative works with, within a tradition of story-telling, while "common sense"—as another mode of apprehending culture—is not reflective or critical. Common sense is a body of culture knowledge that is taken-for-granted, assumed in such a way that knowledge that constitutes it is not easily accessible to critical, conscious thought. Narratives can bring taken-for-granted elements of cultural organization to consciousness, where they can be subject to scrutiny in terms of other values. Whatever else they do, stories allow the teller and prompt the listener to query life, which means querying what we call culture. This can be done to affirm it or to problematize it. Narratives can be used to contemplate cultural life, to celebrate it, or to critique it.

Many narratives, of course, are not critical; they affirm the legitimacy of the status quo and they may help produce the hegemony of certain cultural concepts of reality, such as those which define low caste groups as inferior. In the context of caste life, such narratives may disseminate hierarchy-affirming cultural concepts that settle into common sense, and so tend to escape critical scrutiny, forming layers of unconscious meaning that have political significance. In Brahmanical discourses, such narratives sustain a vision of caste life as objective and unalterable, necessary and moral; this can be done, for example, by portraying hierarchy as an expression of sacred and natural law, perhaps showing the consequences of violating this natural order. Other narratives, however, call into question the morality of the caste hierarchy, and attempt to break down the objectification of hierarchy, and resist the sedimentation of hierarchical meanings in embodied knowledge, common sense, and habitus. They attempt to show that the caste hierarchy, constituted in terms of karma, purity, wealth or birth, is not natural, not necessary, not the only way things could be, and not the way things should be.

Knowing, hearing and telling *anti-hierarchical* stories is a way for some low caste Newars to critique hierarchical ideas and values that construct their own place and identities within the caste system. I believe that such stories constitute efforts to "neutralize" the stigmatizing construction of their caste identity coded and perpetuated by the dominant ideology. In these narratives, they construct meanings that "recode" their experience, allowing them to assert value for themselves and their lives. In such stories, they can mock the pretenses of the high castes, and undermine the moral premises of the dominant ideology. They stress the incoherence, the capriciousness, of the caste system. These narratives also keep alive the idea that social life might be organized according to other moral principles. They may reject or recode concepts of purity and pollution, or any of the other concepts used to organize and justify the caste system.

Narratives and commentary critical of the dominant conceptions of the caste hierarchy stories are not necessarily based on Newar concepts of equality, although they may open up or keep alive such ideas. Opposing the caste hierarchy does not entail rejecting any possible form of social hierarchy. When Newars use stories to cast doubt on the morality and justice of the caste hierarchy, they may propose alternative hierarchies, with different moral foundations. They imagine alternative hierarchies that are "open" rather than "closed," so that movement up the hierarchy is possible. In these alternative, "open" hierarchies, the moral worth and achievements of individuals rather than caste status count for something. These alternative hierarchies are not the hierarchy of caste as understood in terms of purity, pollution or karma.

Like many stories used to make a moral point, these stories unfold in a highly simplified version of the world, only loosely anchored in time and place, where persons are reduced to the schematic simplicity of social positions—much like the child's rhyme we considered in Chapter 3. The encounter of two or three such persons reveals the arbitrary nature of the caste hierarchy. The stories may go on to propose a different set of premises for society. Each of my low caste informants, and even many high caste informants, had one or more anti-hierarchical stories to tell me.

The stories are told in the third person. Little, if any, effort is made to make the physical setting or place of the story tangible and concrete. At most, the story may be located "in a forest" or "in a palace." Time and history are also simplified; the stories often do not take place at a definite moment in time. The events narrated do not occur "in the eighteenth century," or "when I was young." [8] If framed in terms of temporal setting at all, most often the events described simply happened "long ago."

The simplified world of the story is inhabited by kings, Brahmans, beggars, untouchables and so on; or, in other words, by persons incarnated in roles. No effort to convey the complex qualities of individuals in their wholeness is made. The aspect of individual identity that is dealt with is social or political, not psychological—we get to see the social dimensions of individual identities, not the world of feelings of a self responding with emotion to caste life. However, in the interviews in which these narratives were recounted, glimpses of feeling were available in the facial expressions of the teller; I detected, or thought I could detect, anger, distress, hesitation. Asked directly about concepts like karma, or the impurity attributed to them, low caste Newars often responded with anger or discomfort. Their reactions in interviews provide some grounds for saying that they dislike, and find painful, the way they are defined as social persons. The narratives I discuss here can thus be seen as motivated; they do not expressly deal with feelings, with emotions, but perhaps they are "good to tell" because they resonate with the psychological tensions, the emotional costs, the ambivalences, the identity dilemmas, inherent in caste life.

The stories I will discuss mute the personal. Perhaps in this genre—which invokes the stuff of legend and myth—it is rhetorically important that the narrator keep the moral and the affective separate, as a way of tacitly affirming that one repudiates caste on universalizable moral grounds, not in terms of personal grievances or self-interest. It may simply be the stories transport the audience into a world where roles, not actual persons, are the object of narrative reflection. In any event, in the stories I will discuss, suffering is stressed as a universal phenomena of moral concern, not as the personal pain of the narrator. In everyday life, Newars do talk of their personal suffering, speaking of it in what they sometimes term "talk of suffering and pleasure" (*dukhasukhayakha:*).

In the more impersonal morality tales examined here, the characters in the story may have names, but are often referred to by the narrator, or addressed by other characters in the story, by caste titles. The cast of characters presupposes, or represent, hierarchy. For the purpose of the story, they constitute a hierarchy "on the ground," within the world of the story. Dumont's paradigm (1980) of hierarchy works at this level of the story's structure: it takes two, a dyad consisting of a higher and lower actor, to constitute a hierarchy. The stories generally reduce the complexities of a caste hierarchy to the interactions of two or three actors: a low caste or mendicant figure, a Brahman and/or a king. These figures constitute a hierarchy, but the plot shows that the hierarchy in which they are constituted as "persons" is morally defective, or arbitrary.

In essence, the story seeks to reveal a radical gap between a person's social role (place in the caste hierarchy) and a person's moral worth as judged in terms of alternative moral concepts. The narratives distinguish between what the caste hierarchy makes a person, what they are "through and for" the caste system as Bourdieu (1977) might put it, and what this person is as an individual, "in and of" himself or herself, or "through and for" an engagement with higher forms of reality than caste. This severs the link forged in the dominant ideology between place in society and the moral nature of the person. As the story progresses, the person constituted within the caste hierarchy (as proposed by the dominant ideology) and the person seen in the light of the moral (as proposed in the narrative) become radically incommensurate. I would argue that such narrative acts are implicitly self-affirming. For the low caste Newars who spoke to me of caste life, such a narrative is perhaps one way of driving a *difference* between self-identity and social identity, between a complex and fluctuating personal sense of what they are, and a painful sense of how they are constructed as stigmatized actors in the caste system.[9] This struggle was evident in the interviews in which the stories occurred. To establish this difference—to declare to yourself and your interlocutor that you are not what the social system makes you—makes a difference psychologically. I present here stories and discussion by a Brahman, by Kancha, an untouchable Sweeper, and by Krishna Bahadur, from the borderline "impure" Gatha caste.

First Story: The King and the Beggar

It may seem paradoxical for a Brahman to tell an anti-hierarchical story, but we should credit them with a capacity for reflexivity. They should not be reified as nothing but embodiments of a hierarchy in which they have a privileged place, treated more as tropes than as persons, as theorists and low caste critics of Brahmanical ideology sometimes do. In any event, this story does not challenge the Brahman's status; rather, it puts a king in his place, challenging the hierarchy of power that focuses on the figure of the king, although in principle the point the story makes could apply to any high status actor. Without ever mentioning Brahmans, the story places value on the kind of religious knowledge Brahmans may claim; the hierarchy of knowledge (centered on ascetics and Brahmans) is valued above the hierarchy of power (centered on the king).

The story was told in response to the question, "How do you know the dharma?" In South Asia, dharma is a key moral and religious concept. While what dharma means in a concrete, experience-near sense varies in ways that reflect life-experiences and caste standing (Parish 1994), among my Hindu Newar informants the concept was typically invoked to frame discourse in moral terms, to assert that some action is obligatory. It would not be wrong, but would miss many of the subtleties and nuances of the terms, to gloss dharma as social and religious duty, prescribed custom, or moral law. Generally, people use the concept of dharma in ways that propose an objective and non-arbitrary basis for morality and social roles; dharma exists as a standard against which human behavior can be judged. Human beings have dharma that is specific to their social roles; yet dharma may be used to indicate universal obligations or precepts that transcend or encompass the dharma of social roles. In a sense, dharma is the moral order that is the ultimate foundation of the cosmos and human society. People, however, may not know the dharma, and may have to discover it for themselves, or with help from those who do know the dharma. The story:

> Once there was a king. One day he went out to learn the dharma of kings. But a king does not walk like we do. In the past there were no

cars, and people were carried [in palanquins]. For this, a minimum of four persons were needed. Four men set out carrying the king, but one was weak. This man fell on the road, so another was needed. Over there, they saw a man—a beggar. The king called the beggar over, and said to him, "I must go to the rishi's ashram. Carry me." The beggar did not know how to carry a palanquin. Even so the king scolded him, saying "You must carry me, but I'll give you wages." The beggar agreed. Now they again had four men to carry the king. But the beggar did not know how to carry the palanquin. He carried it jerkily, shaking it. The king fell off, and got a cut. The king rebuked the beggar, crying, "What are you doing? I'm cut and bleeding. Carry me properly."

But it happened again. The king hit the beggar his scepter. He yelled, "What are you doing?" He beat the beggar.

Then the beggar addressed the king, "He, Maharaja, where are you doing?"

The king replied, "I am going to learn the dharma."

At this, the beggar told him, "Your mouth says that you are going to learn the dharma, but with your acts you inflict suffering (*dukha*) on me. After I have carried you, you beat me. Is this the form dharma takes?"

Given this reply, the king experienced a shock of realization. "I have come to learn the dharma, and what this beggar says to me is a true thing. He thinks truth. I made him carry me. I have sinned." The king achieved a state of understanding (*bibek:* conscience, discrimination). When he did so, he greeted the beggar with respect, saying "Oh ho, although you are a beggar, what you said has brought knowledge (*gyan*) to me. One should not cause others to suffer. So said the king to the beggar.

The king asked the beggar, "Why did you jump around like that while carrying the palanquin?"

The beggar replied, "On the ground here are insects, many small bugs. Should we walk straight, we will step on them. If we step on them, they will die. To avoid the insects, I had to walk in that way. Since I stepped like that, the palanquin shook. One ought not kill insects, so I did that.

When he heard this, the king got down, and bowed to the feet of the beggar. This is one story. The king learned that you should not give *dukha* to others.

The story neutralizes the arbitrary power of the king. The king has coercive power, but not knowledge of dharma. He lacks proper understanding, I take it, of his role-specific dharma (his dharma as king) and its proper relationship to the universal dharma (which defines the arbitrary infliction of suffering on another as morally wrong). As superior, he addresses the beggar with familiar pronouns and verb forms, harangues him and commands him to carry the palanquin. I visualize this as done with that the blend of commanding and cajoling that high caste Newars often actually use with low caste persons who are unwilling to do something.

The beggar responds with high respect terms of address, pronouns and verb forms, and obeys. The hierarchical dimensions of the relationship, of superiority and inferiority, are sharply marked.

The king is journeying to learn the dharma proper to kings, the *rajdharma*; but he fails to act in accord with a "higher" dharma. This dharma—which we might see as more universal, role-transcendent dharma which "includes" or "trumps" the king's role-specific dharma—mandates justice and non-violence. The king uses power, but does not give justice. He coerces and later beats the beggar, whose motive is obedience to the broader imperatives of dharma which require reverence for all life. He seeks to avoid taking even the life of insects, at the risk of causing some discomfort and pain to the king. The story urges us to believe that reverence for life is a more worthy motive than the kingly virtues of force and command.

The king punished the beggar by beating him. Force is a prerogative of kings. But the beggar responds by pointing out a contradiction between the king's goal of learning dharma and his actions. As a result, the king experiences a sort of "shock of recognition." He realizes the "truth" of the beggar's words and develops *bibek*, a term which Newars often use in the sense of a kind of moral understanding or judgment, or as the agency in the mind that originates moral insight. The king gains knowledge (*gyan*) and expresses his gratitude to the beggar. This insight the king achieves has social consequences. This develops further as the king inquires into the reasons the beggar had for shaking the palanquin. Hearing that the beggar did so in order to avoid killing, the king bows to the feet of the beggar. Their relationship is reversed: the king acknowledges the beggar to be his moral superior. The king is put in his place—subordinate to those who embody the dharma, even if they are beggars. Indeed, the beggar figure here is aligned with the figure of the world-renouncer, or ascetic.

This story is anti-hierarchical in the sense that it places limits on one model of hierarchy—the hierarchy of power, of force, of command that is embodied in the figure of the king. The story subordinates power to dharma. Ideally, dharma should direct the action of the king; it should rule the king. In this sense, dharma is the "king of kings" (Khare 1984).

Dharma itself is portrayed as non-violence; perhaps this identification devalues the royal attribute of force, making the king's rajdharma a lesser dharma. Playing a beggar-renouncer against privileged king implicitly unites those who possess religious insight or knowledge—renouncer and Brahman—against the power of kings. Getting the Brahman into the picture, by way of reasserting their superiority, takes some "overinterpretation," but seems like a fairly plausible implication of the story.

The story constructs a non-royal model of hierarchy. It asserts the superiority of those with an active knowledge of dharma—the king bows to the feet of the beggar in homage to his moral superiority. The story supports a hierarchy based on knowledge of dharma. Since the beggar is aligned with the renouncer, and Brahmans may align themselves with the renouncer figure, the story advances a theme that could be used to legitimate the superiority of Brahmans. Note that purity is not an issue.

The story constructs reality in a way that qualifies the power of kings. The "reality" the story constructs involves the following premises: first, dharma is worth seeking; the story establishes a hierarchy of value, and places the figure of king and beggar within this value system. Second, dharma may not be recognized or properly understood without seeking; it is not an attribute of birth-status, at least not for kings. The intervention of others, as teachers and exemplars, may be crucial for learning the dharma. Third, dharma is a moral imperative which sustains life. Fourth, it also transcends social distinctions, even while defining the duties of particular social stations (so that the dharma of the king may allow the use of force but the misuse of force is not consistent with dharma). Dharma as defined in the story requires that people of all social stations be treated fairly and not harmed. Those who most perfectly embody dharma, however, are superior to others, and the object of hierarchical reverence and respect.

Second Story: A King's Son Is Made a Butcher

Newars often attribute the origins of caste to the actions of kings. I suspect this view of the origin of caste may help some Newars conceive of the caste system as a cultural construction, as something made in society, rather than as an objective reality that cannot be changed. The following minimal story was told by Kancha, the untouchable Sweeper,

> Long ago, it is said, there was a king who had no workers. There were no sweepers. So messengers were sent out to tell people to seize anyone found defecating while facing east, and bring him to the king, and he would be made to kill buffalo. So they got the king's youngest son— or was it the middle son?—and made him a Butcher.[10]

The story posits a time before there were castes, but this time is not made part of "history," as is sometimes done, by placing the origins of the caste system in definite period (such as the reign of a particular king). The story makes the caste order in its inception not totally arbitrary (one should not defecate while facing east, an auspicious direction) but arbitrary in the sense that anyone caught could get assigned to a stigmatizing occupation—even a king's son, even the son of the king creating the caste order. An action, not an innate quality, serves as the basis for recruitment into caste. The king's son cannot be more impure than the king by birth. As for his action, he might not have gotten caught. Furthermore, the need that prompted the effort to place people into castes was economic or functional—the king needed workers—and not based on some principle of just desert or of natural kind. In this story, the king made caste; castes did not arise out of people's innate nature, did not reflect an original state of relative impurity, or even have much to do with a moral biography. The story thus asserts the arbitrary nature of caste hierarchy, and treats it with a certain distancing irony.

Given the premises of the dominant ideology, the narrative, as brief as it is, also poses a fundamental question about the basis of the caste system. Perhaps kings make castes because it is in their "nature" to do so— that is, their actions in constituting the caste system flow from their "biomoral" substance, their essential being. But how can a father and his son have such profoundly different "natures," so that one is a king, the maker of castes, while the other becomes a lowly butcher? The only similarity one can discern is that kings and butchers alike may resort to bloodletting; they are both creatures of force.

A high caste informant might, of course, respond to this story by attempting to close the gap it has opened between "action" and "nature." Perhaps the king's son was different to begin with; maybe his act of defecating while facing east reflected his moral essence, his personal being. He may have sinned in previous life times; he may have shared "substance" with lower caste people, making him deviant. But this reconstruction, I think, distorts Kancha's intent. Efforts to revise what low caste actors mean—to make what they say appear ultimately consistent with the premises of the dominant ideology if "properly" understood, or to make their moral and political discourse seem irrational and misguided—are as much a part of the ideological scene as the tendency for the low caste actors to censor their speech to make it more acceptable to high caste audiences.

While some of the responses to the problem proposed by stories of this kind attempt to reunite "nature" and "action," and so justify the caste order, this is not the only response possible to the rift this story constructs. Many of the efforts to resolve the contradiction this story opens up tend to "soften" the caste system, making it seem more subject to human action. This can take several forms. The caste system may be taken as an arbitrary construction, imposed through willful human acts, instead of as an immutable natural order. This is what I think Kancha intended. Alternatively, the caste system may be seen as a social order that responds, in one way or another, to human action. In this view, the caste system may be taken as subject to manipulation and failure (your present place in society was the result of tricks, or mistakes, or conspiracy). Or the system may be viewed as responsive to ethical modes of action, so that you can, or should be able to, "rise" in the hierarchy. In this view, you should be able to "rise up" in this life, by engaging in moral acts, by obtaining "knowledge," or by transforming one's qualities—if not in this life, then in future lives, through the medium of karma and reincarnation. Use of the karma doctrine, of course, ends up reconstituting hierarchy, by bringing fate and action into alignment.

Kancha, by posing the problem, has not resolved it. He is forced to face the rifts that open up between action, nature and self; his experience flows out of the contradictions of caste life and ideology. He must seek some kind of closure—however brittle and fragile—of the gap between his sense of self (based on "action"), and his social identity and personhood (based on cultural representations of his "nature"), between his insight into the arbitrary nature of the caste, and the need to live his life in terms of that system. He needs to make a living, and this requires that he participate to some degree in caste practices; he cannot afford to alienate the high caste actors who employ him. He needs to find ways to fit himself into the caste system to feed his family. At times in our discussions he seems to justify the caste system as a way of justifying his participation in it.

How does he do this? Kancha told this little story during an interview. I had asked him, "Do you think that the matter of caste is unjust? What's your own idea about this?" Kancha responded by saying that the caste system is simply a reality. "It was made long ago." The image of coming from "long ago" is a validating construct for him—the value of a social form is established by placing it within tradition, by having it come from "long ago." Kancha then went on to *neutralize* the implications of being low caste by excluding his caste from comparison with other, higher castes: "Your own caste is important for you. My caste organizes my social life. A Sweeper is one who follows these ways. And so, I think, you have your own caste." While some may speak of caste in terms of impurity, he speaks of it as a way of life, as a practice, not as an expression of essence. The practice of caste makes social life possible, and constitutes a positive identity he values as well as a stigmatized identity he rejects. "A Sweeper is one who follows these ways." By declaring the value of one's own caste for oneself, Kancha recovers something of value, and neutralizes the implication that he is "low."

The story followed. I am unsure about the significance of telling such a story just at that moment, but, arriving when it did, the story would seem to disconcert the case he was making for accepting the caste system, if that was what he was doing. The story exposes the arbitrary nature of caste roles. How, then, can anyone justify or accept it? Perhaps, however, Kancha saw something else in this story, something that justified, not the caste system itself, but his own stance toward the caste system. He may have felt the story justified his practice of surface accommodation, because it shows how powerless everyone, even a king's son, is in the face of the blind political force that establishes caste roles.

Whether meant as a critique of the caste system, as a justification of his relationship to the caste system, or both, the story marks the limits of his commitment to the caste system. Moments like this, when social actors jettison concepts used to objectify the social order, and invoke ideas that are critical and dereifying, when they shift from asserting the value and naturalness of caste to telling stories that make caste appear arbitrary, show that people have more than one way—the dominant ideology's way—of understanding self and society. In this case, the story expresses a different vision of reality, a vision that contradicts the hierarchical construction of reality that this untouchable works hard and long to maintain, at least outwardly, making a show of diffidence and respect.

He cannot sustain the critical insight. He cannot, after all, do much about it, not unless he is willing to risk the ostracism and retaliation that overt acts of resistance might provoke. Telling a story by itself does not transform the conditions of social existence, whatever inner transformations it may reflect or initiate. Insight into the arbitrary nature of the social order itself often has no immediate, practical effect on life, not in the absence of any social movement that might attempt to put critique into action. Kancha's mind is not totally in the grip of caste ideology, but he insists that to live he must practice caste. He insists he must accept his caste occupation; he must get up early in the morning and sweep the streets. To fit himself into this role—to be an Untouchable in practice— as he must be to survive, means he must find ways to acquiesce to hierarchy, to permit engagement with it. Justifying hierarchy—on his own terms, not precisely those of the dominant ideology—makes a certain sense. His hierarchy-affirming values overlap with those of higher caste actors, but also diverge in important ways. He rejects purity and pollution, but believes Brahmans should be respected for their religious knowledge and ritual practice. He wishes to replicates hierarchy among the lower castes. He believes other castes are lower than his own, and that he should not associate with them.[11] He fears any breakdown of the caste division of labor that might threaten his livelihood. On his own terms, then, Kancha often does endorse the caste system, unlike some of the other low caste people I spoke to, he does not reject it entirely. He seeks ways to make it work and actively participates in the system that oppresses him.

In our discussions, whatever critical comments he makes, he soon reverts to his equivocal defense of the caste system. When he concludes his story, I ask (not really comprehending the implications of the narrative), "But do you think [the caste system] is just?" He responds "It is good. It was made long ago. Although I say I will go up, I cannot go up." This is the effective reality from his point of view. He feels he cannot change his caste status. He cannot act on the insight into the arbitrary construction of the caste hierarchy implied in his narrative, although it may develop in his reflections, making a difference in how he interprets and experiences the world. As a practical matter, he has to live within the political reality of the culturally constituted caste hierarchy. Glimpses of the arbitrary nature of caste relations do not provide him with freedom of action, and do not establish the moral grounds for the making of a different society.

The following story, by a second low caste informant, more clearly calls the caste order into question. The story not only exposes the arbitrary nature of the caste hierarchy, it proposes alternative grounds for constructing social hierarchy.

Third Story: A Brahman Has an Untouchable Guru

This story is told by Krishna Bahadur, a member of a borderline impure caste, the Gatha, who provide the members of a ritual troupe who dance as gods and goddesses in the streets and courtyards of Bhaktapur. He uses his story to make the argument that earned religious knowledge, not one's caste of birth, should be the basis for hierarchy, and that the right to gain knowledge should be based on moral qualities. The argument links moral qualities, religious knowledge, and power. Krishna begins by saying "We must respect those who know."

The story goes like this:

An untouchable—a Cyamakhala, almost the lowest of the low—served a renouncer and respected him as a guru. The renouncer gives him a mantra, a verbal formula that channels spiritual power. (The story thus begins with the violation of a Brahmanical code, since untouchables are not supposed to be given mantras: in this action, the renouncer and untouchable are implicitly identified with each other in opposition to the Brahmans.) With this mantra, the untouchable can cause fruit to grow magically on trees—sweet, ripe, delicious apples, pomegranates, oranges. The untouchable uses this power to feed his family.

A Brahman hears of this, and asks the untouchable to teach him the mantra, showing him more respect (in the way he addressed him) than a Brahman usually shows an untouchable. He begs the untouchable to take pity on him because his family is large and he is poor. Hearing this, the Untouchable says, "I will teach you. And then you will have to respect me as a guru." The Brahman hesitates, but accepts, thinking that he has to eat.

This introduces necessity into the picture. Krishna comments on the Brahman's dilemma and decision: "The Brahman's caste is great, but he would have to respect the Cyamakhala as a guru. He was in a quandary. He knew he did not want to, but he was forced to consider that he had to eat. Finally, he said, 'I will respect you,' and bowed to the Untouchable in respect."

After the Brahman learns the mantra, the untouchable tells him, "Now you know [how to make plants bear fruit]. You can eat and sell fruit wherever you go. Do not lie." The untouchable tells the Brahman he trusts him to tell whoever asks that he has been taught by "that one," the untouchable. The Brahman promises that he will not lie about his. He goes forth and makes his living by selling fruit. One day he sells fruit to a functionary, a soldier, associated with a king's court. The Brahman is asked to take a post in the king's palace and provide the king with fruit. He does so.

There comes a time when the king has to go out from his palace, and he takes the Brahman with him so the Brahman can use his mantra to provide fruit to eat on the journey. During the journey, the king asks the Brahman who taught him the mantra. In Krishna's words, "The Brahman couldn't say this, couldn't say that, since his guru was a Cyamakhala. He was of the Brahman jat, so he was ashamed to say a Cyamakhala" was his teacher. The Brahman lies—he says a respected person, a great man, taught him. He does not acknowledge that an untouchable sweeper was his guru. The King asks for fruit, and the Brahman goes to a tree to produce it, but when he recites his mantra, nothing happens. He tries again, and yet again, but no fruit grows. When he returns empty-handed to the king, the king reproaches him, saying "What are you doing, Brahman? I am not prepared to sit here hungry." The Brahman reports he was not able to produce any fruit. As a consequence of his lie, the Brahman lost the power to make fruit grow. His *siddhi*, his efficacious power, was ended. The king dismisses him, saying, "You are useless. Go." The Brahman then goes hungry, and not knowing what else to do, returns to the Untouchable and begs for forgiveness. Krishna supplies the dialogue.

"Oh ho, Guru, forgive me," [pleads the Brahman]. "Because I have lied. Teach me again." The Guru replies, "Oh ho, it is a sin to teach those you cannot trust. As it is said, once is enough, twice is broken." He refused to teach this Brahman. Straightaway, the Brahman died.

Krishna concludes his narration by saying "This is what *biswas* means."

The word "biswas" is polysemic, carrying meanings we would link to such English words as trust, faith, belief. What Krishna perhaps means to say is that the story tells us what trust is all about. It shows the importance of keeping faith with others—or that it would matter in a just world, which is not what the real world, the world outside the story, is. Krishna may perceive biswas as supplying the integrity that binds people to their word, so that they will keep faith with others, making them trustworthy. I believe he was also implicitly commenting on what the terms of my relationship with him should be.

In this narrative, the dominant ideas in terms of which caste identities are conceived (e.g., low caste actors are impure, low caste actors are repositories of inauspiciousness, low caste actors sinned in previous lives) are passed over in silence, although they are perhaps presupposed in the idea that the Brahman's caste is "great." The story proposes an alternative way of viewing human relations. The narrative floats a possible world—one in which moral worth is the basis for moral respect and social rank. Purity and karma are not directly considered at all. Instead, the narrative reconstitutes the grounds of hierarchy. Social esteem and rank, the narrative proposes, are to be based on empowering knowledge; access to such knowledge is a matter of trust, and granting access to empowering knowledge should, the narrative suggests, be based on directly perceived moral qualities and moral actions.

This is a moral story, and it functions without reference to the ethnophysical theory of impurity and the flow of shared substance that is one of the main bulwarks of the caste hierarchy. Rather, it links untouchability to the ascetic tradition, undercutting Brahmanical hierarchy through a fusing of identity—the figure of the untouchable guru as a source of wisdom and spiritual power is keyed to the figure of the renouncer. This does not fit easily within the value system of the Brahmanical caste hierarchy. The Brahman, an individual of socially ascribed "high" status is portrayed as morally undeserving of religious knowledge and its powers, while an untouchable has the right to possess such knowledge. The Untouchable shows his fitness to possess power by respecting a renouncer, a figure from outside the social world. The terms on which the Untouchable agreed to transmit his knowledge of the mantra to the Brahman were in one sense conventionally hierarchical: he asked to be respected as a guru. This elevation of Untouchable into teacher subverts the social hierarchy with Brahmans at the apex and untouchables at the bottom. The Brahman hesitated, in a quandary, but gave in to the Untouchable's condition out of fear of starving. Thus, the narrative places him in the state of need that untouchables repeatedly declared was their motive for acquiescing to the caste hierarchy—we have to eat.

The Brahman learns the empowering mantra, but fails to keep his word. He could not bring himself to acknowledge that a lowly untouchable was his teacher. By lying, he showed his lack of moral worth, and so lost the power of the mantra.

Since knowledge is available to anyone of worth—even untouchables—this second hierarchy constituted in terms of possession of sacred knowledge is more permeable than the caste hierarchy constituted in terms of purity and impurity. In the hierarchy based on relative purity, one can only fall; but since knowledge can be learned, one can rise in a hierarchy based on knowledge—if that is the exclusive principle defining hierarchy. (Brahmans in fact fuse the two; they supplement their claim to preeminence based on purity with claims to possess, and to have exclusive access to, sacred knowledge.)

The hierarchy proposed in the narrative is based on knowledge that can be attained regardless of caste status, and on moral virtues—honesty, trust and reverence for those who hold knowledge—that can be achieved by any moral person, not just by those who are high caste or "pure." Krishna repeatedly attempts to define the difference between the closed hierarchy of purity and impurity and a relatively open hierarchy of knowledge and virtue. The distinction has great significance for him.

It is easy to see why he maintains this. On the one hand, as a member of a low caste group, on the borderline between pure and impure castes, he feels ambivalent about being excluded and stigmatized; on the other, as a member of the Navadurga troupe—the ritual dancers who embody important Hindu gods and goddesses, a group with vital symbolic and ritual roles within the city—he wants to claim a higher status for his group and himself. He wants to be acknowledged as priestly, as combining sacred power and knowledge in his person. He wishes sacred knowledge, not purity, to define hierarchy. He wants to preserve hierarchy, but not the hierarchy given by purity and impurity. When he focuses on the way that higher castes exclude and stigmatize his own group, he sometimes asserts equality.

In the following passage from an interview, Krishna reveals his ambivalence about hierarchy and equality. He affirms each, in different contexts, yet expresses uneasiness with hierarchy and disappointment with equality. He views equality as useless rhetoric, impotent in the face of the problem of hierarchy. Krishna uses a story to make his point that caste is not a moral order, that people are the same, and that discrimination on the basis of caste lacks moral justification; but the ideal called for in the narrative is unrealizable in the "real world," and he breaks away from the narrative to say, in a rather bitter way, that power, wealth and knowledge are held by some, and not by others—and that is the way it is. He includes me in this—as part of the actual world that differs so profoundly from the ideal of equality and non-discrimination evoked in the narrative. Although Krishna is a Hindu, he draws on Buddhist sources for the narrative. Bhaktapur is predominantly Hindu, but there are a few Buddhist enclaves, and Krishna has some Buddhist friends.[12]

We must keep in mind that Krishna Bahadur *practices* hierarchy; he does not show through his behavior that he accepts as equals the men and women of castes lower than his own. To do so would provoke ostracism as well as criticism. Since he can attribute his conformity to local hierarchical practices to social pressure, we cannot be certain whether he in fact rejects caste as a system, or only his own position in the system. We can only be certain that he is aware of the ideal of equality, and of the tensions between this ideal and reality.

> ("Would you eat boiled rice made by a low caste person?") "I do not accept boiled rice from untouchables. These are the Pore, Cyamakhala [the two Sweeper groups], the Sa:mi [oil-pressers]. You should not eat food prepared by these low castes. If you eat with them, the people around you will talk, will rebuke you—what things they will say. If it is known, the high caste people, and the people of your own caste, will criticize you. And so you cannot eat with untouchables."

After he has stated that he conforms because of social pressure, however, Krishna goes on to declare that "people are the same." He shifts into narrative to construct a foundation for this idea:

> "People are the same. Buddha Bhagavan said they are the same in this world. Once when Buddha Bhagavan was out wandering, he needed water to drink. He was with his friend Ananda the monk. At the time they needed water, they saw an untouchable Sweeper woman was drawing water out of the well. They told her they needed water. She said, 'I won't give you water because I am not of caste.' Ananda then said, 'Woman, I only asked for water, I did not ask for your caste'. . . ."

Krishna then puts Ananda's action in the context of Buddha's teachings. He assumes "the voice" of Buddha, who says to his followers:

"In this world, all men are the same. People are equal. We are all the same. The same God created us all. Do not discriminate by caste.

Here Krishna shifts away from the narrative world to the "real" world. I follow up with some questions (in parentheses).

And what is the use of saying that? Great people have great knowledge. Those who do not have knowledge, do not have knowledge. Those who do not have knowledge cannot be the same as those who have knowledge. You and I cannot be the same. . . . You have much money. If I had a lot of money I would be a little proud in my heart. Any man who has knowledge will be proud. He won't be able to give up his pride.

("In your opinion, men are equal?") "They are equal."

("But according to caste, they are different.") "Different. Men are the same."

("For you?") "My mind is like that. Society is not ready."

("If men are equal, why is there caste?") "It was made to correspond to the degree of understanding that people had. . . . Knowledge is not equal. Understandings are different. Consider the king. He is a man, and we are men, but we cannot be his equals. We have to defer to him."

("If men are equal, why do you have to follow caste?") "If there was no caste, then our affairs could not be put in order. There would be fights."

Krishna invokes the ideas of equality in the narrative, and then distances himself from it. He seems to see it as a powerful and true idea—he frequently reverts to the position that all men are the same—but also as a fragile, useless, ideal that cannot be achieved in the actual world. His words suggest resentment, as did his tone in the interview; in particular, when he says "And what is the use of saying that?" and (bringing it home to me) "You and I cannot be the same." He resents differences in wealth, in knowledge, and in power. He resents the way higher castes treat him in the closed hierarchy of purity and impurity, and would prefer an open hierarchy based on mastery of sacred knowledge in which low caste people could rise, in which his own mastery of sacred knowledge would count for more.

Krishna Bahadur also sees power as a factor in keeping people and groups unequal; even though people are the same, they are forced to defer to those with power. Finally, perhaps the ultimate rationale of the hierarchy is to create order and to prevent violence.

Krishna thinks that it is the actual distribution of "empowering" knowledge in society that makes people unequal; he seeks to affirm the idea that you can rise in the hierarchy by gaining such knowledge. Implied is the idea that knowledge was kept from low castes—that the high castes attempt to keep a monopoly on such knowledge. As a ritual specialist at his own level in the social system, he wishes to claim knowledge to make him high. He asserts a different hierarchy.

Many orthodox Brahmans and members of the other highest castes deny that low castes can rise in this lifetime; they emphasize the impurity, the "essence," of the low castes as an insurmountable obstacle to mobility. Krishna prefers to see "knowledge" and "understanding" as the basis of status. This is ritual or religious knowledge. People do not simply inherit some quantity of purity or impurity; knowledge confers status. Equality and inequality are questions of access and opportunity, not "nature" or "impurity."

Asked whether an untouchable could rise, Krishna answers affirmatively, and explains why:

> "If he was educated, he could go up. And if Brahmans don't study and do their own true karma, by honoring their scriptures and following their rules and rites, then they will come down. . . . A low caste man can rise up. This arrangement is good. It is good because Bhagavan made us and this world. He gave us life. In life, no one wants to be low. They want to be high. To rise up, they have to improve their understanding. They have to gain knowledge, and then they will be high. In the past, because they did not have understanding, they were not educated, they were placed low."

Implicitly, the hierarchy cannot, for him, be unalterable, because Bhagavan made people. He posits an "open," rather than a "closed" hierarchy. Note that the separation of *castes* is constructed—it does not, in his account, arise from some preexisting quanta of purity or impurity. Separation arises rather from a lack of *buddhi*, "understanding," which is something individuals and groups can acquire or lose. "Understanding" is socially developed. Furthermore, although some were made low, no one wants to be low. Krishna identifies this wish not to be low as an inherent feature of life itself; the desire not to be low flows from "the life" that God gives. In this construction, he ethicizes and sacralizes aspirations.

Brahmans and other high caste people attribute their high caste status to the fact they do "karma" which in this context has the sense of "religious acts and rites." This makes them "pure"; but again this is constructed, not an inherent attribute. This claim may be buttressed by invoking karma in the first sense; high caste people will say one must do good works for many generations before one is worthy of being born in a high caste. This argument would seal off their status in this lifetime. But Krishna, a ritual leader of a caste that stands just above castes that are fully impure and untouchable, emphasizes that it is possible to rise through an improvement of understanding, by gaining religious knowledge. He re-invents hierarchy for himself.

Conclusion

Note that all of these Newars' stories deal with problems of recognition. In all three, a hierarchically dominant figure—king or Brahman—fails to recognize another person in a way that provides the complication of the story. In the first story, recounted by a Brahman, a king seeking knowledge of dharma fails to recognize the way the beggar embodies the dharma. In the third story, recognition is withheld from the untouchable when he is not acknowledged by the Brahman as the Brahman's guru— an injustice and a lie that rebound on the Brahman. The second narrative, Kancha's, is the most resistant to analysis in these terms—or perhaps the most subtle and sweeping. The problem of recognition in this story is cast as a problem of misrecognition. The king did not intend to make his son a low caste Butcher. The king's son was not recognized as a king's son: it was not who he was, but what he was doing, that made a difference. The king's son was at the wrong place at the wrong time, just happened to be doing something that was declared the basis for making a person a Butcher. Caste status, the story intimates—in ways, to be sure, that can be neutralized by others who will be able to find ways of making it means something else—is not based on recognition of who a person is, but on being caught up in a net of power (the king's men hunt for someone who fits the criteria the king has given them). What you become in the caste system is determined by power extrinsic to self, not by any quality having to do with "who you are."

I think many low caste Newars seek to declare—to themselves and others—that their caste status does not reflect their moral essence, express their sense of self, or constitute them. They argue that caste practice is not definitive of who they are, is not something that arises out of the very ground of their being, as the predominant ideology of caste maintains. They experience caste as a constructed order imposed on their lives and identities.

In response, they manipulate, reconstruct, and resist their social identities in complex ways, in moral rhetoric, narratives, and fantasies. By showing that there are other ways to view themselves and society, they melt away some of the powerful sense of reality that caste hierarchy has, make it seem less solid, less natural and moral, and less self-defining. People propose other moral worlds, alternative hierarchies, in which they might stand higher. The conditions of life, practices, and ideology that create and sustain caste hierarchy are locked in perpetual conflict with the impulse to escape and alter that hierarchy.

This has fundamental consequences for self-awareness and moral consciousness of self and society. In the case of the Newars, hierarchy embodied in practice is something that people must know and engage, since it is central to their lives. The Newar experience reflects something of the way that human awareness adapts itself to the exigencies of inequality. Let me suggest that most Newars, much of the time, must find ways to make themselves not be fully aware of what, in some important sense, they know—that the caste system is an arbitrary human construction. To get on with their lives in caste society, they must often suppress the kinds of insight and analysis that they display in critical discourse and in anti-hierarchical narratives.

Since the suppression of the critical self may occur more or less systematically in cultural life, I have taken up Fredric Jameson's term "political unconscious" as a heuristic cover term for the phenomena. I suspect I use the term in ways Jameson might deplore—it reflects, for me, a psychocultural dynamic within social systems by which people manage some of the risks of life by modulating what they "know," by keeping knowledge, ideas, and insights out of awareness, and not using them as the basis for actions. This "unconscious" is not an agency or place, but a metaphor for a process of activating and suppressing knowledge.[13]

Cultural models, and the knowledge and values they embody, may have a kind of figure-ground relationship attuned to social practice: what is figure (known) at one moment can be ground (unknown) the next. The process may involve severing, modulating, and reactivating identifications with specific values, symbols, or persons. The term "political unconscious" thus puts a name on a reflexive cognitive process of some significance, inviting us to take note of the ways cultural knowledge (models or knowledge structures, self-images and world-images) can be cycled in and out of awareness and practice in ways that may in part reflect the politics of everyday life (as this in turn reflects the basic political structures of society). An actor's choice of cultural models for interpretation and action is not always politically neutral. In any encounter with others, awareness and behavior may be diverted into safe channels, yet the grounds for critical consciousness preserved in a potential cultural repertoire. This alternative repertoire can be drawn on in critique and resistance.

The concept need not be totally divorced from the concepts of the unconscious developed by Freud and his followers, just because it deals with politics and culture.[14] Yet it should not be treated as a purely psychological concept: what is "repressed" here is not just knowledge of inner states, but also knowledge of social life. I use the term to refer to all the myriad politically relevant ways that people hide and disguise, from others but also from themselves, for reasons having to do with relative power and status, such matters as dissenting opinions about social practices, their feelings for (and against) others, their critiques of culture, society, or self, the dissonant dimensions of felt experience, or chapters of life history. In the process people often obscure much about what they have done or felt, their presence in history, the way they were involved in events or took part in practices incongruent with the manner they now seek to present or think of themselves.

This political unconscious is as fluid and permeable as awareness. What is suppressed and what enters into awareness, what is denied and what is animated, shift in context-sensitive ways, along with the experience, goals, and needs of actors. In caste life, actors invoke hierarchical modes of knowing self and society to make it possible for them to interact with members of other castes, reduce the otherwise painful dissonance, and avoid exposing themselves to the risks that overt opposition would entail.[15]

To displace, disguise, or transform what they have done, felt, or believed, often releases people from responsibility or danger, eases their minds, making it possible for them to uphold certain images of self, and engage life virtually as if none of the suppressed values, realities, events, actions, or self-experience existed. Such forgetfulness is perhaps not blessed, but is often socially and politically convenient, even if (and often precisely because) it exposes the social actor to self-contradiction.

But let us consider the process from the center, as a constructive, rather than just from the margins, where it must also be a defensive process. At the margins, stigmatized actors or actors threatened by objecthood have to deal with the implications of other's visions of society, of morality, of reality and with the dangers and stigma these pose; but what concerns actors centrally are the problems of making a life, whether they are high or low caste. Generally, actors attempt to make lives by making culture, by creating and recreating culture's symbolic and ethical forms in their minds (Obeyesekere 1990), by formulating and animating cultural conceptions in ways that express their own experience and their own interests. A key aspect of this is the effort to generate and sustain a moral vision of social life. Working with cultural meanings, actors seek to define a conscious world that has value and significance for them. To evoke Geertz's striking phrase again, people seek to "inhabit the world they imagine" (Geertz 1983:155). But this may require them to deny the world imagined in a different way. They may need to ignore or overcome meanings and experience that have no place in their conscious world. Building their conscious world, they may create a cultural unconscious. This, too, is a "work of culture." [16]

For example, if read one way, Chapter 1 of this volume tacitly created a political unconscious, similar to that composed through symbolic narrative practices that claim public space for a high caste vision of cosmos and society. In a kind of narrative sleight of hand, by keeping the focus largely on hierarchical constructions, I kept parts of Newar cultural life largely out of sight, out of mind. I played down tensions and disorder, the unrest and protest, the discontents and ambivalence that exist in Newar culture, merely hinting at these while highlighting constructions of hierarchy. Hierarchy's construction was privileged, and we did not get any real sense of what actors thought and felt in most of the chapter. So it always is with analysis of structure, practice, and ideology that does not also explore agency, mind, experience, and consciousness.[17] Chapter 2 restored some balance by presenting some critical, ironic, and utopian reflections on hierarchy.

Just as a narrative can keep much out of sight, out of mind, so can a festival or theory, declaring the seamless reality of its vision, tacitly suppressing alternate visions. In fact, the assertion of order in the ritual journey of the god-chariots attracts a subversive play of disorder. If the narrative of the festival tacitly denies the possibilities and actualities of unrest and disorder—in fact constitutes a political unconscious by refusing to acknowledge social discontents—then paradoxically it is these very narrative and ritual acts of closure that invite the return of the socially and politically repressed. As we will see, the repressed (in the form of social actors acting out) in fact turn out in some force on the margins of the main event, infiltrate where they can, and take some delight in shaking things up, without necessarily being guided by any self-conscious political stance or formal ideology.

Unconscious spaces may be nested inside each other: and what is suppressed, kept from attention at one moment, may be the focus of activity and thought at some other moment. There are relativizing effects, as actors shift perspectives, and animate different, and conflicting, models. Anthropologists, I imagine, need to shift with social actors among diverse perspectives and cultural models. Obviously—many of us now think—ethnography should be more than the transcription of cultural ideology and signifying practice that declares what is real and what is valued by elite actors, by dominant groups. Cultural performances may implicitly divide the world into marked and unmarked regions—but life is lived in both kinds of cultural space, and involves cultural models distributed across the total experiential topography of culture. No culture implodes into its own master narratives, can be contained in the stories that its members claim contain its very essence. Dominant symbolic narratives do not in fact say all that can be said, or declare all that can be known or practiced.

Symbolically and politically, these do have an effect, for in proposing what is real they suppress in narrative consciousness what has no place in that imagined world. Levy (1986) has written of the ways some aspects of cultural experience are "hypercognized," while others are "hypocognized." Such processes of elaboration and muting, of thickening up and thinning out conscious thought, constitutes a dialectic of knowing and not knowing. Building up cultural models in some areas, but "starving" them in others, can have political import, empowering some voices and visions, limiting others. In Bhaktapur as elsewhere, some values, some practices, some actors, are celebrated and raised into intense, mythic awareness. These have their centrality declared while other zones of experience are excluded or muted, unable to claim the public forums needed to shout out and elaborate their own possibilities.

And yet—although critical insights and the work of demystification may have to be suppressed and hidden, even from self—I have shown how some Newars do see caste as arbitrary, as alien to their self-concepts. They reject their construction by others, by caste ideology. This *is* expressed in critical discourse and anti-hierarchical narratives, which should be seen in part as constituting processes of self-construction. A critical consciousness can co-exist with the political unconscious; this critical consciousness, which interprets self and society in ways not simply given in the dominant ideology, can be developed through narrative work.[18] If at times critical models of self and society are driven from awareness, if critical consciousness dissipates with the activation of hierarchical models, then at other moments, hierarchical models and the awareness of self and society that goes along with them will be suppressed, as critical models are activated as salient interpretive schema. The suppression of moral and political awareness thus cuts two ways; the political unconscious of actors has revolving faces, or alternating phases, as actors embrace and animate conflicting models of self and society. The activation of any one model of self and society may require the suppression of other models. Yet the conflicting perspectives of incompatible models are equally elements of the total mental world of low caste men and women.

Inconstant selves in an equivocal world, actors in caste society may shift from resistance to acquiescence, and back again. Moral fantasies and narratives tell us something about how actors experience such shifts in their model of relationship to society, suggesting what is at stake for them: moral conceptions of self are asserted against stigmatized identities, alternative visions of the world shouted in the face of harsh, hierarchical social realities. If actors need at once to adjust themselves to hierarchical realities and rebel against them, then an "inner" politics of self parallels the politics of caste life.[19]

The world view of resistance is as real as the world view of submission. I suspect the self-consciousness presupposed in hierarchical models, narratives, and practices is not any more real, or any more false, than the consciousness implied in non-hierarchical models, anti-hierarchical narratives, and resistance to caste practices. The structure and objective situation of both of these modes need to be recognized, without privileging one as somehow culturally more real than the other, whatever the theories or values of the researcher may be. Actors' narratives disclose both.

What do we make of the morality asserted in the narratives we have considered here? Perhaps like Nietzsche in his *Genealogy of Morals* we should say that these narratives represent "uprisings in ethics" that begin when resentment "becomes creative and brings forth its own values." We have seen evidence that low caste actors resent the way they are constructed and incorporated in caste practices, and such resentment is part of what moves them to reimagine the world. Moreover, the historical reality has been that they could not act, not easily or without putting themselves at great risk; so like Nietzsche, we could say these narratives reflect the resentment "of those to whom the only authentic way of reaction—that of deeds—is unavailable, and who preserve themselves from harm through the exercise of imaginary vengeance."[20] And yet, I think we hear more in these stories than resentment. Low-caste actors may wreak an imaginary vengeance in narrative (the bad Brahman in Krishna's story dies, after all), but they also imagine a better world. These narratives express as much hope as resentment; as much resignation as hope. If we view these narratives as constituting moral fantasies, the strongest desire they disclose is not the desire for vengeance, but the desire for mutual recognition.

Thus I would modify Nietzsche's formulae to read: These narrative uprisings in moral thought begin when resentment and hope become creative, bringing forth stories that explore the problems of meaning and identity, of powerlessness and practice, posed by caste life. These narratives rise up against the social constructions of self expressed in the dominant ideology and implied in caste practice. They are uprisings in ethics and in self-concept.

What the narratives work with are constructions and counter-constructions of the morality of social life, which necessarily stand as constructions and counter-constructions of the social actor, who experi-

ences and interprets these constructions in terms of self. What is contested is the moral grounds on which actors have value, and for low caste
actors and untouchables this is very much a question of self-identity, of
who they are and what meaning they have, for others and for themselves.
The narratives here are thus subversions of constructions of morality that
imply and legitimate stigmatizing constructions of the low caste actor.
The revolt against stigmatizing constructions of self lead to affirmations
of self, whether in the form of a "we" or an "I." Identifying with others,
an untouchable can constitute a self-identity by constituting an implied
community of suffering and solidarity, speaking not about "what I feel,
experience" but about what "we poor people, we Sweepers" suffer or
must do to live. Defining self in opposition, through their stories low
caste individuals such as Krishna and Kancha establish a voice for themselves, and a point of view, that rejects the constructions of the dominant
ideology, opening up affirmative possibilities for self despite the social
reality of caste.

Such narrative work draws on, and helps constitute, a narrative tradition that has the potential for helping constitute a moral and political tradition. In the absence of the power to act, such narratives keep
alive alternative possibilities; they stand as moral fantasies and utopian
thought to social reality, and offer one way low caste actors can construct
themselves in contrast and opposition to their ideological construction
in the caste system. That the consciousness of self and society they imply
may be only part of the consciousness of low caste actors—who may at
times be drawn into and encompassed by the consciousness proposed in
caste ideology and practice—does not detract from its psychological and
cultural significance. At the very least, aside from the way narratives may
help actors adjust themselves to difficult social realities, we need to consider the ways that critical and utopian narratives might keep actors flexible, preparing them to seek and accept, to promote and impel change
should conditions allow it.

By listening carefully, we can come to understand something of the
way that people experience themselves and society, something of the dynamic tensions of the lives they live. We can get at some of the flux and
politics of identity. The dominant ideology is not all that people know.
People have moral fantasies, construct critiques, imagine utopias for
themselves. By listening to people's moral fantasies we can know something of how they might wish to know themselves, in addition to what
they must know of themselves to live in caste society.

By failing to see the pageantry of hierarchy as a form of rhetoric that
asserts certain principles of human existence against other possible principles—that it proposes all castes have their place in the cosmos and the
city not against a backdrop of near-total consensus but in the face of

discontents—we miss seeing the force of the argument made, and fail to see how cultural lives are shaped by rhetorical practices. We better appreciate the moral force, the imaginative power, invested in hierarchy when we see that it has been constructed in the face of opposition and challenges. Uprisings in ethics and action shape the face of hierarchy.

Chapter 5
Holism and Necessity: Conflicting Visions of Caste Life

This caste system is like our body. If our body did not have eyes, we could not see. If we did not have hands, we could not work. Without ears, we could not hear. In the same way, we need people of all castes in society. If we are to eat meat, the Butchers are necessary. We need the Sweepers to clean. We need the Brahmans to recite religious lessons.

(a high caste Newar)

These days anyone, even a Brahman, will make shoes. The question of caste is finished. While our work is good, we do not want. . . . When there is no work, there's no money, and then we cannot eat, we want. So whatever the work is, we have to learn it.

(an untouchable)

Caste does not have a single raison d'être for Newars. They declare that caste is good, natural, traditional; they say it exists because order and interdependence are necessary, or because life must have some structure. They claim it was ordained by Hindu kings, as a form of domination, or out of economic necessity. A Brahman suggested that caste exists because someone must remove filth and human feces from the city.

I do not propose to reduce this heterogeneous assortment of explanations to a single, consistent world view, since I believe to do so would distort the irreducibly plural and dynamic reality of Newar experience and thought. I wish, rather, to begin this chapter by charting the most prominent features of two separate Newar visions of the caste world—which uneasily occupy the same minds and political structure—before we turn to the questions of how the tensions inherent in the coexistence of these radically different views of the world may be given cultural form and played out in cultural practices—where form and practice are, in a deep sense, political.

In the most celebrated of these world views, the caste system is a moral, sacred and natural order. As such it has an objective, unalterable, moral form. When Newars know and experience themselves in these terms, they take the principle of hierarchical interdependence as a moral law, an expression of ultimate reality. It represents they way society "must be." In this moral order, each caste and every individual has a role to play. The "moral self" is encompassed in hierarchical interdependence. Some are stigmatized and some are valued, but this is just, since karma guarantees that people get what they deserve, and because the place people have in society reflects their "nature" or biomoral "essence."

Listening to Newars, I detect a deeper, rawer, more urgent vision beneath this one. Co-existing with the concept of hierarchy as natural order, with its imagery of natural kinds, each fit for its own work, there is a vision based on what people most fear—chaos, disorder, violence, the loss of the protection of society, hunger. Out of this fear is forged a vision of hierarchy as necessary. In this vision, the caste hierarchy is justified because it is viewed as the only real alternative to disorder. It does not really matter whether it is "natural" or not, "moral" or not—the question is, does it protect you from danger?

The fear of hunger also shapes the making of concepts of the moral order. Does it feed you? is a primal question. If caste life makes subsistence possible, it has some legitimacy.

Judged in these terms, the caste system is a moral order, a fragile, limited, arbitrary order. It protects people and makes economic life possible. It does not guarantee that the burdens and goods of life are fairly shared, or that people get what they deserve; it has more basic concerns. Of course, the caste system produces much of the disorder that it offers protection from, and puts some at economic risk, too; but this does not make it any less necessary. Some of my informants recognized that the caste system "protects" them from dangers it creates (caste violence), and all were keenly aware that their economic survival could be held hostage by the social system.

I suspect that the vision of necessity is the driving force in Newar discourse about caste; it is shared by high and low caste informants, and seems to be the most basic justification of the system—any order is better than chaos and violence.

The vision of the caste system as a moral order seeks to transform this world of the necessary. The impulse to do this—to ethicize hierarchy—is surely often authentic, and not just an effort to rationalize and mystify.

Most Newars want to believe in a moral world. They want society to embody principle of justice; they want an ethical world. This leads them to seek to reforge reality, to make it ethical—though this may never be an actuality, but only a collective social fantasy. To maintain their vision of a moral order, and yet keep the actual social order—in which they have a vital interest—going, social actors will delude themselves and others in certain ways. For example, it is an objective fact that someone must be recruited for necessary but stigmatizing occupations, and then kept at work in these defiling roles. "Naturalizing" the arbitrary basis of the division of labor by defining groups as having a nature or fate, a being or essence, that matches their occupation, is also effective to some degree. They can be seen as getting what they deserve; this helps justify forcing them into certain roles.

Of course, people see through this, at least some of the time. Even such semi-transparent constructions of reality, however, serve a purpose—people may elect not to see through them. They therefore provide one of the means by which people can "not know" what they know—that they are collectively manufacturing the relations of the caste system, which exclude, stigmatize, and exploit some. In the case of the caste system, this "social repression" of objective reality allows people to have and engage in certain useful practices without violating their belief in a just, well-ordered world (which, after all, is what they want for themselves).

Those who benefit from the system may more often speak of it as natural and moral; but low caste people may also speak of society in this manner. For they, too, have interests to preserve; without stigmatized work they might have no work at all, and would go hungry. Without a place in society, they would be unprotected from human (and supernatural) violence. The way they echo the dominant ideology reflects a desire to preserve what opportunities and safety they have.

At the same time, they may know they are oppressed. As they reflect on the ways they are stigmatized and deprived, low caste people may come to see the caste system as a form of domination (as will some high caste individuals). As I have shown in previous chapters, they respond to their experience of hierarchy with ambivalence and resentment, with equalizing rhetoric, moral fantasies, and critical discourse. They also implode the moral reference group, develop a self-justifying rhetoric of need, and assert "necessity" against the efforts of the dominant ideology to make hierarchy seem a moral reality.

If my informants are any guide, it is not uncommon for a single person to experience caste as natural, as necessary, and as intolerable. From the point of view of those who live their lives in the caste system, caste is a peculiar, unstable amalgam of fear and hope, of politics and morality, of conflicting constructions of reality, sliding along inside the self like tectonic plates, generating profound inner tensions.

Why Caste Exists: Some Newar Accounts

Newars often explain and defend hierarchy by appealing to concepts of *functional* interdependence. Newars are familiar with the myth of separation and interdependence that tells how four social categories (*varna*) sprung from parts of the body of Purusha, the original man. Shudra came from the feet, Vaishya from the thighs, Kshatriyas from the arms and Brahmans from the mouth of Purusha. The four varnas are thus parts of a whole, and society is like a body. Social units are body parts.

Invoking the metaphorical mapping of body and society, Tej Raj, a Brahman, explains hierarchical interdependence in these words:

> "For the country, there are castes; for our body, we have eyes, head, hands, and feet. In this analogy, the Pore sweepers are the feet. If they were to get rich, they would rise up and become like the head. If this were to happen, it would be an obstacle for the kingdom. It would be a disturbance, a confusion, of the order of things. So we must have the Pore to be the feet. More than the feet even, they must be like the soles of the feet.
>
> If you ask why this is, the answer is—hell exists. Our eyes can see hell; this shit all around us [waving his arms], this is hell. It is dirty, disgusting. If there were no Pore, and you and I would have to remove this filth, then we'd be disgusted. It would be repugnant to us. We would not want to touch it. So the Malla kings, and the learned people of long ago, they made the Pore the caste for cleaning. The Pore clean up all filth and waste. If the Pore are people, as I am a person, then if they were to earn much money, if they somehow became rich, then they would not want to touch this filth. They would not touch it, and then it would get worse. And so the rulers of the past decided that the Pore should not be given much money. The Pore are necessary, but they should not be well off. Since the Pore must be poor, whenever the Pore managed to accumulate any wealth, the kings would take it all away. They would be poor again. Yet the Pore don't know how to get angry. They say: "Our wealth has been seized, but what to do; it happens because of the sins of our past lives." They don't know how to fight with the people who take their wealth."

Not essence but force is used here to explain the caste hierarchy. This Brahman does not appeal to concepts of impurity. He does not attempt to "naturalize" the arbitrary *political* and *economic* foundations of the caste order by invoking person-constituting concepts of "substance" that fit certain people for certain functions. It is not the "moral nature" of untouchables to do unclean work; they are compelled to do so. Indeed, they must be compelled—for if they are persons, then they will not want to do this work.

In this passage, we have a Brahman pointing out that the system of functional interdependence requires someone to be on the bottom—to do the dirty work. He accounts for the position of untouchables in pragmatic, political terms. He frames his discussion of force against the backdrop of a common humanity. He says, "If they are people, as I am a person," apparently acknowledging that untouchables are constituted like him, like any other person. He recognizes that he shares a nature with them; it follows that they have the same desires and dislikes. This means they will be filled with repugnance by the dirt and feces they handle as Sweepers. Far from it being their nature to perform demeaning work, it is their nature, like others, to find such work repugnant. They will not want to do this work; they must be forced to do it. By granting them a common human nature, this Brahman poses the political problem: because they are human, like him, untouchable Sweepers could never be content with their role. This is why, in the past, the state used power to force them to work, and reduced them to the poverty that compelled them to labor as Sweepers. It was necessary to oppress them to overcome their desires. Their humanity is what makes it necessary for force to be used to keep them in their place.

The karma theory enters into the picture as a mystifying rationalization. High caste Newars occasionally explain the low status and suffering of untouchables in this life by saying they sinned in previous lives. The karma theory does not blind this Brahman informant to the significance of political and economic realities. He speaks of it as sapping the will of untouchables to resist.

The Brahman is right to recognize that high caste and low caste actors share some of the same revulsions. Many low caste actors would agree.

Some Newars say that a god or a king made the caste system. Others deny this; they do not believe that the deities had a hand in the construction of the caste system. They see it as a human construction. Castes are thought to spring from an original unity (humankind) or two kinds (male and female) and develop into the manifold parts of an interdependent whole. This development of separate castes makes possible a higher order unity—in hierarchical interdependency—that serves economic and religious ends.

"God made and separated the castes. In the beginning, God made only two castes, male and female. When there came to be more people, God and the kings had people do this kind of work and that kind of work. ("Why did castes develop?") "In the past, there were no workers. Long ago, all were one—there was only one caste. Then the makers of shoes became the Sarki caste, and those who sewed clothes became the Damai caste. The makers of iron tools became the Ka:mi caste. Ka:mi is a little caste [that is, a low caste]. The Dya:la [Pore Sweepers, a respectful term for the informant's group] clean; they have turns at temples [where they collect donations and offerings]. . . . And then the Brahmans, the Shrestha [Chathar], and the farmers— they are great, compared to us they are great. Your own caste is great for you. Some had to do daily worship, and these became Brahmans. Those who worked in the fields became farmers. ("What would happen if there was no caste?") "Caste was made long ago. If there was no caste, there would be no work; nothing could be done. The sweepers would be finished. We, who collect and dispose of dirt and filth, would be finished. For this reason, the castes were separated and put in their places. . . . For this reason, we are the sweepers." (an untouchable Pore Sweeper)

This untouchable fears that there would be no work for him if the caste system was abolished. He would lose his livelihood. Notice the use of "great, big" versus "little" to describe the relative positions of castes; the usage seems to suggest a reality of power and dominance. Some Newars say being stigmatized is not as bad as starving.

When asked about the caste system, Newars often conjure it up by reciting the names of castes, giving descriptions of the role of each caste. Castes are assigned a place in the system according to the role they play. Often, the theme of functional interdependence is stressed more than principles of hierarchy or the notion of domination, although these may be noted. When I ask Krishna, the Gatha, "Why were castes made," he replies:

"The Brahmans were devoted to the gods. They taught religious lessons, they told sacred stories, and so they became high caste. The Tantric priests, they performed rites for the gods and goddesses, and for this reason they became priests. The Joshi write the secrets of the horoscope, while the farmers (*jyapu*) work in the fields. We, who are called the Banmala, we gather flowers in the forest, and we offer these to the gods, and take them to the houses of the Brahmans. And those who hammer and forge iron are the Kau, while the makers of shoes are the Sarki . . . and those who make oil are the Sa:mi . . . And the workers in stone are called Stoneworkers, while the dyers of cloth are the Chipa. The painters [of religious pictures] are the Citrakari. In this way, we were all, each and every one of us, given our occupations."

I detect a ritual of *naming* here. To put a name to a group, and to recite the names of groups, making a kind of litany, is a primordial ritual act; it imposes an order on the world. (Reciting a genealogy is another example.)

I then ask Krishna, "Do you think that the caste system is good or bad? He replies, "Your own caste is good for yourself."

("Why?") "Because if you had another's caste, you would not get along with them." ("How would you not get along?") "You would not be satisfied. Your feelings, your spirit, your mind, would not be in harmony with them. Because, now, we—the high castes won't smoke our cigarettes. We smoke their cigarettes. This is low, that is at the same level, they keep that system. The gods did not do this. The deities do not observe the rules of caste. The gods did not make caste. The caste of the deities is all the same."

("How are low caste and high caste different?") "The high know everything. The low don't know anything. ("If there was no caste, what would it be like?") "If there were no caste, nothing would be certain. Caste is necessary. If caste was finished . . . there must be some foundation for our lives. We must do our rites and we must relate ourselves to each other in conformity with some pattern of interaction. We have to marry. And so we must know how to join our lives with others, how to align ourselves with them. So caste is needed."

There is something equivocal about this testimony. It seems to blend the perspectives of "natural order" and "necessity." This means our interpretation has to be equivocal as well, admitting some uncertainty. When Krishna says that "If you had another's caste, you would not get along with them," is he basing this on a concept of a shared nature or essence? This seems to be supported by his remark that mind, spirit, and feeling would not be in harmony with them. This is a highly plausible interpretation, but we cannot be certain of this. Intimate association with members of other castes may produce dissonance and dissatisfaction, but these feelings may reflect either a conviction of difference, based on cultural models of the person, or an absence of the familiar. We can account for feelings of "harmony" in terms of shared experience just as well as in terms of shared essence. In their relationships, people become used to each other; their interactions are sustained over time, making possible a practical mastery of the patterns of interaction, which are embodied as "self." To interact with others on different terms might then be experienced as a loss of self.

Krishna also speaks here of the caste system as making possible a well-ordered life: "If there were no caste, nothing would be certain." Ritual and social cooperation are based on caste. Without the order that caste provides, chaos would result.

To be low in the caste system is bad; but one's own caste is good because it is the means for carrying on with work, marriage, worship, for attaining prestige, for gaining and maintaining self-esteem, and other goods, however restricted these might be by the general societal distribution of such goods. Furthermore, people know themselves in terms of their engagement with the practices and persons of their own caste. The problem of inequality intrudes on self-identity. This makes for inconsistent, equivocal attitudes. Perhaps because his place in the caste hierarchy is low, Krishna argues against the ultimate, moral reality of caste (since the gods do not make or keep caste), even as he proposes that caste is necessary and meaningful in terms of people's lives. He says, "Your own caste is good for yourself." He claims the members of one caste would not get along with the people of other caste: "your mind, spirit and feeling would not be in harmony with them."

The sudden shift from the idea of harmony to specific behaviors that organize social interaction may not require a very "deep" reading. He may mean only that this type of exclusion, of limited and controlled ostracism, makes people feel uncomfortable. These feelings may be enough to explain his comments on not getting along with and not being in harmony with the high castes; if so, we may not need to search for an underlying model of shared essence. He has simply objectified his experience of exclusion, trying to define this experience and give it meaning.

When a high caste person refuses to share cigarettes or food with Krishna, he declares that Krishna is not his equal. This poses a problem of meaning for Krishna. It makes him uncomfortable. He immediately denies the moral reality of caste, saying that gods did not create it, and do not observe it. By saying this, he implies that the exclusionary practices of the high castes are arbitrary.

Newars often describe the caste system in terms of surface behaviors, rather than underlying models. They speak of caste in terms of what they do and what they experience, not in terms of concepts of substance or essence. Krishna's statement may draw on a "deep" model of the person, but we cannot be certain of this, since his statement does not directly invoke theories of biomoral substance or of impurity. Except for the statement about harmony, it stays close to surface, behavioral criteria, to practices ("the high castes won't smoke our cigarettes") and to the distribution of a key social resource, knowledge ("the high have knowledge. The low don't"). This does not mean that Newars do not understand and practice caste in terms of the idea of unifying and differ-

entiating moral essences, composed of coded-substance or states of relative purity. It is only to suggest that the surface forms, which may express
and be constituted in terms of such an underlying model, are significant
in their own right—they add something to the whole process, and are
experienced in terms of their surface features. These experiences may
help charge the underlying model with meaning or emotional significance. The underlying model may not always be active, or it may be rejected or neutralized by one device or another. The distress caused by
being excluded, and the problems of meaning that exclusion poses, may
not be fully answered from a low caste point of view by the cultural concepts of person and justice that rationalize these practices from a high
caste point of view. The low caste interlocutor of culture may reframe
these practices in terms of other concepts.

Perhaps this is what Krishna was up to in this passage. He seems to be
close to "essentializing" caste when he speaks of mind, spirit and feeling,
but he then shifts away from this, when he focuses on specific practices
that exclude him and declare him to be of lower status than others. If
the biomoral theory of coded-substances which underlies concepts of purity and pollution tends to objectify the system—making it a natural reality—Krishna at this point attempts to deobjectify, to declare that caste
is not a sacred, moral reality, since the gods neither made it nor follow it.
He moves caste into the realm of the necessary; it is a condition of life,
and has meaning, but it does not define people in ultimate terms, and
he does not need to see himself as defined by exclusion, as low.

Krishna's effort to deny moral reality to the caste hierarchy does not
mean he does not find meaning in caste. He does—"Your own caste is
good for yourself." This is a key cultural proposition; my low caste informants repeatedly framed their discussion of caste in terms of this
assertion.

What does it mean? It means that low caste Newars respond to exclusion by falling back on the resources of their own caste. They seek to
develop a coherent, unified, self within their own caste community. The
integrity of this self has to be defended from the implications of the
larger caste system. To do this, low caste informants "implode" the moral
reference group: "Your own caste is good for you." They thus affirm the
possibility of finding meaning in caste (as a web of relatedness) while
denying meaning to hierarchy (as a system of inequalities). Low caste
Newars cope with the stigmatizing implications of their position in the
caste hierarchy by *engaging caste reflexively*. They do not simply learn, and
then execute the hierarchical values of the dominant ideology. While
they know the norms of the caste system, and are perfectly aware of the
values asserted by the dominant ideology of caste, they do not need to
share these hierarchical values with the high castes—in the sense of hav-

ing fully internalized them—in order to participate in the caste system. They seek to "recode" the meaning of caste, to participate in the caste system in terms of values they assert for themselves.

Disrupting Hierarchy

Let me return now to Biska, the ritual journey of the god and goddess that I began to describe in Chapter 1. As I made clear, this festival affirms the value of hierarchical interdependence. It presents a legitimating vision of the social order. In a more muted way, the festival also affirms a common bond between all the people of Bhaktapur within the embrace of the caste hierarchy. Yet this is only part of the story. More significantly for my purposes here, the festival incorporates an element of disorder. The threat of disorder haunts the margins of the festival, sometimes surges forward to disrupt the journey of the god and the goddess that should be as inevitable as the journey of the sun, the passing of time. In some ways, these disruptions may actually help lend significance to the vision of order composed in the course of the festival, but their presence also suggests something fundamental about Bhaktapur's discontents. The hegemony of hierarchy is asserted in the face of these discontents. Implicitly constructed as chaos, disruptive challenges to the festival's constructions of order and hierarchy are used to give felt value and reality to the formulations of order and hierarchy that are contested. This "chaos" is contained by assertions of the power, legitimacy, naturalness and sacredness of the social order.[1]

Constructions of order invite counter-constructions, in a kind of dialectic of rhetorics. Legitimation practices face disruption, only to have disruption reformulated as the disorder of chaos, making fear of the unruliness of the masses a motivation for commitment to the social order. There is no closure here, since challenges to order are perennial. I will first sketch in the "construction of order" in the event, and then suggest how this construction invites anti-structure and protest. I take it as an interpretive premise the idea that complex meaning systems are marked by struggles over the cultural resources for meaning construction. Traces of these struggles become part of the meaning system itself.

Recall that the performance of the festival mobilizes and includes many of the castes of the city—Brahmans, Astrologers, members of the craft and farming castes, Tantric specialists and others. Much of this cooperation occurs "backstage" relative to the festival's dramatic acts, and it expresses in practice the hierarchical interdependence that the pageantry of the festival makes palpable in public space.

During the festival, Bhairav, a fierce form of Shiva, is brought out from his imposing temple, and enshrined in his chariot. The god's temple is in a centrally located square; this square marks the boundary between the "upper" city and the "lower" city. When the god is in his permanent temple, and when he is first brought out and placed in his chariot, he is on symbolically neutral ground, but has to be moved into either the "upper" city or the "lower" city. After the deity is placed in the chariot, groups of men and boys from the opposing halves of the city engage in their tug of war with the chariot, each side seeking to pull the chariot, and the god, into their side of the city. The symbolism is of complementary opposition, and of tension within a whole. (Remember that the Sweepers, in a second "tug-of-war," never get to win, not in living memory.)

After the first tug of war in the city's center, the chariot is pulled up and down the main street of the city, through both halves of Bhaktapur. The Brahman priest who traditionally rode in the chariot with the Malla king's sword told me this was so that all the people of the city could come into the presence of the god (for darsana). Most of the year, only initiates, of the higher castes, attend the god in the secret parts of his temple. Bhairav's consort, the goddess Bhadrakali, rides in a smaller chariot during the festival.

After an interlude of two days, the chariot is pulled downhill, into an area outside the city proper and close to the untouchable Sweepers' quarter. The high castes view this untouchable ward as outside "their" city, since the Sweepers' impurity and inauspiciousness define the purity and auspiciousness of the city. The Pore quarter is on the city side of the Hanumante river; on the opposite shore is one of the main cremation grounds of the city. The untouchables are associated with death. The festival contains re-birth symbolism, so bringing the festivities here makes a point. The opposition is of impurity and death versus purity and life.

Untouchables are not allowed to help pull the chariot within the traditional boundaries of the city. When the chariot reaches the bottom of the hill and approaches the Untouchable quarter, they get a chance to participate by pulling on a separate rope. After the chariots of the god and goddess have been brought to a certain point, the men of Bhaktapur struggle to raise the Yasi(n), the trunk of a large tree from a forest east of Bhaktapur; some pull on the eight ropes attached to it, while others prop it up from below with supports. This god-pole had been given "life" in rituals performed earlier in the day. The lowering of the god-pole will mark the end of the old year, and the beginning of the new year.

Recall that in some interpretations, the god-pole is identified with the god Bhairav, and the ropes are identified with eight protective mother goddesses whose shrines encircle the city. Tantric priests hint at the sexual symbolism of this "erection."

The construction of holism is also evident; individual elements (caste communities) are being organized into interdependent wholes. The untouchables get to pull on one of the ropes used to raise and lower the god pole, thus symbolizing their part in the whole; the "message" is that they are subordinate but have a place in the interdependent whole that is Bhaktapur. The festival acknowledges a common bond, since all the separate groups are needed to put on the festival, but each group is encompassed in hierarchical interdependence.

When the festivities at the bottom of the hill are over, the chariots must be pulled uphill. This requires the mobilization of many men (only men pull the chariots). This tests the solidarity of the people of the city—will enough people join together to get the chariot up the hill? Recent trouble getting enough men to raise the god pole and to pull the chariot uphill suggests some withdrawal from the traditional system, although people are enthusiastic about the tug-of-war and other ritual activities. Once the chariots are pulled back up the hill, the procession stops. At this point, the two chariots are bumped into each other—this is interpreted either as a fight, or as sexual intercourse. The symbolism again is of complementary opposition and of tensions within a whole—male and female are opposites, often antagonists, but are united in sexual intercourse. The god's "semen" is distributed to the crowd in the form of leaves.

Now this is a neat package of symbolism. It asserts order and the dominance of the higher castes over untouchables, who are nonetheless "included." The idea of hierarchical interdependence, of caste diversity encompassed in civic unity within the religious and social order, comes across clearly enough. Ideas and images of sex, death, healing, blessing, motivate the symbolism. But something more anarchic partially compromises this unifying, hierarchical symbolism; it is threatened by the collapse of structure on the periphery of the ceremonies. The sense of celebration is marked. People are animated, in high spirits, some are drunk. The atmosphere is one of a certain festive disorder: the streets are crowded, things have been enlivened by the tug-of-war, and there is a general religious uproar. Animals are slaughtered as sacrifices to the god and goddess; masses of people flow and surge around the chariots. Newars do not usually shove or push others out of their way in crowds, and they do not shove here, but they do push in, with a good deal of intensity, towards the chariots, in order to make offerings. The mood is hardly one of disciplined solidarity, of communion, of reflection upon caste interdependence.

Festivals can stir people up, but fail to get them to accept the ideological image of society that the festival dramatizes. The performance may fail to evoke the moral order; or the meaning of the event can be contested. Occasions when festivals fail, are disrupted, or spin out of control, are interpreted as having meaning. For example, when I was in Bhaktapur, the god-pole raised during the Biska festival broke one year as it was being lowered. This was seen as inauspicious; untouchables were blamed. It was said that they tried to take two ropes, instead of the one reserved for them. The implication from a high caste point of view was that untouchables should stay in their place.

Perhaps the untouchables did nothing at all—or if they did, without any sense of the political implications of their actions. My untouchable informants could not or would not tell me. But they could have pulled it off in the chaos of the event, and if they did not do it, the chaos of the event allows them to be blamed anyway. (From where I was standing in the crowd, I could not tell what was going on.) The disorder associated with the festival produces ambiguity, an inability to determine the validity of interpretations; this state of indeterminacy invites meaning construction, since ambiguous events can be interpreted in different ways, from different points of view. This indeterminacy is what makes possible the construction of meanings that are independent of the "ideal" meaning of the festival. These meanings are not independent of the total context of the festival—a context that is always political and moral—but they are independent of the dominant symbolic rhetoric of the festival, which expresses the traditional elite's construction of "reality."

Festivals are times when some of the most basic images of Newar society are evoked for the people who make up that society. Since the values of order, of interdependence, of hierarchy that are displayed in the festival (and give a hegemonic twist) imply their opposites, it is not surprising that suppressed possibilities tend to break out into the festival—disorder, individual unruliness, breaches of hierarchy. They enter the scene by way of contrast. They can be given meaning.

For example, the opposition of the upper and lower town displayed in the tug-of-war with the chariot is also expressed in outbreaks of fighting between young men from the two halves of the city. This is a long standing pattern, apparently going back centuries, and is found in other Newar settlements as well. Now despite the long traditional history of such conflict, some people in Bhaktapur claim this fighting reflects modern political affiliations. The upper part of the city is said to be more Communist, while the lower part is said to have a greater affinity with the Nepali Congress party. Other citizens of the two halves of the city scoff at this, arguing out that there is little empirical basis for it. But it is an interesting belief, even if it may not be based in fact, since it suggests that the traditional opposition is being used to try to come to grips with modern political oppositions. Since both these political parties were outlawed by the government during the period of my fieldwork, a second opposition was set up between Bhaktapur and the national government. The police became mixed up in this, as symbols of the government; since the police try to stop the fighting between parts of the city, each year the young men of the city stopped throwing bricks at each other and started throwing them at the police.

These riots are not fully political, in the sense of being organized to achieve political goals or expressing a conscious, shared ideology. They do not reflect an overt political agenda or ideology. They have political potential. Riot as an expression of anti-structural sentiment is not so very different from riot as an expression of political disaffection. If Bhaktapur's major civic festivals ideally prompted people to identify with the city, or at least parts of it, they also risked stirring up disaffections with the total system.

The fighting suggests the dangerous side of festivals: when people feel resentful, deprived or disaffected—in some sense, incomplete as selves—they may not seek completion in "communion" or in "submission" to the powers that be, but compensation in violence.

Historical and Structural-Functional Interpretations

The antagonism of the city halves during the Biska: festival has been interpreted in a number of ways. There have been historical and structural functional interpretations.

Historical Interpretations

Some have suggested the possibility that the division of Kathmandu and some other Newar communities into two antagonistic halves reflects the historical merging of separate political communities (Slusser 1982: 91). But even if the opposition of the two halves originated in some historical encounter of polities that later combined, this would not explain the persistence of conflict among spatially defined units in Newar settlements, or the fact that the division is found in so many communities. It seems more likely that the division is dynamically generated by the Newar social system.

Structural and Functional Interpretations

Robert Levy (1990) suggests that the "ritually organized antagonism between the upper and lower city halves served to deflect antagonisms from within smaller local areas, particularly between the groups of economically and socially interrelated *thars* in such areas, antagonisms whose overt manifestations would have been considerably more serious in their consequences." The opposition of the two parts of town may also represent a deflection of antagonism away from the traditional elite (some of who are also insulated by the religious nature of their roles).

In this perspective, the conflict between city halves is seen as a displacement of conflict generated within the social system. The conflict originates in a set of social relations, but is projected into urban space as a struggle with the other city half. This transformation makes it possible to disguise or deny the actual bases of conflict in the community, provides a psychological outlet for anger and resentment associated with caste, class and kinship relations, and helps preserve necessary social relations.

Order, Disorder, and the Dynamics of Meaning Construction

The violence that sometimes accompanies Biska: acquires meaning in terms of the general pattern of meaning construction in the festival. A festival such as Biska: is a series of complex performances, and has a range of meanings (see Levy 1990). But, for our purposes, we can focus on the central meaning of the festival—its "message" about moral order. What I wish to suggest is that if we interpret the festival in terms of order, we must also interpret it in terms of disorder.

Meaning from the Point of View of "Order"

Levy (1990) offers this account of the "message" of Biska:

It is possible to tease out of the drama or dramas of the city's various complex symbolic enactments . . . something like a central import or message, a message that is simple and redundantly presented. For Biska: this seems to be something like this: admire and celebrate the civic order. That order may momentarily and frighteningly sway and lurch, but when the city works together—or refrains, really, from not working together, for the task is not difficult—and accepts the traditional directives of the mesocosmic order, it will all hold together; the space and personnel of the city will remain unified both in itself and in relation to the pulse of annual cyclical time. The main danger to civic order . . . is civic strife, the danger of something going awry in the balance of those human forces that constitute the city. (Levy 1990: 499–500)

This is the "message" of the festival from the point of view of order. The fights that break out during the festival show what could happen, what the dangers to the civic order are, and help force commitment to that order: accept the civic order, or live in a state of siege, as groups in conflict rampage through the streets. But other meanings can be found in the way the festival sways and lurches, in the possibility that it will fall apart.

From the Point of View of "Disorder"

Order always invites disorder; the construction of order shapes constructions of disorder. This makes possible an alternative range of meaning constructions in the context of festivals like Biska:. People who feel their lives are incomplete within a given "moral order" may resonate emotionally with the possibilities of disorder. And so the disorder of the festival is not only a reflection of social structure and function, a way of protecting social units by deflecting discontent away from them, but also a way of knowing chaos, of experiencing possible worlds, of exploring multiple dimensions of experience and being, of encompassing and de-structuring a "moral order" that threatens to keep the self incomplete. The "play" of disorder within festivals makes it possible for people to work through the "warring forces" within meaning systems. It permits people to explore their ambivalences—without making the kind of "non-liminal" commitment to alternative moralities, amoralities, or metamoralities that might lead to general social conflict or personal maladjustment. A festival allows polymorphous and mobile valuations of life, self and society—without necessarily requiring dangerous commitments to these.[2] In festivals, people may be able to act out some of their own deconstructions of the moral order they inhabit.

A rejection of the existing social order, protest and rebellion, are among the possibilities implicit in festivals—possibilities that may become objects of commitment in other contexts. If the first order message of Biska: is to accept, admire and celebrate the moral order, this is framed by a "meta-message." The meta-message sets the conditions under which the message applies. The message of disorder is that people must not be pushed too hard or too far, that their essential needs must be met, and that their worth and integrity must be, at least in some minimal way, acknowledged. And if the message of order flows primarily down from the elite to other groups, the message of disorder flows up: the elite are reminded that the rest of society may be prepared, under some conditions, to find disorder more meaningful and sane than order. Thus Biska:, as a dialogical celebration of order and disorder, concerns the fundamental social compact of the city. It shows what the political order is, as a moral order, and shows what the limits of that order are.

The political forces that contend for power in modern Nepal recognize the significance of festivals. During the period of my fieldwork, the national government and two underground political movements attempted to appropriate the festivals for their own ends. To do this, these modern political forces need to displace the local traditional elites. They want festivals to move people to identify with, and support—not the traditional order—but the modern state that each group seeks to control. They seek to introduce their own symbols and ideological visions into the festivals. The government supplies military bands and high dignitaries. The outlawed parties recruit children to carry placards. The government wants to take over mechanisms for defining loyalties, while the parties want to appropriate and organize discontents. Newar festivals supply both with material to work with. It can be argued that the experience of disorder in festivals has prepared Newars to skirmish with the government; it has certainly helped prepare them to be skeptical of the "constructions of order" promoted by the modern state.

Identifying with Society

The limits of exclusion—of constructing differences and hierarchy—are reached when those excluded resist, rebel, or move away. Commitment to a social order cannot be generated by offering social actors nothing but exclusion and degradation. If the integration of a community is to have some basis other than coercion, then the worth of social actors, their common bonds, their deep relatedness as equals, as persons, and all that this justifies them in demanding of society, must be acknowledged in some way, shape or form. To do this, the process of making differences to justify exclusion and create hierarchy must be suspended; affinity will be stressed instead, to create a sense of inclusion that earns support for the social system. Newar festivals reflect the balance of these opposed processes. Far from coalescing into a simple vision of hierarchical order, Newar festivals also express an ambiguous solidarity. Solidarity in this arena is typically an affair of feeling, of mystique, of psychological participation; it is not based on a set of clearly defined principles. It entails feelings of being part of a whole—of being "at one" with others. This sense of unity can be developed in hierarchical or egalitarian ways, depending on the concepts used to interpret it.

Victor Turner's term *communitas* (1969) captures some of the import of these feelings of affinity and connection. It is a useful working label for a large and complex set of socio-emotional states that may move persons to identify with others, with some group, even when the group stigmatizes them. Turner (1969) remarks that some rituals reveal "however fleetingly, some recognition (in symbol if not always in language) of a generalized social bond that has ceased to be." He posits two models, one of structure and hierarchy, the second of anti-structure and equality.

"The second, which emerges recognizably in the liminal period [of ritual], is of society as an unstructured . . . community or even communion of equal individuals who submit together to the general authority of ritual elders (1969: 96)." I think that both models co-exist cognitively all the time, and get tapped not only in rituals, but in riots. The conflicting models may help organize conflict at the level of action. Consider the risks inherent in states of communitas: people may not enter a state of communion, or submit to the authority of ritual elders, but act out, even rebel, moved by a sense of incompleteness, of deprivation.

Hegemony

To maintain their power in Newar society, the dominant castes must reassert hierarchy, suppressing riots and bringing closure to civic rites. This is not done exclusively in terms of the principle of purity; in the context of festivals, hierarchy is established especially through the possession of religious power and knowledge. The high caste elite controls the secret cult and the secret power of the primary gods and goddesses of the city. The equivalence established transiently in relationship to the divine order is easily disestablished by the priests who mediate between the city folk and the sacred order. Brahmans are themselves god-like, since all lower castes will accept food from them.

The connection that would most threaten the caste system would be sentiments of communitas stirring and uniting the poor under the belief that all people were equal, but denied their share of wealth, power, prestige and freedom of action by the high castes—in other words, communitas combined with resentment. The ideal relation from the point of view of the traditional elite would be communitas binding people to their positions in society and to progressively wider units (neighborhood, temple complex, city) under high caste control. In the traditional system, communal feeling—the sense of membership in inclusive social units—is tapped and mobilized in festivals, but also particularized and contained. "Caste consciousness" combined with an acceptance of the principle of hierarchy is threatening to the immediate status quo, but not to the system as a whole. Thus, while the collective agitation for higher status by the Chipi caste in Bhaktapur challenges the present ranking of castes (they argue that they were ranked low in the past by mistake, and demand recognition of their "true" rank) it poses no danger to the caste system. The more properly egalitarian belief that all people are the same is perhaps less of a threat because it does not define a unified group that can act.

These festivals seem organized to elicit communitas, but also to contain it, under the direction of the dominant groups, the Brahmans and the Royal Group of castes. The communitas elicited at each nested level of society commits people to the social system, from lineage to city; the vision of society expressed promises them a minimum of security and satisfactions, that most people would be reluctant to give up. Their place in the caste hierarchy, however stigmatizing, puts them in contact with sacred powers that protect them. Their place in the caste system also aligns with the moral order, against chaos. By controlling the expressive, emotive side of communitas, the high castes can keep it from being united with a political theory of equality and directed against them in a mass movement. The Brahmans in particular can reassert the structure of hierarchy because they represent the sacred-in-the-social. The sacred upholds hierarchy here: those who can contain and embody the sacred cannot be brought easily into the common measure of humanity. Their purity is coordinate with their numinous "power" or "knowledge," but is not the same thing.

As we saw in preceding chapters, however, some low caste informants challenge even this monopoly on sacred knowledge and authority. Hegemony must be actively defended and maintained, because it is continually challenged. It is not only the structure of domination that is defended; I use the term hegemony to refer not only to the cultural fact of domination, but also to the process by which cultural schemata generate and legitimate practices of domination.

High caste control of civic ceremony—a key means of advancing the hegemony of their world view—is not challenged just in thought and words. A second major Newar festival, Mohani, takes place in the autumn. During this festival, late one night, an image of the goddess Taleju is taken out of her temple within the old royal palace (she is the goddess of the old Malla kings) and carried on a circuit of the city. Her priests and astrologers would determine whether she would go first to the lower city or the upper city. While I was in Bhaktapur, her choice of paths, and the power of the priests to determine it, became contested. A mob of men from both sides of the city gathered in front of the gate from which she would emerge. There they would argue, with each other and with the goddess's attendants, doing a bit of pushing and shoving, too, about which side of the city Taleju should visit first, until one side got the upper hand. The Brahman priest of Taleju, who carries her image, was manhandled, and dragged along—one year one way, the next year the other way. These actions radically challenge the traditional religious authority of the Brahmans and upper castes associated with the Taleju temple, and suggest how the power of the traditional elite is fading.[3] They cannot prevent the crowd that pushes and shoves in front of the temple from rewriting the script for one of the most important religious events of the city. The symbolism is not trivial: Taleju, the king's goddess, is appropriated by the masses.

In this case, as in the fights during the other festivals, a dramatization of social and political structure fails. The failure of the performance symbolizes the collapse of structure, and gives expression to forces that are not fully organized by, or coherent in terms of, traditional culture—or at least not in terms of the dominant ideology. These episodes do not express submission to the caste hierarchy, or dramatize the communion of different castes, but rather express sentiments—acted out in an unruly kind of communitas—that challenge hierarchy. Ritual communitas can express and confirm solidarity, but it can also threaten to spin out of control, becoming a force for change and disorder.

A Dialectic of Tensions: Hierarchy and Its Discontents

This dialectic in which the idea of social order seeks legitimation and hegemony, only to be challenged, disrupted, and resisted, reasserted only to be contested once again, in which the celebration of social harmony invites a disordering play that flows from social discontents, where hierarchy and equality dance in their uneasy complementarity, appears to be carried on by other means, in other forms, in other contexts. It has various incarnations in everyday life, and in the models people bring to everyday life. In this section, I will look at the attitudes people bring to their perceptions of other groups. We have here a politics of everyday consciousness, in which constructions and counter-constructions vie with one another quite generally, shaping perceptions of self and other. The ambivalence in Newar life runs deep: it appears more a dialectic of paradox, where nothing is quite settled—no matter what anyone insists—than a dialectic of synthesis, which finds closure in some ultimate mediation.

Thus, while Newars justify the caste system by appealing to the idea of functional interdependence, they may also resent it. For every construction of hierarchy, there seems to exist a counter-construction, and then a counter-counter construction.

Hegemony and resentment are locked together in mutual subversion. Inextricably intertwined processes of domination and resistance propel developments in each other. The men and women who are part of the whole, the social body, may feel they are deprived, depersonalized, exploited and degraded, may express wariness and doubt, may be angry or ambivalent, may even stigmatize and disparage others to whom they are joined in interdependence. Resentment constitutes a way of knowing; it provokes counter-resentments, and these too animate cultural constructions. Far from being seamlessly constituted by a single structural principle—a passionless, incorporeal, bloodless separation of the pure and the impure—the actual constructive awareness of caste life is highly motivated, embodies a range of values, threats, feelings, and antipathies.

Traditional high caste Newars often depict lower castes in morally disapproving terms. A high caste man, asked why certain castes were the lowest, replied "They are very *candal* [a term implying they are untouchable, cruel and accursed]. They are useless. They will do anything. They live in the burning ground and they take the clothes of the dead."[4] High caste Newars often assert that the lowest castes fail to live a moral life; they claim that low caste behavior is not restrained, decorous, modulated by a sense of what is proper. Low caste Newars, in their opinion, lack a sense of honor (*ijjat*). Stereotypes of the low castes include the idea that they are sexually promiscuous and greedy. In addition to being seen as impure, they are viewed as dirty, rude and vulgar.

Distinctions are made. Some low castes are better than others; the indexical occupations provide one basis for making such distinctions. Castes with "clean" occupations are less stigmatized; masons, carpenters, and other craftsman are less subject to such stereotypes than butchers and sweepers. Farmers (*jyapu*) are often stigmatized and stereotyped, but not in the way, or to the degree, on impure and untouchable castes are.

Harsha Bhakta, a high caste informant who thinks that the conditions of life for the low castes have improved, and who says he welcomes the educational and economic gains low caste groups have made, nonetheless retains much of this disapproving image of low caste people.

"The caste system has always been very strict here in Bhaktapur. The caste system was highly developed, and very rigid. Many rules must be observed. Our caste will not eat with the lower castes. We won't smoke cigarettes with them, or share a hookah with them . . . this is very strict, and we have many such rules.

The government has declared that caste does not matter. The high castes did not really care for that. . . . The Pore Sweepers were untouchable from long ago. They scrape shit and clean filth. They are dirty because of this work, but only because of it. After a day of work, they can go clean up. But they do not do that, although they are better off now, compared to the way they were in the past. It used to be that the Pore could only have roofs of straw, and of nothing else. That is no longer true. Now they have cement and plaster houses. It used to be that once in twelve years their wealth would be taken away from them by the king. If they had houses more than one story tall, these houses would be taken from them. In the old days, after the Sweepers had cleaned shit and dirty things, they did not wash their hands. They would even eat without washing. Now after they have collected shit, they wash their hands and they bathe. They use soap. And if they are also clean, what can we say? In the past, there were thirty-six castes. Four *varna* and thirty-six castes. Now there are only two castes—female and male. Although much has changed, the city of Patan is more conservative than Kathmandu, and Bhaktapur is more conservative than Patan. Of them all, Bhaktapur is still the most strict about caste."

Despite his argument that only their occupation makes Sweepers dirty, Harsha also resorts to a concept of "nature" (*swabhav*). It is their actions that he disapproves of, however, and he uses these to infer their "nature." I am not sure Harsha has objectified their "nature" (which he could do by making use of ideological constructions available to him) but perhaps rather sees their "nature" as socially produced, a result of their own actions and customs (which does not make it any less stigmatizing). I base this judgment on our extended discussions; the passage here is equivocal. Even if he here intends to attribute an objective "essence" to low caste groups, I think the social basis of this construction is transparent.

> "The Pore have Pore's nature, Jyapus (farmers) have Jyapu's nature. But the Jyapus of Bhaktapur cannot compete with Kathmandu farmers. Because it is not in their nature. They do not fit into the society here at all. The low have not come up. Because they do not have language. Because they do not have society. They have not changed. Nowadays the children have, a little."

The key statement here is the charge that they do not have "language" and "society." Harsha could assert that the deficiencies he finds in low caste behavior reflect their "essence" or "being." Perhaps this is implied. He may assume that people's capacity to use language and to regulate their social conduct "properly" are inseparable from their "being" or "nature" as caste persons. This is certainly one view of things that saturates "common sense" in caste society. While this may be a "deep" assumption of Harsha's, he does not bring it into focus here. What is stressed is behavior, what people do.

Harsha is more critical of the Jyapu farming groups than of untouchables. He may feel more threatened by Farmers, who are a majority of the population of Bhaktapur, than by the relatively few Untouchables. He thinks the impure and untouchable castes can be dispensed with; others can be found to do their work, or modern technology can be substituted. He finds the disrespect of the farming castes more disturbing.

In the following passage he tells a story with an interesting rhetorical twist to express his dislike of the Farmers; the story tells of how a low caste Butcher prayed to God to give thanks for being a Butcher, not a Farmer.

Since the Butcher caste is lower than Farmers in the caste hierarchy, telling the story adds emphasis to the disapproval expressed—even the lowest castes would not want to be Farmers. By framing his criticism in terms of what a Butcher thought, Harsha repositions the criticism, making it more general: it is not just what a high caste person thinks of farmers, but what people from all stations of life think of them.

> "What a Bhaktapur Butcher once said of Farmers, of their nature, was this: He went to a holy place, and he said, 'God, I would rather be a Butcher than a Jyapu.' For the Jyapus are that low."

I suspect some of the rhetorical force of this statement derives from the tacit understanding that "no one" would "want" to be a Butcher. (Recall the Sweeper in Chapter 4 who said no one would want to be "born low."). If you would rather be a Butcher than a Farmer, you declare that Farmers are so repugnant to you, so unworthy of respect, that you would rather be hierarchically inferior to them than one of them—thereby declaring your moral superiority. Harsha's point as high caste narrator is that if even Butchers dislike the farmers, it is because there really is something "wrong" with them, something that makes them unworthy of social respect. Harsha continues his criticism of the farming groups:

> "It is true that their nature is not good. They abuse us, by saying whatever they want. They say whatever they like. They don't care about others. 'Your mother's lover. Your mother's lover, your mother's vagina,' and so on, they say things like that. 'Your mother's lover,' they make up such sayings. They say bad things. They make that kind of joke, too, they enjoy that kind of joke." [5]
> When my mother is present, I should not say this kind of dirty thing. If my father is here, I should not talk dirt. But they will say anything."

High caste people begin to construct their images of low caste men and women by evaluating surfaces and performances. Low caste bodies are dirty, the work they do is dirty, and they talk "dirt." It is all of a piece. Essentializing or objectifying this is a possible move in high caste evaluations of the low castes. Yet I think the process of stigmatizing low caste men and women is grounded in the characterizations of performative surfaces and interpersonal behaviors that are so salient in the testimony of informants such as Harsha Bhakta.

The association of dirt with low castes is almost obsessive; low caste bodies are experienced as disgusting. In terms of behavior, what is most stressed are inadequate performances; from a high caste point of view, low caste people do not know how to behave in proper, moral ways. They

feel low caste people have not mastered normative patterns of social conduct and uses of language; this is crucial because only the practical mastery of these discloses a full moral self, and thereby confers dignity and
status.

Harsha Bhakta, for example, in the interview I have quoted from, goes
on to say that farmers do not know how to use the verbal registers of
respect (pronouns and special verb forms) in Newari and Nepali. They
commit, he says, the social mistake of using familiar forms to everyone:
they do not know how to "show respect." (I think some low caste actors
bait and provoke high caste actors by violating the canons of status,
overtly or tacitly).

Harsha goes on to speak of another element of the negative image of
low caste people. The high castes see the low castes as sexually promiscuous. "On their own, they like to elope. They like to run away like that:
they elope and secretly marry. Without any hesitation they go. They don't
care. There is no question of honor (*ijjat*) for them."

Harsha sees the low castes as lacking self-control. He thinks they have
sex whenever they feel like it, without stopping to consider their honor
or prestige or calculate the social implications. Harsha also experiences
the low castes as greedy and grasping: "They are low because they
clamor, 'give us our gifts' [donations due them by tradition], and they
grab at what we offer them." Harsha said this with a pained, disgusted
look.[6]

Many high caste informants know little of lower caste people as persons; they do not know them in terms of their biographies. They recognize roles, not individual existence. The holism of the dominant
ideology contributes this; lower caste men and women are seen as members of a functional category. Without certain castes to do certain tasks,
the argument goes, the practical and symbolic life of the city could not
continue.[7] Individuals are valued when they exhibit characteristics that
help maintain this system: when they are "good" representatives of their
caste. But they need not be fully rounded persons for members of other
castes. One Brahman told me that he knew everyone in Bhaktapur.
Asked if he meant Farmers too, he said, no, not Farmers, and added,
"Farmers all look alike to me. They go work in the fields. I don't know
them." Everyone for him meant the high castes. Farmers he assimilated
to their work.

While I think attention to surfaces—to the stigma of dirt—is central
to the process of generating images of the low caste actor, concepts of
impurity are also crucial. This impurity is not a visible, surface characteristic, but rather a quality or state that can be transferred, which makes
persons what they are. In the case of Newars in the castes I have identified as impure and untouchable, their impurity is associated with their

occupation; but their impurity is not generated only by the kind of defiling work they do. While they absorb impurities from their work, they also receive impurity from others. The primary media for such transfers of impurity are food, touch, or any intimate contact.

High caste Newars sometimes depict their relations with low caste Newars in terms of purity and impurity. They speak of interactions in a manner that seems consistent with an interpretation of hierarchy as the dyadic interaction of higher and lower actors separated by relative states of purity and impurity. The pure is superior to the impure, and the pure and the impure must be kept separate (Dumont 1980:43)—that is, the higher actor will seek to keep the pure and the impure separate. Impurity can and does flow in the other direction, from high to low caste actors.

To put it more precisely, higher caste actors are higher because they give, but do not receive, polluted food from the lower caste actors, while lower caste actors are low because they accept polluted food. (Food is not, of course, the only media for such transactions.) The following passage illustrates this logic. Tej Raj, a Brahman, speaks of the way high caste actors receive services from low caste actors, and give polluted food to the low caste persons performing these services. I ask about what needs low caste people have because they are poor, and Tej Raj answers, in essence, that they need to fit themselves into the caste system.

("But because they are poor, they have needs?") "They are poor, and they have no other work. They sweep and clean, and then they will say to the householder, 'Grandfather, I do not have enough to eat. When I have finished cleaning, please give me a little something to eat.' So they will ask. When Sweepers beg like this, the people of the house will follow their conscience, and will give a little money or a plate of rice or a portion of the food prepared for a feast. They will give the Sweepers polluted food [*cipa*]. The Sweepers will take this. Even though they are given impure food, they accept it. They take it, and are happy." (a Brahman)

Up to a point, this Brahman's testimony can be understood in terms of the "opposition" of the pure and the impure. The opposition is not static; it involves transactions and exchanges. What is crucial is the *transfer* of polluted food: the high caste actors dispose of material they have polluted; the low caste actor accepts this. This separates and ranks the two groups.

While I think that concepts of purity and pollution do supply Newars with one model of and for hierarchy, I do not think this model tells us much about how Newars experience hierarchy. It is easy to *disembody* experience and action when we search for structural templates, for conceptual models. While hierarchy may be conceptually formulated in terms of differences in purity and impurity, actors have to live with the consequences of the way they are positioned in the hierarchy. They must cope with the psychological and political implications of concepts of hierarchy; they have to deal with the way cultural models reflect, shape and distort social "reality." Even in this Brahman's statement the words put in a Sweeper's mouth, "I do not have enough to eat," suggest the economic gap that accompanies differences in purity. This gap is experienced. While high caste actors may stigmatize low caste actors as impure because they take polluted food, low caste actors see themselves as acting out of necessity.

Many low caste informants would deny they take polluted food "happily." Some say such polluted food (cipa) is filthy and disgusting; to be forced to eat it is demeaning. They accept and eat such food out of need, not out of a hierarchical turn of mind, and not out of any ingrained sense that this is the way things should be.

The transaction that Tej Raj describes—a Brahman giving and an untouchable receiving—is consistent with Marriott's "dividual" theory of the Hindu person, if what is given and received is conceptualized as containing "coded-substance" (Marriott 1976). While I think this theory accounts for much of what Newars believe and do, it too runs the risk of disembodying experience. The cultural logic that governs exchanges of polluted food in Newar families, where bio-moral substance is continuously blended and differentiated may also govern the practice of giving cipa to low caste actors, but this logic may pose problems of meaning and expose problems of survival for an untouchable who feels forced to accept the leftover food of high caste patrons.

In theory, accepting cipa food from one's hierarchical superiors should not be problematic. In fact, it often is. The stigmatizing, hierarchy-constituting implications of the system are transparent to most actors: if refusing to accept cipa from someone asserts your superiority to them, then accepting their cipa means you are inferior to them. Since this principle has to be intersubjectively recognized for it to have any value for signaling status, knowledge of it cannot be buried away. People's knowledge of the system is expressed, for example, in the way they use food as the medium for status rivalry. A meal may be what Clifford Geertz once called a "status blood bath." If you can force some one to eat with you, you have achieved status parity, or at least an acknowledgment, however qualified and reluctant, of equality. Moreover, if people as players in the social game are often quite cognizant of the stigmatizing implications, they also experience it as degrading, as sickening. In the face of such embodied knowledge and strategic consciousness, ideologues resort to spin control: the negative consequences of the practice may be denied, and positive aspects highlighted.

Theoretically, taking cipa from superiors has value—a person becomes "at one" with the person who is superior, and receives their nurturance and support. In this perspective, foregrounded in some attempts to rationalize it, the caste hierarchy is a nurturing hierarchy. When the idea of accepting cipa from inferiors is foregrounded, however, the meaning of accepting it changes in a radical way. If ingesting a superior's cipa can be metaphorized as like drinking mother's milk, then ingesting an inferior's cipa is like eating dirt or feces. The idea produces disgust and revulsion. Some people internalize this perspective so deeply they have a revealing visceral reaction to finding out they have ingested an inferior's cipa—they vomit.

Untouchables may reverse the polarity of this, and assert that they want to vomit when they eat the cipa of high caste people. This is rhetoric, but it gets a point across. Untouchables find cipa disgusting, too, like high caste people—the difference is that they may have to eat it out of necessity. Many do not seem to find the prospect of eating their hierarchical superior's cipa much better than eating their inferior's cipa. Whether the transactions involve cipa flowing up or down, they are experienced negatively. Eating high caste cipa, they may assert, is not much better than eating dirt or feces. They do not think eating it will enhance or nurture their substance. They say they would not eat it if they were not poor. Robert Levy (1990) quotes an untouchable, a Po(n)—another name for Pore—speaking of the revulsion he feels.

Cipa is dirtier than feces. . . . When we hear that the *sahu* [merchants] have a feast, we Po(n), we poor people who have nothing to eat, go to the houses of our patrons, and take their cipa, the food that has come out of their mouths, their leftover food. They collect the leftover food after they have eaten and give it to us. While they ate they mixed everything by hand, and when they chew the food they drop some of the food from their mouth. They mix and gather that kind of food for us, and we have to eat it. It may even have been on the floor. Their thrown away things are our meal, in which we get dust and hair, and everything. The main point is that we eat dirty food. (1990:385)

At the very least, we can dismiss the idea untouchables are always "happy" to eat cipa. Notice the stress on being poor; eating cipa is what "poor people with nothing to eat" must do.

Low caste informants are in the position of responding to the stigmatizing images of them, as well as to their relative lack of access to economic and other resources.

"Just as doctors have to clean when they perform an operation, so do we clean. Our caste has to handle dirt. A doctor has to touch blood and pus while cutting into a wound, and he, too, has to clean everything that is dirty. [An untouchable Sweeper]"

Here the stigma associated with being a Sweeper is countered with the observation that high status modern physicians also handle impure materials. Asked how he feels about the concrete rules (not being able to enter a high caste house, share food, and so on), he responds:

> "My heart is not uneasy. This is the way it has always been for me. My caste is important for me. Your caste is important for you. The Brahman's caste is important for the Brahman. There is no worry in being part of your own caste. In this [discrimination by high castes], there is no suffering (*dukha*).
>
> We have to work. If there is not enough to eat, we get weak. Only this is suffering (*dukha*). If there's no work and we can't eat, we won't be strong, our stomachs won't be full. Yes, we have to work, to eat, to drink. No work, pain, nothing to eat, pain. Going hungry, this is suffering. . . . Everyone is the same. Those with money, the high caste, the shopkeepers, they have money. All the farmers have much money. They are not hungry. They have paddy rice and they have parched rice—they have everything. Brahmans have money. I don't have anything. I am a body with nothing, and so I suffer. We don't have rice. We have suffering.
>
> ("They sometimes say that the Dya:la [the respectful, polite name for informant's caste] are impure. When that is said—[He interrupts])—"I don't get angry.
>
> ("Why [not]?") "Because it has been so from long ago, and so I do not get angry." (a Sweeper)

Note that anger is evidently the responses he expects me to expect, the response he perhaps expects in anyone. He moves quickly to neutralize it—treating anger not as justified, but a dangerous emotion. I imagine anger may be a threat to his way of reconciling himself to social reality: anger destabilizes his moral adaptation, and must be overcome by fatalism before it becomes an issue in the social scene, disrupting an equilibrium with society as vital to him as it is oppressive. More broadly, an effort is apparent in his words here to limit comparison of the situations of different castes: "My caste is important for me. . . . The Brahman's caste is important for Brahmans." This is a defensive maneuver, a "sealing off," a contraction, of the reference group. Would the informant insist there was no psychological pain—no *dukha*—in his situation, as compared with that of high castes, no deprivation, if he did not experience such deprivation? He seeks to maintain a certain perspective on this by pointing out that real suffering is absolute deprivation—hunger.

By emphasizing the solidarity and significance of one's own caste, informants downplay rank—and so neutralize some of the implications of the caste hierarchy. One does not have to take the point of view of the "whole" in evaluating self—one can adopt the point of view of a "part," of one's own group. From a personal point of view, this *implosion* of the reference group (a shift from the perspective of the "whole," the system of ranked castes, to "part," one's own particular caste) establishes an equivalence among otherwise ranked castes—castes are ranked in relationship to each other, but what is important, informants suggest, is their place in your own life. Every one's own caste is important to them. A caste is a vehicle for living a life; there is no point in comparing and ranking them, since every caste permits its members to live their lives.

He invokes necessity to justify his life and actions. Brahmans and farmers have money and rice; they do not go hungry. He fears hunger. He lives in a world of raw, naked need. The dominant ideology of hierarchy is largely meaningless in this world.

When he says he does not get angry because his caste is impure, he explains that this is because the caste system began long ago. He wants, I think, to distance the threat to himself, and justify his participation in the system. He prefers to see caste as an unalterable feature of the social world. He has not internalized the values of the dominant ideology; these are simply irrelevant. The caste system is simply a fact of history and tradition; it is an imposed order. He does not need to justify it in terms of the dominant paradigm. He does not feel compelled to respond with indignation or action, either—the caste system exists outside the scope of his powers. I think Kancha resents the system; but he thinks resentment is futile. Being angry does not feed you.

Kesar Lal, from the "impure" Jugi caste, shows more anger. I ask him about to account for the existence of the caste system.

("Why was caste made?") "We did not make it. This was made by King Bhupatindra Malla [a medieval king]."

("Do you have pride in your own caste?") "No."

("Why not?") "That is not necessary, this is not a necessary thing."

("Is it good or bad that caste was established?") "We have to say good. We have to go on carrying our own worries [or troubles]."

("In your opinion?") "Although I don't like caste, I did not make it. It is a thing from long ago, it is not mine. If it was made nowadays, then we could fight and say "Why are you doing this to me?" It is a thing from long ago. So even if we shouted against it, we would not win. There is nothing we can do." (a Jugi)

Kesar Lal perceives caste as unnecessary and as unchosen. It is not self, not part of his own nature or being. "I did not make it. It is a thing from long ago, it is not mine." Caste is not of his making; it is something done to him. He experiences it as an imposed order. This is implied by the rhetorical question "Why are you doing this to me?" The question gives the grounds on which he would challenge the system if he could; but it was made long ago, and it is futile to struggle against it. "Even if we shouted against it we would not win." Note also how he proposes the necessity of splitting his attitude into a public face and a private attitude: "We have to say good. We have to go on carrying our own worries." Although more angry in word, tone and demeanor than Kancha, Kesar shares a feeling of powerlessness. "There is nothing we can do." His powerlessness is a fundamental reality: to survive he must find ways to live with inequality.

We can end this chapter with a sort of parable about the relationship of economy, purity, and resentment in Newar caste life. The parable puts the shoe on the other foot; it repositions positioned subjects. Asked about the relationship of money and caste, a Brahman informant told the following anecdote. A high caste family accepted a loan from a much lower (but still water acceptable, "pure") caste. This family then invited members of the high caste family to a feast. At the feast, boiled rice was offered to the high caste people. "They looked at each other; but because they needed the money, they ate." The next day friends saw them bathing at the river. Asked why they were purifying themselves, they replied, "Last night we ate shit."

Chapter 6
The Indian Untouchable's Critique of Culture

To expect untouchables to live in an unequivocal world is perhaps to expect the humanly impossible. People who have to eat do not always concern themselves with intellectual consistency. They may not care if their views are rational or coherent. Bring on the food, they may think—even if it is "mixed with dirt and hair," "dirtier than feces," even if accepting "the food that comes out of other mouths" stigmatizes and declares one's inferiority. We are poor, they will say, so we have to eat it. Not intellectual coherence, but pragmatic necessity may reign supreme for them. Living lives of quiet and unquiet desperation, they do and think what it takes to live.

High caste actors draw contrasts between what they are and what untouchables are. In doing so, they construct a "crushing objecthood" for low caste actors (Fanon 1967): exclude, distance, stigmatize, and subordinate them. In ideology, in everyday attitudes, we can see such a process of constructing an identity, a nature, for the untouchable: as dirty, filthy, impure, depraved, as some one who "must have" sinned in a past life. We might dispute the cultural basis of the identity "given" untouchables by high caste actors, debating whether it is a social personality mentally leveraged into social existence by the opposition of the pure and the impure, or an identity framed conceptually by ideas of a biomoral nature of coded-substance, or a typification of the "other" scraped off the concrete surface of the stigmatizing roles they play in cultural life, or all of these, but agree that it is an identity culturally constituted.

For many high caste Hindus, the untouchable embodies the other. What then are untouchables to themselves—both other and self?

Self-contradiction, as in the way Krishna both rejects and affirms hierarchy, places himself within it and beyond it, may be unavoidable. Low caste actors often have an ambivalent multiple consciousness of self and world; they are part of, but not part of, the dominant culture that constructs them as other. They must be seen in terms of their contradictions, in terms of the quandaries they live.

No doubt, untouchables sometimes fall into the trap of embodying the other in their own eyes, may see in themselves what high caste actors see, may let high caste ideology guide the formation of self-concepts. But if untouchables are absolutely constituted out of culture, how do they sometimes come to reject this second nature, and seek to alter self and society, reform culture, and emancipate self from external and internal constraint?

Unless we imagine that persons do not need culture to address the most basic questions of existence and self-identity, that human selves do not find themselves challenged by the way society defines them, we must address such questions. The source of their own cultural identity, the basis of their critiques and resistance, may also be issues for those untouchables who pursue social and self-emancipation. Fanon (1967), for one, makes clear that these are key questions: people do not magically stand free of the cultural attitudes that stigmatize them, but respond to the threat, the challenge, posed. Confronted with the images others hold of them, they do not just internalize, or just resist: they internalize and resist. Rather than seeing the untouchable as born a creative resister in the cradle, or passively created by the dominant culture, we need to see how they struggle to achieve identities and open up cultural spaces for themselves. Almost unavoidably, any untouchable as an individual self is inhabited, haunted, subverted, by the high caste, collective version of himself, even if, even as, this image of self is rejected. This is the dialogue with culture that untouchables are—it defines them, as other to caste Hindu and other to self, and they respond, redefining themselves, re-imagining culture and self.

Untouchables identify with and struggle against meanings they embody for others; they project themselves into ideology and into critique, finding identity in both. However, whatever critique of caste ideology the untouchable makes, that critique develops within a cultural self that ideology helps constitute and shape, or that it subverts and threatens, perhaps having all these relations to self at once. The critique is critique from the inside, from within self, from within a culture, in intimate ways.

I think this is true—up to a point. In this chapter, I want to pursue this line of inquiry, and also reverse its polarity. While I will reflect on the way the untouchable—indeed, any member of any impure caste—is made to embody the other in "Indian" culture, I will also discuss the way the untouchable treats the caste Hindu as their other. Doing so, untouchables—defined in part by the opposition of pure and impure—define who they are in opposition to their collective definition, in opposition to "the Brahman," the "Hindu," the dominant order and its ideology.

They formulate a critique of the dominant culture that constitutes them as its other.

In this chapter, my aim is to use what I learned from low caste Newars to "read" the discourse of Indian untouchables as a critique of caste culture. Perhaps they provide keys that will give us wider insights. This untouchable critique has been recorded in several important works, notably Mahar (1972), Joshi (1986), and—especially important for this discussion—Khare (1978, 1984) and Freeman (1979). Since I must interpret from somewhere—interpretation "from nowhere" is not an option, for we all come from somewhere to the understandings we have—I will mobilize insights from several Western theoretical traditions to seek an illuminating engagement with untouchable thought and feeling.

My stance is deconstructive, at least in part. Like many others exasperated by this term's misuse and by excesses associated with it, I have at times wished it would go away—but I find I need the concept, or something like it, to sustain a necessary project: to conduct multiple interpretive readings of multiple indigenous "readings" of Hindu-Indian culture, where such indigenous "readings" radically contradict each other, while also suffering from radical self-contradiction. In a certain sense, the untouchables I seek to understand have a deconstructive stance towards "Hindu" culture. Untouchables often subvert normative and dominant interpretations of culture. They question the ethical, ontological, and existential status of key cultural constructs; they endeavor to examine the way these are produced and understood, taken up in life and put into practice. They take pieces of culture apart and reassemble them, amending and supplementing culture in the process, giving a "spin" to symbols and meanings that they lack in the dominant community.

Of course, such readings—as moral and political discourses—contradict each other. We now envision culture as contested, as well as shared. But people efforts to invest—or at least inflect—symbols with moral and political meaning may also bring together incommensurate interests and perspectives. The grounds on which untouchables dispute the dominant ideology are often equivocal. The caste system generates such self-contradictions: a person who does not want to be lower than others may want to be higher, and the person who resents the superiority of higher caste may also resent efforts by those lower to claim equality with him or her. People have interests in emancipation and interests in domination. Moreover, untouchable and high caste actors alike find identity within culture. When they seek to redefine themselves, they draw on culture, as they do in pursuing their conflicting interests. There is no unequivocal closure to this process, at least not about caste. Even while rejecting caste and subjecting its cultural underpinnings to critical scrutiny, the critique of the culture of caste is based in culture; it cannot filter out all the elements that help constitute hierarchy, cannot subject everything at once to effective conscious critique. The critique of hierarchy virtually always, I believe, incorporates hierarchical premises in itself, which tend to permit equality, protest, critique itself, to be restructured back into hierarchy, muting their force, often effectively encapsulating them.

Moreover, as critique supplies a surrogate or alternate ideology—a "counter-ideology" of the kind Owen Lynch (1969) has documented among the Jatavs of Agra—this too becomes subject to critique. The low caste thinker formulates culture-as-critique, and generates a minority ideology that faces critique by the high caste actor who seeks to defend his "culture." Both sets of actors look for contradictions in each others' cultural productions, and both discourses involve self-contradiction. This tempts the analyst seeking a unified, singular culture to construct a coherence for culture that it may not possess. This is especially a problem in conceptualizing non-dominant "meanings" that may co-exist in the same mind with a dominant ideology—the temptation may be to overlook them or dismiss them, to not conceptualize their significance. This is not justified, since "conflicting" schema and "non-dominant" ideology can have sociological and psychological significance, and may be used by different actors to produce different "readings," different understandings, of the culture they "share."

The caste Hindu and the untouchable may "have" the same culture, but "read" it in different ways, and animate it as a vehicle for thought and life in radically different ways. Their readings overlap, but also diverge. Shared concepts have contested meanings in "Indian" culture; we need to explore both the shared forms and their disputed significance. We should certainly not dismiss the untouchable's point of view, or fail to assess its sociological and psychological significance because it is self-contradictory and equivocal, or because it is often restructured "back into" the hierarchical institution and ideology from which it emerged, reflected on, criticized and resisted more or less strongly. Ultimately, for social actors, culture lacks the intellectual coherence, the consistency and rationality given by a single master principle such as Dumont postulated for Indian culture, and out of which he constructed *Homo hierarchicus.*

The world of caste is a world of oppression. Caste status condemns many to a life of fear. It exposes them to deprivation. The meanings they impose on caste-bound life, and the ways they find meaning in it, are not reducible to the various ideological forms of caste hierarchy, with which anthropologists have been so concerned. Much effort has been expended on defining the form of hierarchy; much less effort has been made to understand the total experience of the caste world.

Nonetheless, some important work has been done, and can be compared to the Newar material, giving us a wider view of the problems of meaning posed by life in caste society. Several areas seem especially worthy of further exploration and interpretation.

First, the world of caste is a world of dissimulation. "Distorted communication" based on denial of mutual recognition (this in Habermas' sense) arguably stands at the heart of the caste system. Low caste people must act as if they do not know themselves in any other terms than those given by the hierarchical model for an interaction, disguising whatever dissident thoughts they may have; they must cast themselves in the roles and social persona assigned them.

Of course, a concept of "distorted communication" poses the problem of what "undistorted" communication would be. Habermas (see McCarthy 1978) has discussed this in philosophical terms; here, I mean that low caste people clearly possess premises for interaction in their cultural repertoire other than the ones given in dominant hierarchical models; they claim frequently that they would prefer to act on these alternatives if it did not expose them to danger or deprivation. This possibility is rarely open to discussion or negotiation with high caste actors, however, except on those relatively rare occasions when low caste people have power over high caste persons (which is often temporary coercive power which brings on dissimulation, evasion and deception on the part of the higher caste actors). Moreover, while low caste internalize as self-images the images of them held by dominant groups, their self-image is not simply the product of this internalization, but include much other material besides—derived from family life, friendships, or from their "counter-ideology" (Lynch 1969). A high degree of self-contradiction, of dissimulation, is thus typically involved in their social presentation of self in hierarchical interactions. Untouchables, in particular, must be what they are not, and do what they do not wish to do—their desires and sense of self are overwritten, unheard. Moreover, they must adopt the language and engage in the interactions and communicative process, in which they are not fully heard, but are defined. If this does not qualify in some sense as "distorted" communication, I do not know what does.

If we ask, what is the context of this? I think we are led to the obvious conclusion. The world of caste is a world of violence and deprivation. In this context, the language of hierarchical models is often used to articulate not the consensual grip of hierarchical models, but the experience of domination, violence, and deprivation those models formulate, organize, and legitimize, because it is the only language permitted, and the key to surviving. I would argue that low caste people often appropriate the language of hierarchy, give it a different "spin" in their own minds, define how it is to be interpreted with tacit or explicit metacommunications—ranging from an exaggerated obsequiousness to a fatalistic shrug and declaration that "We have to eat" to irony—and so inflect the idioms of hierarchy to express their sense of deprivation, powerlessness, and resentment.

Low caste individuals and communities have other ways of dealing with the stigma and oppression they face, and with the dominant ideology of hierarchy. Khare (1984) shows that they may distinguish the role of the untouchable ascetic vs. caste-oriented ascetics and renouncers as a way of "liberating" some of the root concepts of the South Asian cultural tradition. In their efforts to work out a critique and counterideology, they lay claim to the key symbol of the renouncer (Khare 1984).

Another area that calls out for further exploration and interpretation is the sexual politics of caste. A gender hierarchy is "locked into" the caste hierarchy: what are the dynamics of this?

"Distorted" communication and the practices of domination are not passively accepted by low caste people. The critique of Hinduism by untouchables (Khare 1984) is a cultural critique of culture. Untouchables attempt to work out a critical language for their cultural experience under the cultural and political hegemony of caste, and seek to develop a "counter-ideology," for themselves (Khare 1984; Lynch 1969). The critique and counter-ideologies are not "outside" of culture, but a dynamic aspect of it. The critique of culture is one of the most important cultural practices in any culture. It should not, I believe, be set aside as residual.

Pragmatic strategies for living—what Khare (1984) terms the "pragmatic ethos" of low caste groups—constitute a language of necessity that disputes the dominance of the language of hierarchy. Furthermore, the low caste rhetoric of the ideal—as moral fantasy, as an element of critique—constitute a language of the ideal that disputes the dominance of hierarchy.

Thus what we find in untouchable minds is not a single language, hierarchy, based on a single master principle, the opposition of pure and impure, but a tangle of languages with which actors interpret the world in a variety of ways. Since this is the case, we cannot, I think, explain the dominant role of the language of hierarchy in the dominant ideology of caste society by arguing that this language determines what people know and experience, what they think and how they perceive the social world—all these other languages are "good to think," too, and render social experience intelligible and meaningful. We must, I think, see the language of hierarchy as privileged in terms of the cultural production of the value and legitimacy of those political and economic structures with which the ideology of hierarchy has co-evolved historically. Dumont and others approach the ideology of hierarchy as a "structuring structure," which gives form to social life, but it is also a "structured structure," which takes form from other structures (Bourdieu 1977). Thus the language of hierarchy is not a language unto itself, something that develops in splendid isolation from politics and history, unfolding in passive minds like a vine in a garden. It is also a veiled language of power. As such it dissembles, disguising the arbitrary foundations of a social order, masking the workings of power even as it asserts and justifies domination. It helps discipline consciousness since—"like a garrison in a conquered city"—it recalls the possibilities of violence constitutive of the social order.

Dissimulation and Violence

We have seen several examples of dissimulation. In the preface, I showed how Mahila acted one way in public, another way in private with me. In Chapter 4, we saw how efforts are often made to conceal one's caste background by taking high caste names and other tactics. Such dissimulation does not always have to represent a conscious policy; sometimes dissimulation is deliberate, and other times represents the activation of cultural knowledge in frame-sensitive or context-sensitive ways. In these frames, as actors participate in hierarchical interactions and practices, they may accept the structuring of behavior and the disciplining of consciousness entailed by the context. Doing so, actors may not always actively "know what they know"—that is, they are not acting on knowledge and values they possess consciously (and can articulate) in other settings, where they may be overtly critical of caste, but on the basis of knowledge and values relevant to the particular hierarchically structured context with which they are engaged. Other knowledge and values are kept "out of frame"—and perhaps "out of mind"—for the duration of the interaction.

We need an example. I will give one from a study of caste life that is a useful antidote to the formalism and abstraction of many anthropological studies of caste systems. This work takes us beyond the analysis of the structure and ideology of caste society; the analysis of the dominant ideology is surely a necessary task, but not the only necessary task. We need also to explore the actions and experience of actors within structure and ideology.

James Freeman's intimate and disturbing life-history of an Indian untouchable does this. While the untouchable who is the focus of the study is not in the least "representative" of all untouchables—many of whom would condemn his acts and mode of life—nonetheless his story of his life reveals much about what is involved in living a life "at the bottom" of caste society.

The untouchable's name is Muli. He is a member of the Bauri caste, and he lives in a twenty caste village on the outskirts of the Indian city of Bhubaneswar, the capital of Orissa in eastern India, far from the Kathmandu Valley. Yet like Mahila, although the Bauri are not Sweepers, Muli lives in a segregated ward, apart from the high caste neighborhoods, of the village.

His caste, the Bauri, live on the edge of starvation as well as at the bottom of the caste system. Only 20 percent of the village, according to Freemen, "live comfortably, without fearing starvation" (35). Muli's family belongs not to this group but to the worst off: the 20 percent who continuously face the threat of starvation, "lacking both food reserves and cash to pay for even the cheapest of medicines." Muli has faced starvation in his life, and recalls his childhood "as a time when he was always hungry." Mostly landless and dependent for subsistence on immediate earnings, the Bauri of Muli's village have been slow to learn new skills and acquire jobs in new sectors of the economy because they do not have the resources or savings to live off while they get training or seek new employment.

High caste villagers stigmatize the Bauri in many of the same ways high caste Newars stigmatize those from impure and untouchable jat, and justify their caste standing using many of the same concepts (e.g., untouchables must have done something wrong in previous lives, are inherently polluting, are polluted because of their occupations) (Freeman 1979: 50). Like low caste Newars, Bauri resent their treatment and reject high caste concepts of the caste system (52). While they often act in conformity to the rules of caste, they also confront and challenge high-caste actors. "A Bauri insultingly tells a Brahman who cheats him that if he is so greedy for the Bauri's property, why doesn't he also eat the Bauri's excrement?" The Bauri are not always prepared to admit that caste differences have any reality in cultural terms (as the separation of the pure and impure). One of Muli's friends tells Freeman that "the only difference" between the Bauri and the largest of the higher castes is that the higher caste has more money.

Freeman (1979:3) describes the first time he saw Muli. A "gaunt forty-year-old with betel blackened teeth," Muli was "sitting in the dusty road in front of one of the small thatched roof tea shops in the village, with his glass and saucer placed conspicuously beside him—a silent signal to the shopkeeper that an untouchable wants to buy some tea." Three men sit on the benches in the shop, drinking tea and gossiping. The ten-year-old boy whose job it was to refill tea cups ignores Muli for several minutes, and then addresses him in insulting and offensive language, asking him what he wants. Muli points to this cup, and when he gets his tea, pays the boy who has so sharply defined him as an inferior: "from a proper distance," Freeman writes, Muli "dropped two coins into the boy's outstretched palm." He drinks some of his tea—obtained through this ritual of abasement. When he wants to leave, he must continue with the ritual performance that defines him and mediates his social existence: "Suddenly he stood up and shuffled off, crouching to show respect, so that as he passed by the men in the tea shop his right hand trailed in the dust." Clearly, Muli knows how to show deference and to display his own status. Elsewhere, however, he mocks high caste pretensions, and portrays them as unworthy of respect. He knows how to ridicule, and even devises strategies for turning the tables on the high castes by making them dependent on him.

Muli is skeptical about the purity complex. Freeman writes that

Muli's belief in the concept of ritual pollution, applied only to limited situations. While he believed that a corpse polluted immediate relatives, he ridiculed the idea that Bauris pollute higher castes, and he even questioned whether higher-caste people themselves really believe it, since he saw them disregard such notions when they became inconvenient. (Freeman 1979:378)

Such attitude towards high castes, and the images and experience that nurture this skepticism, represent knowledge and values; but not the knowledge and values expressed in crouching in front of high caste actors. Does Muli experience but conceal this other knowledge of caste life as he crouches before high caste people? Is this knowledge active in his mind as he drags his arm in the dust to show "respect"? Does he conceal his attitudes towards caste in the way he might conceal amusement by putting a hand to his mouth to cover a smile or laughter? Or does he conceal this knowledge also from himself—and practice a form of self-deception?

It may not, of course, be a matter of either-or. An untouchable may crouch and think how much he resents the caste system—humans can do things with irony. Dissonant or dissident knowledge may be active in the way an actor experiences or evaluates a situation, may inflect the meaning of an interaction. But I suspect if such knowledge is present and active too often or too overtly it would threaten the frame of hierarchical interaction with dissolution.

Now, untouchables might not want the frame for their interactions with high caste actors to dissolve in this way, since it might expose them to violence or deprivation. Despite changes in law, despite modernization, despite reform movements, the world of caste continues to be a world of violence and deprivation for multitudes of untouchables (Joshi 1986).

We have seen that low caste Newars fear the loss of employment; they also fear reprisals, economic and physical. The regime of fear and violence is even more severe in parts of India, where more than 10,000 violent attacks on untouchables per year have been reported; even more no doubt go unrecorded (Joshi 1986:99). In fact, as untouchables in India break down barriers of discrimination and break out of the place assigned them in society, the incidence of violence against the more than 100 million untouchables in India seems to increase (Joshi 1986:2).

Thus, the untouchable's world is not only one of discrimination, but of intimidation. Where high castes have power over low castes, caste relations are ultimately enforced with beatings or economic sanctions, and in extreme cases by murder or massacre (Joshi 1986:99). The sense of responsibility untouchables sometimes exhibit is the product to a moral code, to be sure, but also reflects a fear of being beaten or isolated. Their desire not to "pollute" others may be voiced in the idiom of impurity and sin (*pap*), but they are sensitive to this because they are sensitive to the structures of violence and deprivation that constitute their world. In my experience, low caste people will often follow up the statement that it is a "wrong" or a "sin" to pollute others or violate the rules of inter-caste contact with a statement that they will be beaten or sanctioned if they do so. Their moral intuitions have objective social and political, as well as cultural and psychological, origins.[1]

Pragmatic Strategies of Living—The Idiom of Necessity

As part of their commentary on their lives and practices, Kancha and other low caste Newars often said: "We have to eat." We should take this both literally, and as a critical statement. It defines the idiom of necessity. They have to eat, and so are forced to do much that they do not want to do; this is a fact, but also coercion that robs them of freedom, a violation of what ought to be. Reality is what it is, and shapes their engagement with caste practices—their words acknowledge this. By saying, "We have to eat," however, they also declare that they should not be forced to base their actions and lives on brutal necessity.

The realities are stark. At one point, Muli's family was eating one meal every other day. No one would loan them rice. They dug up roots to eat and stole yams from fields. His wife took to "selling" berries, which Freeman observes is a slightly disguised way of begging. "Buyers exchanged rice for berries, knowing that the seller was poor and probably starving" (220).

The idiom of hunger complements the idiom of purity in South Asia. Can you have the structures and practices we find in South Asia, based on the opposition of the pure and the impure, without power and desperation? The idiom of hunger gnaws away at the cultural coherence given in the idiom of purity; where the analyst can enter into an abstract universe, the social actor confronts a world that is often desperately concrete. The primal language of this concrete world is hunger, spoken before, and around, and through the idiom of purity, which is—for many—only a supplement, a deformation, of the idiom of necessity.

Perhaps this is not easy to see, although it should be, since low caste actors call it to our attention. Untouchables like Kancha invite us, urge us, to see their actions not solely in terms of the dominant cultural code, but in terms of their experience of having to do what it takes to live. What a behavior counts as, what it means, in terms of the purity complex, and the meaning it has in terms of their struggle to live, are often radically different.

Low caste actors ask us to do what they do—to reinterpret their conformity, to translate it into the idiom of necessity, the language of pragmatic survival strategies. They cue us, but it is easy to miss these cues if we are not sensitive to the ways shared practices can have different meanings. If we grasp the indigenous meanings of the purity complex, we may be tempted to think we have an adequate account "from the native's point of view" and fail to respond to cues about alternate interpretive models for actions constituted in terms of the opposition of purity and impurity. Since we already understand these actions in terms of other indigenous meanings—which we have had presented to us, or constructed ourselves, as the "culture" that accounts for those practices— we may overlook interpretive possibilities that mean much to the people we wish to understand.

With untouchables, we may have to "translate" the meaning of their conformity to caste rules into the terms and concepts they themselves use to interpret it, which give a different "spin" to things. We can only do this by paying very close attention to the fine-texture of their communicative practices—and by not giving in to the temptation to ignore their inflections of the language of domination. It is easy to privilege the dominant ideology, to take it too literally, and grant it monopoly status as the foundation of cultural reality and world view. Untouchables know and articulate it, but also inflect, question, and reinterpret it. We should not stop with the way they "share" hierarchical meanings and fail to examine the way they dispute those meanings, giving a one-sided account of a "culture" that is constituted in multiple ways by warring forces of cultural production. For many untouchables, the language of their experience is the language of necessity, of what you have to do to survive. They find the coherence and rationality of their actions in this. Thus, when low caste actors seem to "speak" the language of purity and impurity in their acts, they may really be "speaking" the language of necessity. Their acts have more than one possible interpretation, because they have more than one interpretive language; thus we must be prepared to "translate" back and forth—rather than accepting things at face value. After all, untouchables in their more reflective commentary give us the key for this translation. "We have to eat." Thus, I would argue that many low caste actors voice their self-knowledge—often kept "out of mind," lost in the fluctuating awareness/unawareness of the political unconscious—of deprivation and violence through their conformity to caste rules, which they interpret and evaluate in the idiom of necessity. They conform to the code of behavior of the purity complex, but what their conformity "means," what it "says," if we interpret in terms of the totality of their experience, is something like "Behave so, or you won't eat. What will people think? You might be beaten; you might not get work. You will go hungry."

Let us expand our inquiry here, and bring in yet another case, another set of untouchable voices. This time we will go to Lucknow, the capital of Uttar Pradesh in northern India, where R. S. Khare did fieldwork with the Chamars, an urban untouchable group. Khare's work regrounds our understanding of untouchable culture and life. It compels us to deal with the ideas untouchables have of, and for, themselves, even as we try to see how they exist in and through the ideology of other groups. Khare's insightful study reveals untouchable identifications and dialogues with cultural symbols and meanings. Dialogues proposing "what they are," flow from their own experience and rebound from high caste perspectives, propelling some Chamar into a dialogue about what might be, and a critique of what is.

Khare explored cultural consciousness in three different Chamar neighborhoods in Lucknow, each one embodying a somewhat different aspect of Chamar experience. In one, many residents held highly desirable jobs, not just for Chamars but for most of the city's population, including jobs as educated professionals, as skilled workers, and as government employees. Shopkeepers and vendors rounded out this relatively prosperous community. In contrast, in the second Chamar neighborhood, the greater part of the working inhabitants were day laborers, leather-workers, and small vendors. Not only did they have lower paying and much less prestigious employment, but inhabitants of this second neighborhood could not get the city government to protect them from the flooding of the open drain along which their neighborhood extended. They felt neglected by the city's officials and abandoned even by politicians from their own community. If alienation and deprivation are themes in this community, these inspire an urgent interest in reform expressed in various ways in the community. Several active reformers and radical ascetics lived in this neighborhood. The higher number of Buddhist households in this neighborhood reflect the advocacy of Buddhism as an alternative to Hinduism by some untouchable leaders. The third neighborhood, on the outskirts of the city, Khare describes as a kind of urban hamlet, a village-like settlement where reform consciousness was more muted. Here, one group, of those who worked in the city, pulled the community towards the prospects, lifestyles, and social change the city represented (perhaps most powerfully symbolized by consumer goods: bicycles, radios, cameras, motorcycles). Most of the rest, who worked as field laborers, remained more oriented to a strategy of accommodation combined with mild reform within the horizons of a more-or-less traditional Hindu social universe, a position rejected by the younger and more urban-oriented.

One of Khare's key interests is in the meaning for the Chamar of the low caste ascetics found in all these neighborhoods, and the way some Chamar see reform ideology as supported by, as growing out of, the values and practices of low caste asceticism.

Untouchable Ascetic Versus Caste-Oriented Ascetics and Renouncers

Khare (1984) maintains that asceticism as a significant cultural form is shared by untouchable and Brahman alike, but that its meaning differs for them. In untouchable ideology, the ascetic emerges as a contested concept—and as a key symbol they seek to seize for themselves. Within their critical discourse, the untouchable may define the role and meaning of the ascetic in ways that distinguish it from the concept of ascetic in high caste thought and experience.

Untouchable critics of caste culture may seek to "liberate" the concept of the ascetic. Khare (1984) writes that they attempt to distinguish a "culture of the deprived" from the culture of upper caste Hindus and thus "free the genuine content of Indian asceticism from the caste Hindu's distortion." Delivered from Brahmanical Hinduism, the ascetic embodies untouchable hopes and aspirations—he figures in their minds as a "moving utopia," represents "a forceful moral critique of a caste-ordered society," "subverts unjustified inequality," and launches "alternative symbolizations" of the social world (23). Compare this to Krishna's use of the figure of the untouchable ascetic in narratives that project and support the idea of alternative ways of constituting the social world and hierarchy.

Khare discusses five central features of Indian asceticism (1984, 24–25):

1. Identification of the personal self and ultimate-sacred self.
2. The ascetic is beyond the moral categories and controls of society: not immoral, but amoral.
3. Egalitarianism.

These three, he suggests, are not as contested as other characteristics of the ascetic complex. The stress placed on the last two qualities of the ascetic, he argues, characterize the untouchable's concept of the ascetic.

4. The ascetic achieves an "ultimate" spiritual state from which he can know and reveal the "root of morality that upholds the length and breadth of the entire Indic tradition."

The untouchable ideologist, says Khare, stresses this ability to reveal the basis of morality, while he maintains it has variable significance for caste Hindus.

5. The ascetic is a symbol of self, representing an aspect of an ideal self; and as such the ascetic is treated as "a moral image immanent in all humans." Untouchables and Brahmans alike told Khare that "the yogi and bhogi [the ascetic and enjoyer of life] reside in everyone." The self-image the ascetic embodies is supposed to be cultivated over the long term as self-control.

Again, Brahmans and untouchables share the concept but make different uses of it. The untouchable uses this idea to sustain arguments for equality and mutual recognition. In his study, Khare quotes Jigyasu, an Untouchable intellectual and writer, on the role of ascetics.

Ascetics as gurus have always been very important to the Chamar. We have lived in their company in villages and cities for centuries. For the people whom the Hindus has systematically isolated and excluded, the Untouchable or low-caste ascetic was a guide, a doctor, a teacher, a benevolent companion, and a true friend. We, the Chamars, did not have ambivalence toward the ascetic. He was always more on our side than any Brahman. Even if we did not dislike the Brahman, he did. A Brahman ascetic, on comparison, was congenial only out of his benevolence; if he did not care for us, there was nothing that we could do to change his mind, except try to win him by our genuine devotion to a Hindu deity. The common Chamar is still too much in awe of a Brahman ascetic, though it is unnecessary and out of ignorance. The awakened Chamar should suspect the Brahman ascetic, especially these days. He could do so only if he put distance between himself and all things Brahmanical. The Chamars routinely bring their families into close contact with a sympathetic ascetic. Again, unlike the Hindu, they do not know ambivalence toward him. The Hindu householder fears the ascetic's wrath, but craves his miraculous blessings. He is caught forever in his own doubts about the nature of the sacred. Actually, this is a trap Brahmanic thought has produced and maintained. Spared of this, the Untouchable ideally approaches the ascetic with full, unwavering faith. The householder interiorizes the ascetic. The Untouchable has little difficulty in doing so, for both the Untouchable and the ascetic receive little from society, the first under denial and the second under self-denial. But both the Chamar householder and the Untouchable ascetic impart critical lessons to each other: The Chamar reminds the ascetic of worldly reform and of restoring will within the oppressed; the ascetic reminds the Chamar of his true spiritual heritage and individual worth. (1984: 26, diacritics omitted).

For Jigyasu, not all ascetics are equal. The best of them, he indicates, the ones not dominated by Brahmanical premises, "symbolizes hope in despair and reminds us of social justice based on spiritual equality." He distinguishes this kind of ascetic from those who affirm Brahmanical (or caste Hindu) ideology:

Those [ascetics] still dominated by the Brahmanic rites and viewpoints are counterproductive; those unwilling to see a fundamental difference between the social justice of the caste system and of the spiritual order [atmavadi dharma] are of limited value. The ascetic of the spiritual order clearly see how the Hindu weaves a cobweb along castes, gods, Brahmanic rites, karma, *maya* [illusion], and *samasara* [rebirth] that he begins to view social exclusion and justice as a form of dharma.

The ascetic tradition of true persuasion, however, needs to be carefully rescued from the surrounding Brahmanic forms and images. The mentality of this ascetic, who is most often not a Brahman, is best tested when he fights for the social justice denied to others. He does not believe in Hindu gods and their discriminatory rites. . . . He is a true wanderer and a true renouncer. He is free himself and makes others free. (1984:34, diacritics omitted).

The caste Hindu is "other" here—portrayed as ensnared by the illusions he has woven to oppress others, while the untouchable and ascetic engage in a dialogue in which each "imparts critical lessons" to the other and seek emancipation. Khare (1984:26) argues that the untouchable thinker seeks to formulate an alternative cultural ideology for untouchables. "He strives to make the ascetic *the* independent variable within the Indian spiritual and social order, for the ascetic reveals to him the roots of all his caste-engendered deprivations" (1984:26). To achieve this state of revelation, Jigyasu portrays the ascetic as a key symbol in a liberation ideology, but maintains this key symbol must be rescued from the mystifying distortions of Hindu culture—the "cobweb" of castes, gods, rites— that have obscured the potential for emancipation and transformation embodied by the ascetic. This requires a critical stance. Not all ascetics have equal value. The untouchable and the "true" ascetic (who is un-mystified and demystifying) exist in a mutual dialogue, each "remind-ing" the other of critical values: Jigyasu says "the Chamar reminds the ascetic of worldly reform of restoring will within the oppressed; the as-cetic reminds the Chamar of his true spiritual heritage and individual worth."

Like Jigyasu, some Newars align ascetic and untouchables. In Krishna's story, the untouchable ascetic guru is true and generous, while the Brah-man is deceptive and unfaithful. The Brahman desires the untouchable's teaching, and accepts the provision that he will acknowledge having an untouchable guru, but betrays this trust. In his acceptance of caste dis-tinctions by denying his teacher was an untouchable, he loses the power he has gained. He loses his power—and falls.

We should interpret this in light of Krishna's general theory of hierar-chy. As the Brahman can fall, so can the untouchable "rise up." The key is knowledge, not birth status. Knowledge is learned, and can be held and wielded by ascetics, and by ritual leaders such as himself. His denial of status as birth right aligns Krishna with the critique of the Chamars—arguably, this idea is as "good to think" for low caste people as purity and impurity are for high caste people.

The untouchable internalizes the ascetic, Jigyasu says. This sheds an important light on Krishna's stories. In Krishna's story the Brahman did not—and could not, because of his caste standing—truly internalize the ascetic who was an untouchable, while the untouchable had internalized it from *his* ascetic teacher. Krishna's story converges with Jigyasu's cri-tique: the untouchable and the ascetic are united in a way the Brahman and renouncer cannot be. They portray the ascetic tradition as belong-ing to the untouchable. This depiction carries with it a forceful argu-ment that knowledge and moral action, not birth status, should be the basis of social life. Jigyasu repatriates the moral concepts embodied in this tradition, bringing the idea of spiritual equality to bear on social injustice. He does not treat the ascetic pursuit as sealed off in socially transcendent "otherworldliness," but as a position from which concerns of the social world can be addressed. Not directly part of the caste world, the ascetic tradition provides a cultural basis for political engagement and for moral critique of that world.[2]

Of course, the high castes also align themselves with the ascetic and draw him into their construction of the world. The renouncer is a re-source in an ideological struggle, a tug of war between opposing view-points. High caste concepts have hegemony—are diffused throughout society, seem natural, shape common sense, and generally have a strong grip on millions of minds—but alternate views make inroads; reformist thinkers like Jigyasu subject dominant views to critique and suggest alternative ideologies, which over time are picked up by others, who extend or apply them.[3]

Thus, as a key cultural symbol, a fluid symbol that can be "thought" and "read" in various ways, the ascetic renouncer is enlisted on both sides. Let us look at the ascetic-Brahman alignment. Fuller (1992), in his superb effort to summarize popular Hinduism—which is Hinduism as it is in caste society, that is, for the most part, Hinduism in which the ideology of hierarchy has achieved some degree of cultural hegemony, forming an integral basis for religious thought and practice—discusses the way Brahman and renouncer are assimilated to each other. We can compare his remarks with Jigyasu's:

> A vital aspect of the relationship between Brahmans and renouncers is that the former, although they are mostly householders living in the world, have come to be partially assimilated with the latter, so that the "ideal Brahman" is or is like an ascetic renouncer . . . the ideological significance of the Brahman-renouncer assimilation is indisputable. In particular, it means that the social and religious supremacy of Brahmans partly depends on their likeness to renouncers. Hence Brahmans can represent themselves as independent of inferiors, just like renouncers who ideally avoid all entangling ties with members of the society they have left, even though the Brahmans' purity is still partly preserved by the lower castes who carry out polluting tasks for them. Paradoxically, therefore, Brahman supremacy is a function of both their asymmetrical, complementary relationships with inferior castes, and their ideal detachment from such relationships. (1992:18)

This helps us see what is at stake in Jigyasu's and Krishna's re-visioning of culture. By assimilating the renouncer to the untouchable while rescuing the renouncer from the Brahman, a key basis of the social and religious supremacy of Brahmans is called into question. Jigyasu and Krishna might argue that Fuller has merely stated the Brahman's ideology, since they want to assert that the actual role of renouncer is to neutralize and subvert the Brahmanical synthesis of a world in which the Brahman has supremacy.

Indeed, a critique of academic studies of Indian society and religion by untouchables might be very interesting. They might accuse us of doing little more than transcribing cobwebs. They might detect, and criticize, a tendency to leave them out of the picture.

Fuller (1992), for example, does not mention the assimilation of untouchable and ascetic; the untouchable is seen in relation to the Brahman in terms of the purity complex and the caste society (17), but not in relation to the ascetic renouncer. In fact, Fuller's remarks on the linking of Brahman and renouncer are found under the subtitle "Brahmans, Renouncers, and Kings." These three figures are presented, in Fuller and other academic discussions, as crucial figures in Hindu culture, and they certainly are; but so is the untouchable, about which much less is said. Hinduism is virtually defined in terms of the figure of Brahman, renouncer, king—but not in terms of the untouchable, who defines the Brahman's purity, but is otherwise often represented, if at all, as a marginal figure. Even the single dimension of untouchability that is analyzed—symbolic impurity—is often treated rather one-dimensionally, when in fact it is a multi-faceted reality (Levy 1990).

Arguably, as Dumont's work first forced us to acknowledge, but left hanging in abstraction, the untouchable as "other" is the invisible fourth that completes this trinity, an essential figure against which all the other figures define themselves. Without the untouchable, would the "three hierarchical models" (Burghart 1978, cited in Fuller 1992:16) represented by the other figures, each of which can claim superiority to the others in some contexts, coalesce into any kind of unity? Or, at least, the unity they do have? Brahman, renouncer, king—they share an identity as non-untouchable: the king's power against the untouchable's powerlessness; the Brahman's purity against the untouchable's impurity (or: knowledge against ignorance); the renouncer's freedom against the untouchable's subjugation to a social world of suffering. Nonetheless, the untouchable is often relatively neglected in studies of Hindu society and culture.

No doubt this is because the untouchable is not celebrated but stigmatized. Yet if untouchables have an essential role in defining the high caste Hindu self, we must explore this; to neglect the untouchable is to attempt to understand Hindu culture without analyzing the way culture has produced the images of self and other by which identity is ultimately defined. Actual untouchables embody stigmatized otherness—which is more than impurity. Thus, our unit of analysis should be at least fourfold, as in Figure 1. The untouchable is opposed conceptually to the other three—perhaps we should say the other three are opposed to the un-

FIGURE 1. The symbolic value of the untouchable for high caste actors.

Social centrality and power	*Set apart (transcendent vs. stigmatized)*	
Brahman	Renouncer	*Sacred knowledge and power*
King	**Untouchable**	*Secular functions*
Protected self	***Symbolizes what is reflected in self and for self:***	
	filth, impurity, ignorance	
	servitude, suffering, powerlessness	
	unrestrained sexuality	
	inauspiciousness and misfortune	

touchable. The untouchable embodies filth, impurity, and inauspiciousness; embodies suffering; embodies moral degradation; and actualizes in
tangible ways everything the high caste householder, Brahman, and king
are not and do not want to be or suffer. In Hindu Newar culture, I believe, from the perspective of the higher castes, one may coherently desire to become a renouncer, although this is typically discouraged, but
the desire to be an untouchable would be deviant and irrational, an incoherent wish. If the renouncer can be assimilated to self, the untouchable cannot. The renouncer is a potential self, but the untouchable is
what one rejects in, and for, self.

The untouchable becomes a cultural symbol for many high caste actors—meanings are imposed on actual untouchables, whatever their
own sense of self. The untouchable is a tangible symbol of the contents
of the political unconscious, an embodiment of much that is rejected in
the high caste Hindu self: impurity and inauspiciousness but also powerlessness. Their political and economic oppression is legitimized in concepts and sentiments that are animated by fear and loathing that derives
from the cultural psychology of caste life.

If the householder-renouncer opposition pits "this worldliness"
against "otherworldliness," the opposition of Brahman/untouchable
(and with it all high castes against all impure castes) is not merely a matter of abstract quanta of purity and impurity: the untouchable exposes
the underside of this world to the eyes of the high castes, revealing the
full potential horror of thisworldly existence. One Newar Brahman, remember, said the Pore live a hell on earth, the ultimate in filth and impurity and suffering. One Newar Sweeper echoed this, with no apparent
irony, when he defined "hell" for me as "our excrement." Thus the opposition of Brahman and king with untouchable contrasts the protected
moral world of the high caste householder with a kind of existential
horror-in-the-world: the untouchable's living hell. The renouncer an-
nounces an exit and holds out the promise of salvation; renunciation for
the high caste Hindu may assuage guilt or guarantee continued transcendence of the untouchable's world, but for untouchables the concept of
salvation may be infused with meaning deriving from their interest in
emancipation from the caste system.

Sexual Politics and Gender Hierarchy

Another area that needs more exploration is the relationship of caste
hierarchy and gender hierarchy. In some respects, gender differences
may be a more important model of differences than caste differences;
moreover, caste can be used to think about gender, and gender about
caste. Indeed, for some Newars, not the opposition of pure and impure

or of Brahman and untouchable, but the opposition of male and female seems to be the most basic prototype of hierarchy. God, they say, originally made only two castes—male and female. All the rest came later— as surplus difference, the mere construction of kings, history, society. The original difference of male and female is the key to order; the caste hierarchy can go, but the gender hierarchy is natural and necessary.

Regardless of the way they are used as templates or prototypes, the caste hierarchy and gender hierarchy may reinforce each other in powerful and systemic ways. In the caste system, high caste people may avoid having social intercourse with lower caste people—eating with them, inviting them into one's home—but high caste males do not necessarily avoid sexual intercourse with low caste women.

Muli's life-story reveals something of the sexual politics of caste life; it also reveals an interplay of insight and collusion that is as much part of untouchable experience as Jigyasu's demystification. Indeed, the contrast with Jigyasu is telling. We can hardly equate the two. Where Jigyasu is principled, Muli is compromised. Jigyasu is a moral critic, who attempts to generate a deliberately critical and political moral ethos as a way of furthering the emancipation of the untouchable from caste culture. Muli acts within a "pragmatic ethos"; for the most part, he is just trying to survive or get ahead, and he will lie, cheat, and pander to do so. In fact, Muli is a pimp—he supplies women to high caste men. He is not a sympathetic character. Yet Muli's life bears witness to some of the actualities of untouchable experience, of what is, where Jigyasu represents a critique of what is, and a vision of what should be. Greedy and grasping, dissimulating and self-serving, often desperate, ill and hungry, Muli virtually embodies the high caste image of the untouchable as other. Certainly, he does not embody the values Jigyasu finds in the figure of the ascetic. Survival, not justice, personal advantage, not collective emancipation, are the lief-motifs of Muli's life. Muli is very much in, and of, the social world at the bottom of the caste system. But the way he is "in the world" reveals much. With Muli, we cannot romanticize the untouchable, but we can see his state of oppression and the quandaries it poses. We can see the flicker of critical insights in Muli's responses—tentative and equivocal—which intellectuals such as Jigyasu build on and build into a critique of culture.

If Jigyasu constructs a vision of moral and spiritual equality, Muli, I think, exposes equality in other forms. As a pimp, he explores the equality of desire. Lust does not follow the contours of caste divisions; it crosses caste boundaries. Muli is a pimp for money, but also finds a kind of fascination in the way sexual desire makes men the same. They all want women—the women he can supply. They befriend him, and moderate—without letting fully lapse—some of the ritual distancing of hierarchy. From Muli's point of view, this common denominator of desire makes high caste men like any other men, and makes them dependent on him. Can we afford to ignore this possibility in our analysis?

I think not. Consider the following episode from Muli's life-history. Muli arranges for a high caste doctor, Doctor Babu, to meet an untouchable woman, Koki. When they go into a field, Muli hides and watches them.

> That first time, I watched them at work, out in the taro field in the evening. I hid behind a hedge where they didn't see me. Afterward, Koki went home, while Doctor Babu washed himself, using a water pot he had with him. Then he changed his clothes, borrowing one of my shoulder cloths. When I saw why, I laughed. His own shoulder cloth was wet. He threw it in my face playfully and said, "It was very nice, thank you."
>
> When I saw him the next morning, I turned my face away. He asked, "Why aren't you talking to me? Are you angry with me?"
>
> I replied, "I'm not angry. I am shy to see your face. When you came today, a laugh came to my mouth."
>
> He asked, "Why? What happened? You are not a woman hiding from a man. Speak up."
>
> I said, "You are a man. I am also a man. I saw everything of your work last night, a doctor, out in the taro field. You put on my cloth, the cloth of a Bauri boy. You acted according to my directions, creeping into the field, and so I can't help laughing." (Freeman 1979:152)

Why does Muli laugh? At the incongruity of the situation? Which provides some kind of cathartic release for someone so powerless, so accustomed to humiliation? Muli has an injured foot, and the episode continues with the doctor treating it; the doctor has been cultivating a relationship with Muli by treating him, since he wants Muli to supply him with women. Thus, the doctor tells Muli, "You may be laughing now, but anyway, I must give you an injection and change the bandage on your foot." Muli reflects: "I thought to myself, how funny it was that our positions had reversed. Respected Doctor Babu was pressing to treat me."

Muli recounts other times when he overhead or witnessed high caste actors having sex with lower caste (and impoverished) women. As the above episode suggests, Muli's voyeurism may have as much to do with caste as sex; what matters to him may not just be that he witnessed a man and a woman having sex, but that he saw and heard a high caste man having sex with an untouchable woman. Arguably, whatever frission he experienced as voyeur—and these episodes seem to have significance for him—may have as much to do with equality as with sexuality. When

Muli says to the doctor, "You are a man, I am also a man," he asserts they are the same in a sexual context, building on and reframing the doctor's comment that Muli is not a woman hiding from a man, that is, that coyness is a female characteristic, not a male one. (In fact, untouchables and women as subalterns are perhaps more alike than different in this; each hides much from those with power over them.) The comment invites frankness, and Muli takes advantage of it. He agrees he is a man, like the doctor; giving a spin to the doctor's comment, Muli asserts that he and the doctor are alike, equals at least in this way—as men. The context of this declaration is explicitly a sexual one: Muli says he saw "everything" of the doctor's "work" in the taro field. The doctor has been exposed in this sexuality, as the same as a Bauri boy. After sex, he even wears the Bauri boy's clothes. The transposition reveals equality—and yet is strange. It produces laughter in Muli's mouth.

If sexual desire exposes a human common denominator however, it also exposes vulnerabilities that Muli can attempt to manipulate. Muli not only finds the reversals of roles (and power) incongruous—"funny"—but, I think it is fair to infer, pleasurable. Ultimately, he may want to encompass the equality of sexual desire he has discovered in the taro field, restructuring it into a hierarchy, one in which he has the power and gravity that attracts people into dependent relationships with him: perhaps what matters most to Muli is that the high caste sex client is dependent on the pimp.

Both the caste hierarchy and Muli's response are implicated in a gender hierarchy. High caste men seek untouchable women; untouchable women need and want money; and some of these women are willing to have sex for money or gifts. Muli, by acting as a go-between, makes the exchange of sex for wealth possible. Women become the medium for transactions within a world that is stratified by caste, class, and gender. Muli can attempt to make high caste men his "friends," and dependent on him, only by supplying women. Muli and his high caste clients alike take advantage of women's poverty. For high caste men, untouchable women are primarily sexual objects—not even potentially wives. For Muli, the same women are tools for constructing relationships with high caste men. Muli is instrumental for some of the women as well—they use him to meet high caste men, and to provide cover for what they are doing. Muli helps them circumvent restrictions on the freedom of women.

The Critique of Culture

Caste life—at least life at the bottom of the system—imposes a kind of "flight or fight" structure on consciousness. Individuals shift, sometimes abruptly, between acquiescence and resistance. The knowledge supporting one state is not always fully available when a person is in the other state, and does not form the sole basis for social action.⁴ Instead, multiple states of consciousness, mediated by different and often conflicting values and cultural models, organize a variety of activities and interactions. Life is lived in contradiction.

Being able to suppress critical insights and ideas enables people to maintain contradictory views needed to adapt to the contradictory imperatives of social reality. Shifting models enables a person to engage and know the world in several different ways. Such shifts may effect a radical disjuncture between what people know, as self-reflective beings, as critical, thinking subjects, and what they *must* know as pragmatic actors in order to make lives for themselves within hierarchical social structures.

Life in a hierarchical society is not easy for anyone. The pressures of living within a stratified social system are enormous—each actor is the object of redundant processes and structures of control. While actors benefit in basic ways from the political creation of order (some, of course, more than others), they also risk much, because force, violence, scarcity and isolation—feared, anticipated, threatened, imagined, experienced, or remembered—can crush, starve and wither, bringing death, defeat and pain to social actors too eager to press their interests or to transform their society.

Thus political and economic realities generate a culture of dissimulation. Since this often involves significant—but highly variable—degrees of self-deception, I think we can properly speak of a "political unconscious" here: a psycho-socio-cultural process of hiding knowledge from others and self. In this process, much of what people know and experience may be suppressed, at least in particular contexts, in ways that help them symbolically restructure their world, making it possible for them to engage the social world in several different and contradictory ways by enabling them to hide what they think, know, and feel from themselves and others. Psychologically, this may help make life more bearable for some. But the social and political implications are even more crucial. A culture of dissimulation and the "political unconscious" it generates adapt people to hierarchy by providing a way of managing the risks of knowing too much, too clearly. They develop because the "critical self" must often be suppressed.

The way untouchables are part of Hindu tradition, but not part of it, draw on it, but are not "at home" in it, stands as a case study of the tension between ideology and critique, structure and transformation, and perhaps sheds light on what is at stake for understanding cultural life in the debate between Gadamer and Habermas (McCarthy 1978; Nicholson 1991; Misgeld 1991).

The way untouchables view themselves shows us how the dominant culture does not provide "a home" for the total, dynamic system of low-caste self-concepts, even though the untouchable "mind," through the multiple languages it uses to know itself, in some sense grows out of this culture. The effect is general and divisive: a person cannot be "at home" in another caste. Recall that Krishna observed, in effect, people would not be at home in other castes.

Untouchables forge a critique of culture out of culture by assembling and disassembling cultural schema to constitute new values and meanings, practices and perspectives. Dispossessed, alienated, they may interpret themselves "out of" the dominant tradition; they may formulate a critique of the dominant ideology—a hermeneutic task which also relates them to tradition, since they must draw on culture to critique it.

As a result, the process of critique may be self-subverting. Liberation from the "Hindu" caste tradition requires a critique, but this critique can only take its departure from a tradition; alien traditions—Western liberalism, Marxism—may be adopted for this purpose, but fail to resonate or have mass appeal, precisely because they are alien. Thus critics and "counter-ideologies" must forge their material out of a pre-existing tradition, if they want to disseminate it widely and if they want it to have wide appeal to people who are already enculturated, who are prepared, therefore, to find certain kinds of meanings meaningful. This means critiques will make use of premises that are also premises of what is rejected and criticized; this facilitates slippage back into dominant ways of thinking, feeling, acting, and may have the net effect of bringing consciousness back into the fold of hierarchy—another source of the equivocal quality of low caste "critical discourse" and "protest movements." This may not be as important as what Khare calls the "practical ethos"—untouchables do what they have to do in the face of extreme deprivation, and to prepare themselves to do so maintain a stance of flexible adaptability as a key cultural attitude—but may facilitate the shifts from one mode of thinking to another within this ethos.

Achieving critical distance—which involves breaking through the common sense, taken-for-granted qualities, is a process of raising habitus into consciousness and making it an object of discourse—seems integral to powerful critique, although I would not rule out the possibility of critique itself inhabiting pre-reflective modes of thought, as a habitus, an unconscious interpretive schema. We often know when things do not "feel right," and may feel moral outrage at some circumstance, without being able to articulate why, even though our "feelings" reflect "embodied knowledge" of a fairly sophisticated, culture-laden variety. If we know more than we can say, we may be able to develop a critique unconsciously, and orient ourselves to action on this basis. Of course, it is hard to see how this could become moral-political rhetoric and discourse, but it is easy to see how rhetoric and discourse could resonate or feed on such unconscious interpretive schema.

To some extent, for untouchables, critical distance is supplied objectively, with their experience of discrimination and exclusion. This poses the problem, but this alone will not melt away the world view that has been established; nor does it guarantee that meanings will not be produced that afford ideology a new grip on mind and experience, giving dominant groups an edge in their struggle with others to achieve or subvert hegemony. Oppression does not guarantee a critical self. Yet a critical self does sometimes crystallize.

The concept of a critical self seems to be one lacking in psychology and the social sciences, but I think it is necessary if we wish to understand many aspects of cultural life and behavior. What does it mean to reject cultural tradition, if self is given in tradition, or even merely shaped by it? Take Krishna. Can we really understand him if we do not explore his identification with a critique of culture? Does it not—in part—define who he is? Does it not give him a divided self? For he must reject what he is, and perhaps teeter precariously on the edge of not knowing himself, risk meaninglessness, which I suppose might lead him to affirm a caste identity—dancing on the edge of a void, not knowing who you are, where you came from, or where you are going, is not done lightly. If you are not what society, thinking itself in you, thinks you are; if you are not what your culture presents to you as yourself (low caste, untouchable) and represents you as in society, constituting a social reality premised on you being what society takes you for; if you do not have the reality, the being which you thought you were and which provided the only coherence for self you have ever known—then what are you? Who are you? Whether one embraces or resists the self-representations cultural tradition and cultural experience provide, whether one celebrates and defends these images of self, taking them as self-image, or subjects them to relentless critical scrutiny as not self, or both, there are consequences.

Arguably, the critique of culture is a key cultural practice. Accounts of culture that ignore indigenous processes of reflecting on and critiquing culture are one-sided, and portray cultures as less dynamic and more unified than they are. Indeed, the critical self may be a universal, at least of complex hierarchical societies. Muli and Jigyasu, in any event, as different as they are, reflect in their own ways on the experience of untouchables, and generate critical insights into the dominant culture, and in some important respects treat the high caste Hindu as their Other.

We can now return to the question posed by Chapter 3, regarding the travails of way "India" has been constructed in academic discourse. In the light of the material presented here, what is India? "India" is not caste, though caste is a vital—and oppressive—institution. It is not the opposition of pure and impure—which may be subverted in terms of a pragmatic ethos. It is not hierarchy—although hierarchy has cultural hegemony. Nor is India reducible to holism. Individuals exist, and value themselves. Krishna, Kancha, Muli, and the others know themselves as persons, have goals, pasts, a sense of self that goes beyond caste identity. They value relationships, but we cannot say they have no being, no reality, no self-awareness as individuals within the nexus of relationships in which they find themselves. Traditional South Asian cultures cannot be reduced to the language of the purity complex, of hierarchy, of holism, because there is more to cultural life than the purity complex. Constructing hierarchy as a dominant image ultimately distorts cultural life. India is multiple; it cannot be captured in a single image. India is a place where men and women use conflicting languages to imagine themselves and confront existence—as they do in Nepal and elsewhere. We must learn to hear that people have to say in the idiom of necessity, and what they voice in the language of critique. We should not construct their "culture" only out of the language of the dominant ideology; nor should we attempt to impose a consistency—which we label "culture"—on their experience that it does not possess (Sapir 1934, 1938; Bourdieu 1977).

Conclusion: The Politics of Consciousness

Living in a caste society, men and women must often suppress much of what they know about themselves and each other. Finding ways to neutralize their awareness that others are, in many ways, like themselves, they cultivate a consciousness of what divides people from each other in the garden of castes planted by long-dead kings.

This poses paradoxes, since it multiplies the ways that people can know the world. They see that others are like themselves; but they learn to know differences. Encountering someone on the street, they see a person with a body and a face, who speaks, certainly bleeds blood, perhaps loves and suffers. But what if this person is Mahila on his way to his work as a Sweeper? He exists for others, an untouchable, an absorber of impurity and inauspiciousness, whose dirty hands signify his nature and his sin. He passes another person, but a high caste person, a Brahman, endowed with purity, power, and knowledge. Brahman and untouchable walk the same streets but between them lie the differences that define them.

Caste ideology constructs and legitimizes these differences: it provides a theory for defining self and other, for justifying society. Others are not like self, caste ideology asserts; they are essentially different kinds of humanity, separated by essence, opposed by substance, and ranked by nature. Their "natures" repulse each other. Hierarchy is simply the natural order of the cosmos and the city, reflecting the way the universe is, and ought to be. And yet, this construction of reality, this process of organizing "difference" into a hierarchy of value that can be felt as palpably necessary and natural, co-exists with a recognition, at once cognitive, empathic, and cultural, that others are "like self." To overcome this recognition, actors committed to, or merely entangled with, the caste order must cultivate a sense of "reality" that makes the hierarchical construction of others seem objective and moral, making it possible not only to see that others are not like self, but to know that the untouchable deserves his fate, his hell on earth, while higher castes deserve their good fortune, their place in society. Doing so makes it possible to feel that inequality, the fact that others face different life-chances, is justified.

This reforging of perception reduces the dissonance of seeing others suffer. If others were like self, a moral response to their plight would be called for. For low caste actors, the art of seeing others as different kinds of persons may help reduce the dissonance of knowing others enjoy advantages and fulfillment denied self, since one does not have to compare self with other. If perceived in this way, other lives have few implications for self.

I have little doubt such a process of neutralization does sometimes take place, precluding the development of caste and class antagonism. And yet the potential for seeing others as like self, as equals, remains. It can be recovered. Any hierarchy, any claim of privilege, however constituted or justified, can be neutralized in the moral imagination. This is what Newars intend to achieve, if only ephemerally, by asserting: "I am person, and you are a person, too." I have shown how some low caste actors seek to escape the implications of their caste status by invoking various ideas of human equality and solidarity, by disrupting and contesting constructions of hierarchical order. By doing so, low caste actors ethicize resentment, and—if only briefly—throw off the psychological burden of being low, small, impure, inauspicious, stigmatized, and powerless. This helps protect a core of self-esteem. People may not be able to invoke an equality that can be put into practice, but equality and solidarity have meaning for them, as does disorder itself, as it ephemerally lifts them out of their objecthood.

But even Newars who reject hierarchy at one juncture, often insist on it at another. The Newar case strongly supports Andre Beteille's insight into the interplay of hierarchy-constituting and hierarchy-dissolving moments in human societies and consciousness.

I find it false to represent the opposition between equality and inequality as a contrast between two societies in two different parts of the world. On the contrary, each society is an arena within which the two interplay, and if we fail to examine this interplay within societies, the comparisons we make between societies will be shallow and misleading. We can talk about *homo hierarchicus* and *homo equalis* only if we recognize that there is something of both in every society and perhaps in every human individual. (Beteille 1983)

The dynamics of this interplay of hierarchy and equality need to be taken into account in the interpretation of caste. They exist in the moral system, and our account of it would be one-sided if we dealt only with systematic ideological efforts to make hierarchy seem natural, unifying, and consensual. What is experienced seems far more open-textured. From a human point of view, this possession of "something of both" means the moral world has no fixed structure, but always remains in flux, like a kind of moral kaleidoscope. Cultural consciousness of self and society constantly forms and dissolves in fluid variations on the themes of hierarchy and equality, within social, political, and economic structures that constrain powerfully and yield only grudgingly to pressure for change.

What drives this dynamic? The short answer is: power and symbols. Ultimately, the power of the state and the state of the economy do. Concrete interests in domination (which run up and down the system, as well as emanating from the state and dominant groups) drive efforts to achieve and sustain hegemony. A hierarchical "turn of mind" alone cannot sustain caste hierarchy—it arouses too much resistance. Hierarchy needs enforcing, as well as ideological buttressing. This can drive resistance into the psychological underground of culture, where it appears in moral fantasies, in oblique narrative critiques, in moments of disbelief and anger. An account of such power, an analysis of the structures of force, violence and economic life, is essential for understanding caste and its psychology.

Naked power does not, however, account for everything. Something of the commitment to caste life can be explained only in terms of the cultural shaping of experience and self. The symbolic construction of caste life has some power to evoke conformity—despite the resentments and resistance generated by the caste system—by making this way of life seem natural, sacred, and necessary. Symbolic constructions of hierarchy can help render the critical self problematic, by attempting to starve or subvert the reflections on experience that animate critiques of culture and society. Symbolism is no doubt often cheaper than force, and can be more convincing than violence—for violence demystifies.

Despite their power, I do not think that symbols and meanings can eliminate the critical self or abolish discontents. People continue to reflect on their experiences, and tell stories about possible worlds. They scrutinize the moral and political grounds of society, and may achieve insight into the capricious nature of the social world they live in. They may resent injustices, and resent their powerlessness in the face of such injustices. Since they often are powerless, however, or feel threatened, sometimes the only way to respond to insight is with amnesia, keeping critical ideas suspended or hidden, from self as well as from others.

This paradoxical combination—insight encompassed in amnesia, insight struggling with the need to forget, to not know, to acquiesce—generates the moral discourse that defines the private horizons of many

Newar actors. Powerless in the public realm, one of the few things they can do is to find meaning within their private horizons, in moral fantasies, or by disrupting the closure of constructions of order, whether the festivals that celebrate it or the everyday interactions that embody it. They retreat into alienation and its culture, and yet in fits and hitches challenge the world. Perhaps this is adaptive, allowing them to survive, to live lives within a hierarchical public world. The meanings that accumulate within their subjective worlds may make it possible for them to act when transforming action becomes possible; their moral fantasies define what they can find meaningful, and this prepares them to engage not the actual world but possible worlds.

I have argued that South Asian values of solidarity and equality have not been incorporated into analysis and interpretation as the active principles they are. Dumont, who has proposed that Indian civilization has a special affinity with hierarchy, acknowledges that hierarchy and equality co-exist: "my intention was not to claim that in India there has never been the slightest trace of equality as a tendency or even as a norm . . . nor to fail to recognize more or less modern movements." He wished, rather, "to isolate the predominant ideological note of a social system in relation to its morphology" (1980:xxi) This is a reasonable point: one does not want to collapse hierarchy and equality into a false equivalence. I agree with Dumont that one cannot give dominant values and "repressed" values the same weight in analysis. We can, however, look at their different roles, if we are interested in the dynamics and process of cultural life, and not just in "ideology" and "morphology." However differently they must be weighted in analysis, as one is "foregrounded" and the other kept out of focus—in a precarious equilibrium between consciousness and the poltical unconscious—the question of *how* hierarchy and equality are related does arise. Ignoring the role of the ideologically less salient principle is unwise, especially if that is what dominant discourses seeks to obscure. Indeed, equality's overdetermined ideological absence makes it a shadowy, subversive presence in Newar moral discourse.[1]

Consensus and Diversity

Some anthropologists have argued that high and low caste actors share the same understanding of, and the same commitment to, the values of the caste hierarchy (Moffatt 1979; Dumont 1980). Moffatt argues against diversity in this domain, and offers an explicit statement of his belief that high and low castes are as one in their hierarchical views: "We are arguing, in common with Dumont [that] Untouchables and higher-caste actors hold virtually identical cultural constructs, that they are in nearly total conceptual and evaluative consensus with one another" (1979: 290)

The data I have presented suggests either that he overstates the consensus of high and low castes, or that the Tamil communities he worked with and Newars are very different. Perhaps he missed seeing the way that informants, in moral discourse, manipulate, relativize or neutralize dominant ideological constructs, and shift between points of view.

Others have maintained that high and low castes do not uniformly share values and beliefs (Berreman 1971; Mencher 1974; Kolenda 1964; Khare 1984). In this view, diversity and dissent within a cultural matrix, not consensus, is the reality. People share some parts of a culture, but not a nearly "total" consensus with each other.

And yet, it cannot be denied that low caste men and women at times subscribe to the same hierarchical values as high caste actors. Even untouchables often give every indication of believing in hierarchy—some of the time. Just as you can challenge Moffat's assertion of near-total consensus, so you can upset arguments for near-total dissent and divergence in understandings of caste life by showing that low caste people do subscribe to values of hierarchy: they use, in ways that seem authentic, and profess commitment to, in ways that seem quite sincere, concepts of purity and pollution, of karma, of "high" and "low," that stigmatize them.

I have tried to take this controversy a step farther, by showing the crux of the impasse: cultural consciousness *is* equivocal, *is* ambivalent. The warring forces of meaning unleashed in moral and political discourse vie with each other in actor's thoughts and actions, offering alternative identities and commitments. Empirically, people are often profoundly inconsistent about what they believe. They have motives for subscribing to hierarchy, and motives for resisting it: if they create a world by distinguishing Brahman and untouchable, and all the grades in between, there are also moments when they neutralize the values of hierarchy, and recover other values through assertions of human solidarity or equality, or by acting out a momentarily liberating chaos. The observer can catch them at different moments. Analytically, we need to base our interpretations on both moments.

The appearance of "nearly total conceptual and evaluative consensus" among high and low caste actors seem to be a methodological artifact, an analytical objectification of the dominant discourses. Such discourses themselves are directed to occupying and holding consciousness, establishing not only cultural, but psychological hegemony within a total context where violence and deprivation silence many who might speak against hierarchy and its ideological justification. Any ethnographer can frame interviews so that they tap knowledge of the dominant ideology of caste hierarchy, and yet not tap the *range* of personal and collective responses to caste life. But the range of responses may draw on dramatically different sets of cultural values, or be based on personal reflection and thought—and most likely, on both. The way that informants perceive the encounter with the ethnographer shapes the response made to the ethnographer's questions. An interview may be defined by informants as a context in which a performance of a certain sort is called for; they may decide that the purpose of an interview is to display knowledge of the ideal norms of caste, and not an occasion in which to discuss their own experiences or personal convictions (cf. Berreman 1972; Spiro 1984; Briggs 1986). This is not to say that the rejection of caste is somehow "more real" or "authentic" than the affirmation of caste values; it is only to say that there are conflicting elements in the way people see and understand their social worlds, not one "true" value.

My view is that high and low castes share culture in the sense of "knowledge of" values, propositions, rules and scripts, but that men and women of different caste status reinterpret shared culture in terms of their life-experience. Knowing about a value is not the same as being committed to it. Informants can explain cultural principles that they have not adopted as personal attitudes or beliefs. They can tell the anthropologists about cultural ideas that do not structure their perceptions of the world, or sense of self (Spiro 1984).

I do not deny that the dominant framework of ideas and institutions make a difference: they do exert a grip on minds. Hierarchy's cultural hegemony is the product, after all, of efforts to shape and discipline consciousness in politically significant ways, not of a passive body of culture that people are free to ignore. Dominant concepts of reality present themselves as reality, backed by the full force and faith of the most powerful elements of society, including, most critically, the state. My point is that such constructs are not simply internalized and enacted, ensuring a simple consensus.

Not simple consensus or absolute divergence, but transformations of problematically shared cultural constructs characterize human understanding in caste systems. These transformations are shaped in part by the way actors struggle with the quandaries and exploit the opportunities of cognitive and political structures. Even within caste systems, understanding is relative and pluralistic, not fixed and univocal. What people think and feel about caste life—the way in which they understand and engage it—shifts relative to varying contexts. Actors in different positions in the caste system experience and evaluate the symbols and ideas that give form to that system in different ways. For low caste actors, it often seems prudent to present the high caste version of reality.

To recognize hierarchy as a key principle in a culture does not require us to reify hierarchy and find in it the explanation of all cultural data.

Nor does hierarchy provide an explanation of itself. A cultural ideology may, of course, totalize. It may define hierarchy as an objective fact that organizes all of life, as being part of the natural order of the world, a moral fact that is beyond inquiry. It exists because it exists; it has always been so; that is the way it is. Such beliefs are important data for the anthropologist. But they are not the whole story.

The act of selection of indigenous understandings is always the observers' act. By reifying conceptions selected from dominant ideologies and hegemonic formations, taken from one set of informants, and not another, while they are taking one stance available to them, and not another, by not listening closely enough to hear the murmurs of ambiguity and ambivalence in lived lives, one can produce an image of consensus and unity that obscure the real complexities of cultural life.

Replication of Hierarchy: Neutralizing and Recovering Cultural Perspectives

Moffatt (1979) offers as evidence of a cultural consensus of high and low caste people in south India the phenomena of "replication." Untouchable groups—those who are "excluded for reasons of their extreme collective impurity from particular relations with higher beings (both human and divine) . . . recreate among themselves the entire set of institutions and of ranked relations from which they have been excluded by the higher castes" (1979:4–5). We have seen that some Newar untouchables attempt something like this, but have not achieved it. They have not recreated the entire set of institutions, and there is ambiguity about who is the lowest in the system. In my experience, those untouchables nominated by others as the lowest of the low often reject the honor, deny that they are lowest, and propose that someone else is still lower. They take advantage of the social fluidities and cognitive ambiguities that exist at this level of the social order to do so. But the impulse to replicate hierarchy is present, and the claim made that others are lower than self.

I want to suggest the possibility, at least, of a more complex reading of replication, one that does not read quite as much "consensus" into it, but that still recognizes it as participation, even as collusion, in the caste system. The close-ups of person-centered analysis shows something more subtle than does the structural analysis of service transactions between untouchable groups.

High and low castes neutralize and recover different aspects of their shared cultural knowledge. Neutralizing and recovering are interpretive and rhetorical moves. People shift among cultural perspectives to try to achieve a better fit between shared "culture" and unshared experiences, histories, desires, self-images and world-images.

A psycho-social dynamic drives this. Low caste actors may seek to neutralize stigmatizing implications of hierarchy by adopting an egalitarian perspective. But when they feel threatened by groups that are still "lower" groups, they may reject equality and solidarity and affirm hierarchy. One can hardly romanticize this. Neither can one deny the central tension of equality and hierarchy.

Replication may serve material interests, and not just reflect a deep cultural consensus as Moffatt suggests. Moreover, we need to explore the psychological principles involved. Stigmatizing others lends a semblance of value to self, gives one's life some meaning by contrast (Sartre 1963). To replicate oppression is to distance it—perhaps even to gain a kind of emotionally significant pseudo-power over it. The subordination of others reassures self, and implies a solidarity with those with power over self. Anna Freud's principle of identification with the aggressor suggests a possible psychological mechanism that would alter the meaning of hierarchy in the context of replication. As Victor Turner said of this mechanism, "identification also means replacement. To draw off the power from a stronger being is to weaken that being" (1969:174). By identifying themselves with the values that threaten them, low caste actors may defend themselves psychologically against the threat of hierarchy.

If my reading of the testimony of Bhaktapur Newars and my sense of them as persons-in-culture does justice to their felt experience, they seek to find the unity of self in culture (Parish 1994): the crowds that throng the city's streets to watch the god pass by in his chariot are not tenuous figments of the cultural order, having no autonomous existence, mere shadows of hierarchy's ideology, incapable of dissent or self-definition. Yet they do exist in a dialogue with culture. I do not doubt that this dialogue often leads people to assume the identities presupposed in ideology, to acquire ideology as a language for self and society, with all this entails. Yet I believe some relatively autonomous self-definition occurs in what is, I maintain, a dialogue, often a debate, an argument with and against culture, conducted in cultural terms, yes, but not in a way that forces an endless repetition, allowing nothing new to be said.

Without suggesting any absolutely fixed course for this dialogue, I would suggest that the formulation of self-identity can escape closure in Brahmanical ideology, and that an actor may instead find his or her identity in critique. Moreover, despite the contradictions and dissimulation they must live with, I believe the direction of self-development in the lives of those I knew in Bhaktapur is not toward dissipation and fragmentation, as when self can find no means to anchor itself, to "take hold," to ground itself in affirmative images of self and world.[2] After all, critique is as cultural as ideology, and finding a home for self in either places the self in culture. I would not postulate that they achieve any final closure in any part of culture; nor would I wish to argue that non-cultural aspects of psychological experience don't make a difference. I would argue instead that these selves grow out of, and into, a culture, even if they reject large parts of it. The critical self has as a place in Newar culture, as a potential ordering core of identity, just as the ideological self does, and often in the same person. Achieving a viable relationship with their status and its ideology—to find what we might think of as breathing room—is a basic motive and conflict for caste actors.

In fact, their dilemmas, their experience of self-contradiction, may give them a depth of identity quite unlike what might be found in more affluent societies; they do not have the option of indifference, of narcissism, because their quandaries of identity and survival press in on them, forcing them out of themselves, if only in dissimulation and not always in empathy. Subsequently, they may plunge more deeply "into" themselves. Caste society poses the question of who you really are, of what value attaches to self. Of course, there may be no answers for the questions of identity—not easy ones, anyway.[3]

For this very reason, for some, the task of defining some core of self-identity takes on a certain primordial urgency. It is something that has to be done, like appeasing an angry god or finding enough to eat.

The testimony of some low caste actors indicates a felt need to defend an identity from threats implied or embodied in the dominant cultural order. The refrains one hears in interviews suggest this: "your own caste is good for you"; "I am a person, like you" (said with an edge of anger); "those other people are lower than me."

In knowing themselves in terms of their caste identities, people face various possibilities of incompleteness and dissolution: if they are low caste, they lack access to much that is defined as the grounds of a full and esteemed life; if they are high caste, they could fall, be degraded, lose themselves—become like low caste people. At the same time, caste is valued for the order, identity and measure of security it gives. Without caste, there might be chaos; people would not know how to live a social life. Without caste, violence might break out.

If hierarchy means that untouchables experience themselves as incomplete, then to replicate hierarchy is a way to try to restore and complete the self by taking possession of hierarchy. Recall that when I asked one untouchable why members of his caste had begun to perform life cycle rites previously done only by upper castes, he angrily defended their right to do so by saying all people, Brahman and untouchable alike, had "the same flesh, the same blood." I wondered why he resented the question and reacted defensively. Did he think it was a challenge to his right to perform those rites? He asserted equality—the same flesh, the same blood—but what makes this significant? Why place a value on being of the same physical substances, in blood and flesh? If hierarchy threatens some persons with radical incompleteness, then asserting that they are the same as those who are "higher" expresses a desire to be whole. It is a way of standing forth as complete, against the background of others' incompleteness.

By replicating hierarchy, and adopting high caste values and practices, untouchables avoid the full psychological consequence of being the lowest. The stigma of being the lowest member, the terminal degraded object in the system, is passed on. This sustains hierarchy, but modifies one's existential place in the system. Perhaps one should say the system is, for untouchables, transfigured—by replicating hierarchy they come to have one, rather than another, self-identity.

And so, despite my doubts about how to depict the psychological process involved, I do not think that one can necessarily infer from the way very low caste groups attempt to replicate hierarchy that they share, in some deeply consensual way, the commitment to the values of hierarchy of the dominant castes. The use that low castes make of such replicated relations may be profoundly different, and reflect, not consensus, but the psychodynamic of their life-experiences and their own self-interest.

Caste and self have different meanings for actors who occupy different positions in society. The meaning of hierarchy co-develops with the meaning of self; the psycho-existential realities of this process are not the same for high and low caste actors. When interpreting caste systems, we need to take this "inner" relativism of culture into account, and seek to discover how socially positioned subjects reformulate and reframe the meaning of shared symbolic and social forms. For this task, I believe person-centered ethnography remains indispensable.

I think replication is best seen as a subtle fusion of resistance and collusion. If so, replication is a highly ambiguous form of resistance, since it denies hierarchy (my own low position, defined by others) by reproducing it (elevating myself by making others lower, defining my own status relative to others). It is a form of resistance because it denies hierarchy the meaning it has for the dominant castes; it appropriates and redeploys hierarchy. Of course, this plays into the caste system, ultimately reinforcing it, by affirming the principle of hierarchy, so it is also a form of cultural collusion. This is hardly surprising. Cultural resistance is often compromised. It is often, perhaps typically, encapsulated within a structure of collusion, making it less threatening to the social order. Collusion is often what makes resistance possible.

What replication—and the controversy it generates about the relative status of groups—does is introduce an element of ambiguity. Ambiguity is generated in other ways—by claiming that one's status is an accident, or that a mistake was made, and that one should have a higher status. All this is a step away—perhaps a big step away—from seeing the entire system as arbitrary in premise and practice. Yet it does start to demystify the system, to make it seem less natural, less necessary, more arbitrary. It is a safe step away from more dangerous knowledge, from admitting that caste has no other basis—from seeing it is arbitrary all the way up and down.

Stepping up to dangerous knowledge requires taking a political leap of faith. Low caste actors are often unwilling to make this risky jump, at least not in public, because of the violence or loss of income they might experience. What is surprising, perhaps, is that so many were willing to make stronger declarations: arguing that we are all persons, caste is an imposed order. But these declarations do not have the same practical significance as the discourse of replication: they are not ways in which they can have their cake and eat it too; replication both deflects some of the implications of hierarchy and appropriates hierarchy for use by the low caste person, transforming it into something that can be mastered and exploited.

Thus, while the way that "replication" reproduces the form of hierarchy may suggest that values are shared by all castes, this "consensus" may be more apparent than real, an artifact of certain assumptions about culture. If culture is shared, if people engage in the same practices, we expect to find people in agreement; we speak of Newar beliefs or the Newar family structure. If we fail to adequately problematize the idea of "shared culture," we may fail to explore the ways "shared" practices in fact express different meanings and motives, needs and goals (Spiro 1987, chap. 5). We may create expectations about consensus (which we often then proceed to fulfill) by assuming that people simply internalize values and enact them, and fail to assess the ways people transform and redeploy values in practice and in their psychological worlds.

We may overstress consensus because we view all actors as the more-or-less passive products of culture, ideology, and social structure. In actuality, the motives for—and meaning of—the replication of hierarchy among Newar untouchables may not reflect a "near total" evaluative and conceptual consensus, an internalization of the ideology of caste, or a passive submission to caste practices. Rather, they may reflect a dialectic interplay of resistance and collusion. In this interplay, practice and consciousness mirror dominant cultural concepts of reality, and resonate with the social force that stands behind those concepts, but the relevant community of social actors also begins to rewrite, to take control, of these concepts, to deflect some of their implications, introducing a subtle element of dissonance into the shared discourse of hierarchy.

In addition to the subtle elements of resistance that may be attached to replication, we should not overlook the material advantages that might be gained through exercising power over subordinate groups, or the way replication might be a form of strategic communication with the high castes. Moreover, to say that low caste people at times reject the cultural values that disadvantage them is not to say that they will guide their actions by egalitarian principles. They may pursue their own interests, even exploit others. Equality would not serve them in this. The values of caste hierarchy may offer the means of justifying their pursuit of relative power and material advantage, just as it does for the highest castes.

The Fragility of Equality, the Ambiguity of Justice

Equality as a cultural force is paradoxical, and not just because it serves as the logical foundation of hope and anger among those who feel oppressed by society. Unstable and potentially explosive, equality as a key complex of meanings in a critique of oppression does blend powerful resentments, fears, aspirations, self-images, and reflective critical analysis into an unstable mixture. We have seen that concepts of equality are not absent in Newar society or in India although they are not dominant; egalitarian insights have survived one of the most sustained and total efforts to drive equality from human consciousness—they persist in breaking into consciousness even in the caste system, surely one of the most enduring hegemonic enterprises in all of human experience. Yet equality is a fragile idea. It is often—perhaps typically—abandoned in practice for some system of rank. People retreat from egalitarian social experiments. The leaders of egalitarian movements accumulate wealth, status and power. Low caste men and women maintain that all people are the same, but seek to exclude others while gaining what advantages they can. Even in contexts where it is normative, equality is often violated. It breaks down inside castes, as Pocock notes: "although all the members of any caste are in theory equal, in fact they are very conscious of their standing in each other's eyes" (Pocock 1973:1). In Indian civilization, it evens breaks down within spiritual groups whose members have supposedly renounced the social world, and with it, social hierarchy (Burghart 1983). Thus even world-renouncers, viewed by some Newars as embodying a spiritual equality, may establish a hierarchy among themselves. Equality may survive suppression, but wither away where unopposed.

People have to live their lives in terms of incommensurate values and goals. They fashion different versions of their own lived world—and equality does not exist in all those versions. It has moral force only in some. Perhaps equality has no real content, and suggests no principles of relationship, no devices for ordering existence, no way of securing and protecting interests. Perhaps equality is a principle for collapsing structure and order, not for making or maintaining it.

"I am a person, and you are a person too," Newars say. "I bleed blood, and you bleed blood." These words invite the collapse of distinctions; they disavow differences. Since they repudiate differences, they deny any basis for exclusion or hierarchy. This is consistent with Williams' (1969) observation that equality is a kind of empty concept; however fleshed out, it resolves ultimately into the assertion that people are people. This makes them alike, but it does not attach much meaning to being a person, and ignores the equally valid observation that people are different. The "emptiness" of equality undoubtedly bothers some. On the one hand, it does not seem practical, since it offers no basis for putting together a complex society that requires a complex division of labor; on the other hand, it does not seem realistic—differences seem so apparent, and have such an aura of actuality about them. (Of course, this aura of actuality could be a cultural construction; we must be wary of common sense, of self-evidence.)

I think, however, that these philosophical objections to the idea of equality miss its moral force, and sociological significance. The "emptiness" of the concept is what gives it the power it clearly has in critical discourse. In the conceptual "emptiness" of equality ("I am a person, and you are a person") all differences dissolve. All that is left is mutual recognition. When our common identity as persons is asserted in this way, differences are made to appear arbitrary, unnatural or irrelevant. This is what makes equality a powerful concept for men and women with grievances against the structure of society. They use it to liberate themselves, and to propose the reforging of social relations.

Equality is thus a destroyer and preserver, not a creator, of social worlds. Let me put this another way: equality is a sometimes powerful critical concept, but not a very constructive one. It is used most powerfully to judge social life, not to constitute it. It does not so much tell you the way things should be, mapping out a social order, but rather declares that something is wrong or right in the way the social world works. The elementary sentiment of equality has a kind of signal function: it alerts people to problems in social existence. The concept of equality provides a kind of ideal template for justice—by declaring that all members of society are the same, the person who invokes the idea of equality proposes that society must fairly and fully recognize the interests, needs and aspirations of all. Comparing reality to this ideal sheds light on what is wrong, and offers a powerful critical platform, but it does not supply a viable plan for constructing society, or for getting things done.

As Isaiah Berlin (1981:90) has noted, absolute equality has rarely, if ever, been a positive goal. People do not desire to be forced to be "the same" anymore than they want to be excluded and stigmatized on the basis of "being different." Taken beyond its critical uses, equality potentially creates injustices by denying differences that people want to take account of. This opens the way, of course, for reinventing hierarchy.

Equality is paradoxical, too, because it is fragile and yet durable. The ideology of hierarchy developed in traditional South Asia was as forceful, as focused, as finely tuned an attack on the *possibility* of equality as the world has ever seen; but the idea of equality survived in the minds of social actors. What is the basis for the persistence of equality in hierarchical cultures, and of hierarchical attitudes in contemporary complex societies with egalitarian ideologies?[4]

I think equality and inequality are inseparable, inter-linking forms that arise almost universally in human groups because they arise almost universally in human minds. They have a cognitive, embodied, basis (Johnson 1993). This is not to deny that Australian Aborigines (say) are more egalitarian than Newar Hindus, although foraging peoples such as the Aborigines have ways of constructing hierarchy (Myers 1986). The elaboration of the forms is radically different; their histories and contexts are radically different. A particular society may move from less to more equality, or less to more inequality, or produce different concepts of equality and hierarchy. (France after the French revolution was a different society with respect to hierarchy and equality, but not one in which hierarchy or equality was absent.) It is true—at least from a certain point of view—that hierarchy may have greater scope and significance in one society, while equality is more pervasive and salient in another. Yet even the most hierarchical cultures apparently cannot eradicate the ability to conceive of equality; nor have Western cultures with egalitarian ideologies eliminated hierarchical commitments, interests, emotions, and aspirations.

While ideology cannot entirely grasp and shape actors and their thoughts, the interpretive powers people possess as persons-in-culture are necessary but not sufficient conditions for the transformation of social existence. The structures of power, of economic life, and of history do not melt away before moral fantasies or a cultural tradition of critical discourse. But the potential for change originates in mental life. Only acts of cultural reinterpretation make change possible. Transformation begins in the politics of consciousness.

I urge us to look at cultural life with a strong sense of structure and a strong sense of human agency. If cultural constructions of "reality" in some sense constitute the world people inhabit, these are, after all, ultimately human construction themselves, made in history and in practice (Ortner 1989). I find the alternatives inadequate: many social theorists have had a strong sense of social structure, but a weak sense of human agency; others have had a strong sense of agency, but a weak sense of structure. Some have seen the diversity within culture, but not "the diversity within the human actor" (Trawick 1990:139). I believe that agency and structure can be powerful simultaneously, generating mental tensions and social stresses. Actors push against, probe, assault the social and political structures and cultural formations that constrain them, construct them, limit them, often to no avail. Their struggles dissipate in disappointment. But if structures erode, because of internal or external changes, dramatic movement can happen—a seismic disturbance, a social quake. Structures of life and feeling are crucial; like God, the sense of reality is not mocked, even if this God is only an apotheosis of society (Durkheim 1965). But neither do agency and imagination vanish. Agency and imagination can be expressed within an iron cage, even if it only leaves the actor with bloody hands and a sense of futility. Strong agency stirs within strong structures. Strong minds engage powerful and encompassing cultural formations—such as the ideology and practices of caste hierarchy—at once animate and energize these, yet also resist and subvert them.

Yet if ideology and the social body it legitimates has its limits, so does human creativity. The interpretive powers of women and men, and their capacity to make culture, while hardly trivial, are not infinite; people cannot at will transform the conditions of their social existence. If they could make utopia in a day, I do not doubt they would have done so. Newars— Brahmans, untouchables, farmers—are keenly aware that they cannot simply create a new order by finding new meanings for the world. They continue to search for moral meanings for their world anyway—because life continues to pose problems of meaning, to make them suffer (Weber 1958).

As economic and political structures organize life, they produce emotional pain, economic suffering, existential misery, anxiety and despair. They limit people and make them incomplete. They produce resentment and rage that may be directed at cultural practices. Thus, the structures that organize and constrain life provoke criticism and reimagining; they inspire the critical self. They help create the conditions for their own transformation. Therefore, no human social structure is stable, and none can be understood on the basis of their social and conceptual structures alone, considered in static terms and without reference to human agency and experience. While social structures constrain, and force their own enactment, they are themselves social and historical formations. In any society, the relative predominance of hierarchy over equality, or of equality over hierarchy has specific social origins in such processes (and in the structuring structures it produces, which alter further historical developments).[5]

Hierarchy and equality belong to a curious class of concepts. They are shaped by history and culture, and yet are not reducible to history and culture. Even though they are always embedded in culture and have a specific social history, hierarchy and equality seem to have transcultural features that place them beyond the compass of radical cultural and historical relativism. They appear to have a kind of "deep" conceptual structure; they are not just ideological constructs, but rather are grounded in what people *can* know of themselves and society. The roots of equality and inequality seem to be intertwined deep in the human mind; they seem to develop together as a result of the mind's encounter with the basic conditions of social existence. Human beings are conceptually ambiguous; their ambiguity makes both equality and hierarchy possible. We can easily enumerate ways humans are alike: everyone possesses, as one of my Jugi informants noted, noses, eyes; we all bleed blood and not milk. Alternatively, it is easy to find or invent differences: in skin color, in patterns of conduct, in cultural or physical characteristics that may be real or fantasized.

Holism Versus the Individual Body

The hegemony of hierarchy is, in part, the product of efforts to deny, break up, efface, and limit challenges to inequality. It is a response to a threat, not a set of ideas that have spontaneously generated themselves in a political vacuum. The threat is not just the opposition of disenfranchised groups. The threat goes much deeper; it lies in consciousness itself, in the ways people are able to reinterpret society and to invoke ideas of equality and human solidarity. Equality must be overcome in the mind of the Brahman as well as the untouchable.

Ideology meets potential threats at the level of individual consciousness. It must be deployed to guard against the mind's capacity to reflect on the meaning of differences and likenesses, against an agent's ability to ask probing questions of culture.

Ideology is, among other things, an effort to intervene in the critical and reflexive work of minds. In every society, people engage in a process of making and unmaking differences that justify hierarchy under an abstract principle of justice, to treat like cases alike and different cases differently, that has rational appeal in many different cultures, perhaps universally. In this discourse, a hierarchy is a moment in a complex cycle of inventing, valuing and unmaking human differences and similarities.

Inventing hierarchy may be the cognitively harder task in this cycle; constructing hierarchy invariably require cultural amplification and elaboration. The construction of equality may be less cultural (at least in some aspects), though by now it should be clear that equality takes shape and acquires moral force in terms of distinctive cultural concepts. Taking a purely psychological perspective, some might argue that the human mind naturally develops the capacity to perceive and evaluate situations and ways in which people are "the same"—we simply recognize their embodied reality, that they are like ourselves. The elementary form of equality does not require that we attach any further meaning to this recognition of alikeness, although people may. Constructing hierarchy, in contrast, always involves attaching evaluative, social meaning to differences.

Of course, if we argue that people have some "natural" capacity for recognizing the way human beings are alike, we would also probably accept the notion that people possess some natural cognitive capacity for perceiving and processing differences as well. This seems quite likely. But hierarchy is more than difference. The ability to recognize differences does not explain the way differences are composed into a hierarchy: recognizing differences is not the same as ranking differences.

Whatever the mind makes of differences, the *ranking* of differences into a social hierarchy is always a cultural and political process, not some kind of automatic reflex of a culture-free mind. This means that hierarchy and equality may not be perfectly symmetrical concepts; they may have different logical structures and different paths of development within culture and individual consciousness.

I give the equality implied in mutual recognition priority in justice discourse only in a limited sense, and I may be ethnocentric—or too influenced by my Newar friends—in doing so. But let me at least note the possibility. It seems to me the equality of mutual recognition has a powerful appeal because it "balances" relationships, and because it constitutes a powerful vehicle for critique. In one-on-one interactions, if I have the same power as another, I am unlikely to let myself be defined as not a person, as not having interests, as not deserving equal consideration of my circumstances, and so on. Only if I lack power—the power to communicate my position, and the power to force a hearing, or am motivated by some other compelling consideration, would I surrender this equality. I might do so out of love or empathy, but I would resist coercion. Even if I have privileges and advantages others do not possess, a higher status and better access to moral and economic resources, and even if I believe in my superiority and the legitimacy of my more favored place in society, I would still want others to treat me on the basis of mutual recognition—as a person—and resent it when they do not. In my experience, Brahmans and untouchables feel the same way. On this, as with the judgment that no one would want to be born low caste, they seem to agree.

Of course, this does not imply a universalized ethic of equality, or an identification of equality with justice: as we have seen, hierarchy can be seen as justice, as giving people what they deserve, as treating different cases differently. Yet justifying a legal code or social ethic that treats people differently in this particular way takes much cultural work, arguably requires, in fact, what we have called a cultural hegemony with "a lock" on "common sense" as well as on major social, political, and judicial institutions. Even in the face of this, however, concepts of equality are available, and may supply the starting point for critique.

Many might disagree with any attempt to privilege equality, and I recognize some of the difficulties. The notion that the recognition that people are alike, and so equal in a presumptive way, is more "self-evident," and possibly more culture free, than concepts of hierarchy, may itself have a cultural basis. It may be an illusion, based on an ethnocentric or idiosyncratic sense of what values are "self-evident." [6] The kind of analysis it would take to unravel this issue is beyond the scope of this work. The key point here is that opposing perspectives of equality and hierarchy, of the social whole and the concrete individual, are available to Newars, and they use each one as if it were necessary and natural, self-evident and unchallengeable.

The chart in Figure 2, which I derive from the interviews with Newars from which I have quoted in preceding chapters—suggests the disjuncture in Newar thought between perceiving a basis for equality and constructing a basis for hierarchy. Whatever their source in mind or culture, concepts for "seeing that" people are alike and "seeing that" people are different coexist in Newar culture. The chart presents two arguments. One argument reduces people to empirical individuals ("bodies")— this nullifies hierarchy. The other arguments obviates equality: it is "holistic" in form, and relies on a metaphorical equation of society with a body.

Notice that both arguments provide justice, but one as equality, the other as hierarchy. For if justice consists in treating like cases alike, and all people are essentially alike, then they deserve the same treatment, and for their fates to differ in radical ways is an injustice. But if justice consists in treating different cases differently, then, since castes are different categories of people, as different as the parts of a body, justice requires different treatment, and incommensurate fates are just. Newars may assert either view, depending on the premise they adopt.

Here equality and hierarchy are not symmetrical in construction; the denouement of hierarchy is somewhat more complex. (The two forms are also not symmetrical in terms of enactment and social force, since, of course, hierarchy and holism are dominant forms.) The construction of hierarchy begins with a metaphor, not an empirical proposition. Dumont (1980) and Shweder and Bourne (1984) identify holism or socio-

FIGURE 2. Concepts of equality and hierarchy in Newar thought.

Equality	*Hierarchy*
1. Propositions: PEOPLE HAVE BODIES Bodies are the same	1. Propositions: SOCIETY HAS A BODY Castes are like body parts
2. Device: Enumerate body parts, or appeal to uniform physiological substance ("same blood, same flesh")	2. Device: Assign function to body part and assign analogous function to social group
3. Implication: People are the same CANCELS HIERARCHY	3. Implication: Castes are different. People of different castes are different. CANCELS EQUALITY
4. Corollary: People deserve the same respect, treatment, and status.	4. Corollary: Castes do not deserve the same respect, treatment, or status.
5. Proponents: Mostly low caste	5. Proponents: Both high and low
6. Relation of individual to caste: Functional	6. Relation of individual to caste: Synecdochic, part for whole.
7. Justice implication: Treat like cases alike.	7. Justice implication: Treat different cases differently.

centric thinking as characteristic of Indian culture. As Shweder and Bourne (1984) note, "in holistic sociocentric cultures like India the human body, conceived as an interdependent system, is frequently taken as a metaphor for society as a whole" (1984:191). Thus the Newars share a social trope found widely in South Asia. Alongside this—and subversive of it—is the argument that people have bodies, and so are the same. Holistic/sociocentric thinking and hierarchy are socially dominant forms, but do not constitute the only mode of thought. The alternative argument, based on individual bodies, has some salience and power.

There are counter-arguments as well, of course. When I told a high caste Hindu of these low caste arguments, the claims "people have bodies," "people bleed blood," and so on, he responded by saying that animals bleed blood too. A Buddhist Newar asked by Stephen Greenwold (1978:502) whether members of impure castes are permanently impure, replied "Yes and no." He said that all people can become pure in theory, by attaining the "knowledge" (*gyana*) of Buddha, but that "once a living creature takes birth in an impure family, he really can never become pure in this life. Nothing comes of nothing. A duck's egg always produces a duck." In this conception, birth is destiny. One can hardly imagine a stronger assertion of hierarchy based on the concept of impurity; yet he goes on to say as well that "caste is really a matter of the king. The king

can make untouchables clean and people of clean caste, untouchable."
Occasionally, power trumps purity. This dialectic of construction and
counter-construction is complex, and cannot be captured in a single
model, but requires us to see how actors use multiple models, animating
them in relationship to each other: purity, power, equality, all contribute
to the actual constructive awareness of self and caste society.

Holism requires differences, and calls them into being—castes are different as the parts of a whole are different.[7] The South Asian evidence
shows that holism, with its organic metaphor, is also able to overcome
equality and to construct hierarchy. Yet although holism is clearly invoked to justify hierarchy, Newars may, as we saw, envision equality in
terms of holism, too; all persons may have a deity dwelling inside them,
so that their differences are transcended in a higher order spiritual
equality.

The ongoing dialectic is open-ended, with all kinds of possibilities for
rhetorical riposte and counter-attack. I can easily imagine high caste
Hindus drawing on Western folk concepts of "blood" as natural substance to meet the arguments of "I bleed blood, and you bleed blood,
too." They would say, "Yes, I bleed blood, and you bleed blood—but I
bleed different blood." Blood, they might argue, contains different essences, enjoins different codes of conduct, and therefore positions
groups in society in different ways. They might domesticate (acculturate)
the Western concept of "blood," making it fit their concepts of the
person.

Like Dumont, I have argued, however, that Newars treat the question
of differences and hierarchy in a framework of order, not just of substance. People are different in a fundamental way, not just because their
substance, their being, is different, but because their different roles and
qualities are necessary for an ordered existence. What they do is just as
important as what they are: the interplay of concepts of being and doing
reinforce each other. Kolenda (1964) and Sharma (1973) quote South
Asians, who, like many Newars, view hierarchy most saliently in terms of
functional interdependence, not substance or purity.

As important as holism is in Newar culture, it is not their only way of
being. They recover something of themselves in the act of dissent, and
perhaps make themselves incomplete in other ways as they do so. They
must shift perspectives and throw themselves into flux—which may be
one of the conditions of human existence, at least in complex societies.
There is no finality. For any number of reasons, the untouchables who
assert equality may find themselves affirming hierarchy.

It is important to note that the "people have bodies" argument both
is hierarchy-neutralizing and has to do with the moral equivalence of
physically embodied individuals—it is not holistic equality, the moral

equivalence generated by being absorbed in, part of, a deity, nor is it the moral individualism of the ascetic. Although Newar concepts of equality can be sociocentric, they can also be individualistic.[8] It is this very *diversity* that has been relatively neglected in studies of caste and culture in South Asia. As Appadurai says, speaking of holism, "Ill-served by the trope of part and whole are those aspects of social life that have uneven degrees of saliency in the life of a community, which flow in complex ways into each other, and which make up indeterminate, ever-shifting configurations in and among themselves" (1989:759).

The arbitrary foundations of the caste order are made to seem natural by the various devices in caste ideology that *make* differences. In the process of constructing hierarchy, *empirical* differences or similarities *can* be assigned meaning and value. But this process—of selecting and evaluating perceptible differences, so that they mean something—is only one way of constructing hierarchy and equality. It can work the other way. Someone can learn to see, not just that I am dirty and poorly dressed, but that I am impure, a fit receiver of inauspiciousness. Many of the differences and alikenesses used to constitute hierarchy and equality as values are forged in culture, not found in the empirical world—the god that dwells in the heart is not an empirical proposition in the way that the assertion that everyone bleeds blood is.

In either case, equality and hierarchy are interwoven in culture just as similarities and differences are interwoven in perception. The possibility of focusing on one persists even when the focus is on the other. Human beings are conceptually ambiguous. Anytime any one proposes that two groups are different in a way that should (or does) make a difference— justifying the privileges some possess, and the disadvantages others experience—someone else will challenge the grounds on which this is done. Anytime someone maintains that people are the same, someone else—or the same person in a different mood—can counter with an account of their differences. Newar caste rhetoric (and Western discourse about equality and inequality as well) turns on this infinite loop of making and unmaking differences, of asserting sameness and finding differences.

Despite qualifications to his central argument, Dumont, in his account of *Homo hierarchicus*, is caught up in the same recursive process of making differences and alikeness, self and other, hierarchy and equality—he simply distributes these across civilizations, India and the West. He is right to see that caste ideology *makes* differences—that purity and impurity are differences constituted in culture, not found in nature; they are not empirical differences that are given value, but differences that culture creates *as* values. This was a key insight. But alternative hierarchies and equalities can be constructed as well; by reifying just one ideological moment, one particular construction of hierarchy, that of a dominant ideology, Dumont was able to make a sharp contrast between Indian civilization and the West. Dumont packaged empirical differences into a seemingly telling contrast; but his project resonates with a need, variously expressed in the West and elsewhere, to give definition to a sense of self through contrasts with others. In sharpening contrasts, one risks overlooking the actual, complex textures of difference and alikeness. Dumont's comparative approach runs a grave risk—of slipping easily from structural *analysis* into the *heuristics* of Orientalism.

In responding to critics, Dumont (1985, 1987) himself acknowledges the need to hedge and qualify his conclusions, while maintaining that hierarchy exists in a pure form in India. But when others read Dumont, they focus on the sharp contrasts, and the idea of the South Asia as *homo hierarchicus*, not on the hedges and qualifications. To take an example, in an otherwise critical and penetrating book, Marcus and Fischer cite Dumont as raising the question of cultural variations in the concept of the person, "on behalf of all hierarchical societies affirming explicit premises of inequality. . . . In these cases, the individual, while a physical entity, has no autonomous sociological status, and is conceived as but an integral part of a larger unit" (1986:45–46). But conceived by whom? In what context? In terms of whose ideology? Are we denying Newars agency? Newars conceive of themselves as parts of larger units, their families, their castes, the caste system, their cities; but they know themselves as autonomous individuals within the matrix of these groups and communities. How can we say the individual has no autonomous sociological status? As in the Western world, they have no autonomous sociological status in some ideological formations; but they act in society, think in society, and feel in society—and we can fail to see this only if we mistake ideological constructions of reality for social reality itself. The interplay of multiple ways of knowing themselves, and the tensions the coexistence of these alternatives generates, are of great psychological and sociological significance. The method of sharp contrast of single ideologies obscures this.

In my view, hierarchy and equality are always available to human minds; people everywhere place some value on the way people are alike or different. At root, hierarchy and equality are transcultural categories—since they have to do with fundamental possibilities of relatedness and otherness—and yet they are also cultural, for they are always given meaning and value in culture. The universal and the cultural both matter.

Whatever cognitive universals moral concepts embody (D'Andrade 1990, Johnson 1993), they take shape and form in cultural practice and thought. The justice of the Hindu caste system (untouchables get what they deserve because they committed sins in previous lives) is not the justice of democracy in class-bound industrial societies (where many believe the homeless have done something to deserve their fate). There is an important family resemblance (people "get what they deserve"), but the differences (concepts of pollution, karma, and reincarnation) make a difference, too.

Now, all this does not leave "justice" congealed in an unchanging culture that determines absolutely what people think, feel, and do. Culture changes. People remake it. The power, the possibility, the resources, for re-telling moral concepts always exist within cultures. This makes possible the reconfiguring of moral consciousness. The moral visions that take shape in culture can be contested (for example, by using moral narratives to render problematic their claimed connection to "deep" universals), sometimes transformed. The concepts of justice embodied in hegemony, forged in ideology and action, represent particular political transformations of justice and can be subject to reflection and retransformation. Ideas have cultural histories, after all—even moral constructs do. They wear out, and lose their grip on consciousness, as the conditions of life change, or people generate new images of world, society, self. As people withdraw commitment, disengage, change their deeply cultural minds by drawing on culture in different ways, existing moral visions may dissolve—and others arise to take their place. New visions may connect "deep" moral universals to human life in new ways.

Equality and hierarchy are asserted and challenged in ideology and critique, in the cultural dialogues of what people are, and in the equally cultural dialogues of what might, and should, be. We need to explore these dialogues, the way they deploy concepts of hierarchy and equality, and the way the dialogue of self-identity engages both these dialogues. Different cultures create or understand equality and inequality in different ways, but their "interplay" is important even where hierarchy has been worked out almost obsessively, as it was in Nepal; until the 1950s the caste hierarchy in Nepal had the full support of a Hindu state backing it up. And yet, Newars have developed cultural and personal images of equality. When someone says, "[the god] Vishnu is in my heart. He is in your heart also. He is in the heart of others. He is everywhere. Since he is everywhere, we are with everyone. We are all the same," can it be doubted that the speaker has a rich, highly developed idea of equality?

Recall Kesar's controlled rage. The god in my heart, he said, wants what the god in your heart wants. I want, he argued, what you want. He does not, I'm sure, imagine that social equality can be achieved—quite the contrary. In pointing out what his heart-god wants, he asserts neither an empty piety nor a pie-in-the sky fantasy, but the foundation of a sense of self. In the face of inequities, he preserves his belief in his humanity, as represented by the fragment of divinity within him, that unites all people.

And yet Dumont says that "What no Indian religion has ever fully attained and which was given from the start in Christianity is the brotherhood of love in and through Christ, and the consequent equality of all, 'an equality that exists purely,' Troeltsch insists, 'in the presence of god'" (1985:99). Perhaps Dumont is right and there is a comparative thesis in this: cultures that transpose love from the family to the monotheistic divine sphere have made possible the universalization of equality, and have lent moral force to the concept of equality. (The metaphor of 'brotherhood' is cross-fertilized with another trope, lifting moral solidarity above kinship amity, for the equality of all is established "in the eyes of God.") Yet the equality in and through Vishnu in fact attains as great a universality. Indeed, since Vishnu inhabits the hearts of women and men, one might even suggest this vision of universal equality potentially achieves a greater universality, since the "brotherhood" is not "everyone." But as the use of the gendered metaphor reminds us, although ideas of equality are not unique to the West, they do have concrete histories within cultures, and reflect specific cultural attitudes.

I have come to view the interplay of hierarchy and equality as rooted in something the human mind *does* when confronted with the problem of life in society. The work of culture in constructing hierarchy is to make differences (of race, of gender) mean something in a social context; or, more subtly, to *make differences*, such as differences in purity or auspiciousness, that *can* mean something in a social context—and to *make* these differences make a difference. But if hierarchy is one product of culture, then equality is another. If in the West, people can be equal in the eyes of one transcendent God, then Hindus can be equal by virtue of the god that dwells in each person. If Westerners conceive of the equal rights of autonomous individuals, then Hindus can evoke a sense of shared divinity.

I am not arguing for some symmetry of equality or solidarity conceptions across cultures: but I am arguing against simple contrasts, and I am arguing for the need to explore the specific dynamic relationship of hierarchy and equality in any culture. The Hindus I know are not, as Dumont's work implies, a distinct cultural species of human kind, a *Homo hierarchicus*, who are hierarchical out of a deep consensus about values, but are rather people who live socially and politically situated lives, and who in their lives, have cultural models of both hierarchy and of equality or human solidarity. Politically dominant values do determine what can be enacted. But this does not stop people from trying out different ways of knowing themselves, in moral fantasies, in rhetoric, or in the anonymous and ambivalent communitas of festivals.

Dumont recalls that equality is possible in India; but he does not seek to work out the relationship it has with hierarchy. He acknowledges equality as an afterthought to hierarchy; he does not see the way these are entangled in India, the way that hierarchy cannot achieve the closure and finality he (and Brahmanical ideology) ascribe to it. He sees the West as making people the same, and India as making them different; but people make themselves the same, and different, everywhere, as they live lives within cultures, and respond to political and economic circumstances. South Asians can subvert the Brahmanical hierarchy, conceive of alternative hierarchies, assert equality, and reassert hierarchy—they shift among values and perspectives. Different values are made salient in different ways at different times for different purposes—by actors in different life situations, drawing on different dimensions of their culture.

Nothing I have said diminishes the importance of the dominant concepts of caste life and of the constraints on action they create as they constitute a public "reality" for social actors. Understanding these is essential. What I argue is that there is more going on than many anthropological accounts acknowledge—and that much of this "more" is systematically obscured and distorted by the dominant ideologies of caste life. By looking at the constructions of personal voices—where people seek to say what they think and feel—I think we see how much more there is. People do not know and experience themselves and the world in terms of the "single vision" proposed by the dominant construction of reality. They know and experience themselves in terms of multiple, conflicting visions of world and self.

Every complex culture carries within it multiple critiques of itself. A complex culture also contains cultural possibilities—visions of world and self—that can be actualized or, if not actualized, used to subvert, challenge, and vex the dominant order. Such visions and critiques are not the ideology that organizes public life or the political system, but they have sociological and psychological significance. They may be more or less dormant possibilities; or they may be highly developed in the imagination and experience of some actors, more real for them than actual social reality, like the phantom limbs of an amputee, culturally experienced without having social existence, much less the power to challenge the dominant order. Visions and critiques, however, cast shadows and light on the cultural world of the dominant ideology, puncturing common sense, challenging the hegemony of dominant concepts of reality, making the unthinkable thinkable, enabling some to reinvent the world and self.

Some people find it very hard to be "at home" in a cultural tradition. Untouchables—and those like them in any hierarchy—can try harder, but may find that the harder they try, the harder it gets, for efforts to integrate themselves into the dominant culture, to embody its central values, may develop into an exercise in self-contradiction (Fanon 1967). They are trying to be what they are not, in terms of social definition; and if they try to be what they are, by social definition, they are nothing they would want to be, and not what they know themselves to be, at other moments. They may well give up, and seek emancipation from the stigmatizing web of meanings they find around them—as some untouchable's seek to brush away the cobwebs of castes, gods, and rites, as Jigyasu said of the culture he rejected. People are not totally passive creatures of culture; they are also agents of cultural lives.

"Critical understanding of self," wrote Gramsci, "takes place . . . through the struggle of political 'hegemonies' . . . first in the ethical field and then in politics proper, . . . [leading to] the working out of a higher level of one's own conception of reality" (Gramsci 1971:333).[9] I think that Kesar, like Krishna and many others, has arrived at the point Gramsci speaks of: as Kesar breaks with dominant concepts of reality, he breaks through into critical consciousness, thus altering his sense of self, making himself a different kind of social actor. Neither Kesar nor Krishna have totally broken free from the grip of hierarchy, but the horizons within which they define self and evaluate society do extend beyond the dominant conception of reality. They generate a critical, if ambivalent, consciousness out of elements of their culture, and so provide themselves with the moral grounds on which to reject the justice, the identity, the social reality, that the established order offers.

This is true of many others in caste society. They dream of possible worlds. Doing so, their reflective concepts of self and society—which surely help them define who they are, help constitute their felt self-identity—"achieve some degree of autonomy" from social and cultural constraints, "if only in fantasy and imagination" (Spiro 1984:330).

In part, such fantasies are surely the stuff selves are made of. Immanent in culture, they nonetheless allow what Spiro (1984) calls the "self-reflective ego" to transcend or disavow some elements of culture. A person, a Kesar or a Krishna, can be a moral agent in consciousness by proposing a world in narrative and fantasy, in moral discourse, even if they cannot translate much of this into practice. They can be moral agents in their irony and anger if not always in effective social action. We cannot identify the "self" of such actors with the ideology or discourses of the cultural order, and pretend self does not exist as well in their ironies, their anger, their aspirations, their critiques of social practice, their moral fantasies.

I suspect moral fantasies are also the stuff political cultures are ultimately made of, the stuff of demagoguery and moral suasion alike, of resistance and reaction. In fantasy and imagination, we find discontents voiced and symbolized. As Kenneth Burke said: "Only those voices from without are effective which can speak in the language of a voice within" (1969:39). Fantasies represent formations of experience, bodies of felt meaning, that those who seek dominance or emancipation may each draw on and seek to direct to political ends.

Of course, these fantasies—as subterranean moral projects, as veiled or overt critical theories, as the implicit utopias and critiques of people who would change the world if they could—reflect conditions of life characterized by relative powerlessness in the here and now. People engage in them because they cannot act freely and fully to achieve what they want and what they perceive as justice: moral fantasies and utopian narratives are sublimations of moral and political desires, prosthetic utopias that compensate psychologically for the amputations experienced in social reality. If powerlessness runs deep enough and lasts long enough, there may be no other compensation for what invisible hands and dead hands have done in the iron cages of history.

But dreams of possible worlds imply possible futures. In some possible futures, if history shuffles the deck in a way that creates opportunities for their expression, these utopian and critical imaginings and the models of self and society they play with may help animate self-making, culture-making, and history-making.

People use culture to stir things up, to challenge and dream, as well as to define themselves and reality in terms of the dominant order. Some may not want to be "at home" in a culture that oppresses. They may seek emancipation—away from the cobwebs, out of the cage—if only in fantasy. Inching towards their very own brave new worlds, they may examine their iron cages with the attention to the minutiae, the details, and overall design of the cultural construction they live in that only those seeking a way out can muster. If, doing so, they have achieved critical consciousness, they may appreciate how powerless they are. And yet, by stirring things up, by challenging the dominant ideology, by groping for different ways to think and feel their experience, by imagining possible worlds, they may confront the dominant order with the disturbing possibility of change and transformation.

Postscript: The Problem of Power

People in caste society wrestle with problems of meaning and necessity inside the belly of the beast—inside the dominant construction of reality.

Let me explain. I have been concerned with moments of apparent insight and blindness, with the ways social actors know and fail to know their social worlds. In my person-centered research, I have been forced to recognize the "political forging" of consciousness as a central social process. It is a process through which dominant groups attempt to substitute symbols and meanings for coercion and violence, achieving legitimacy by constructing visions of the social order that are institutionalized in social practices, embodied in symbolic performances, and granted the status of common sense and objective reality.[1] But I have also been concerned with the ways actors break with dominant concepts, break through the limits of the cultural world constituted by those concepts, and reject dominant concepts of reality, even as they live their lives within the world and reality formed in terms of those concepts.

To understand this dynamic, the concept of cultural hegemony seems useful, although it presents dangers to which I will turn shortly. The notion of cultural hegemony has roots in the thought of the Marxist theorist Antonio Gramsci, but has been adopted and developed by many others, including literary and culture theorist Raymond Williams (1977); anthropologist Sherry Ortner in a study of Sherpa history and religion (1989); political scientist David Laitin in a study of Yoruba culture (1986); and anthropologist Daniel Linger (1992) in an article on protest and rebellion in a city in northeastern Brazil. These scholars use the concept in different ways; what they all share is a recognition of the political dimensions of culture.[2]

"At the heart of Gramsci's notion of hegemony," writes Daniel Linger, "is his most vital insight: culture is political." The grip of culture on consciousness has political roots and consequences. While we cannot reduce culture to politics, neither should we assume culture is always neutral;

often enough culture embodies and animates political discourse, justifying, even determining, who gets what. Every effort to forge a world view—by setting up a dominant "concept of reality" and attempting to diffuse it throughout society by shaping and socializing minds[3]—sets loose a politics of consciousness, which may take unexpected turns, and always contains within it the possibility of resistance and opposition.[4]

"Civilization," wrote Freud in his work on its discontents, "obtains mastery over the individual's dangerous desire for aggression by weakening and disarming it and by setting up an agency within him to watch over it, like a garrison in a conquered army" (1961:70–71). I wish to shift the ground of the metaphor a bit. It is not just a "natural" bodily propensity for aggression that is weakened and disarmed by "setting up" in minds cultural models that construct visions of self, society, and reality. Just as significantly, culture established subjectively in persons may suppress and redirect socially dangerous desires for justice and emancipation—desires which if acted on might threaten to disrupt the cultural order. To put it another way: for a group's ideas to achieve hegemony over the mind, competing ideas must be neutralized or co-opted. When cultural meanings possessing political significance compete in minds, then concepts of justice have a special place, a pivotal value—the city stands or falls with these concepts because they coalesce, formulate, and sustain the possibilities of the idea of a moral order, and shape identifications with the actual social order, organizing resistance or assent to social practice. Concepts of justice may have to be redeployed if a particular political vision of reality is to have real-world force.

I do not know whether the sense and sensibility of justice that must be overcome culturally for ideology to get a grip on the mind is the product of innate mental capacities (the result of psychological development, as some Western psychologists maintain) or acquired in the course of cultural life (as others might argue). The origins of "justice consciousness" may not matter much in practice; what matters is the real-world politics of consciousness, as this involves efforts to compose and disseminate legitimating visions of justice. Whatever the source of justice beliefs, what often matters most in practice is being able to suppress, or transmute, or redirect them.

Desires for justice or social transformation can be controlled by installing concepts of reality, systems of meanings, and knowledge of fear, violence, and deprivation within the person to watch over their often subversive desires and dissident thought—"like a garrison in a conquered city." And yet, discontents may persist, and even turn creative, generating new visions of justice, of what life should be like. Disenchantment may embody a desire for emancipation and may propel culture-making, leading actors to challenge existing visions of social life, if only in thought or talk, and moving them to formulate new visions, if only in fantasy.

Since this often arouses resistance in society and self, the mind is the scene of political struggles to determine what can be thought and felt, and what cannot. As a result of this struggle, what justice means can change: if equality is justice from one perspective (treat like cases like, as a classical formulation has it), hierarchy may embody justice from another perspective (treat different cases differently). If I am a person, like you, I should hear your claim to justice; but if I believe you are different in morally relevant ways, if you are an untouchable, a handler of excrement who must have sinned in past lives, then I may believe you deserve your social fate, so that inequality is perfect justice.

But if I am an untouchable I may resist this, in thought if not in action. This conquest of mind succeeds (if it does) through the force of rhetoric in public discourse, by means of the shaping of common sense and communal activity (Linger 1993). It succeeds because the active partisans of an ideology have control over resources for interpreting experience and are able to coordinate their control over meanings with their power over other resources, including control over the implementation of key cultural practices. The ability to occupy and hold the mind is not absolute, however; it meets resistance, often fierce resistance, within political and social arenas to be sure, but also within self. Resistance may continue even when a ideology becomes dominant in a practical sense; even then, those political desires that have been repressed and driven underground may reemerge or take alternative forms. This may in turn trigger additional effort to suppress or redirect them, within society and within self. An actor's multiple moral-political consciousness is thus the product of responses to conflicting cultural models.

Gramsci raised the question of actors' participation "in a conception of the world mechanically imposed by the external environment," that is, by social groups. Now one might think—after reading the work of Dumont (1980) and Moffatt (1979)—that caste hierarchy constituted a hegemony that totally dominated traditional consciousness, that these hegemonic cultural formations had, in India, abolished all resistance, all alternatives. That is, of course, not quite true, as the testimony of many social actors reveals. Yet, while falling short of total hegemony, the values and practices of the caste system surely achieve a practical dominance. I do not think recognizing this detracts in any way from what I have said about the psychology of caste: it is hierarchy's hegemony that sets up the psycho-existential quandaries that have been one focus of this study.

doxa but no hetero dox

A sense of self may dissent from cultural life. In caste society, social life coalesces around the values and practices of caste hierarchy; but psychological life may coalesce around a rejection of these values. This does not mean that the social world shrinks into insignificance. The dominance, the hegemony, that caste hierarchy achieves remains social reality. As an untouchable Sweeper, Mahila experiences this every day. His diffident public face reflects the dominance of caste values in Bhaktapur.

Indeed, Mahila *is* hierarchy: a living symbol of it. The pageantry of hierarchy fills the public world during festivals: everyday interactions reflect it; persons embody it. Even the actors who most vehemently resist hierarchy represent and embody it to others as they walk the streets, become type-specimens. In these ways and others, hierarchy dominates public space, occupies and organizes cultural consciousness.

Hierarchy has hegemony: it is resisted. We have seen that the cultural media—pageantry, common sense, the interactions of everyday life—in which hierarchy is cultivated are also where it contested: pageantry is disrupted; what common sense makes natural, fantasy makes arbitrary; the premises of everyday life are reimagined in narratives. On occasion, someone will stand up and challenge the way they are not being recognized as human beings. In the face of this, hierarchy sustains itself and its dominance only through the sustained effort of those with a stake in it (who may be those who at other moments reject it). It follows, I think, that the meanings and practices that constitute hierarchy have a precise political value, even when this goes unrecognized in analysis. I believe they achieve their political effect, in part, by seizing and shaping the sense of justice, by determining what constitutes a just world. Hegemony can be exerted in many ways, across many cultural domains, but I feel it has a special relationship with ideas of justice, as I suggest above. Hegemony can be achieved in the fullest sense only by controlling concepts of justice.

Yet even more than this, to achieve and sustain hegemony over minds—to elicit assent, not just grudging accommodation—constructions of the world must make it possible for actors to find meaning in their lives. At its most powerful, hegemony is subtle domination, a package of meanings that elicits much active consent, not just acquiescence, even on the part of those most disadvantages by the world it constitutes. They must be able to find themselves in it, find meaning in it. Unless it offers them lives, a construction of the world will not generate the moral commitments and social identifications that sustain a social order.

To say that slaves are inferior by nature and thus can be bought and sold, or that peasants are brutish and insensitive, fit only for the drudgery of agricultural labor is naked ideology. Hegemony may be less direct, harder to perceive. It may emerge with a vision of a meaningful existence, of a moral order: A paean to an aristocratic way of life, a narrative celebration of their graceful lifestyle, or their vision of a good life, which upholds and brings into focus the human face, the value, the meaningful experiences of a way of life may nurture hegemony insofar as it presupposes the subordinated presence of others—servants in the hall, serfs or slaves in the field, untouchables on the edge of the city. These unspoken others haunt the celebration; their existence is implied. To rhapsodize about the dominant way of life is to put these shadowy figures in their place.

The discourse does not have to be about stratification. In America, as the ethnic mix of communities changes, some people also rhapsodize about the ethnic neighborhood; recalling how it used to be asserts the way it should be, and recognizes—without necessarily accepting—the way it is becoming. This too puts people in their place—it says some do not belong. This belief can organize action—even violent action. In these cases, memory is hegemony, organizing convictions about the world that set people in opposition to each other, giving practices of exclusion social meaning and moral significance.

Cultural images of self and society that achieve hegemony—that stand as powerful and pervasive self-images and societal images from which people take meanings that integrate them into social practices—may animate behavior and attitudes long after a deliberate, conscious ideology has been exhausted and abandoned. Someone may reminisce about what his long-suffering mother did in the kitchen—lingering over the memory of loving meals patiently cooked and served—long after women have been accorded equality of opportunity in the "official" ideology of a society and economic reality has dictated that they seek paying jobs. This may be a hegemonic performance, to the extent it charges social relations with moral meaning, and declares the way relationships should be, assigning burdens to some, privileges to others. This performance might reflect an ideology, but it is not quite the same as ideology. True, an ideology is a system of ideas, values, and meanings, and all of these contribute to the process of forming a cultural hegemony; but hegemony is a "lived system of meanings and values," which may not consciously be held, in the way a formal ideology is, but rather saturates "the whole process of living" (Williams 1977:110).

The difference between ideology and hegemony is the difference, then, between formulating an idea discursively and experiencing a state of consciousness, a feeling, a commitment, a sense of reality. Hegemony takes form in the feelings that suffuse practice, not just in terms of those conscious values that are codified as "official" beliefs. Hegemony interlocks with ideology, but not only with ideology. It also grows out of what Williams (1977) has termed "structures of feeling." What people know and experience reflects the way their process of living has been saturated with meaning. Life itself then presents a vision of what is real and good, evoking commitment to social practices and identification with the concept of self that is required by those practices. Such commitments and identifications can occur despite a consciously critical stance, since what persons feel and do may fly in the face of what they believe (even if their conscious critical values are predicated on a rigorously worked-out counter-ideology). The dialectic of ideology and hegemony often produces painful self-contradiction.

Since the domination enacted through values that achieve cultural hegemony is frequently indirect and unintended, social actors do not necessarily feel responsible for it. They can subject their motives to the most searching scrutiny, and not find a guilty mind—for they do not have one. They do not know what they have done—or they manage not to know what they know. Cultural hegemony may achieve some of its effects by way of the political unconscious: identifying with the meanings of the moral order may leave one blind to the consequences of one's practice. How can only doing what you should and must be blamed for social evils down the line? Often, a sort of cultural maze of blinds and baffles distance and protect one set of social actors from the impact of their beliefs and practices on another set of social actors.

The hegemony of interlocked cultural models and social practices that sustain caste separation and domination is a matter of tactic politics, a body of rhetoric that is not fully aware of itself, a consciousness-making and reality-defining discourse that almost subliminally shapes political attitudes. It may be a nascent ideology, the matrix out of which explicit political beliefs grow; or it may be derived from a developed ideology, perhaps so deeply internalized that its political origins are no longer recognized. In either case, what is crucial is that some conceptions and values assume the status of common sense, nature, objective reality, biological fact, the sacred. People see them as inviolable. It follows that they will feel threatened by those who repudiate this world view.

Like untouchables who affirm the caste hierarchy, people often actively and "willingly" participate in practices that stigmatize them, and collude in their own exploitation. To join in "naturalizing the arbitrary" (Bourdieu 1977) permits those oppressed by the arbitrariness of the social order to find meaning—moral meaning—in their fate. This is often more tolerable than the naked truth—that their fate is wholly arbitrary, and has no meaning—and the despair it offers.

Hegemony is an expression of the power to make culture. Dominant groups seeks to shape and dominate consciousness through the cultural production, legitimation, control and diffusion of values, symbols and meanings, creating a sense of reality that reinforces, ethicizes, and naturalizes social practices that "position" social actors in relation to each other. One suspects self-validation is a key motive, perhaps as important as the desire for social control.

When power is concentrated, as it once was in Bhaktapur, a particular group may leave its mark on the models and practices that shape social relations: kings and elites build temples, interpret texts, make laws, define reality in ways that make them at home in the world, leave them in charge, places them at the center of the city if not at the center of the universe. Through political and moral and cultural leadership they claim their place in the cosmos and society, and put others in their place.

What mediates, what renders palpable and makes persuasive such claims, is the construction of concepts of reality and the forging of consciousness in terms of those concepts, in ways that produce at least a measure of active commitment to social practices. To lock together values and practices in a way which will carry actors along, which will produce active commitment, a cultural formation must be more than a system of coercive domination; it must be a vehicle for life. It cannot only exploit; it must appeal to people on other levels, perhaps satisfying a need for symbolic experience and moral meaning. The demand for symbols and meanings may, of course, itself be stimulated and shaped by cultural practices, and thus be an integral part of the process of socializing for ideological responsiveness. Several points follow from this general perspective.

1. Since the hegemonic formation is part of a way of life, and is often not recognized as an instrument of domination, it has a reflexive authenticity for social actors.
2. Since it is not an instrument of domination for them—and they do not clearly see the violence it does to others—it does not violate their justice concepts. This makes it possible for them to believe in a just world.
3. Since it is their way of life, authentic and meaningful for them, they will defend it on moral grounds.
4. They will see attacks on it as attacks on themselves and their (moral) way of life. Even implied threats—the very possibility of other constructions of reality, of other way of ordering life—may be viewed with suspicion or enmity. To see the arbitrary foundations of one's own life as natural is to make unnatural other cultural worlds: if I apprehend my world as natural, moral and sacred, then I may react to other worlds as unnatural, immoral and unsacred, an anti-reality. The inhabitants of such anti-realities may be demonized, as if their existence threatened moral reality and self with dissolution.
5. Thus a zone of violence may develop on the margins of hegemony, as people defend their "reality" or assert it against others. Patterns of violence may develop within a society in the grip of hegemony, when people are moved to defend what they accept as natural,

necessary, moral, sacred. Hegemony thus both replaces violence (with symbols and meanings) and yet can generate violence (against other worlds of meaning). By instilling a particular sense of reality, values that achieve psychological hegemony define what is worth fighting for, dying for, killing for. To make the arbitrary seem natural, necessary, and moral is often to demonize other cultural worlds or actors, and to make this demonization seem self-evident, a matter of "common sense." Coercion and violence can acquire a certain felt legitimacy, whether mobilized for or against a dominant order.

6. Cultural hegemony as a lived process may generate psycho-existential complexes in actors (Fanon 1967). Every hegemony has its discontents.

Alas, so does every theory. We grasp at the concept of hegemony to free us from the distortions of the idea of hierarchy, but what prevents this concept from distorting in turn? Nothing: the concept of cultural hegemony can be, and is, used in ways as totalizing and petrifying as anything done with the concept of hierarchy. We want to use the concept to liberate us, in general from the idea that culture knows no politics, and, in the South Asian case, from the intellectual hegemony of Dumontian concepts of hierarchy. And yet we risk simply imposing another intellectual hegemony upon ourselves, reifying and essentializing in another mode. We may continue to neglect questions of human agency and draw away from people's efforts to make lives for themselves. Simply exchanging yesterday's megaconcept for today's, one fleeting monomania for another, without changing our deeper interpretive attitudes serves neither us nor actors: it continues the habit of reducing the richness and variety of cultural life to the one-dimension tolerated by the currently dominant modes of theorizing.

Perhaps every theory will be famous for fifteen minutes (if I can be forgiven the irony of echoing Andy Warhol) and nothing will ever change, because the more "theory" changes, the more it remains the same. Concepts come and go, but the habit of congealing cultural life into "one idea" remains. The hedgehogs rule, while the foxes bark from the margins.

Thus, I confess to growing feelings of ambivalence regarding the concepts of power, culture, and person that are deployed with the concept of hegemony, or that may gravitate to it. What I fear is that the concept of cultural hegemony will be engulfed in theory and ideology (as these blur together) that reify and absolutize the concepts of power, forming at least a proto-hegemony, a contender for dominance in cultural debates about social life, as these implode into academia. It is easy to export

Western concepts of power. It is harder to do justice to the cultural life of power in cultures that have radically different concepts of reality, agency, and society (Dirks 1987).

Using hegemony and resistance as founding concepts may prompt the analyst to reduce life to power in various ways. I do not just mean reducing cultural life to the cultural politics of class conflict, although if done badly I think this produces a crude caricature of the real pain and politics of life. But more than this I worry about the interpretive ethos: using these concepts, we may tend to account for social life in purely manipulative political and oppositional terms, minimizing what is shared, exaggerating conflict, in a new idealism of power, half romanticism, half cynicism. While recognizing the politics of culture, the way culture makes power, and power makes culture, remains essential, I think we should be wary of slipping into the interpretive stance that power is all there is, that power is the body and soul, the animating principle, of cultural life. Much Western social thought draws on a metaphysics of power that I believe we should not uncritically incorporate in theory and ethnography.

Social actors do "make culture." The kings and elite of Bhaktapur made imposing temples, organized rituals, filled urban space with art, architecture, and pageantry that embodied their vision of the universe, and of their place in the universe. They had the power to do so, and, like one of those dragons that swallows its own tail, exercising this power to animate a vision of the cosmos in public space no doubt helped nurture their power. In some circumstances, power feeds on power, on itself, virtually self-generates within culture. Often, those with the most power get to make the most culture, and this gives them more power, making it possible for them to fill social space with their cultural productions, relative to the relatively powerless. Recognizing this, I am not objecting to a cultural analysis of power, but to the metaphysics of power that often infiltrates it.

Of course, not only kings and the elite make culture. Ordinary people—who may be extraordinary—do as well. But king or untouchable, poor farmer or wealthy merchant, I do not think they make culture and history out of nothing, or that they make all of it, or that they do it only for the power, only out of political motives—as if they did not have other motives. I become skeptical when power becomes theoretical touchstone, the raison d'être ascribed to all cultural practices, to all processes of meaning construction, the hidden agenda of all moral discourse and social practice. I do not think the human world and human agency are so mired in what I believe Foucault himself once called the "monotony of power."

So while I welcome the focus on the ways culture is political, and make use of it, I dissent from the idea that power somehow stands outside of culture and constitutes it, that all else dissolves into power, a notion that creeps easily into power-focused analysis. Theorists who set their sights on power, who employ it as their touchstone, run the risk of seeing it everywhere, of making it their transcendent category, their essence of essences, a master concept. The concept of power needs to be decentered: not out of existence, but away from this tacit metaphysics.

No doubt the concepts of hegemony and resistance can succumb to the narrowest metaphysical and metaphorical construction of power found in Western thought, where power becomes the "metaphoric key" for everything: culture 5 power, self 5 power, morality 5 power.[5] After all, there is analytic power in this narrative construction of power: it illuminates an aspect of things. Problems develop when one term of the metaphor—power—becomes the dominant term, the master-concept that absorbs everything into it. This metaphoric keying of human life and culture to power is not mere hoary Nietzscheism, vulgar Marxism, or fashionable Foucaultism, but a cultural legacy taken up again and again, the key term of a very Western mode of thought. Demystification achieves a kind of hegemony, replacing the richness and variety of cultural worlds with a monologue proclaiming that power, exhausting, monotonous power, is all there is.

Perhaps most of us would reject such an exaggerated, hermetically sealed, vision of life. We don't live it, after all; and we do see more in the lives of those we study. Our quandary: we cannot pretend culture has no political import; but neither can we reduce culture to power. The challenge for theory and analysis is: how do you sustain some sense of a lived dialogue between a culture's lived ethical, moral, and religious values, its politics, and the workings of social power, without collapsing one into the other, and without keeping them so separate they cannot sway and affect each other?

The trick is to see how politics develops as an integral part of cultural life without making culture "nothing but" power. I hope that if used with a little humility, hegemony and resistance can be illuminating concepts with which to explore cultural life. Ideally, they can spur polythetic comparisons (Appadurai 1992) and inspire the polytheistic analysis of diverse cultural worlds (Shweder 1991, chap. 1). While forged in Western thought, these concepts can help focus attention on the "poetics of power" of other cultures (Dirks 1990). But they cannot replace a wider view of what cultural life involves.

Resisting the "single vision" created by overinvestiment in a single concept may help us reclaim areas of human life for inquiry and puzzlement. The single-minded focus on a single master concept—whether the reified term is hierarchy or hegemony—is part of what makes them relatively uninteresting and I think ultimately misleading when it comes to understanding the full dynamics of cultural subjectivity, or moral consciousness, and many other aspects of human cultural life that are touched by the politics of cultural life, but not totally reducible to power. Inflated concepts of power displace and exclude from analysis many of the fragile spaces of possibility in which people try to make lives for themselves.

Drifting, gravitating toward the familiar, critical concepts can become paragons of cultural values, and may turn unwittingly and naively affirmative. Rather than directing a withering skepticism at our use of concepts, what passes as a critical stance may simply re-reflect the ways we "know," or want to know, ourselves. Indeed, at times, it seems, Western cultural concepts of the person may "trump" critical thought. What underpins some theory is a vision of persons as sovereign agents who reveal their nature in resistance to power. In other cases, we find an opposing, but equally and prevalent and Western vision: a concept of the person as a social construction, as the locus of discourse, as a subject-position, whose every feeling and action reflects the workings of power, leaving no room for personal agency, for human nature, for individuality, choice, randomness.

We often treat actors as narrowly as our theories allow, sometimes slicing them so thin they seem almost non-existent, even in our ethnographic accounts of social and cultural life, where one might expect thicker descriptions. Why? Perhaps because we overvalue our theories and the ethical-existential stances they represent—even when they conjure up one-dimensional images of actors that fly in the face of ethnographic reality.

"The treatment of the blue-collar worker in academic discourse," writes Claudia Strauss, "is only slightly worse than that of the 'individual,' who is alternately apotheosized as a creative resister or 'decentered' our of all theoretical consideration" (1990:325). I agree, and I think both maneuvers might be seen as complementary moments in a Western discourse. Fitting others into our cultural and theoretical polarities, we may at one moment subtract from them all agency and independent life, while at another moment adding back and supplementing precisely those characteristics we wish to supplement in self. I find it significant that those socially subordinate often get this double treatment, but it represents a general trend in theory and interpretation. By degrees, this process may assimilate others, whether low caste actors and peasants in India, "third world" women (Mohanty 1988), or blue-collar workers, to concepts of the person entirely familiar to us: they become one-dimensional surrogates for ourselves, what we want to be or fear we are, imagined and projected, reflected and refracted back at us.

In the work of Dumont and his followers—who we can take as representing certain habits of thought found in a dominant current in twentieth-century culture theory—the "individual" and the political activity and moral thought of caste actors are all equally displaced, virtually decentered out of existence. In such theory, the individual self or person is made to disappear with theoretical gestures—as when Dumont says individual persons "exist empirically, but . . . have no reality in thought, no Being" (1980:272). But if individuals in all their individuality as agents and subjects of cultural life and low caste actors as thinkers and doers are "decentered" out of all theoretical and ethnographic consideration in such seminal studies, the subordinate actor is elsewhere indeed virtually apotheosized as "creative resister." In this body of theory and interpretation, they are reduced to a singular image and assigned an autonomy that places them outside their own cultures and lives, as when the brilliant historian Ranajit Guha views the peasant rebel not only as an empirical person or member of a class, but as "an entity whose will and reason constituted the praxis called rebellion" (1983).

Studies in this second mode seem to reconstitute the individual subject and agent, but not as the subjects and agents of the cultural lives they actually live. Addressing herself to the work of Ranajit Guha (1982, 1983) and other "subaltern studies" scholars, Rosalind O'Hanlon suggests their approach involves substituting a kind of generic subject for specific cultural subjects in all their diversity and multivalence. She suggests that these scholars end up substituting historically specific Western concepts of the subject and of agency for culture-specific and life-specific forms of subjectivity and agency:

the classic figure of western humanism—the self-originating, self-determining individual, who is at once a subject in his possession of a sovereign consciousness whose defining quality is reason, and an agent in his power of freedom—is readmitted through the backdoor, in the figure of the subaltern himself. (1988:191)

We could respond to this by "decentering" the individual subject and agent once more, of course, but this would put us back to square one.

In fact, compared to the expunging of agency from social analysis, there is much to be said for incorporating "the creative resister" into our interpretive practice, as long as we do not let it dominate our thinking. Examining ways people seek to reimagine themselves and their world, the ways they act as agents and act on cultural forms, seems indispensable, because it captures a key aspect of cultural life. Individuals are up to things in their activities, and are often neither so tightly constrained they cannot act volitionally at all, nor so embedded in culture they cannot rethink some of their practices. Such agency does not do away with the structure of the caste hierarchy, of course, but it is part of the story of cultural life. I think we can handle this. Our problems really begin when we take part for whole, a facet of life for totality. It does not matter whether we inflate agency and deflate structure, or vice versa: we end up with distortions.

At times, people do resist, and this resistance declares something crucial about what and who they are. These acts and what they signify are key aspects of their identity, existence, and culture. But when the image of creative resister is reified and celebrated as the single, dominant images of peasant subalterns and untouchables in India or of blue-collar workers in the US, I think it distorts. Actors resist in myriad ways, but they do more, and less. If actors are seen *only* in terms of a pre-formulated imagery of resistance, we risk not taking account of much that is important to them. We need to resist the temptation to use a theoretical megaconcept—hierarchy, hegemony, resistance—to reduce actors to a single facet of their multi-faceted existence, to flatten them out in our discourse, making them one-dimensional, rendering them homogeneous, even while we need to continue to find ways to document and portray the ways they resist and conform, socially, psychologically, and politically.

In reality, we can neither apotheosize caste actors, turning them into one-dimensional proto-revolutionaries, nor proclaim them culturally perfected collaborators in the social order that oppresses them. We need a richer and more nuanced, if less heroic, sense of the way people creatively resists and yet actively cast themselves in the roles that objectify them and help animate the practices that oppress them.

Certainly, the lived realities of caste life do not resolve themselves easily into (cultural) hierarchy overcoming (natural) equality. We do not always find creative resisters, unambiguously endowed with will and reason, who affirm universal and self-evident rights revealed by reason, acting in the face of social oppression, affirming equality, as we might prefer.

Nor of course do we find an Eden of cultural harmony in the garden of castes, in which consensus has overcome alienation and "culture" speaks with one, hierarchy-affirming, voice. We do not find much fulfillment for such moral and political wishes or for theoretical single-visions in the landscape lit by the fitful flashes of illumination that the anthropological literature offers; the world that critical psycho-ethnography reveals is charged with ambivalences and tensions. Looking closely, we find cultural concepts of hierarchy locked into an uneasy complimentarity with cultural concepts of equality and mutual recognition, each continually subverting and transforming the other.

This process is what has sociological and psychological reality. If we wish a full understanding of caste actors we must engage their critical

ironic, utopian, and egalitarian concepts as well as their hierarchical constituting ones, without assuming any of these are precisely the same as
our own.

Our analytic task has to be to reconcile agency and culture (or to shed
some light on why they cannot be reconciled), and integrate them into
a more powerful vision of lived cultural life. In a passage from his *Prison
Notebooks*, Antonio Gramsci asked two complementary questions:

Having first shown that everyone is a philosopher, though in his own way and
unconsciously, since even in the slightest manifestation of any intellectual activity,
in "language," there is contained a specific conception of the world, one then
moves to the second level, which is that of awareness and criticism. That is to say,
one proceeds to the question—is it better to "think," without having a critical
awareness, in a disjointed and episodic way? In other words, is it better to take
part in a conception of the world mechanically imposed by the external environment, i.e., by one of the many social groups in which everyone is automatically
involved from the moment of his entry into the conscious world. . . . Or, on the
other hand, is it better to work out consciously and critically one's own conception of the world . . . choose one's sphere of activity, take an active part in
the creation of the history of the world, be one's own guide, refusing to accept
passively and supinely from outside the moulding of one's personality? (1990:
47–48)

Let me develop a point I make in the last chapter, because I think although it is an obvious point to some, it also flies in the face of the habit
of decentering the individual out of existence that characterizes much
theory, modern and postmodern. For those who have misplaced it,
Gramsci restores the thinking subject: "everyone is a philosopher," he
says, "though in his own way, and unconsciously." Like Melford Spiro
(1984), Gramsci raises the question of the way actors relate themselves
to the conceptions of the world their society offer. I think Spiro's interest
in psychology complements Gramsci's interest in politics. Having understood the power of culture, the way it contains a conception of the world,
and of one's self, both these theorists invite us to move to what Gramsci
calls "the second level," and explore the role of awareness and criticism,
and of the self-reflective ego—which in some sense represent consciousness raised in counter-point to "the world mechanically imposed by the
external [social] environment." I do not doubt that this conscious and
critical self remains grounded in culture, with roots that reach down into
the political and psychocultural unconscious. But can it not have a relative autonomy, neither quite the product of the dominant conception of
the world, nor pristine and culture-free? Of course, by placing his questions on opposite sides of an either-or, Gramsci phrases his point too
neatly, implying that one either takes part in cultural hegemony, derives
an identity and world view from it, or that one moves beyond it, forges

one's own conception of the world. This may be too heroic. Many actors live, I maintain, in a shifting zone of interpretation between dominant conceptions and their own conceptions of self and world. We can catch them at multiple sites in this zone, as they reposition and reformulate their consciousness.

We get this shifting, multiple consciousness when an individual internalizes several images of the world and self, of equal or varying degrees of significance for self. You may internalize cultural conceptions of the world in several ways: either make them part of yourself as a key motive or only vaguely have in them mind as you go about your affairs; either make them the foundation of an emotional world and seek to embed self in the cultural world they constitute, or else have only a faint knowledge and fainter feelings for them, be largely unmoved by them (Spiro 1984). At the same time, you may not be able to avoid the need, as Gramsci says, to "work out critically and consciously one's own conception of the world."[6] You may even work out your own conception of the world in opposition to dominant concepts: the genesis of self may lie not wholly in the internal replication of external culture, but also in processes of psychological accommodation and resistance, in some variation on what Gregory Bateson long ago termed "schismogenesis."

In any event, the self may not reflect the dominant ideology. The appealing simplicities of Dumont's vision dissolve. It does not crystallize an essence for a civilization. Yet if we must recognize now that this elegant theory overreached itself, since actors refuse to resolve into the simplicities it requires, we at least gain a more dynamic sense of actor's lives and consciousness: *Homo hierarchicus* stands encompassed in *Homo dialecticus*.

I believe that the dialogues actors have with culture generate what Kenneth Burke terms "a complex individual of many voices." His example of the basic rhetorical structure of this many-voiced self does not work so badly for a caste system: "here," he writes, "is the purest rhetorical pattern: speaker and hearer as partners in partisan jokes made at the expense of another" (1969:38). Clearly, caste relations involve partisan identifications: self against other, and as partner in jokes and self-affirmations made at the expense of others, yet always, we should recall, also at the expense of self. Thus I define myself every time I define another, yet every time I collaborate in casting stigma on someone else, I place myself in a system where I am similarly constituted.[7] The basic motives involved in the caste system—keeping others "out" of one's own group and "down" in their place, but making those a little "higher" recognize self as equal, and so on—are all "internalized" by actors. Thus "the same person can participate" in all the stances involved, producing a self "of many voices." I have tried to show something of how this self speaks for, yet also against, the caste hierarchy. A multiple consciousness does pervade the system, reflecting the way "the rhetorical pattern" of self-definition slides from collusion to rebuttal, and back again, variously identifying self "with" the system and "against" it. Virtually everyone is in turn speaker and hearer and victim of the partisan joke: excluded and stigmatized.

In my mind, these multiple voices reflect a lived dialogue with culture. What motivates the inconsistent, shifting "voices" is the goal of making a life. What these voices speak is "culture" in a double sense—not only do they reflect the structure of caste relations, they animate meanings needed to make a life within a caste world, compose possibilities, seek to defend what they can grasp. Thus, while recognizing the power of hegemony to shape actor's consciousness, I do not think actors are mere conduits for culture, or reflections of culture: we may conceive of them so when we take as our only point of departure the first of Gramsci's question, of how a dominant culture shapes people, analyzing hegemony but neglecting to proceed with the inquiry into their critical consciousness. Of course, people do absorb culture: they breathe in the cultural atmosphere, define what it means for them. The question is, do they do more? Are they totally passive in their relation to culture, or do they add to it, vary it, develop and make it their own, infuse it with their meanings and experience? I have concluded that they can; we need to pursue Gramsci's second question, and use ethnography to explore the way actors work out their own conceptions of the world, their own relationship to dominant cultural forms. We need our psychoethnography of "the politics of consciousness" to address the ways actor's slip out from under hegemony and construct their own concepts of the world. As long as the concept of culture in culture theory admits nothing outside itself, we cannot easily theorize or pursue this.

Long after Edward Sapir (1934) voiced the need for it, we still await the full emergence of a concept of self in the study of cultures. Despite the achievements of psychological anthropology, we have yet to see the emergence of a concept of self in the study of the politics of cultures.[8]

We arrive then at what, perhaps, should always have been obvious, and perhaps would have been, had it not been for the development of certain kinds of culture theory that deny agency and reflective consciousness.[9] Dumont's theory is merely an example of a habit that has achieved a significant degree of hegemony from time to time in the scholarly world. It is for this reason that I have risked stating the obvious and doing so as forcefully, as redundantly, as I have.

It is not my intent to minimize the importance of culture. In the hands of actors, in the form of models that mediate relationships and understandings, culture is powerful indeed. It need not, however, imply a passive actor. Women and men may speak against the cultural conceptions that define reality; to do so they may need to find a cultural voice, to take hold of a piece of their culture, reinvent it, make it a platform for their dissent. This does not detract from their agency.

Actors may also speak for culture, may raise their voices and conscious-ness in defense of the values and traditions of cultural life. Gramsci's "second level" of awareness is not only the plane where actors forge cri-tique and counter-ideology, but also where they forge self-conscious ide-ology, consciously defend their practices, affirm philosophies of life, seek preeminence for these models of self and society. On this plane, an in-dividual may in fact speak for and against culture, may seek integration into dominant conceptions, yet seek also to alter fundamentally the re-lationship of self and culture. Individuals may seek to give self a new foundation by advancing new premises for culture. Certainly, my reading of many Newars is that they try both to relate themselves to cultural pat-terns, and tried to define these in terms of their concerns and lives, not just absorbing culture or losing self in culture, but also variously con-necting their lives to culture, seeking to evade culture's grip, striving to assert themselves significantly, with or against culture (Sapir 1934). For understanding them, Gramsci's dichotomy, a sharp "either-or," with he-gemony on one side and freedom on the other, misleads. This formula-tion does not capture a sense of actors' ambivalences, of the exigencies of practical life, of their struggles, of their psychological work, all of which shape a shifting, multiple consciousness of self and society.

To define this, we need a kind of meta-principle—some sense of shift-ing ratios, of a dialectical engagement—that would allow us to see how actors constitute themselves in concert with culture, and yet also contest it, to capture a sense of how they find identity within dominant concep-tions of the world and yet seek to shed these, to unravel them, as they shift perspectives, or confront problems of living. Perhaps, in the words of Kenneth Burke, an actor's basic relationship with cultural forms may simultaneously

be treated . . . as a concerto of principles mutually modifying one another, . . . [and] . . . as a parliamentary wrangle which the individual has put together some-what as he puts together his fears and hopes, friendships and enmities, health and disease, or those tiny rebirths whereby, in being born to some new condition, he may be dying to a past condition, his development being dialectical, a series of terms in perpetual transformation. (1969:38)

This is *Homo dialecticus*, and I feel this appellation fits caste actors bet-ter than *Homo hierarchicus* ever did. In concertos where social values and personal experience come together, crystallizing mutually integrating images of world and self, and in wrangles where they don't, actors have lives. In these lives, men and women do not simply flow into the forms of hegemony, with inner lives that are the passive products of discourse. Nor do they automatically take a stand of resistance, as if they were moral and heroic by virtue of some essence. I suspect most people, most of the time, are simply trying to make lives for themselves.

Of course, there are exceptions. Of course, too, culture, and history, and politics do shape the fundamental possibilities of life. But these in turn are themselves shaped by people's efforts to make their lives happen, to fashion something, however small and fragile, out of their life-chances.

Making culture and making history may at times simply be incidental to the task of fashioning a life—and not a romance of will, reason, and praxis. As Fanon (1967) puts it, people resist and rebel because it has become impossible for them to breathe. If they make and remake cultures for themselves, it is as a way of finding air to breathe.

The desire to live, to make a life, to make a better life—these motives stretch like a thin, taut, thread from despair to hope, from Muli's wife begging and Muli pimping to Kesar building his business so he can declare his independence from caste, to Krishna's narratives of possible moral worlds, and on to moral and political activism.

This set of motives implies a sense of moral purpose. Seeking food for hungry mouths, meaning for themselves, air to breathe, refuge and shelter and hope, people set out to make what lives they can in the world they find around them: to draw life out of culture.

What actors do as they seek to draw life out of culture reverberates in the lived worlds others inhabit. This may yield a harvest of tragedy, irony, and ambivalence.

Notes

Introduction

1. In writing this paragraph, I was influenced in part by the theophany in the Bhagavad Gita. Arjuna, shaken to the core of his being when Krishna discloses his cosmic form, cries out at what he sees:

I see your mouths with gaping teeth,
As if they were the fire of time.
I do not know the way, and I have no refuge. . . .
. . . .
You lick all around you
as you devour
all the worlds with your flaming lips.
O Vishnu, the whole universe
is filled with fire
And scorched
by your fierce light.

Tell me,
who are you
who have this terrible form?

Who are you? is a question we might ask of human history, if we could experience the totality and horror of it in an epiphany, representing it to ourselves in the form of a god, as Durkheim claimed we represent society to ourselves. But this would be a terrible god. How much death and suffering, oppression and injustice, can the human mind bear to contemplate, much less experience? How many holocausts? One can almost imagine that humanity might choose to represent society to itself as a deity, but not history, that truly terrible form. And the answer to the question whispered to history, Who are you?, must, of course, in some sense be — humanity, ourselves.

2. As are also the fears and threats imagined with the same sense of possibility, where possibility is taken as a threat to what is, when what is, is what should be (Bourdieu 1977; Parish 1994, Postscript).

3. While colonialism in India no doubt altered and may have intensified the indigenous cultural stress on hierarchy, the case of Nepal as a relatively independent society shows that Hindu states and populations cultivated caste hierarchies

for reasons of their own, reflecting social, political, and cultural dynamics that existed independently of colonialism. No doubt British rule in India cast a shadow of some sort on the development of Nepalese society at the national level, especially perhaps with respect to the political elite, and through them the discourses of colonialism and considerations of regional politics must have affected the total dynamic of Nepalesse society. But the realities of caste life cannot seamlessly and without distortion be absorbed into the master narrative of colonialism, as if history was only a tale told from the top down, with no counterpoint of local voices.

4. Habermas (1977); Gadamer (1993 [1960]:567–71)

5. Even when taking ideas from other cultures, people typically put them to work in dialogues with pre-existing understandings; they do not start over from scratch.

6. While concealing may be a deliberate, conscious choice, it is not always so, but just what one does—a protective maneuver triggered by the presence of another who has higher status. Since the critical self is gone from consciousness in this context, people may be quite sincere when they profess commitment to an ideology or practice they reject on other occasions. Methodological problems evolve, of course: a difficulty here is that we may learn not to believe people even when they declare their most fundamental convictions just because we have learned to believe that subalterns disguise what they actually think (Hale 1994: 204, 272n8). In reality, people may choose to reveal as well as conceal.

7. Gellner and Quigley (1995), a book published too late to be discussed here, offers a fuller view of the Newar caste system.

8. Gadamer speaks of the "dialogue that we are." McCarthy (1978:192), suggests that Habermas in effect proposes a complementary dialogue, writes that "Habermas speaks of the dialogue that is not yet but ought to be."

Chapter 1

1. The mask is an image of Betadya, Bhairav's "vehicle" (Levy 1990:469).

2. I assume here that I can read facial expressions signaling "disgust" across cultural boundaries. Work by Paul Ekman (Ekman and Friesen 1975) and others suggests that some facial expressions are universal.

3. I draw on Levy (1990:464–500) here, as well as on my own research. I omit many important details not relevant to the theme of the book.

4. As they have in the past, if the accounts of Brian Hodgson, British resident in the nineteenth century, are any guide.

5. In those both outside the city and related to counter-structural Tantra.

6. Other Newars disputed this construction, arguing that inauspiciousness, bad influences, cannot be transferred from one person to another person. I would suggest the "transfer" motif is present in at least a veiled form in a number of ritualized transactions.

7. In a sense, the city's rites "capture" the body for the sacred order, uniting feeling and meaning, supplying cultural symbols with animating experience, creating the "condition of possibility" through which people might begin to identify self with religious values. They may also come to feel that the social order "must" embody sacred values, and has legitimacy insofar as it celebrates and affirms such values. Actors through their "felt" identification with the values of the religious order may also identify themselves with, or identify themselves against, the social

order, depending on its perceived relation to religious values. I echo Weber and Durkheim here because I think they got it right, in part.

8. My phrasing of this contrast derives partly from Sapir (1934).

Chapter 2

1. Newars with a modern education might make use of such a vocabulary of "rights." Schools may also introduce or supplement notions of equality. Skinner and Holland (in press) note that some school books introduce themes of national unity that involve bridging established notions of difference.

2. In some respects, this testimony recalls certain aspects of *bhakti* cults of India (Hopkins 1966; Singer 1966). Khare (1984:84) in his study of the untouchable Lucknow Chamars quotes an ideological formulation by Achutananda: "I believe that all human beings are equal, and brothers . . . ; the feeling of high and low is illusion. Humans become high and low by their own individual virtues and vices. Human heart alone is God's temple, hence to practice equality toward the entire humanity is the "supreme religion" (quote marks in original). There are resonances with a style of thought found in the Bhagavad Gita: "Yoked in Yoga, he sees himself in all creatures, all creatures in himself—he sees everything the same" (Bhagavad Gita, VI:29, trans. J. A. B. van Buitenen 1981:97). Sargeant quotes the commentator Ramanuja on this passage from the Gita: "A person who has brought his *atman* [self] into Yoga, will see similarity in all *atman*s when separated from *prakriti* (material nature); he will see that all beings are in his own *atman*; in other words he will see that his own *atman* has the same form as the *atman*s of all other beings and contrariwise, so that he has seen all that is *atman* when he has seen one *atman*" (1984:300). On the Newar "heart-self" as locus of divinity, see Parish (1994).

3. I agree with R. Rosaldo (1989) that the preoccupation with "thickness" may at times tell us more about anthropologists than about other cultures. This preoccupation may lead to neglect of meanings that have "force" but are not culturally elaborated. I am not sure that Rosaldo and I employ the term "force" in precisely the same way—he speaks of emotional force, while I derive my conception in part from D'Andrade's (1984) seminal discussions of directive, evocative, and constructive force. Nonetheless, Rosaldo makes with some rhetorical force a point I see as relevant to equalizing rhetoric in Newar moral discourse: "By and large, cultural analysts use not *force* but such terms as *thick description, multivocality, polysemy, richness*, and *texture*. The notion of force . . . opens to question the common anthropological assumption that the greatest human import resides in the densest forest of symbols and that analytical detail, or 'cultural depth' equals enhanced explanation of a culture, or 'cultural elaboration.' Do people always in fact describe most thickly what matters most to them?" (1989:2). The answer is no, I believe. It is not necessarily the case that culture must be "thick," layered, obscure, needing the analyst's interpretive cunning to make it clear and accessible. People may speak simply and forcefully to each other. Of course, some cultural domains may be a forest of symbols, best approached through "thick" description: elaborate, rich, dense, layered, opaque or polysemous to insider and outsider alike. I would add, too, that statements with moral or evocative force may be voiced in different ways by different actors, even when not elaborated on by them—force and multivocality may be related in different ways than force and elaboration. Moreover, in some cases, elaboration may surround force, thickness

may call it into being. We need to recognize both force and thickness, in all their guises and relations.

4. This interpretation reflects a more technical analysis of the cognitive spaces of meaning construction in the passage, drawing on the work of the linguist Gilles Fauconnier (1985). Generally, from a high caste perspective, if untouchables are impure, inauspicious, and dirty, then self is pure, auspicious and clean. By characterizing myself as pure and auspicious, I make it possible to stigmatize others through contrast. Vincent Crapanzano sums up the dialectical process of "selving self" by "othering others" in these words: "One casts the other . . . in order to cast oneself. And, I hasten to add, one casts oneself in order to cast the other." (1990:401) The pun is apt.

5. Of course, it is possible, indeed probable, that some notions of equality are modern introductions. For example, Skinner and Holland (in press) note that phrases such as "All people's blood is red" are found in school books used in "Moral Education" classes. What seems ultimately most important, however, is not where the words in which people speak of equality comes from, but that people are prepared to find them meaningful. That people have seized and made such concepts their own, suggests, I think, that these ideas resonate with concerns that did not arise elsewhere, but grow out of lived experience in caste society. We cannot just answer affirmatively the question, Is this a modern introduction? and leave it at that, but must also ask, Why is this idea good to think? Why does it come to have felt significance? But I tend to think the modern formulae for equality are often glosses on preexisting sentiments, and that felt ideas of human equality and solidarity have been incarnated in rather diverse cultural idioms. As Kenneth Burke says: "only those voices from without are effective which can speak in the language of a voice within" (1969:39).

Skinner and Holland note that the educational curriculum in Nepal at once constructs differences and unity in the interest of promoting a vision of a nation-state. While students may connect emotionally with this process in a variety of ways, some reflexive form of what I believe Margaret Mead once called "anticipatory socialization" would seem to be involved. Students imagine (or are led to envision) a future; they imagine themselves in the socially unified, educated, progressive, "modern" world of the developing nation-state, with the stigma and superiority of caste and ethnic group transcended. That this nonetheless entails a stigmatized "other" (uneducated, "traditional," older) who is not part of this world may slip past with little scrutiny (Skinner and Holland, in press).

6. The "translation" may be between different cultural perspectives, or between a dominant ideology and cultural and personal experience not constituted by the dominant ideology. If we accept that culture contains multiple perspectives, this seems self-evident, but anthropologists have not always viewed culture as "not all of a piece."

7. However limited in effect (Juergensmeyer 1982), efforts to reform the social order recur (Malik 1977, Joshi 1981.)

8. One could argue that equality is nothing but the collapse of hierarchy, and so is a derivative principle—you only get equality by reversing, destructuring and inverting hierarchy. But this poses a chicken and egg problem. Which comes first? Is it equally plausible to argue that hierarchy is nothing but dissolution of a more primary equality—that you only get hierarchy by perturbing, overcoming, and destructuring equality. The point here is that Newars seem to move from a perspective in which hierarchy contains equality to one in which equality contains hierarchy—from conceptions of a hierarchically ordered whole in which

ranked solidarities are embedded, to perceptions of an undifferentiated common ground of being, a matrix out of which hierarchy emerges, and into which it can collapse.

Chapter Three

1. We would no longer say, as Hegel did, that "India as a land of desire formed an essential element in general history. From the most ancient times, all nations have directed their wishes and longings to gaining access to the treasures of this land of marvels, the most costly which the earth presents, treasures of nature" (quoted in Singer 1972:16). India is no longer "opulent and fabulous," a land of marvels and treasures. Contemporary images of India often emphasize poverty, stagnation, underdevelopment. Post-colonial (but not politically neutral) discourse defines India as peripheral to the world order. The contrast of Indian spirituality and Western materialism persists; caste remains a dominant image.

2. In this Dumont appears less sophisticated than some of the Hindus he characterizes, who seem able to shift fluidly between whole and part (Khare 1978).

3. Quoted in Joshi (1986:97), where it was translated by Gail Omvedt.

4. Fuller (1992:16) acknowledges that Dumont's work endows the purity complex and the caste system "exaggerated prominence"—calling to mind Inden's observation about the dialectic of exaggerations by which we in the West have "imagined" India—but his own study seems to me too protective of the concept of hierarchy, neglecting works on resistance, e.g., Khare (1984).

5. The general view I take should apply to ideologies of equality as well as of hierarchy. If I am right, relations of inequality should break out even in the most egalitarian settings. Emphasizing and ranking differences is always possible, and so I would expect to find that hierarchy and equality as contending visions virtually everywhere, both where the dominant ideologies are hierarchical, and even where "official" ideologies are egalitarian—whether on an Israeli kibbutz, or among Hindu renouncers.

6. Parry's view is that equality does have a place in traditional India, as an autonomous value. He gives the examples of a concept of "brotherhoods of equals," and of egalitarian principles that regulate certain systems of land tenure (1979:315–317). I wish to stress not only such social forms, but moral discourse that regenerates equality as a cultural schema.

7. See, for example, to mention only a few: Berreman (1971), Menchner (1974), Appadurai (1986, 1992), Dumont (1980, 1987), Beteille (1983, 1986, 1987); also Lynch (1977), Kolenda (1976), Barnett, Fruzetti, and Ostor (1976).

Chapter Four

1. Unlike the assertions of equality, this is not a view my informants seem articulate about, yet it is my inference that such a view of the world is psychologically real for them, and influences their actions, identity, and emotional experience. What is unvoiced cannot be quoted, however significant. It can be recovered in part from observations of practices, e.g., as implicit in life cycle rites (Parish 1994) that bind each caste person to his caste, making it "known" as a vital part of self.

2. Rosser (1978:88) errs, I think, in seeing the Newar system as bipolar, that

is, as segmented into two blocks by the "water line," although he is correct in suggesting that the system is segmented into blocks, not continuous, when it comes to political and economic relations. But dominance is not clearly marked by the water line, and the system is not bipolar. The high castes dominate the farmer block (the conglomeration termed *jyapu*) as well as the impure *jat*, if not in the same way; and the sequence of domination is continued in the relationship of *jyapu* to groups lower than *jyapu*. Nor is the "water line" quite as "precise, clear, immutable" as he states.

3. Non-Newar castes found living with Newars include Dhobi, Sarki, Gaine, Damai and others.

4. For this to happen, the breach must become public and his group be able to enforce the norm—a rapidly fading state of affairs.

5. The clothes of the dead are thrown at a special place called the *chwasa*, which is often a crossroads.

6. According to Rosser (1978), there are definite strategies for consolidating their movement into higher status. They must emulate the lifestyle of higher status people, discontinuing contact with low caste people, drop their membership in low caste associations and seek memberships in high caste associations (perhaps offering financial incentives for acceptance), and attempt to arrange for his children (or himself) to marry within a higher status level. Rosser traces these steps for farming castes; they are harder for people of castes lower than farmers to achieve.

7. On stories as moral discourse, see Shweder and Much (1987), Narayan (1989).

8. Of course the internal unfolding of events and responses is necessarily ordered by time, by the temporal quality of the acts that take place within the story. This is one of the essential qualities of a narrative.

9. The particular implicit distinction between self and person I make here (a blurred one in any event) is inspired in part by reflections on a discussion of Ameile Rorty's typology of ways of construing 'persons' in Bruner (1986:39–41). My concept of you as a person—which exists within a zone of action and interpretation in which actors engage in social practices—does not necessarily correspond to your concept of yourself, although you may have to take account of it. Personhood in this sense is a kind of objecthood, perhaps even a "crushing objecthood" (Fanon 1967), produced socially. It can be distinguished from the self as an interpreting agent and locus of self-experience. An individual may repudiate his or her own social construction. Thus the untouchable as dramatis persona in the symbolic drama of the caste order is not the untouchable as self who may experience this as repugnant or oppressive. Although the distinction is easily overdrawn, and fails to suggest the ambiguity and ambivalences involved, I find it analytically useful because it suggests how some actors/selves may detach themselves from, and re-value the value that society places on them—and seek to identify themselves with the revaluation.

10. This story may be a transformation of an episode from the story of how King Harisimhadeva brought the Goddess Taleju to Nepal. In this story, as Levy (1990:236) records it, the king sees a man defecating while facing east, indicating that he is not of twice-born status, and assigns this man the role of killing buffalo. The killing of water buffalo during sacrifices to Taleju are done by the Nae, the Butcher caste, and this episode accounts for this.

11. None of these castes would accept his claims, however, and most rankings

by other groups agree in placing his caste below these groups; Kancha's claim reveals resistance to accepting this consensus.

12. Newar Buddhists practice caste, despite the more universalistic and egalitarian traditions of Buddhism.

13. I recognize that "political unconscious" is an awfully grand-sounding term for what are no doubt elementary cognitive processes in the cultural life of complex societies. However, I think the term is justified by the way it calls attention to what seem to me two key aspects of social cognition. First, it focuses us on the social and political implications of the way constructive knowledge gets socially formulated and deployed; second, it grounds this in cognitive and psychocultural processes, in the ways minds or psyches, persons or selves (or whatever terms you wish to use) acquire and use cultural knowledge. What people know and feel about their circumstances at a given moment depends in part on what cultural knowledge has been activated, and what has been suppressed, mentally and socially. This may seem a very simple insight—and it is—but it is not one that can be formulated or explored on the basis of many traditional theories of culture. These theories represent culture as highly integrated and unified, as a structure or system that constituted consciousness for actors. They leave little room for agency or conflict. Yet we have very little empirical basis, I think, for assigning a single consciousness to actors: we do so when we identify actors with culture, and treat culture as static, unified, thing-like. The notion of a multiple consciousness of self and society and a political unconscious follow from a cognitive definition of culture.

In this view, culture exists not as a totally shared and unified field (a structure or system) but as units (schemas, models) that can be active or inactive in minds and specific cultural contexts (D'Andrade 1995). Where culture conceived as a unified system tempts us to think of it as existing in all minds in the same way, culture in cognitive theory exists in minds in different ways: cultural models are distributed across actors, and are not held (internalized) in the same way by all actors.

Actors possess different cultural models, and different degrees of commitment to or involvement with these models (Spiro 1984). When culture is not defined as a unified structure, but rather as a population of cognitive models, different questions can be asked (D'Andrade 1995). How are these models distributed? How are they activated? How do actors shift between models? In other words, the kinds of questions I have been raising in this work emerge. The question of the political unconscious simply addresses the political implications of a basic process in cultural cognition: certain cultural models or theories out of all those held by an actor at certain moments occupy and hold awareness while another set does not, while at another moment the reverse is true.

If we locate meaning in cognitive models rather than public symbols, even what is shared may have different meanings: actors may interpret the "same" value or symbol by animating different models. These different models may conflict—can imply very different worlds, very different scripts and purposes—and be used to contest each other. If different actors can have different models of self and society—a proposition which many would affirm today, at least for actors who occupy different positions in society—there is no reason to think the same actor cannot apply different models to themselves and their cognized worlds. Thus, the particulate view of culture formulated in cognitive anthropology prepares us to recognize conflicting models in the phenomenology of actors.

Of course, if culture lacks the near-total integration some classical theorists attributed to it, this does not imply that culture is not partially integrated. Rather than being unified in an overarching structure or system, some cultural models/ schema form networks, while others do not; some models are hierarchically incorporated in other models, and some not. Areas of relative (and dynamic) integration do exist: but not so that any absolute unity exists in culture or consciousness. Similarly, rejecting the notion that a culture forms a single consciousness-constituting structure does not require us to deny cultural consciousness to actors. When actors shift among cultural models, they do not stop being cultured: but what mediates action and consciousness from moment to moment is not some reified totality, "culture," or disembodied "discourses" or "practices" but rather cultural knowledge accessed, animated, and brought to life, in goal-oriented, context-sensitive ways by persons-in-culture.

In certain respects, cognitive theory combined with the sharp focus on persons and their dynamics found in cultural psychology seems a more realistic and powerful approach than either "objectivist" theory or "practice" theory, since both these approaches typically lack robust and nuanced concepts of mind, self, and experience, and fail to theorize adequately the inner diversity of actors (Trawick 1990) or the dialectical engagement of persons with their "lived worlds" (Holland and Skinner in press). In general, psychological anthropology and practice theory would appear to have much to offer each other. Neither sees culture as unified and transcendent. Where practice theory suffers from a certain vagueness about actors and their motives (Ortner 1984, 1989) (so that they tend to be seen as having interests but lack fully formed subjective lives, thought-processes, and psychodynamics), psychological anthropology often tends to neglect the political dimensions of cultural experience. The person-centered ethnography developed in psychological anthropology (Levy 1973, Levy and Wellenkamp 1989, Hollan and Wellenkamp 1994) could serve to flesh out the views of actors taken in practice theory, offering a richer, more nuanced view of their lives, agency, and self-experience.

14. I think the concept might be developed along the lines of some of Gregory Bateson's ideas (1972).

15. The amnesia that replaces insight into the arbitrary nature of the caste hierarchy may serve as a psychological defense for some, for whom the problem, the impasse created by the fact that alternative social relations cannot be enacted, is too painful and disorienting to be confronted for long. Greenblatt (1980) quotes from More's *History of Richard III*: "men must sometimes for the manner sake not be aknowen what they know." Simulation of "not knowing" is a kind of first step into the political unconscious; but some people enter it more deeply, keeping what they know not only tactically out of sight, but also strategically out of mind.

16. Used as the title of Obeyeskere's important book (1981), the phrase "work of culture" is found in Freud (1965:100): "Where id was, there shall ego be. It is a work of culture, like the draining of the Zuider Zee." But cultural work can also render unconscious what might otherwise have a role in conscious purpose and adaptation.

17. Burke (1969) might say this has to do with the analytic habit in the social sciences, strongly carried over even into interpretive studies, of keying analysis to scene rather than to agent. Yet both are key.

18. If telling stories is one way of doing this, singing songs may be another.

Holland and Skinner (1995) show how songs sung by some Nepalese women during the festival of Tij critique social practices.

19. In terms of the psychology of self, the shifting mode of actors' relationships
to society, the qualitative variation in their identification with and opposition to
social practices, and the successive triggering of alternative cultural models in
response to such shifts and variation, may shape the development of self-identity
and the organization of psychological processes. The displacement of self-consciousness and world-perception from one mode to another, from submission to
resistance, may provoke or redirect processes of identification and rejection, defining what is perceived as ego-alien or as having relational value, and influence
psychological defenses and processes of self-identity differentiation. Shifts in the
basic premises of one's relationship to social practice, in the way one envisions
one's relationship society, may sway felt evaluations of self, perhaps reordering
the way persons feel about themselves and their lives, reconstituting their expressive behavior and "personality" styles (cf. Riesman 1983), or restructuring their
goals and motives as they activate schema to help them flesh out their stance
toward society (Strauss 1992). The context-sensitive activation and suppression
of conflicting modes of relationship and models of self and society may affect the
unity and (in)consistency of the self (Ewing 1990).

20. Comparing several translations of Nietzsche's *Genealogy of Morals*, I, 10, I
have decided I like the rendering in Jameson (1981:201) best, perhaps because
"uprising" suggests to me a rising up into consciousness and a raising of consciousness, which I think are appropriate secondary images not conveyed by "revolt in morality". A caution: the theory of resentment can be used to "contain"
actors in a stigmatizing image—as irrational creatures of envy, capable of nothing
but ill-will and rancor. The theory of resentment may in such incarnations serve
to structure the political unconscious of dominant groups, blocking out any empathy for, or realistic appraisal of the situation of, low-status, poorer actors. In
these cases, the imagery of resentment may tell us more about anxieties and guilt
of dominant groups—grounded perhaps in their unconscious feelings that the
hatred of the oppressed is justified—than it does about the actual range of moral-
emotional experience in low status people. See Jameson (1981:201ff) on this
point.

Chapter Five

1. On resistance in ritual, see Dirks (1994). Mariott (1966) describes the "anti-
structure" of a festival in an Indian village. See also Linger (1992, 1993). In
the festival of *Gai Jatra*, some Newars produce explicit critical commentary in the
form of caricature and satire.

2. Of course, it may be a person's "real" commitments that are expressed in
the festival.

3. It is worth noting that there is a police station, an outpost of the modern
nation state, a few hundred feet from where this all took place; but the police sat
in their barracks. I doubt that they had much of a brief for the traditional local
elite. Since the police ignore the uproar, it becomes a safe protest against the
local traditional elite.

4. He is referring to the traditional right of certain low castes to take the
clothes of the dead which have been disposed of at specified places.

5. These insults and jokes are a stylized part of a festival, *Gatha muga: ca:re,* or *Ghantakarna,* during which some hierarchical codes are violated.

6. That is, Harsha's facial expression corresponded with a "disgust face" blended with anger, as identified in cross-cultural studies (Ekman and Friesen 1975.)

7. One threat modernization presents to the caste system is that those who benefit least from the system will pull out in pursuit of new opportunities. In the same way, local elites shift resources into the modern sector in order not to be left behind; but if successful they may continue to patronize the local system, while low caste actors with access to the modern sector have little reason to continue in stigmatizing roles.

Chapter Six

1. "Sin" (*pap*) and impurity cannot be reduced to an identity, although a sin may be treated metaphorically as an impurity.

2. It is instructive to compare these views with Dumont's discussion of renunciation (1980, appendix B).

3. This is a critical enterprise, but one that takes place within culture. We do not need to posit a mind entirely separate from culture to account for this. People rework cultural symbols and schema, work out their implications, cross symbols with other symbols to generate new meanings, transpose symbols, shift them into new contexts, activate schema in new contexts, unite separate schemas to create new schema, and so on.

4. I do not, of course, rule out "blended" states of consciousness; empirically, these exist, as when a low caste person exaggerates conformity to caste rules as a way of resisting through irony.

Conclusion

1. We need to avoid the "fallacy of equal traits" that would give the same weight to dominant and non-dominant symbols, but we also need to avoid constructing cultures in terms of a "fallacy of unanalyzed interplay" where no analysis is made of the interactions of dominant and non-dominant forms.

2. As Nepal's social transformation proceeds, this may well change, and I think you can see signs of this, as youth finds no continuity between past and future in the rites and practices that offered world-images and self-images to their grandparents, but do find self-definition in the newer rites of consumerism and education.

3. The equivocal, shifting self-concepts of actors in caste society should not be equated with the shallow, fragmented, "postmodern" selves claimed by some to chararcterize the West. In certain streams of postmodern theory, "the subject" becomes a "subject position"—the product of "discourse," so radically "decentered" in some versions that neither subjective life nor agency have any real meaning (see Rosenau 1992 for an overview.) It is hard to see how discontents and resistance could grow out of this. How would a "subject position," a mere "site" seamlessly constituted by discursive formations, without any psyche, hence without any capacity for insight or the experience of alienation, do so? Such theorists of a postmodern (non)self seem to imagine subjectivity and mentality

as nothing more than an emptiness filled with flickering images from the video bazaar: presumably discontents are just another flicker on the screen, do not involve pain that moves actors to evaluate their relationship to society, and are not potentially creative, capable of driving "uprisings in ethics."

See Holland and Skinner (1995) for a useful critique of "subject position" theory.

4. Hierarchy does not vanish in "the West," anymore than equality does in the South Asia. Egalitarianism in principle does not preclude inequality in practice. This is partly a matter of pragmatics, of accepting authority to get something done, and of political domination. But there is more to it than this. Inequality seems to have deep emotional significance for some in the supposedly egalitarian West. Ernest Gellner, for one, remarks that, despite the seeming power and pervasiveness of egalitarian thought in industrial societies, many "value inequality, not simply as an unavoidable means towards other social ends, or an incentive, or a way of providing the leisure required for progress, or a concession—but as good and above all a thrill in itself." Gellner discerns such an attitude in the work of the novelist Evelyn Waugh to make his point: "Waugh . . . conveys that positively sexual frission, the skin-tingling titivation engendered by radical inequality, by the brazen and confident denial of the equality of man which profoundly excites both the active and the passive partner, the higher and the lower, so to speak, in the ecstatic union of inequality" (1987:92). This sexualization of dominance in Western culture and elsewhere is of great cultural and sociological significance.

In any event, contradictions in values and consciousness are elementary features of cultural life in complex societies. Not only do "public" symbols and the "order" they construct have "private" ambivalences attached to them, they constitute the terms of "shared" social quandries and cultural ironies, with which actors struggle in a variety of ways (Linger 1992, Obeyesekere 1981).

5. For example, the technological organization of work life, requiring mobility and a certain open-ended sort of education, may well contribute decisively to the formation of the particular variety of egalitarianism found in certain Western industrial societies. The economic interests involved will be defended in the legal and political arenas. One can think of a range of other social factors that promote or require egalitarianism. Gellner (1987) sets out a list of candidates.

6. The expression "self-evident" itself suggests the possible cultural basis of this argument in American democratic thought, and I use it deliberately here to signal this possibility.

7. Obviously, Dumont's insights into holism remain crucial, if partial.

8. Appadurai (1986:758) suggests that holism is an assumption deeply implicated in Western social theory: "the idea of the "whole" is so deeply embedded in Western thought and its values about truth, form and determinacy that it seems unquestionably natural."

9. By "political hegemonies," I take Gramsci to mean conflicting cultural models of life, self, and society which contend for social preeminence and actors' commitments that are ultimately grounded in political structures and struggles.

Postscript

1. I draw on Laitin here: "the political forging . . . and institutionalization of a pattern of group activity in a state and the concurrent idealization of that schema

254 **Notes to Postscript**

into a dominant symbolic framework that reigns as common sense" (1986:183). I assume that not only the state, but any powerful group can attempt to construct a hegemony. Ortner also speaks of cultural schema and social practices as components of hegemony: she identifies a particular Sherpa schema that "interlocks with various social practices to form a hegemony, a closed and mutually reinforcing world of social practice and symbolic form in which the two levels constitute, reinforce, and naturalize one another" (1989:81).

2. It is more than possible that Gramsci, or scholars specializing in his work, might not recognize the concept of hegemony as contemporary thought develops and applies it in new ways; but there is something to be said for letting an idea develop freely, as people see what they can do with it, rather than restricting discussion to exegesis alone.

3. Laitin speaks of a "Gramscian paradigm of hegemony and political action" and proposes that the first postulate of this paradigm is that "Hegemony creates a unified moral order or, in the words of Gwyn Williams, 'an order in which a certain way of life and thought is dominant, in which one concept of reality is diffused throughout society'" (Laitin 1986:105). Obviously, I do not believe that the moral order of a society is typically "unified" except in ideological visions; and I also think the "diffusion throughout society" may often be problematic. What groups attempt, and what they achieve, are often quite different.

4. This being the case, dominant groups do not rely on symbols and moral meanings alone to sustain the social order. While they may seek to substitute symbols and meanings for coercion and violence, the substitution is never complete or absolute. Often, symbols and meanings merely provide a legitimizing framework for coercion and violence

5. The term metaphoric key derives from Kenneth Burke, via Kelly-Byrne (1989).

6. Spiro would proably insist that one also works out a world, and relates self to culture, on the basis of unconscious motives, many of which reflect the nature of mind and body

7. The Brahmans do not escape, since they too are stigmatized, not in the idiom of purity, but in the idiom of moral character: refer to Krishna's narrative of a Brahman who had an untouchable guru in Chapter 4.

8. Burke's ideas about the "dramatic" structure of social thought seem relevant here. Looking at the history of theory, there appears to be a tendency to polarize agency and culture, first splitting one off from the other and then setting them in opposition or zeroing out one as an analytic term, rendering it passive: either it is will and reason, or it is social and cultural constraint that are made the active principle. We can change our terms, but not our tune, choosing surrogate concepts for culture, make our focus "hegemony" or "discourse," but still see the cultural term as active, the self as passive. While the reverse may occur, I don't think it has not been the dominant trend in the twentieth-century social sciences. Whatever terms we select, we face the same conundrum.

While these terms inflect the meaning of the concept of culture in importantly different ways, they inhabit the same conceptual territory as the culture concept: despite the inflections, I suspect culture by any other name will perplex as deeply. All three terms have thorns, for the innocent and the incorrigible alike.

Recognizing that we are involved in setting the ratio of agency to culture that we use to construct our accounts of cultural life, and that where we set this and other ratios are in some ways thought-experiments, might be benefical. It may be that cultural life involves incremental slips and catatastrophic shifts in these ratios, too, so that one predetermined setting will never be able to do justice to social, cultural, and psychological life.

9. Some will protest this was always obvious, and we can only acknowledge that it was, to some—the wise and the innocent. Theory means innocence lost, but does not guarantee the arrival of wisdom or humility. I should say, too, that the restoration of agents in an intellectual world that virtually defines itself by the dissolution of "the agent" does not mean we can attempt a dissolution of "culture"—as if this would reveal a pristine agent—nor does it mean that we can neglect the cultural being of the self, ego, agent.

Bibliography

Acharya, R. and H. Ansari. 1980. Basic Needs and Government Services: An Area Study of Bhaktapur Town Panchayat, Nepal. CEDA, Tribhuvan Univeristy, Kathmandu, Nepal.

Appadurai, Arjun. 1986. "Is Homo Hierarchicus? Review Article." *American Ethnologist* 13: 745–61.

———. 1992. "Putting Hierarchy in Its Place." In G. Marcus, ed., *Rereading Cultural Anthropology*. Durham, NC: Duke Univ. Press.

Bailey, F. G. 1957. *Caste and the Economic Frontier*. Manchester University Press.

———. 1960. *Tribe, Caste and Nation*. Manchester: Manchester University Press.

Bateson, Gregory. 1972. *Steps to an Ecology of Mind*. New York: Ballantine.

Barnett, Steve, Lina Fruzzetti, and Akos Östör. 1976. "Hierarchy Purified: Notes on Dumont and His Critics." *Journal of Asian Studies* 35(4): 627–46.

Berlin, Isaiah. 1991. "Equality." *Concepts and Categories*. New York: Penguin.

———. 1979. "The Hedgehog and the Fox." In *Russian Thinkers*. New York: Penguin.

Berreman, Gerald. 1971. "The Brahmanical View of Caste." *Contributions to Indian Sociology* n.s. 5: 16–23.

———. 1972. *Hindus of the Himalayas: Ethnography and Change*, Second edition. Berkeley: University of California Press.

Beteille, André. 1983. *The Idea of Natural Inequality and Other Essays*. Bombay: Oxford University Press.

———. 1986. "Individualism and Equality." *Current Anthropology* 27: 121–34.

———. 1987. "Reply to Dumont." *Current Anthropology* 28: 672–76.

Bougle, Celestin. 1971. *Essays on the Caste System*. Cambridge: Cambridge University Press.

Bourdieu, Pierre. 1977. *Outline of a Theory of Practice*. Cambridge: Cambridge University Press.

Bruner, Jerome. 1986. *Actual Minds, Possible Worlds*. Cambridge, MA: Harvard University Press.

Buitenen, Johannes A. B. van. 1981. *The Bhagavadgita in the Mahabharata*. Chicago: University of Chicago Press.

Burghart, Richard. 1983. "Renunciation in the Religious Traditions of South Asia." *Man* n.s. 19: 635–53.

Burke, Kenneth. 1969. *A Rhetoric of Motives*. Berkeley: University of California Press.

Chattopadyaya, K. P. 1980 [1924]. *An Essay on the History of Newar Culture*. Kathmandu, Nepal: Educataional Enterprise Pvt. Ltd.

Crapanzano, Vincent. 1990. "On Self-Characterization." In J. W. Stigler, R. A. Schider, and G. Herdt, eds., *Cultural Psychology: Essays on Comparative Human Development*. Cambridge: Cambridge University Press.

D'Andrade, Roy G. 1984. "Cultural Meaning Systems." In R. A. Shweder and R. A. LeVine, eds., *Culture Theory: Essays on Mind, Self, and Emotion*. New York: Cambridge University Press.

———. 1990. "Some Propositions About the Relations Between Culture and Human Cognition." In J. W. Stigler, R. A. Shweder, and G. Herdt, eds., *Cultural Psychology: Essays on Comparative Human Development*. Cambridge: Cambridge University Press.

———. 1995. *The Development of Cognitive Anthropology*. Cambridge: Cambridge University Press.

Daniel, Sheryl B. 1983. "The Tool Box Approach of the Tamil to the Issues of Moral Responsibility and Human Destiny." In C. Keyes and E. V. Daniel, eds., *Karma*. Berkeley: University of California Press.

Dirks, Nicholas. 1987. *The Hollow Crown*. Cambridge: Cambridge University Press.

———. 1990. "The Original Caste." In M. Marriott, ed., *India Through Hindu Categories*. London: Sage Publications.

———. 1994. "Ritual and Resistance: Subversion as Social Fact." In Nicholas Dirks, Geoff Eley, and Sherry Ortner, eds., *Culture/Power/History*. Princeton, NJ: Princeton University Press.

Dumont, Louis. 1965. "The Functional Equivalents of the Individual in Caste Society." *Contributions to Indian Sociology* 7: 85–99.

———. 1980. *Homo Hierarchicus*. Complete revised English edition with appendices. Chicago: University of Chicago Press.

———. 1985. "A Modified View of Our Origins: The Christian Beginnings of Modern Individualism." In M. Carrithers, S. Collins, and S. Lukes, eds., *The Category of the Person*. Cambridge: Cambridge University Press.

———. 1986. *Essays on Individualism*. Chicago: University of Chicago Press.

———. 1987. "On Individualism and Equality." (Comment on Beteille 1987). *Current Anthropology* 28: 669–72.

Durkheim, Emile. 1965. *The Elementary Forms of the Religious Life*. New York: Free Press.

Dumont, Louis and David Pocock. 1959. "Pure and Impure." *Contributions to Indian Sociology* 3: 9–39.

Ekman, Paul and Wallace V. Friesen. 1975. *Unmasking the Face*. Englewood Cliffs, NJ: Prentice Hall.

Ewing, Katherine P. 1990. "The Illusion of Wholeness: Culture, Self, and the Experience of Inconsistency." *Ethos* 18(3): 251–78.

Fauconnier, Gilles. 1985. *Mental Spaces: Aspects of Meaning Construction in Natural Language*. Cambridge, MA: MIT Press.

Fanon, Frantz. 1967. *Black Skin, White Masks*. New York: Grove Press.

Freeman, James M. 1979. *Untouchable: An Indian Life History*. Stanford, CA: Stanford University Press.

Freud, Sigmund. [1961]. *Civilization and Its Discontents*. New York: W. W. Norton.

———. [1965]. *New Introductory Lectures on Psycho-Analysis*. New York: W. W. Norton.

Fruzzetti, Lina, Akos Östör, and Steve Barnett. 1983. "The Cultural Construction of the Person in Bengal and Tamilnadu." In A. Östör, L. Fruzzetti and S. Barnett, eds., *Concepts of Person: Kinship, Caste, and Marriage in India*. Delhi: Oxford University Press.

Fuller, C. J. 1992. *The Camphor Flame: Popular Hinduism and Society in India.* Princeton, NJ: Princeton University Press.

Fürer-Haimendorf, C. von. 1956. "Elements of Newar Social Structure." *Journal of the Royal Anthropological Institute of Great Britain and Ireland* 86, part 2: 15–38.

Gadamer, Hans-Georg. 1989 [1993]. *Truth and Method.* Second revised edition. New York: Continuum. Originally published as *Wahrheit und Methode,* 1960.

Geertz, Clifford. 1973. *The Interpretation of Cultures.* New York: Basic Books.

———. 1983. *Local Knowledge.* New York: Basic Books.

Gellner, David N. 1992. *Monk, Householder, and Tantric Priest: Newar Buddhism and Its Hierarchy of Ritual.* Cambridge: Cambridge University Press.

Gellner, David N. and Declan Quigley. 1995. *Contested Hierarchies: A Collaborative Ethnography of Caste Among the Newars of the Kathmandu Valley.* New York: Oxford University Press.

Gellner, Ernest. 1987. *Culture, Identity, and Politics.* Cambridge: Cambridge University Press.

Gold, Ann Grodzins. 1988. *Fruitful Journeys: The Ways of Rajasthani Pilgrims.* Berkeley: University of California Press.

Gramsci, Antonio. 1971. *Selections from the Prison Notebooks,* ed. and trans. Quinton Hoare and Geoffrey Nowell-Smith. London: Lawrence and Wichart.

———. 1990. "Culture and Ideological Hegemony." In J. Alexander and S. Seidman, eds., *Culture and Society.* Cambridge: Cambridge University Press.

Greenblatt, Stephen. 1980. *Renaissance Self-Fashioning.* University of Chicago Press.

Greenwold, Stephen M. 1974. "Buddhist Brahmans." *Archives Européennes de Sociologie* 15: 101–23.

———. 1978. "The Role of the Priest in Newar Society." In J. Fisher, ed., *Himalayan Anthropology.* The Hague: Mouton.

———. 1975. "Kingship and Caste." *Archives Européennes de Sociologie* 16: 49–75.

———. 1981. "Caste: A Moral Structure and a Social System of Control." In Adrian Mayer, ed., *Culture and Morality.* Oxford: Oxford University Press.

Guha, Ranajit, ed. 1982–1983. *Subaltern Studies I & II.* Delhi: Oxford University Press.

Habermas, Jurgen. 1977. "A Review of Gadamer's Truth and Method." In F. R. Dallmayr and Thomas McCarthy, eds., *Understanding and Social Inquiry.* Notre Dame, IN: University of Notre Dame Press.

Hale, Charles R. 1994. *Resistance and Contradiction: Miskitu Indians and the Nicaraguan State, 1894–1987.* Stanford, CA: Stanford University Press.

Harper, Edward, ed. 1964. *Religion in South Asia.* Seattle: University of Washington Press.

Hodgson, Brian. The Hodgson Collection, India Office Library, London. Manuscripts written while British Resident in Nepal, 1822–1844.

Höfer, A. 1979. *The Caste Hierarchy and the State of Nepal: A Study of the Muluki Ain of 1854.* Innsbruck: Universitätsverlag Wagner.

Hollan, Doug W. and Jane C. Wellenkamp. 1994. *Contentment and Suffering: Culture and Experience in Toraja.* New York: Columbia University Press.

Holland, Dorothy and Debra Skinner. 1995. "Contested Rituals, Contested Feminities: (Re)forming Self and Society in a Nepali Women's Festival." *American Ethnologist* 22(2):279–305.

———. In press. "The Co-Development of Identity, Agency, and Lived Worlds." In J. Tudge, M. Shanahan, and J. Valsiner, eds., *Comparisons in Human Development.* Cambridge: Cambridge University Press.

Hopkins, Thomas J. 1966. "The Social Teaching of the Bhagavata Purana." In M. Singer, ed., *Krishna: Myths, Rites, and Attitudes*. Honolulu: East-West Center Press.

Inden, Ronald. 1990. *Imagining India*. Oxford: Blackwell.

Jameson, Fredric. 1981. *The Political Unconscious*. Ithaca, NY: Cornell University Press.

Joshi, Barbara R., ed. 1986. *Untouchable! Voices of the Dalit Liberation Movement*. London: Zed Books.

Johnson, Mark. 1993. *Moral Imagination*. Chicago: University of Chicago Press.

Juergensmeyer, Mark. 1982. *Religion as Social Vision: The Movement Against Untouchability in 20th-Century Punjab*. Berkeley: University of California Press.

Kelly-Byrne, Diana. 1989. *A Child's Play Life: An Ethnographic Study*. New York: Teachers College Press.

Khare, R. S. 1978. "The One and the Many: Varna and Jati as a Symbolic Classification." In S. Vatuk, ed., *American Studies in the Anthropology of India*. New Delhi: Manohar.

———. 1984. *The Untouchable as Himself*. Cambridge: Cambridge University Press.

Kolenda, Pauline. 1964. "Religious Anxiety and Hindu Fate." In E. Harper, ed., *Religion in South Asia*. Seattle: University of Washington Press.

———. 1976. "Seven Kinds of Hierarchy in Homo Hierarchicus." *Journal of Asian Studies* 35(4): 581–96.

Laitin, David. 1986. *Hegemony and Culture*. Chicago: University of Chicago Press.

Leach, Edmund. 1954. *Political Systems of Highland Burma*. London: Athlone Press.

Lerner, Melvin J. 1980. *The Belief in a Just World: A Fundamental Delusion*. New York: Plenum Press.

Levy, Robert I. 1984. "Emotion, Knowing and Culture." In R. A. Shweder and R. A. LeVine, eds., *Culture Theory: Essays on Mind, Self, and Emotion*. New York: Cambridge University Press.

———. 1990. *Mesocosm: Hinduism and the Organization of a Traditional Newar City in Nepal*. Berkeley: University of California Press.

Levy, Robert I. and Jane C. Wellenkamp. 1989. "Methodology in the Anthropological Study of Emotion." In R. Pluzchik and H. Kellerman, eds., *Emotion: Theory, Research, and Experience*, vol. 4, *The Measurement of Emotions*. New York: Academic Press.

Linger, Daniel T. 1992. *Dangerous Encounters*. Stanford, CA: Stanford University Press.

———. 1993. "The Hegemony of Discontent." *American Ethnologist* 20: 3–24.

———. 1994. "Has Culture Theory Lost Its Minds?" *Ethos* 22(3): 284–315.

Lynch, Owen. 1969. *The Politics of Untouchability*. New York: Columbia University Press.

MacDonald, Alexander W. 1975. *Essays on the Ethnology of Nepal and South Asia*. Kathmandu, Nepal: Bibliotheca Himalyayca.

Mahar, J. Michael, ed. 1972. *The Untouchables in Contemporary India*. Tucson: University of Arizona Press.

Malik, S. C., ed. 1977. *Dissent, Protest, and Reform in Indian Civilization*. Simla: Indian Institute of Advanced Study.

Marcus, George E. and Michael M. J. Fischer. 1986. *Anthropology as Cultural Critique*. Chicago: University of Chicago Press.

Marriott, McKim. 1966. "The Feast of Love." In M. Singer, ed., *Krishna: Myths, Rites, and Attitudes*. Honolulu: East-West Center Press.

————. 1976a. "Hindu Transactions: Diversity Without Dualism." In B. Kapferer, ed., *Transactions and Meaning*. Philadelphia: Institute for the Study of Human Issues.

————. 1976b. "Interpreting Indian Society: Diversity Without Dualism." *Journal of Asian Studies* 36: 189–95.

————. 1989. "Constructing an Indian Ethnosociology." *Contributions to Indian Sociology* n.s. 23, 1.

McCarthy, Thomas. 1978. *The Critical Theory of Jurgen Habermas*. Cambridge, MA: MIT Press.

McHugh, Ernestine. 1989. Concepts of the Person Among the Gurungs of Nepal. *American Ethnologist* 16: 75–86.

Mencher, Joan. 1974. "The Caste System Upside Down, or the Not-so-Mysterious East." *Current Anthropology* 15: 469–93.

Mines, Mattison. 1988. "Conceptualizing the Person: Hierarchical Society and Individual Autonomy in India." *American Anthropologist* 90: 568–79.

Misgeld, Dieter. 1991. "Modernity and Hermeneutics: A Critical-Theoretic Rejoinder." In Hugh J. Silverman, ed., *Gadamer and Hermeneutics*. New York: Routledge.

Moffatt, Michael. 1979. *An Untouchable Community in South India*. Princeton, NJ: Princeton University Press.

Mohanty, C. 1988. "Under Western Eyes: Feminist Scholarship and Colonial Discourses." *Feminist Review* 30: 61–88.

Narayan, Kirin. 1989. *Storytellers, Saints, and Scoundrels: Folk Narrative in Hindu Religious Teaching*. Philadelphia: University of Pennsylvania Press.

Nepali, Gopal Singh. 1965. *The Newars*. Bombay: United Asia Publications.

Nicholson, Graeme. 1991. "Answers to Critical Theory." In Hugh J. Silverman, ed., *Gadamer and Hermeneutics*. New York: Routledge.

Obeyesekere, Gananath. 1981. *Medusa's Hair: An Essay on Personal Symbols and Religious Experience*. Chicago: University of Chicago Press.

————. 1990. *The Work of Culture: Symbolic Transformation in Psychoanalysis and Anthropology*. Chicago: University of Chicago Press.

O'Hanlon, R. 1988. "Recovering the Subject: Subaltern Studies and Histories of Resistance in Colonial South Asia." *Modern Asian Studies* 22(1): 189–224.

O'Flaherty, Wendy, ed. 1980. *Karma and Rebirth in Classical Indian Traditions*. Berkeley: University of California Press.

Ortner, Sherry. 1984. "Theory in Anthropology Since the Sixties." *Comparative Studies in Society and History* 261: 126–66.

————. 1989. *High Religion: A Cultural and Political History of Sherpa Buddhism*. Princeton, NJ: Princeton Univ. Press.

Parish, Steven M. 1994. *Moral Knowing in a Hindu Sacred City*. New York: Columbia University Press.

Parry, Jonathan. 1974. "Egalitarian Values in a Hierarchical Society." *South Asia Review* 12 (2): 95–121.

Pocock, David F. 1973. *Mind, Body and Wealth: A Study of Belief and Practice in an Indian Village*. Totowa, NJ: Rowman and Littlefield.

Raheja, Gloria. 1989a. *The Poison in the Gift*. Chicago: University of Chicago Press.

————. 1989b. "India: Caste, Kingship, and Dominance Reconsidered." *Annual Review of Anthropology* 17: 497–522.

————. 1990. "Centrality, Mutuality, and Hierarchy: Shifting Aspects of Inter-Caste Relationships in North India." In M. Marriott, ed., *India Through Hindu Categories*. London: Sage Publications.

Ramanujan, A. K., trans. 1973. *Speaking of Shiva.* New York: Peguin.

————. 1990. "Is There an Indian Way of Thinking? An Informal Essay." In Ian M. Marriott, ed., *India Through Hindu Categories.* London: Sage.

Ricoeur, Paul. 1990. *From Text to Action.* Evanston, IL: Northwestern University Press.

Riesman, Paul. 1983. "On the Irrelevance of Childrearing Practices for the Formation of Personality." *Culture, Medicine, and Psychiatry* 7: 103–29.

Rosaldo, Renato. 1989. *Culture and Truth.* Boston: Beacon Press.

Rosenau, Pauline M. 1992. *Post-Modernism and the Social Sciences.* Princeton, NJ: Princeton University Press.

Rosser, Colin. 1978. "The Newar Caste System." In C. von Fürer-Haimendorf, ed., *Caste and Kin in Nepal, India, and Ceylon.* New Delhi: Sterling.

Sapir, Edward. 1934 [1985]. "The Emergence of the Concept of Personality in A Study of Cultures." In D. G. Mandelbaum, ed., *Selected Writings of Edward Sapir in Language, Culture, and Personality.* Berkeley: University of California Press.

————. 1938 [1985]. "Why Cultural Anthropology Needs the Psychiatrist." In D. G. Mandelbaum, ed., *Selected Writings of Edward Sapir in Language, Culture, and Personality.* Berkeley: University of California Press.

Schwartzman, Helen B. 1978. *Transformation: The Anthropology of Children's Play.* New York: Plenum Press.

Sartre, Jean Paul. 1952 [1963]. *Saint Genet.* New York: Pantheon Books.

Sharma, Prayag Raj. 1977. "Caste, Social Mobility and Sanskritization: A Study of Nepal's Old Legal Code." *Kailash* 5(4): 277–79.

Sharma, Ursula. 1965. "Theodicy and the Doctrine of Karma." *Man* 8(3): 347–64.

Shweder, Richard A. 1991. *Thinking Through Cultures: Expeditions in Cultural Psychology.* Cambridge, MA: Harvard University Press.

Shweder, Richard and Edmund J. Bourne. 1984. "Does the Concept of Person Vary Cross-Culturally?" In R. A. Shweder and R. LeVine, eds., *Culture Theory: Essays on Mind, Self, and Emotion.* Cambridge: Cambridge University Press.

Shweder, Richard, Manamohan Mahapatra, and Joan G. Miller. 1987. "Culture and Moral Development." In J. Kagan and S. Lamb, eds., *The Emergence of Moral Concepts in Young Children.* Chicago: University of Chicago Press.

Shweder, Richard and Nancy Much. 1987. "Determinations of Meaning: Discourse and Moral Socialization." In W. M. Kurtines and J. L. Gewirtz, eds., *Moral Development Through Social Interaction.* New York: Wiley.

Singer, Milton. 1966. "Radha-Krishna Bhajanas of Madras City." In M. Singer, ed., *Krishna: Myths, Rites, and Attitudes.* Honolulu: East-West Center Press.

————. 1972. "Passage to More Than India: A Sketch of Changing European and American Images." In *When a Great Tradition Modernizes.* Chicago: University of Chicago Press.

Skinner, Debra and Dorothy C. Holland. In press. "Schools and the Cultural Production of the Educated Person in a Nepalese Hill Community." In B. A. Levinson, Douglas E. Foley, and D. C. Holland, eds., *The Cultural Production of the Educated Person: Critical Ethnographies of Schooling and Local Practice.* Buffalo: State University of New York Press.

Slusser, Mary. 1982. *Nepal Mandala: A Cultural Study of the Kathmandu Valley.* Vol. 1. Princeton, NJ: Princeton University Press.

Spiro, Melford E. 1987. "Social Systems, Personality, and Functional Analysis." In B. Kilborne and L. L. Langness, eds., *Culture and Human Nature.* Chicago: University of Chicago Press.

————. 1984. "Some Reflections on Cultural Determinism and Relativism with Special Reference to Emotion and Reason." In R. A. Shweder and R. LeVine, eds., *Culture Theory: Essays on Mind, Self, and Emotion.* Cambridge: Cambridge University Press.

Stiller, Ludwig. 1973. *The Rise of the House of Gorkha: A Study in the Unification of Nepal 1768–1816.* Kathmandu, Nepal: Ratna Pustak Bhandar.

Strauss, Claudia. 1990. "Who Gets Ahead? Cognitive Responses to Heteroglossia in American Political Culture." *American Ethnologist* 17(2): 312–28.

————. 1992. "What Makes Tony Run? Schema as Motives Reconsidered." In R. D'Andrade and C. Strauss, eds., *Human Motives and Cultural Models.* Cambridge: Cambridge University Press.

Toffin, Gérard. 1978. "Intercaste Relations in a Newar Community." In J. Fisher, ed., *Himalyan Anthropology.* The Hague: Mouton.

Trawick, Margaret. 1990. *Notes on Love in a Tamil Family.* Berkeley: University of California Press.

Turner, Victor. 1969. *The Ritual Process.* Chicago: Aldine.

Van de Veer, Peter. 1987. "Taming the Ascetic: Devotionalism in a Hindu Monastic Order." *Man* n.s. 22, 680–695.

Wadley, Susan. 1975. *Shakti: Power in the Conceptual Structure of Karimpur Religion.* University of Chicago Studies in Anthropology Series in Social, Cultural, and Linguistic Anthropology, University of Chicago.

Weber, Max. 1958a. *The Religion of India.* New York: Free Press.

————. 1958b. "Social Psychology of the World Religions." In H. H. Gerth and C. Wright Mills, eds., *From Max Weber: Essays in Sociology.* New York: Oxford University Press.

Williams, Bernard. 1969. "The Idea of Equality." In J. Feinberg, ed., *Moral Concepts.* Oxford: Oxford University Press.

Williams, Raymond, 1977. *Marxism and Literature.* New York: Oxford University Press.

Wikan, Unni. 1980. *Life Among the Poor in Cairo.* London: Tavistock.

Name Index

Subject Index

Agency, 59–60, 211–12, 236–37; and culture, 254n8, 255n9
Ambivalence, 8, 65, 101–5, 130–32, 149
Anger, 169–71. *See also* Resentment
Ascetics 49–51, 177; low caste, 184–90; in narratives, 127–30; and untouchables, 189–90; and king, 189; and Brahmans, 188–90. *See also* Renunciation

Bauri (caste), 179
Begging, 111; disguised, 181. *See also* Hunger; Necessity
Bhagavad Gita, xxi–xxii, 243n1, 245n2
Bhaktapur, 4–6, 19–24
Bhakti, 46, 83, 245n
Body, and the sacred order, 164, 247n7
Buddha, 131–32
Butcher (caste), 164; and structures of feeling, 23
Brahmans, 38–39; cultural roles, 54–55; in narratives, 127–30; and king, 24–25, 189–90; and untouchables, 188–90

Caste: anthropological preoccupation, 6; ambiguities of caste status, 113–15; in Bhaktapur, 27–28, 29, 162–63; and exclusion, 26–28, 34; and Hindu state, 26–28; and impurity (*see* purity and impurity); in Kathmandu Valley, 4–6; and social mobility, 113–15; and moral order, 5–6, 143; multiple models of caste relations, 70, 78, 88, 91, 142–43 (*see also* Diversity); and multiple social identity, 113–15; Newar castes, 4–5, 25–30, 107–10; psychoexistential quandaries posed

by caste life, 7–8, 101–5; and resentment, 28; and stigma, 26–28, 162. *See also* individual castes
Chamars (caste), 61, 183–84, 245n
Chariot festival (Biska), 19–20, 24–25, 29–33, 39–40
Cipa (polluted food), 166–68
Colonialism, 94, 243–44n3
Communitas, 158–59
Comparative method: global vs. polythetic 66–68, 97; dangers of sharp contrast 219
Consciousness: politics of, 7–11, 161; and resistance, 8. *See also* Critical consciousness; Multiple consciousness
Consensus and diversity, 201–4, 208, 227
Counter-ideology, 10–11, 175
Critical consciousness, xx, 11–15, 77, 92, 223; and psychoethnography, 10
Critique, xvi–xvii, 59–62, 77, 80–81, 195–96; of caste system, 80–81, 174, 193–97; of culture, 11–15, 174–?, 193–97, 222; and ideology, 10–13, 175–76, 205; indigenous critical theory, 11–15; and resistance, 11; of social and cultural life, xvi, 11–15; of theory, xii, 16
Culture: and agency, 254n8, 255n9; cognitive theory of, 249–50; and critique, 11–15, 77; cultural models, 249n; and differences, 214, 218; and discourse, 254n8; and emancipation, 173; and hegemony, 254n8; and identity, 172; and "meta-culture," xxi; and mind, 252n3; and multiple ethos of caste system, 142–43; multiple models, 42; resistance and dominant order, 224; "thickness" vs. "force," 249; and values, xi–xiii